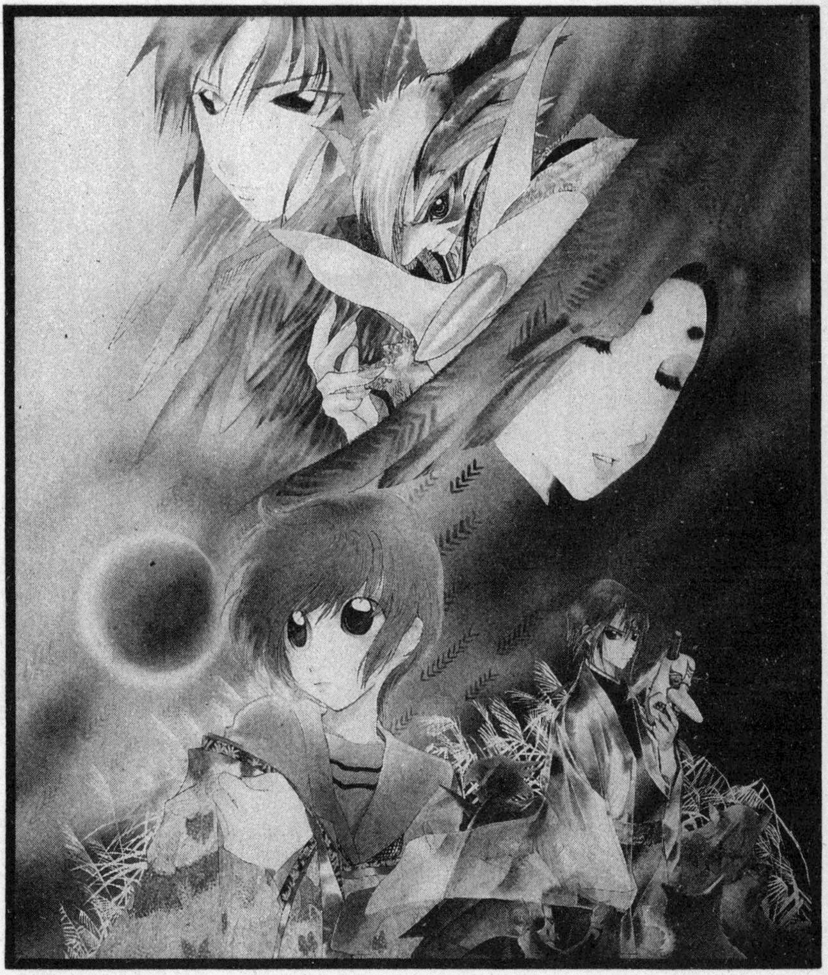

Crescent Moon Vol. 4
Haruko Iida
Script by
Red Entertainment / Takamura Matsuda

Translation - Nan Rymer
English Adaptation - Stuart Hazleton
Copy Editor - Suzanne Waldman
Retouch and Lettering - Eva Han
Production Artist - Jacqueline Del Monte
Cover Design - Patrick Hook

Editor - Bryce P. Coleman
Digital Imaging Manager - Chris Buford
Pre-Press Manager - Antonio DePietro
Production Managers - Jennifer Miller and Mutsumi Miyazaki
Art Director - Matt Alford
Managing Editor - Jill Freshney
VP of Production - Ron Klamert
Editor-in-Chief - Mike Kiley
President and C.O.O. - John Parker
Publisher and C.E.O. - Stuart Levy

A 🐸TOKYOPOP® Manga

TOKYOPOP Inc.
5900 Wilshire Blvd. Suite 2000
Los Angeles, CA 90036

E-mail: info@TOKYOPOP.com
Come visit us online at www.TOKYOPOP.com

ISBN: 1-59182-795-7

First TOKYOPOP printing: December 2004
10 9 8 7 6 5 4 3 2
Printed in the USA

Crescent Moon

Haruko Iida.

Original Works By

Red Company/Takamura Matsuda

Volume 4

HAMBURG // LONDON // LOS ANGELES // TOKYO

ONE DAY, FOUR MYSTERIOUS YOUTHS APPEAR BEFORE HIGH SCHOOL JUNIOR MAHIRU SHIRAISHI. INSTEAD OF BEING HUMAN, THESE YOUTHS ARE NOT ONLY MEMBERS OF THE "LUNAR RACE," BUT MEMBERS OF THE RING OF THIEVES, "THE MOONLIGHT BANDITS," WHO ARE CURRENTLY ALL THE BUZZ IN TOKYO. FROM THESE YOUTHS, MAHIRU LEARNS SHE IS THE DESCENDENT OF "THE MINISTER OF THE LEFT'S PRINCESS," WHOSE ANCESTORS WERE RESPONSIBLE FOR STEALING THE "TEARDROPS OF THE MOON" SO MANY YEARS AGO. IT IS ALSO BECAUSE OF THIS HERITAGE THAT MAHIRU POSSESSES THE ABILITY TO DRAW OUT THE HIDDEN ABILITIES AND POWERS OF THE LUNAR RACE. ASKED BY THE FOUR TO ASSIST THEM IN THEIR QUEST TO RETURN THE TEARDROPS OF THE MOON, MAHIRU MOVES IN WITH THEM TO LIVE AND WORK AT THEIR NIGHTCLUB, CALLED THE MOONSHINE.

MEANWHILE, INSPECTOR KUSAKABE, WHO LEADS THE INVESTIGATION AGAINST THE MOONLIGHT BANDITS, HAS APPROACHED AN ORGANIZATION NAMED "DAWN'S VENUS," FAMOUS FOR ITS MYSTICAL ABILITIES IN CAPTURING AND TAMING DEMONS. IT IS AT THE WORLD PERFORMANCE FESTIVAL THAT THE LUNAR RACE AND DAWN'S VENUS CLASH IN BATTLE BEFORE MAHIRU'S EYES...JUST AS THEY HAVE FOR HUNDREDS OF YEARS. LEARNING THIS SAD PIECE OF HISTORY, MAHIRU MAKES THE DECISION TO DO HER BEST TO BECOME A BRIDGE BETWEEN THE HUMANS AND THE LUNAR RACE.

BUT UNBEKNOWNST TO MAHIRU, THE SEER OF DAWN'S VENUS IS NONE OTHER THAN HER CLASSMATE, KEIKO. THE TWO, UNAWARE OF EACH OTHER'S ROLE, DEPART ON A CLASS TRIP TO KYOTO TOGETHER, DURING WHICH KEIKO AND HOKUTO WITNESS MAHIRU AND MITSURU, IN TENGU FORM, TOGETHER......

MAHIRU SHIRAISHI: A JUNIOR IN HIGH SCHOOL. MAHIRU POSSESSES THE ABILITY TO AWAKEN AND DRAW OUT THE HIDDEN POWERS OF THE LUNAR RACE.

未完月

The Story So Far...

NOZOMU MOEGI: A VAMPIRE. DESPITE HIS BLONDE HAIR AND BLUE EYES, HE SPEAKS WITH A KANSAI - DIALECT. HE'S A SMOOTH TALKER AND LOVES THE LADIES.

MITSURU SUOU: A TENGU. DUE TO HIS COMPLICATED UPBRINGING, MITSURU NOT ONLY HATES THE HUMAN RACE, BUT DISTRUSTS THE LUNAR ONE AS WELL.

MISOKA ASAGI: A FOX DEMON. ALWAYS COOL, CALM, COLLECTED AND STOIC, MISOKA TAKES ACTION FAST AND IS REGARDED AS THE UNSPOKEN LEADER OF THE GROUP.

AKIRA YAMABUKI: A HAPPY-GO-LUCKY WERE-WOLF, AKIRA IS LOATHE TO DWELL ON ANYTHING TOO SERI-OUSLY OR TOO DEEPLY FOR LONG.

OBORO KUROSAKI: OWNER OF THE BAR MOONSHINE.

KATSURA SHION: PIANIST FOR THE BAR MOONSHINE.

SHIROGANE: RULER OF THE LUNAR RACE, AND THE CURRENT EMPEROR OF THE MOON. HE IS ALSO OBORO'S NEPHEW.

KIMITERU KUSAKABE: A POLICE INSPECTOR INVESTIGATING THE MOONLIGHT BANDITS.

YOUHEI NISHINO: DETECTIVE KUSAKABE'S SUBORDINATE. HE'S A POLICE SERGEANT.

HOKUTO KOUDOKUI: LEADER OF THE DEMON EXTERMINATION AND CAPTURING TROUPE, DAWN'S VENUS.

MUTSURA HAYASHI: A MEMBER OF DAWN'S VENUS.

KEIKO HIMURA: A MEM-BER OF DAWN'S VENUS KEIKO HAS THE POWER OF PROPHECY. SHE IS ALSO ONE OF MAHIRU'S CLASSMATES.

Crescent Moon

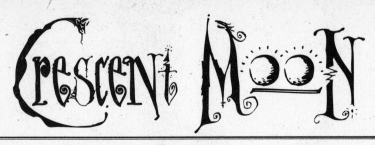

Contents

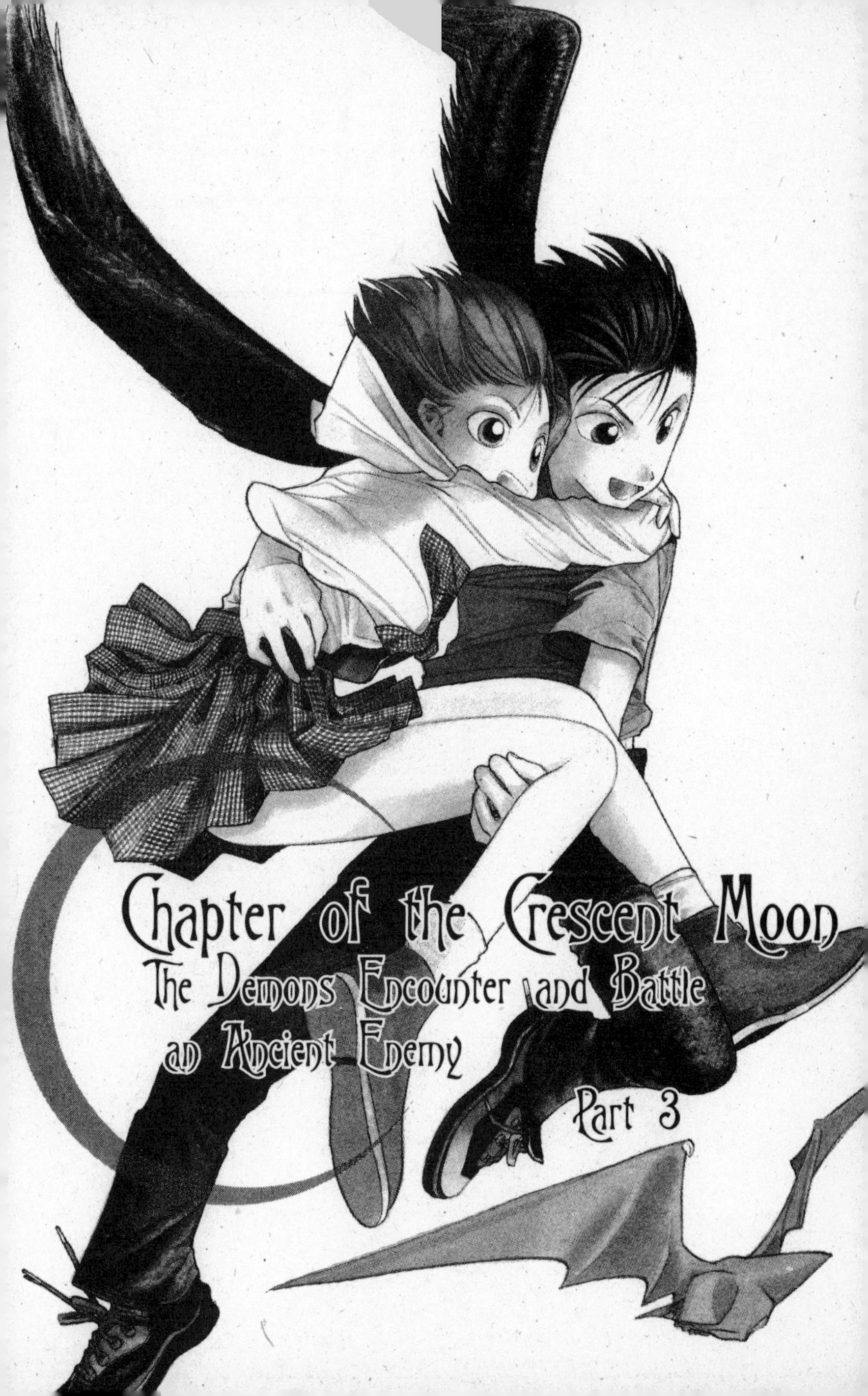
Chapter of the Crescent Moon
The Demons Encounter and Battle an Ancient Enemy
Part 3

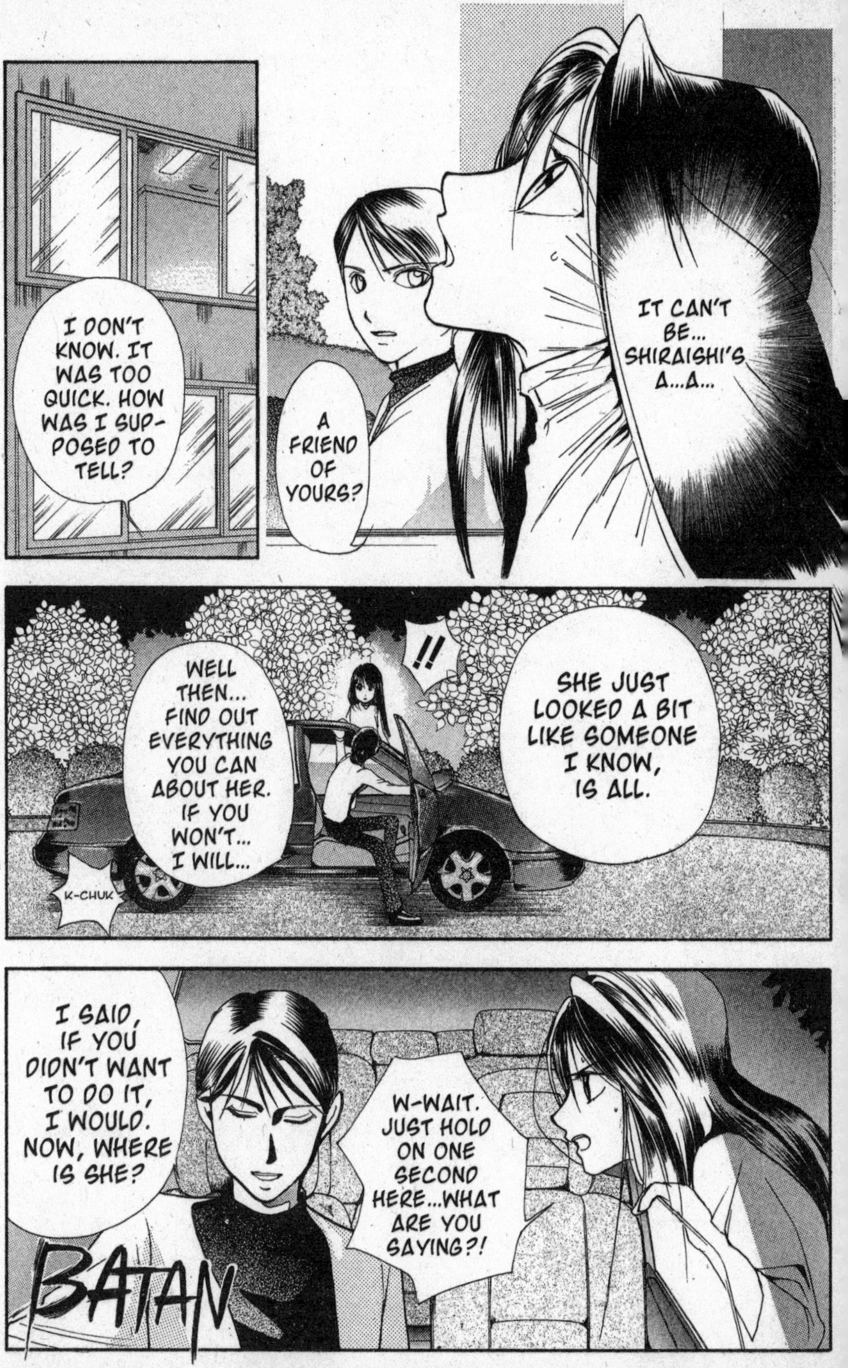
IT CAN'T BE... SHIRAISHI'S A...A...
A FRIEND OF YOURS?
I DON'T KNOW. IT WAS TOO QUICK. HOW WAS I SUP-POSED TO TELL?
SHE JUST LOOKED A BIT LIKE SOMEONE I KNOW, IS ALL.
!!
WELL THEN... FIND OUT EVERYTHING YOU CAN ABOUT HER. IF YOU WON'T... I WILL...
K-CHUK
W-WAIT. JUST HOLD ON ONE SECOND HERE...WHAT ARE YOU SAYING?!
I SAID, IF YOU DIDN'T WANT TO DO IT, I WOULD. NOW, WHERE IS SHE?
BATAN

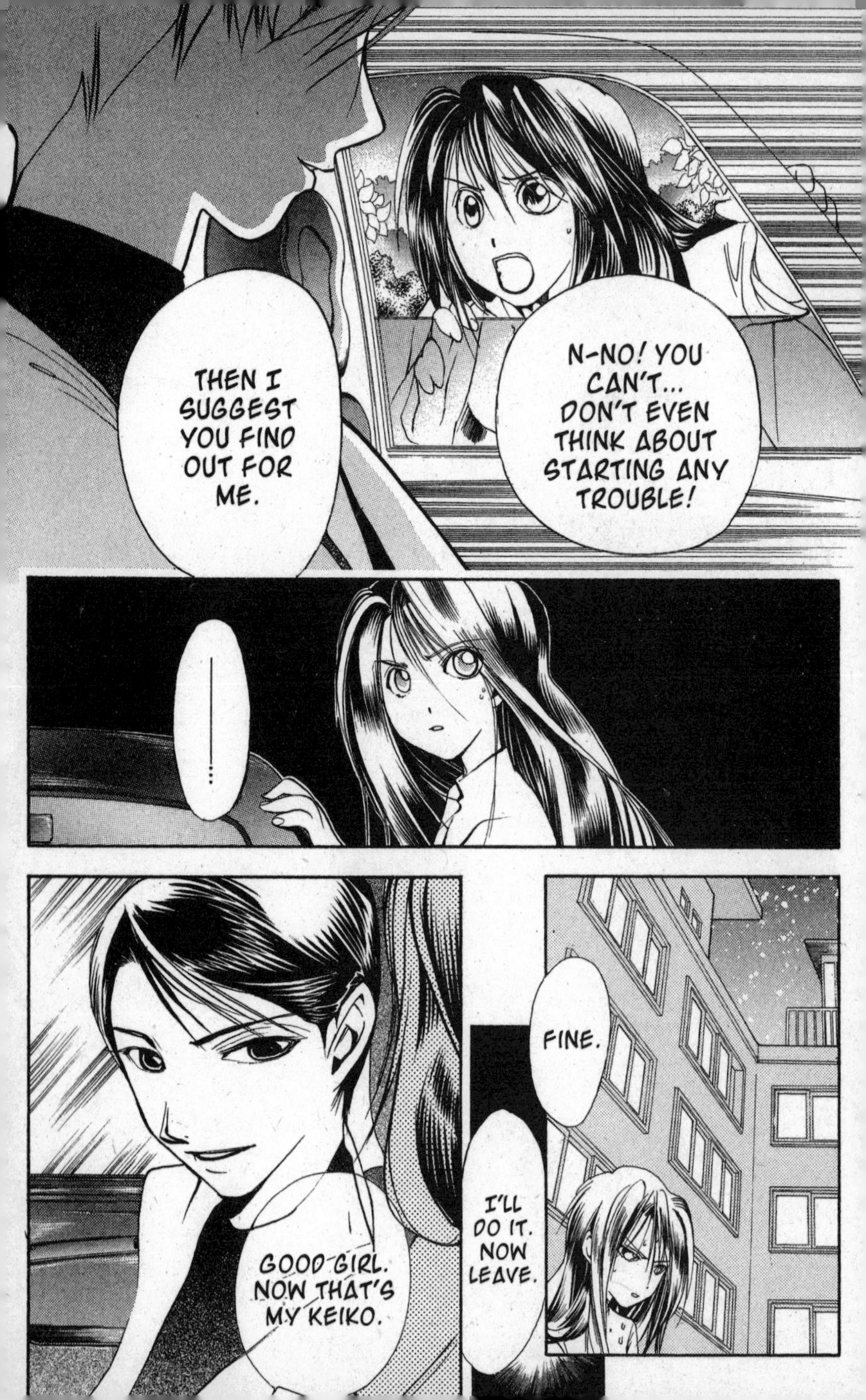
N-NO! YOU CAN'T... DON'T EVEN THINK ABOUT STARTING ANY TROUBLE!
THEN I SUGGEST YOU FIND OUT FOR ME.
......
FINE.
I'LL DO IT. NOW LEAVE.
GOOD GIRL. NOW THAT'S MY KEIKO.

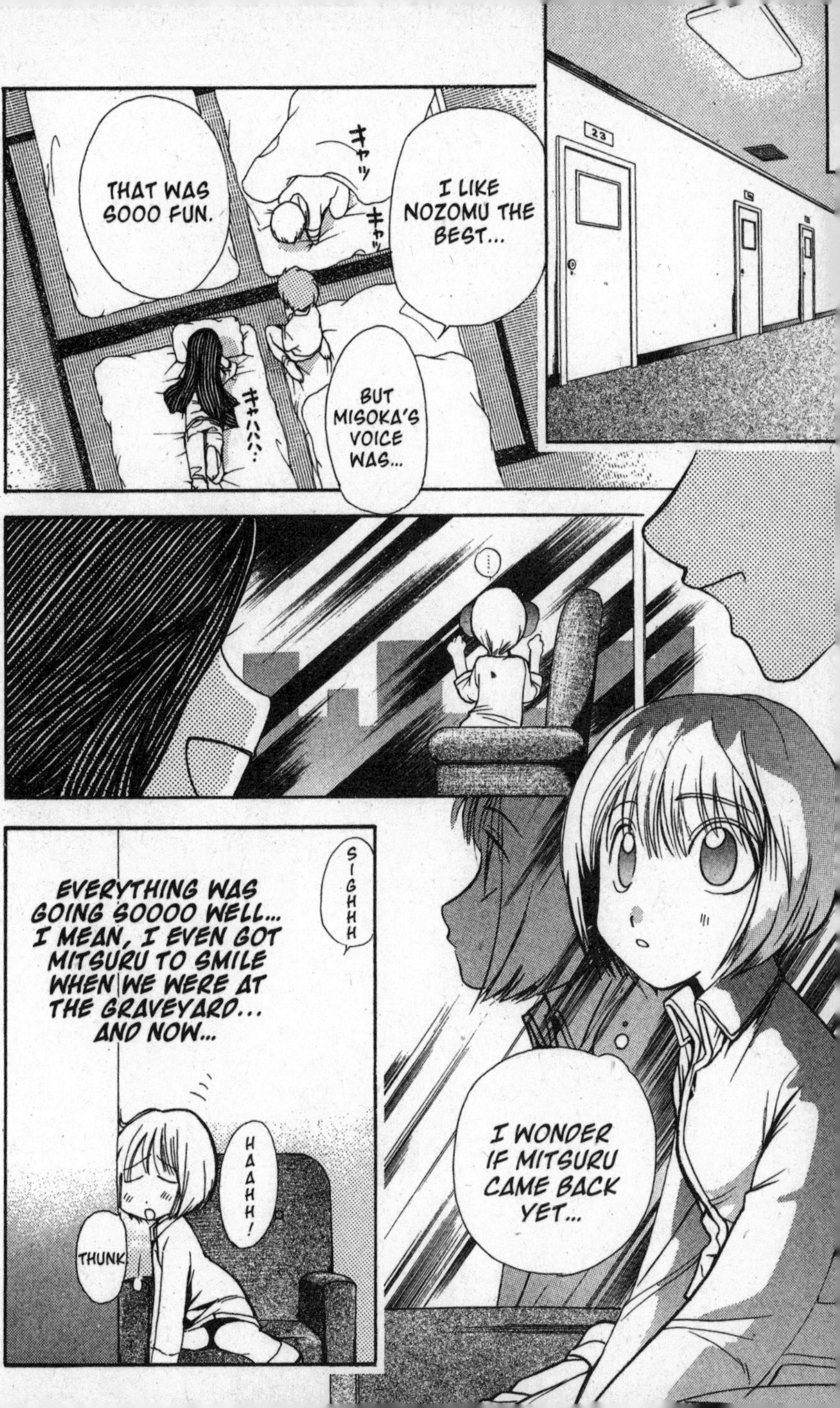

I LIKE NOZOMU THE BEST...
キャッ
キャッ
THAT WAS SOOO FUN.
BUT MISOKA'S VOICE WAS...
キャハハハ…
I WONDER IF MITSURU CAME BACK YET...
...
SIGHHH
EVERYTHING WAS GOING SOOOO WELL... I MEAN, I EVEN GOT MITSURU TO SMILE WHEN WE WERE AT THE GRAVEYARD... AND NOW...
HAAAHH!
THUNK

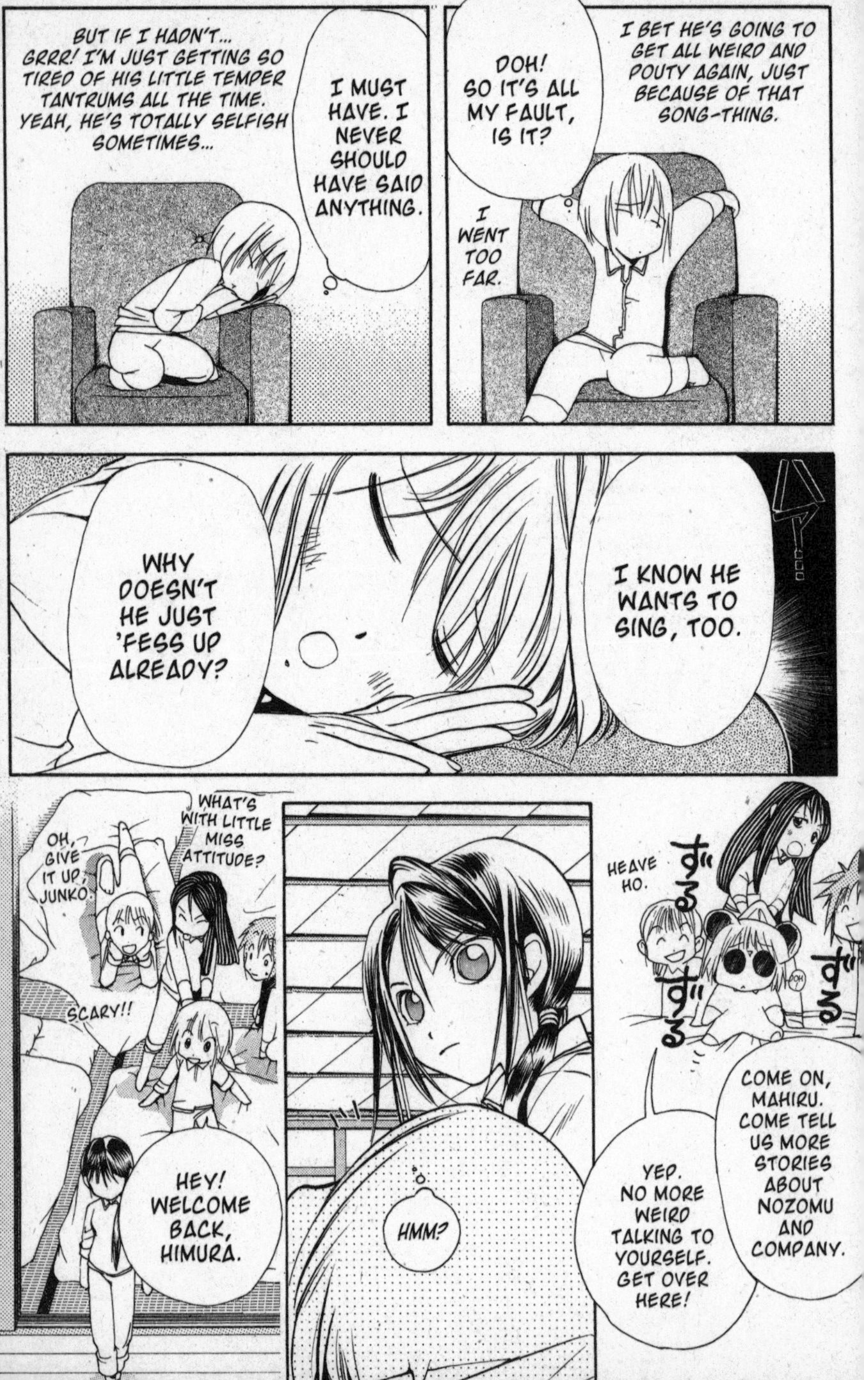
I BET HE'S GOING TO GET ALL WEIRD AND POUTY AGAIN, JUST BECAUSE OF THAT SONG-THING.
DOH! SO IT'S ALL MY FAULT, IS IT?
I WENT TOO FAR.
I MUST HAVE. I NEVER SHOULD HAVE SAID ANYTHING.
BUT IF I HADN'T... GRRR! I'M JUST GETTING SO TIRED OF HIS LITTLE TEMPER TANTRUMS ALL THE TIME. YEAH, HE'S TOTALLY SELFISH SOMETIMES...
I KNOW HE WANTS TO SING, TOO.
WHY DOESN'T HE JUST 'FESS UP ALREADY?
ずる
ずる
HEAVE HO.
ずる
COME ON, MAHIRU. COME TELL US MORE STORIES ABOUT NOZOMU AND COMPANY.
YEP. NO MORE WEIRD TALKING TO YOURSELF. GET OVER HERE!
HMM?
WHAT'S WITH LITTLE MISS ATTITUDE?
OH, GIVE IT UP, JUNKO
SCARY!!
HEY! WELCOME BACK, HIMURA.

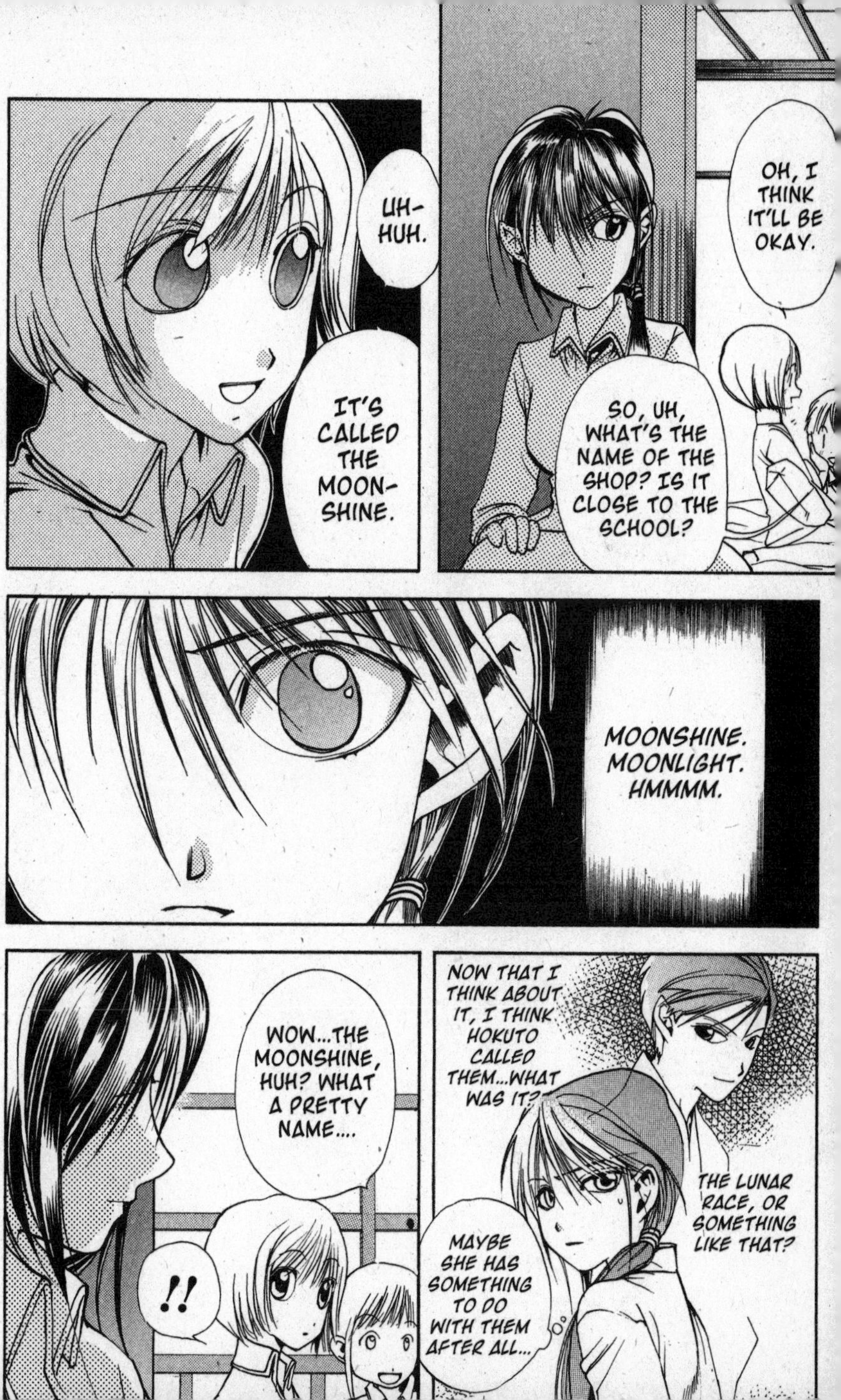
OH, I THINK IT'LL BE OKAY.
SO, UH, WHAT'S THE NAME OF THE SHOP? IS IT CLOSE TO THE SCHOOL?
UH-HUH.
IT'S CALLED THE MOONSHINE.
MOONSHINE. MOONLIGHT. HMMMM.
NOW THAT I THINK ABOUT IT, I THINK HOKUTO CALLED THEM...WHAT WAS IT?
THE LUNAR RACE, OR SOMETHING LIKE THAT?
MAYBE SHE HAS SOMETHING TO DO WITH THEM AFTER ALL...
WOW...THE MOONSHINE, HUH? WHAT A PRETTY NAME....
!!

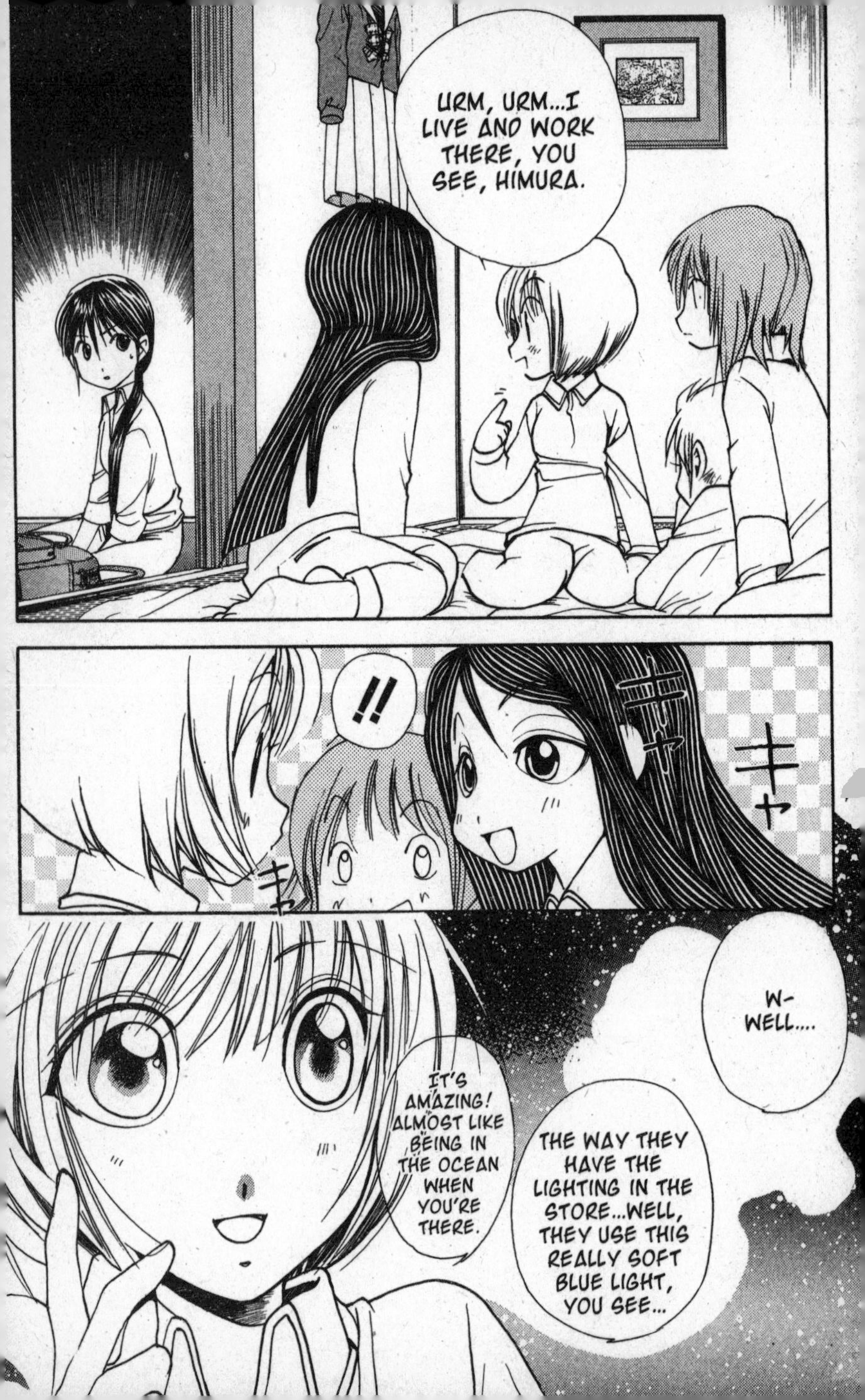
URM, URM...I LIVE AND WORK THERE, YOU SEE, HIMURA.
キャ
キャ
!!
キャ
W-WELL....
THE WAY THEY HAVE THE LIGHTING IN THE STORE...WELL, THEY USE THIS REALLY SOFT BLUE LIGHT, YOU SEE...
IT'S AMAZING! ALMOST LIKE BEING IN THE OCEAN WHEN YOU'RE THERE.

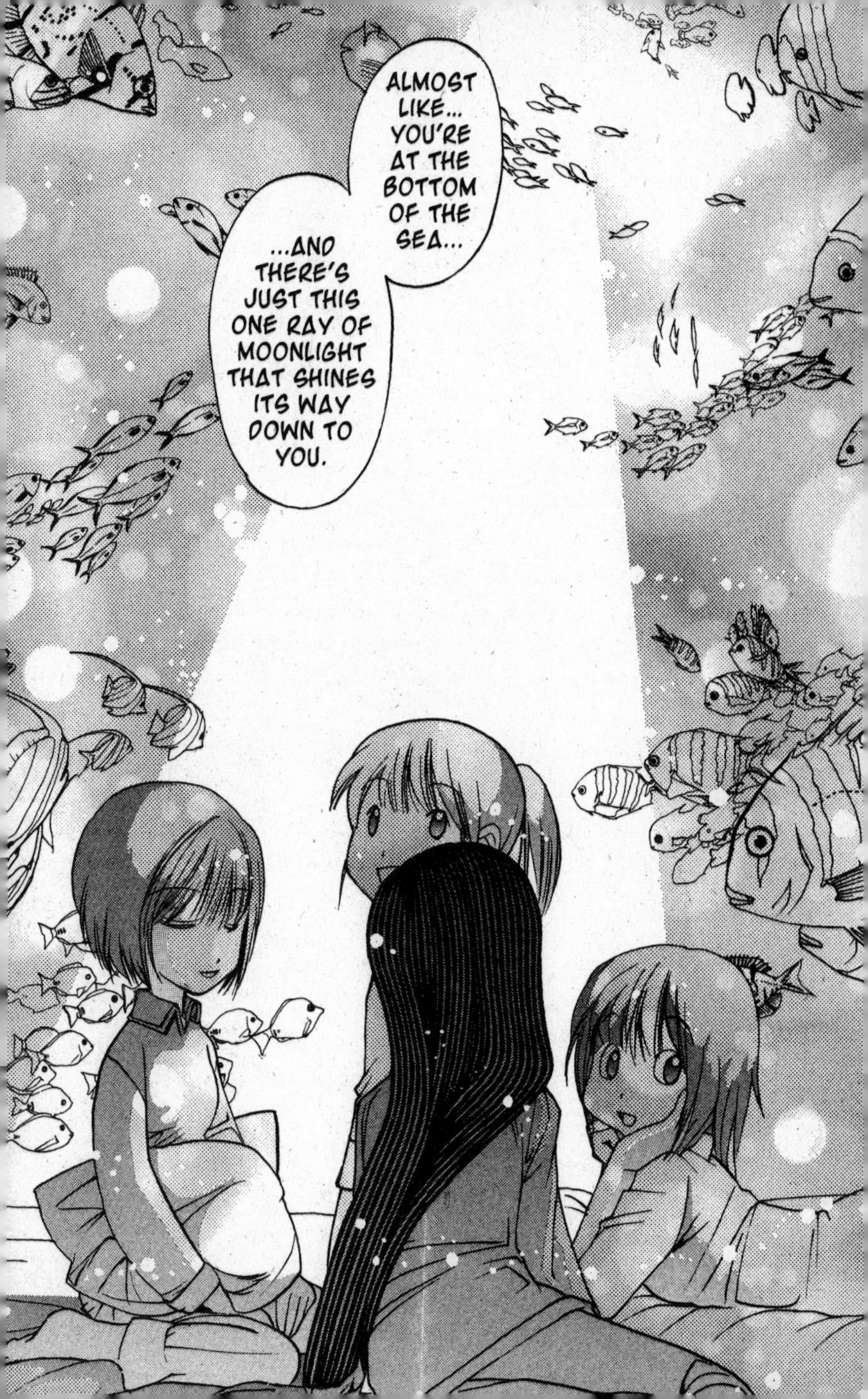
ALMOST LIKE... YOU'RE AT THE BOTTOM OF THE SEA...
...AND THERE'S JUST THIS ONE RAY OF MOONLIGHT THAT SHINES ITS WAY DOWN TO YOU.

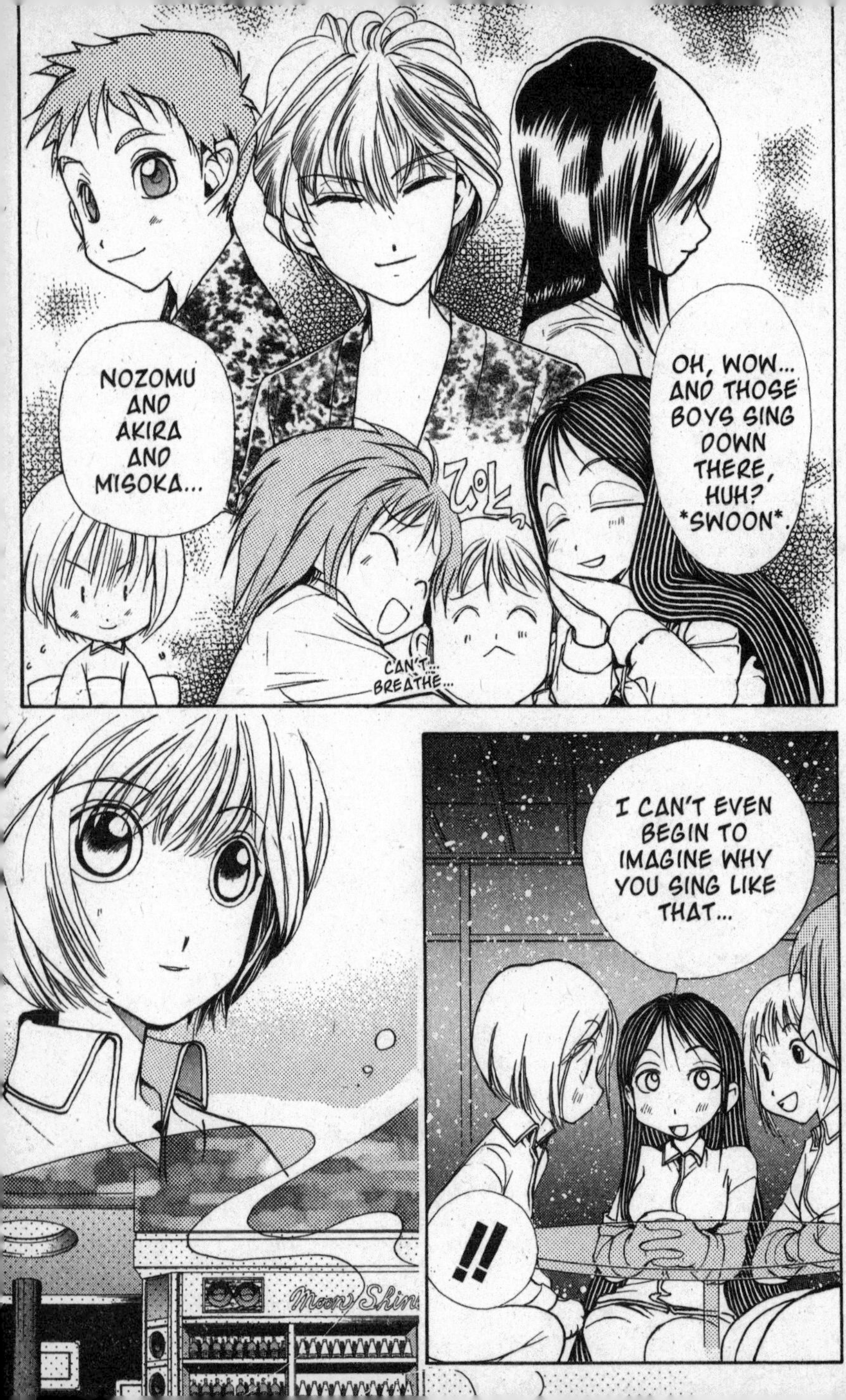
OH, WOW... AND THOSE BOYS SING DOWN THERE, HUH? *SWOON*.
NOZOMU AND AKIRA AND MISOKA...
CAN'T... BREATHE...
I CAN'T EVEN BEGIN TO IMAGINE WHY YOU SING LIKE THAT...
!!
Moon Shin

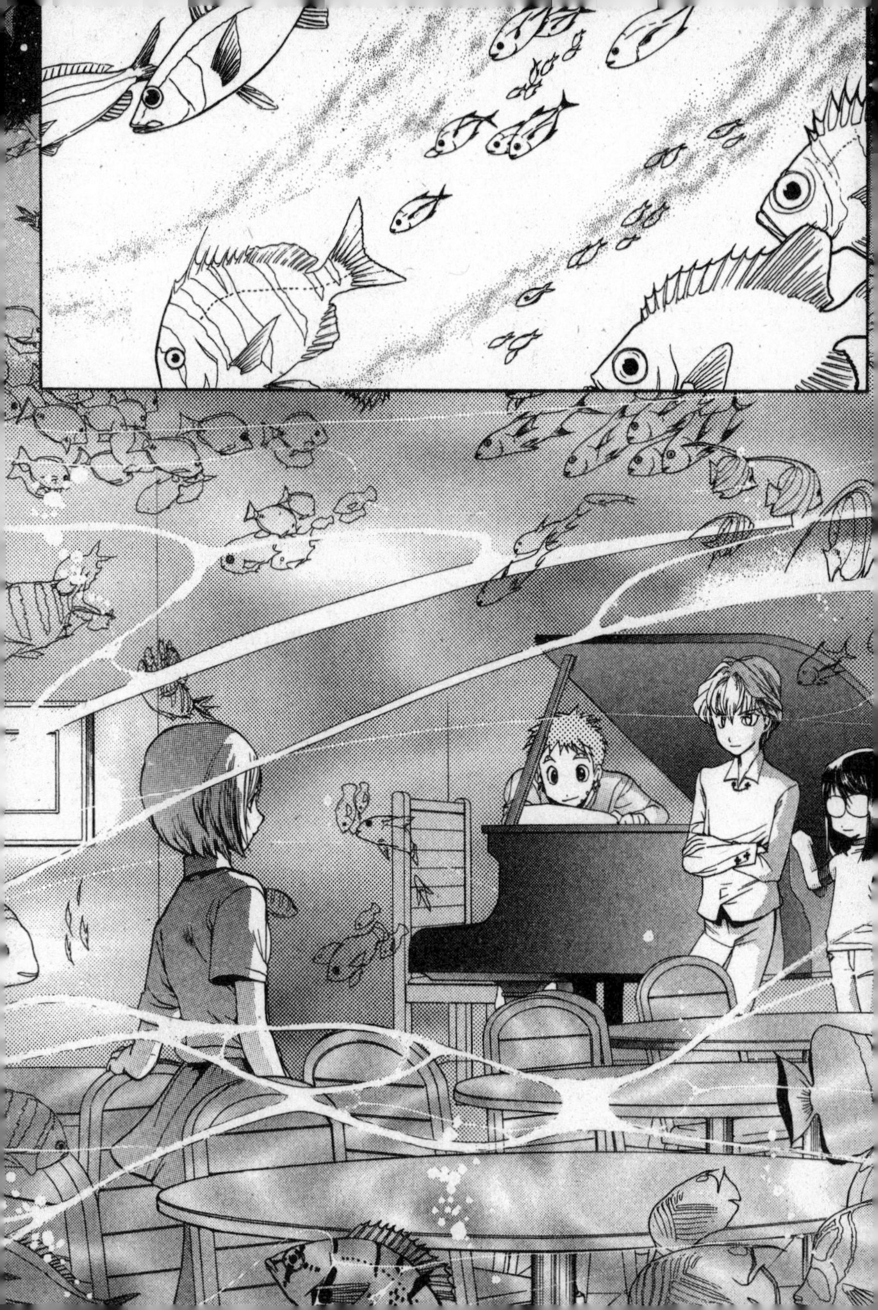

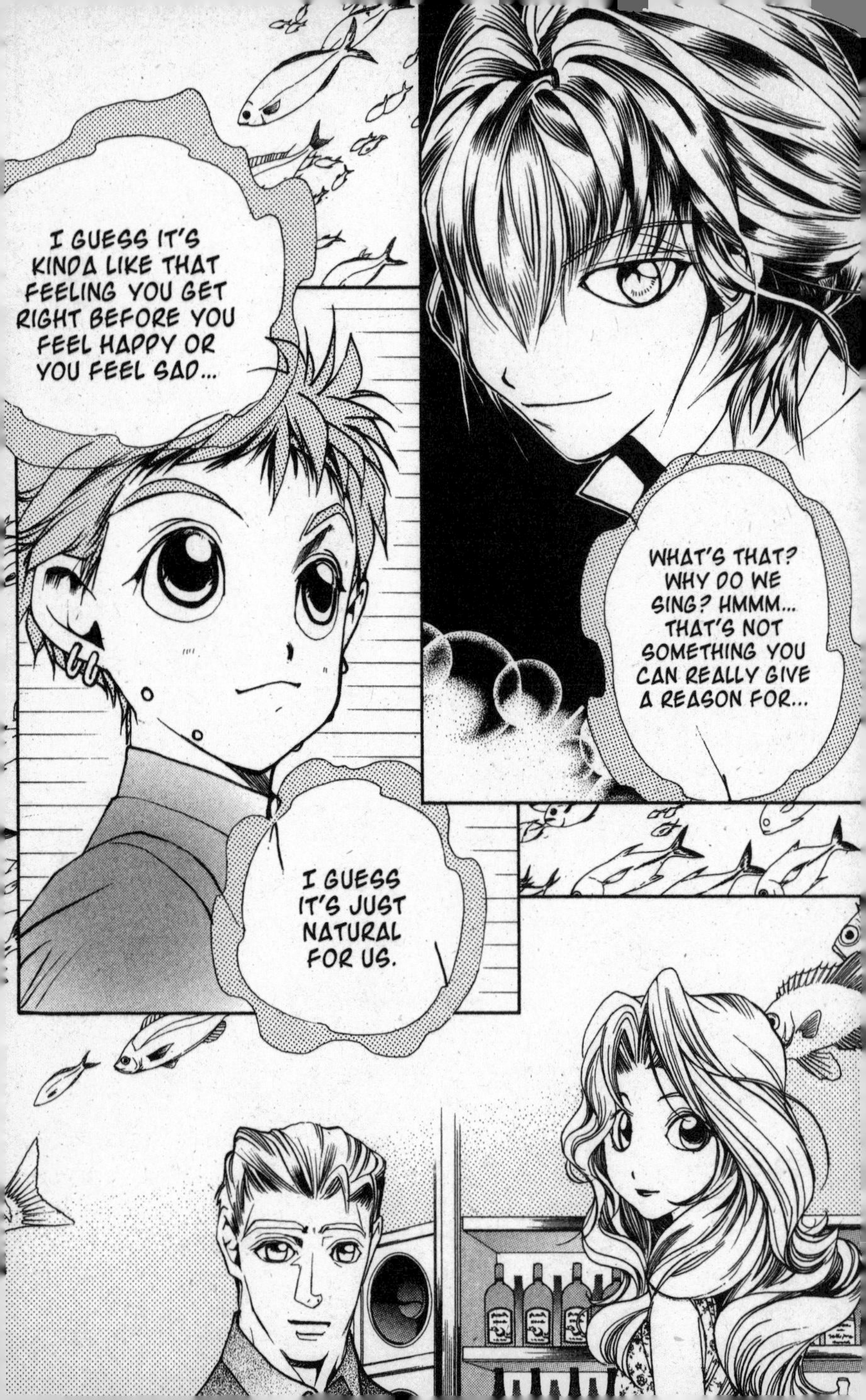
WHAT'S THAT? WHY DO WE SING? HMMM... THAT'S NOT SOMETHING YOU CAN REALLY GIVE A REASON FOR...
I GUESS IT'S KINDA LIKE THAT FEELING YOU GET RIGHT BEFORE YOU FEEL HAPPY OR YOU FEEL SAD...
I GUESS IT'S JUST NATURAL FOR US.

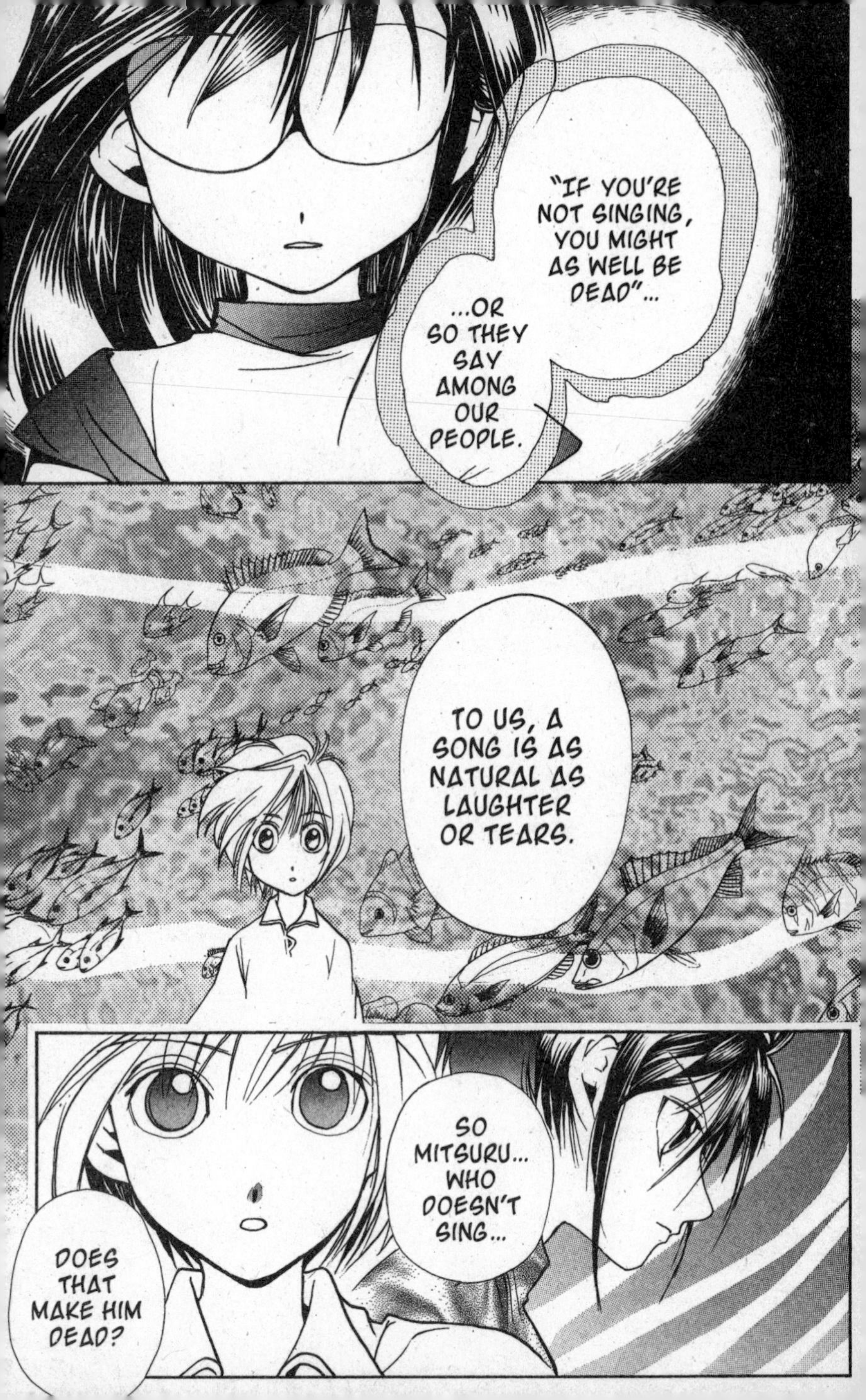
"IF YOU'RE NOT SINGING, YOU MIGHT AS WELL BE DEAD"...
...OR SO THEY SAY AMONG OUR PEOPLE.
TO US, A SONG IS AS NATURAL AS LAUGHTER OR TEARS.
SO MITSURU... WHO DOESN'T SING...
DOES THAT MAKE HIM DEAD?

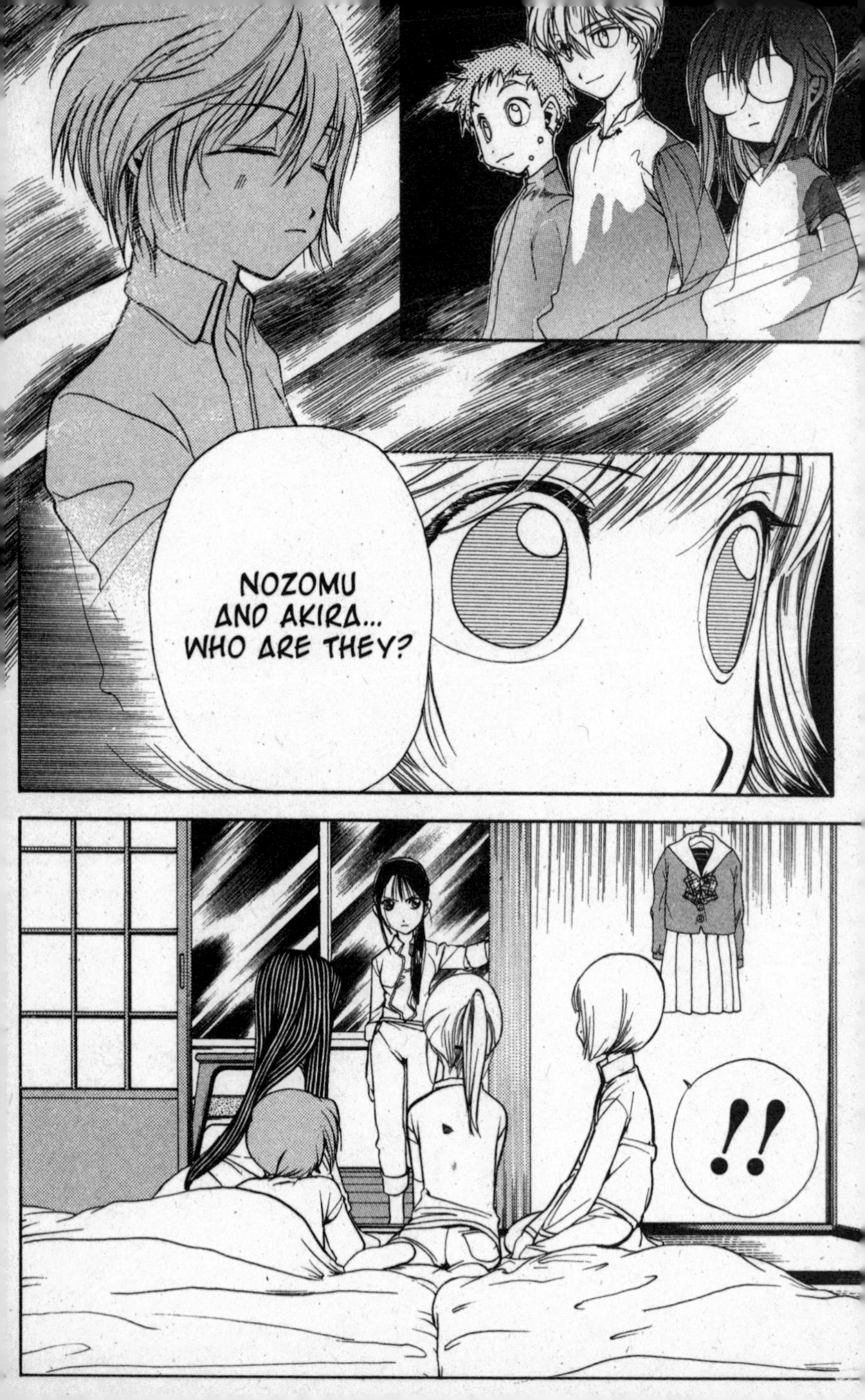
NOZOMU AND AKIRA... WHO ARE THEY?
!!

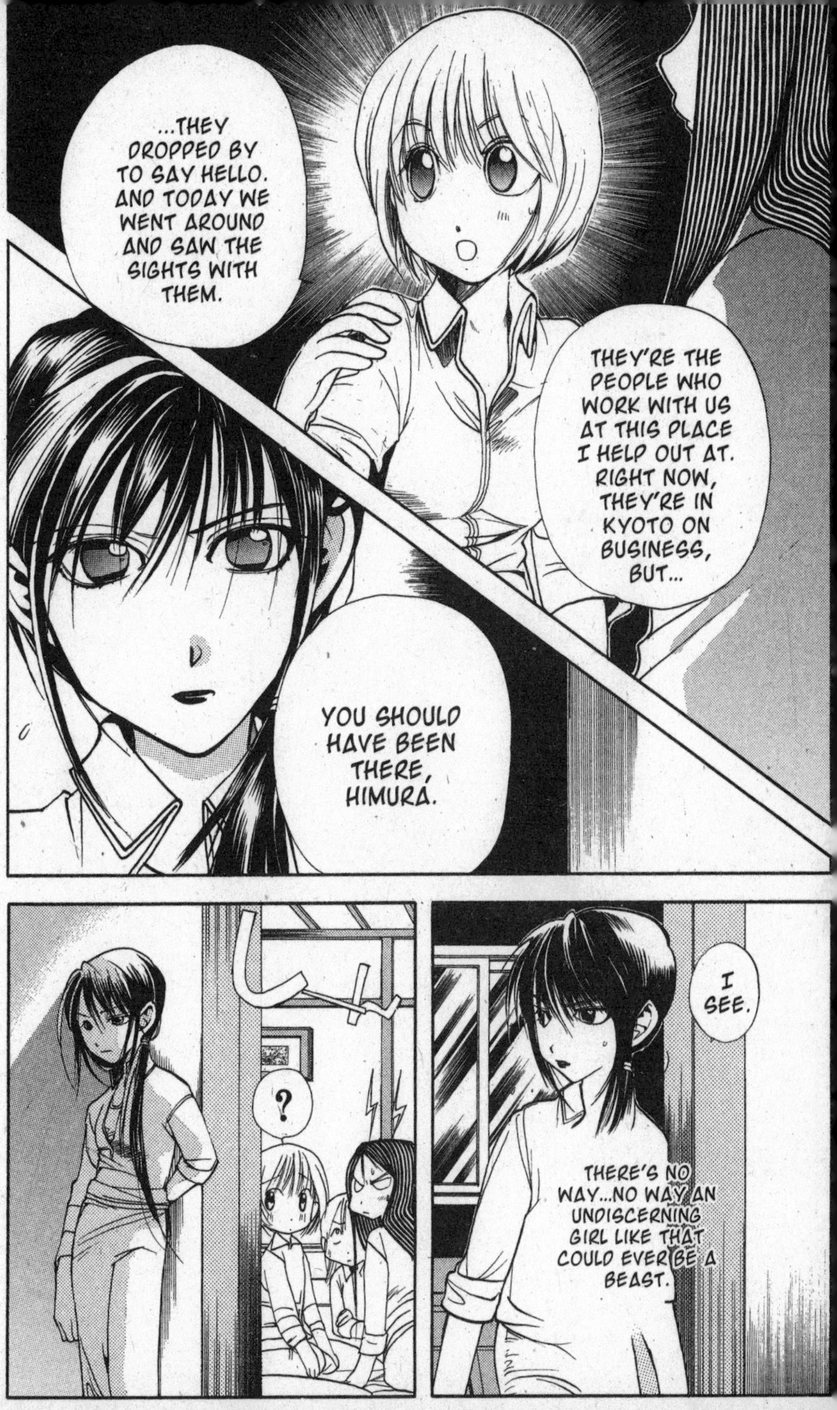
THEY'RE THE PEOPLE WHO WORK WITH US AT THIS PLACE I HELP OUT AT. RIGHT NOW, THEY'RE IN KYOTO ON BUSINESS, BUT...
...THEY DROPPED BY TO SAY HELLO. AND TODAY WE WENT AROUND AND SAW THE SIGHTS WITH THEM.
YOU SHOULD HAVE BEEN THERE, HIMURA.
I SEE.
THERE'S NO WAY...NO WAY AN UNDISCERNING GIRL LIKE THAT COULD EVER BE A BEAST.
?

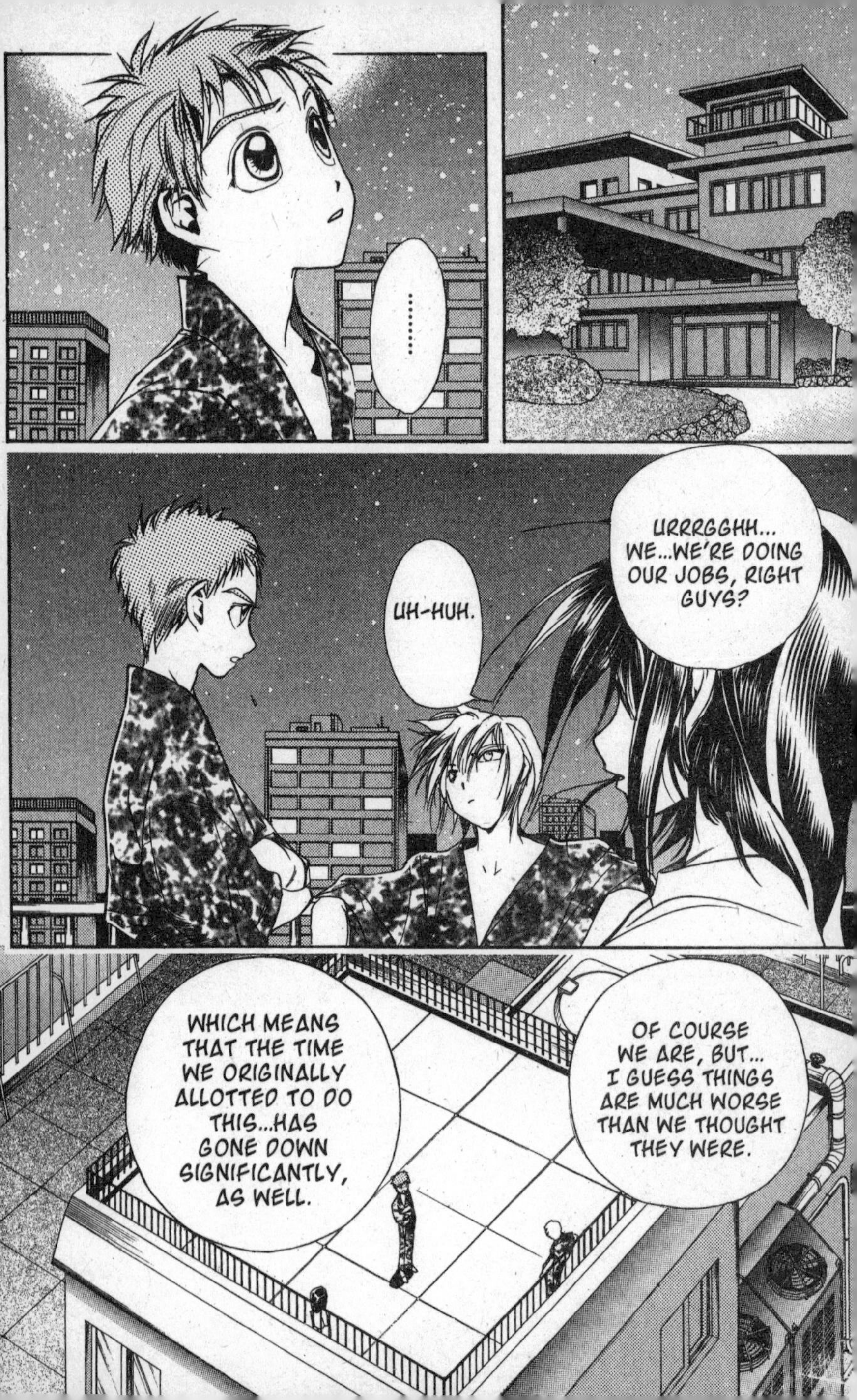
....
URRRGGHH... WE...WE'RE DOING OUR JOBS, RIGHT GUYS?
UH-HUH.
OF COURSE WE ARE, BUT... I GUESS THINGS ARE MUCH WORSE THAN WE THOUGHT THEY WERE.
WHICH MEANS THAT THE TIME WE ORIGINALLY ALLOTTED TO DO THIS...HAS GONE DOWN SIGNIFICANTLY, AS WELL.

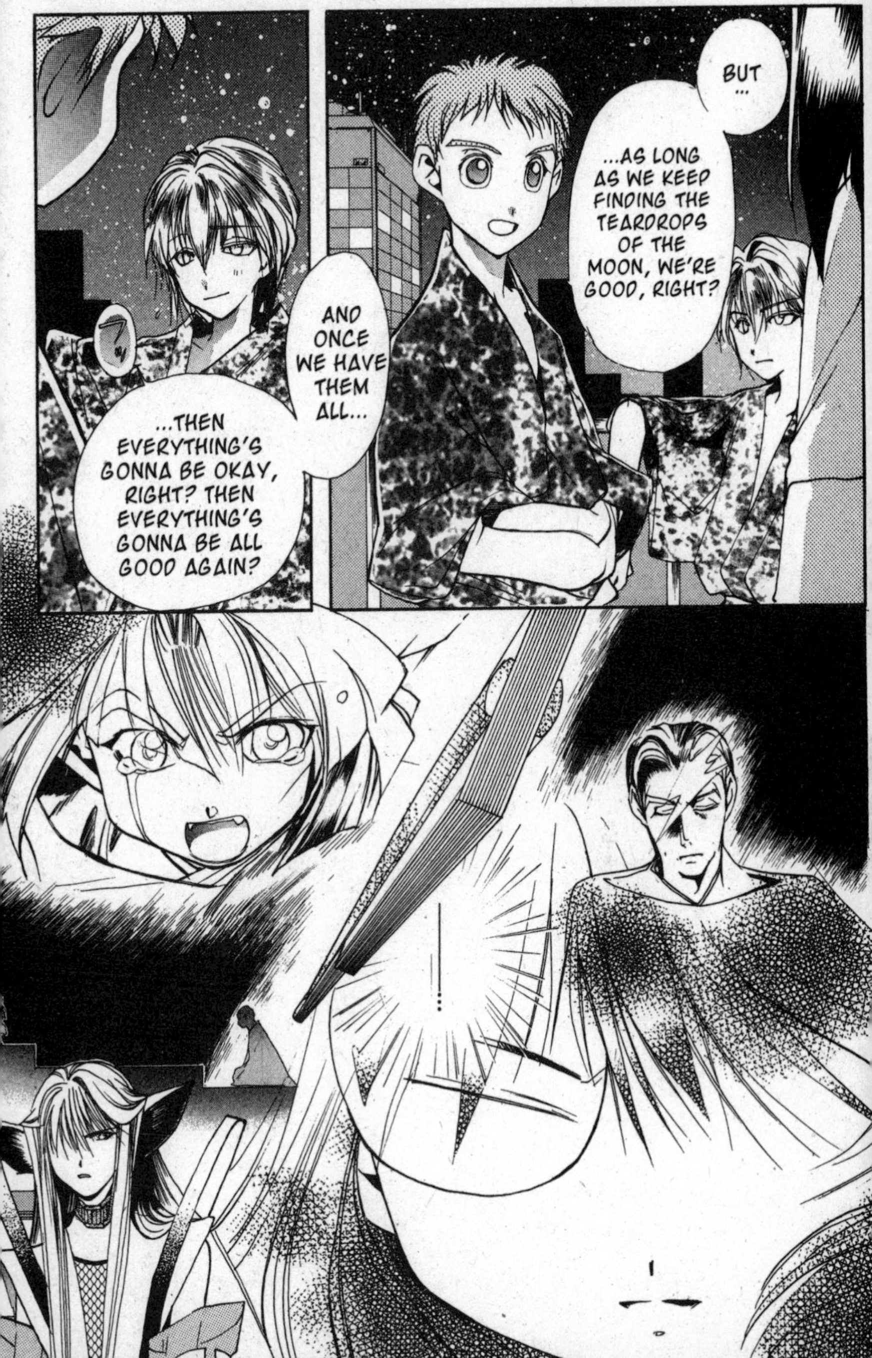
BUT ...
...AS LONG AS WE KEEP FINDING THE TEARDROPS OF THE MOON, WE'RE GOOD, RIGHT?
AND ONCE WE HAVE THEM ALL...
?
...THEN EVERYTHING'S GONNA BE OKAY, RIGHT? THEN EVERYTHING'S GONNA BE ALL GOOD AGAIN?

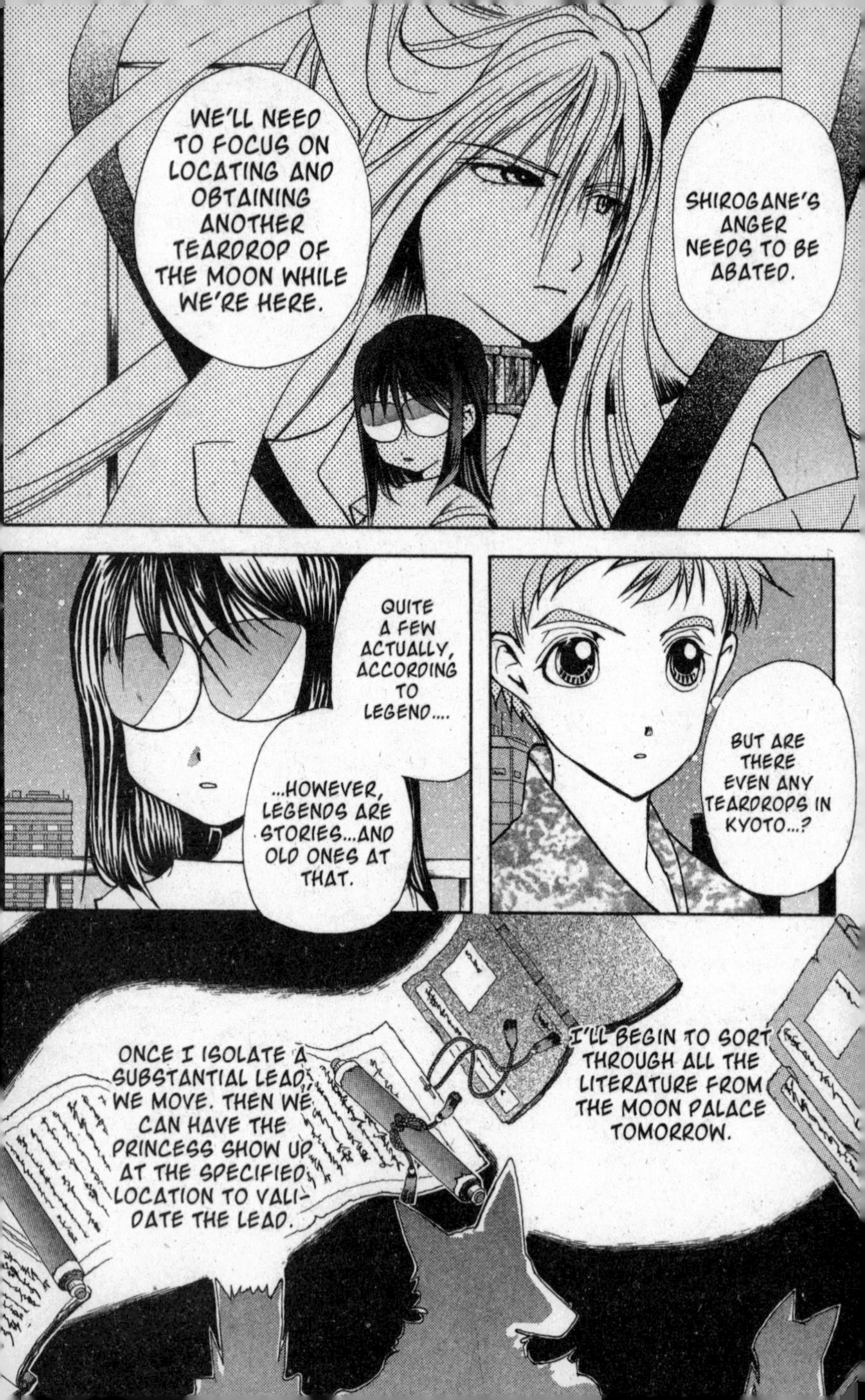
SHIROGANE'S ANGER NEEDS TO BE ABATED.
WE'LL NEED TO FOCUS ON LOCATING AND OBTAINING ANOTHER TEARDROP OF THE MOON WHILE WE'RE HERE.
BUT ARE THERE EVEN ANY TEARDROPS IN KYOTO...?
QUITE A FEW ACTUALLY, ACCORDING TO LEGEND....
...HOWEVER, LEGENDS ARE STORIES...AND OLD ONES AT THAT.
I'LL BEGIN TO SORT THROUGH ALL THE LITERATURE FROM THE MOON PALACE TOMORROW.
ONCE I ISOLATE A SUBSTANTIAL LEAD, WE MOVE. THEN WE CAN HAVE THE PRINCESS SHOW UP AT THE SPECIFIED LOCATION TO VALI-DATE THE LEAD.

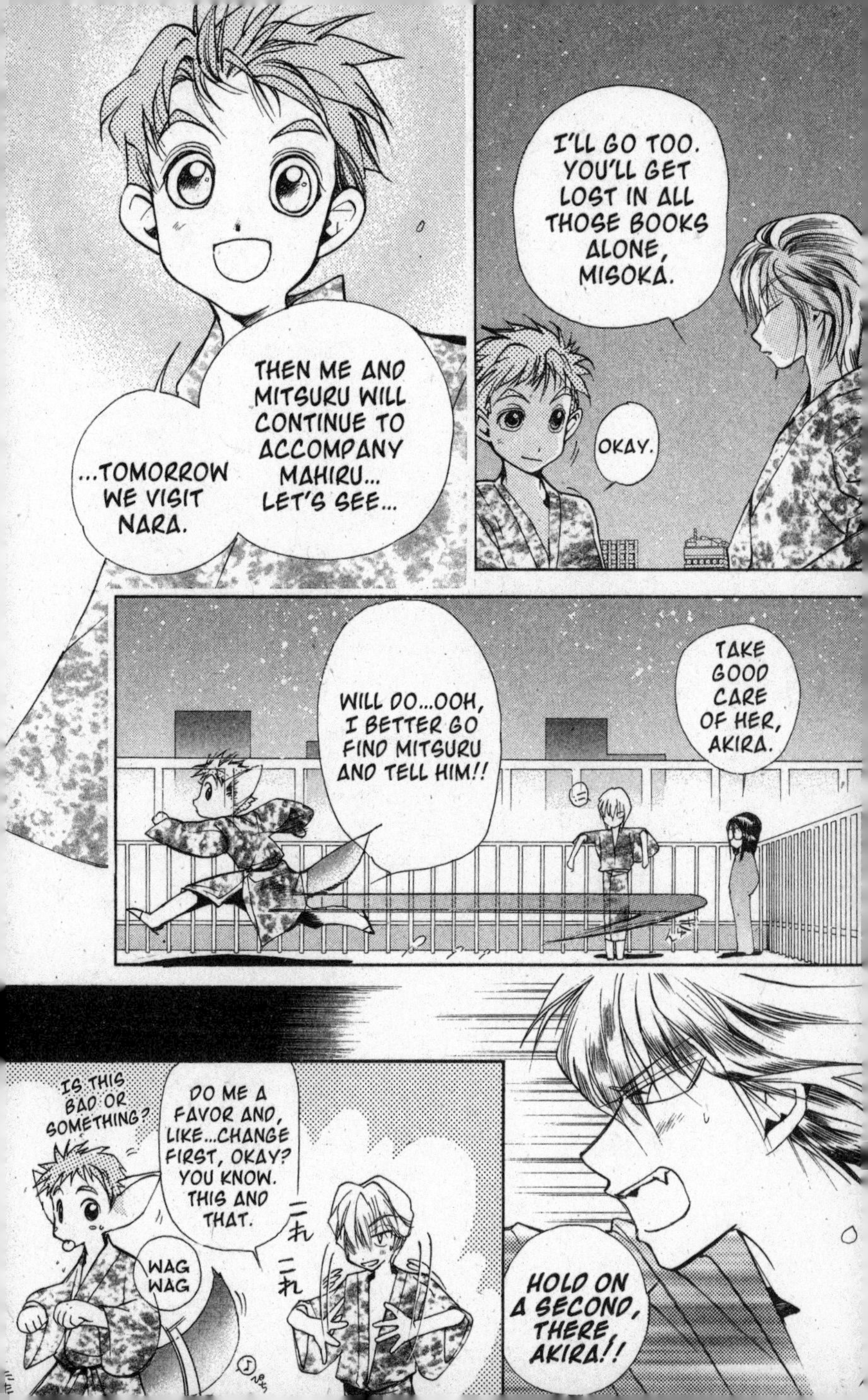
I'LL GO TOO. YOU'LL GET LOST IN ALL THOSE BOOKS ALONE, MISOKA.
OKAY.
THEN ME AND MITSURU WILL CONTINUE TO ACCOMPANY MAHIRU... LET'S SEE...
...TOMORROW WE VISIT NARA.
TAKE GOOD CARE OF HER, AKIRA.
WILL DO...OOH, I BETTER GO FIND MITSURU AND TELL HIM!!
HOLD ON A SECOND, THERE AKIRA!!
DO ME A FAVOR AND, LIKE...CHANGE FIRST, OKAY? YOU KNOW. THIS AND THAT.
IS THIS BAD OR SOMETHING?
WAG WAG

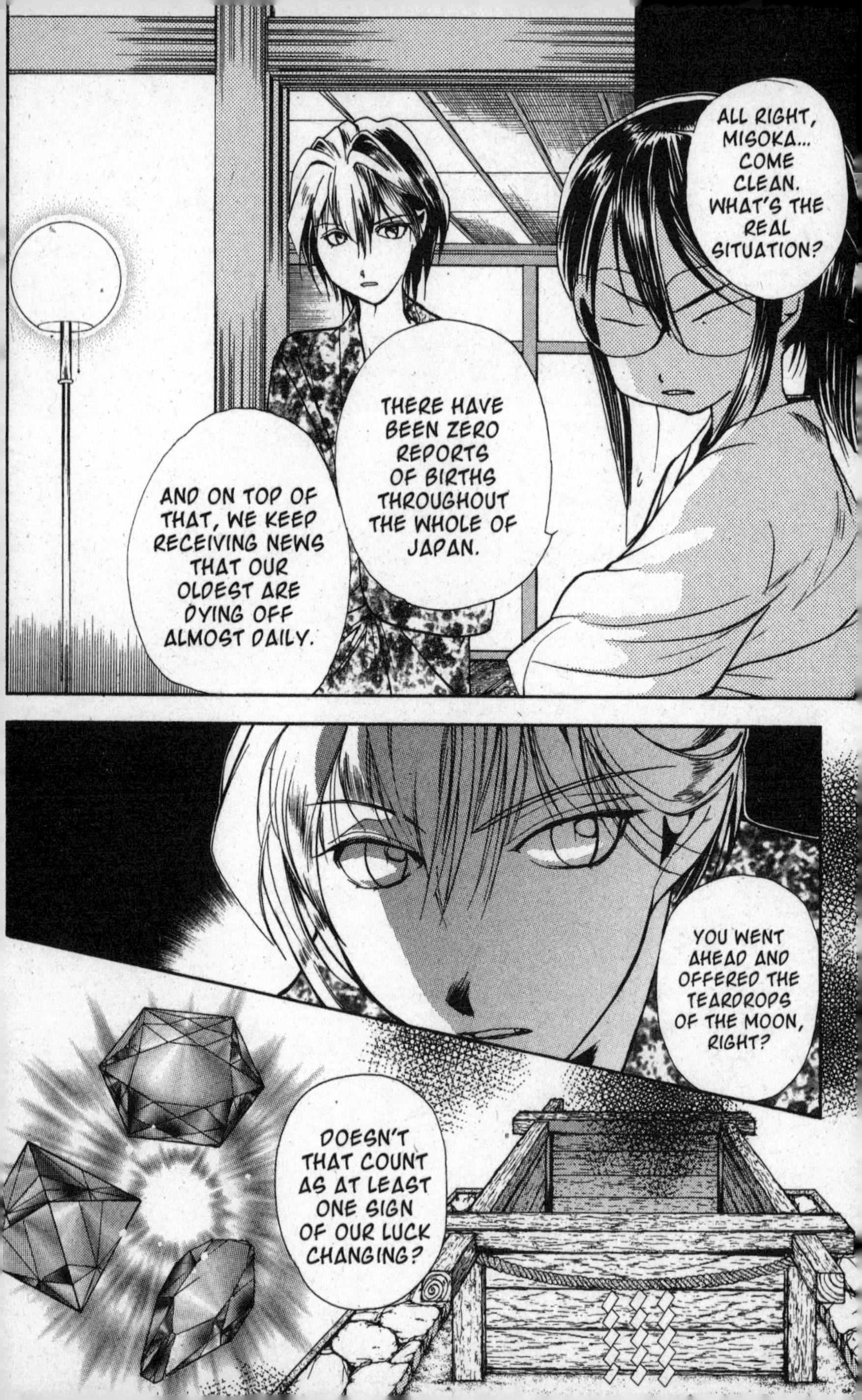
ALL RIGHT, MISOKA... COME CLEAN. WHAT'S THE REAL SITUATION?
THERE HAVE BEEN ZERO REPORTS OF BIRTHS THROUGHOUT THE WHOLE OF JAPAN.
AND ON TOP OF THAT, WE KEEP RECEIVING NEWS THAT OUR OLDEST ARE DYING OFF ALMOST DAILY.
YOU WENT AHEAD AND OFFERED THE TEARDROPS OF THE MOON, RIGHT?
DOESN'T THAT COUNT AS AT LEAST ONE SIGN OF OUR LUCK CHANGING?

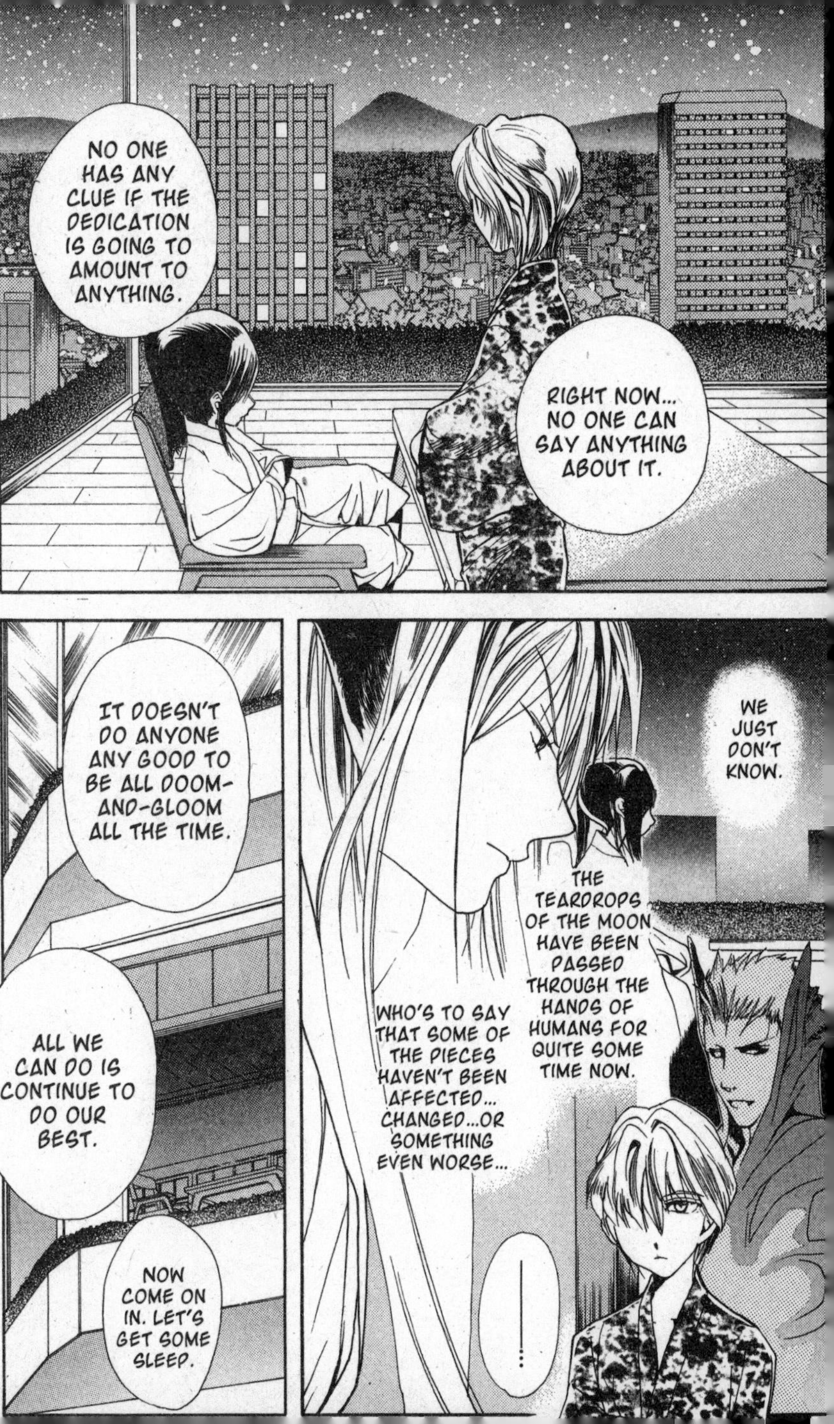
NO ONE HAS ANY CLUE IF THE DEDICATION IS GOING TO AMOUNT TO ANYTHING.
RIGHT NOW... NO ONE CAN SAY ANYTHING ABOUT IT.
WE JUST DON'T KNOW.
THE TEARDROPS OF THE MOON HAVE BEEN PASSED THROUGH THE HANDS OF HUMANS FOR QUITE SOME TIME NOW.
WHO'S TO SAY THAT SOME OF THE PIECES HAVEN'T BEEN AFFECTED... CHANGED...OR SOMETHING EVEN WORSE...
......
IT DOESN'T DO ANYONE ANY GOOD TO BE ALL DOOM-AND-GLOOM ALL THE TIME.
ALL WE CAN DO IS CONTINUE TO DO OUR BEST.
NOW COME ON IN. LET'S GET SOME SLEEP.

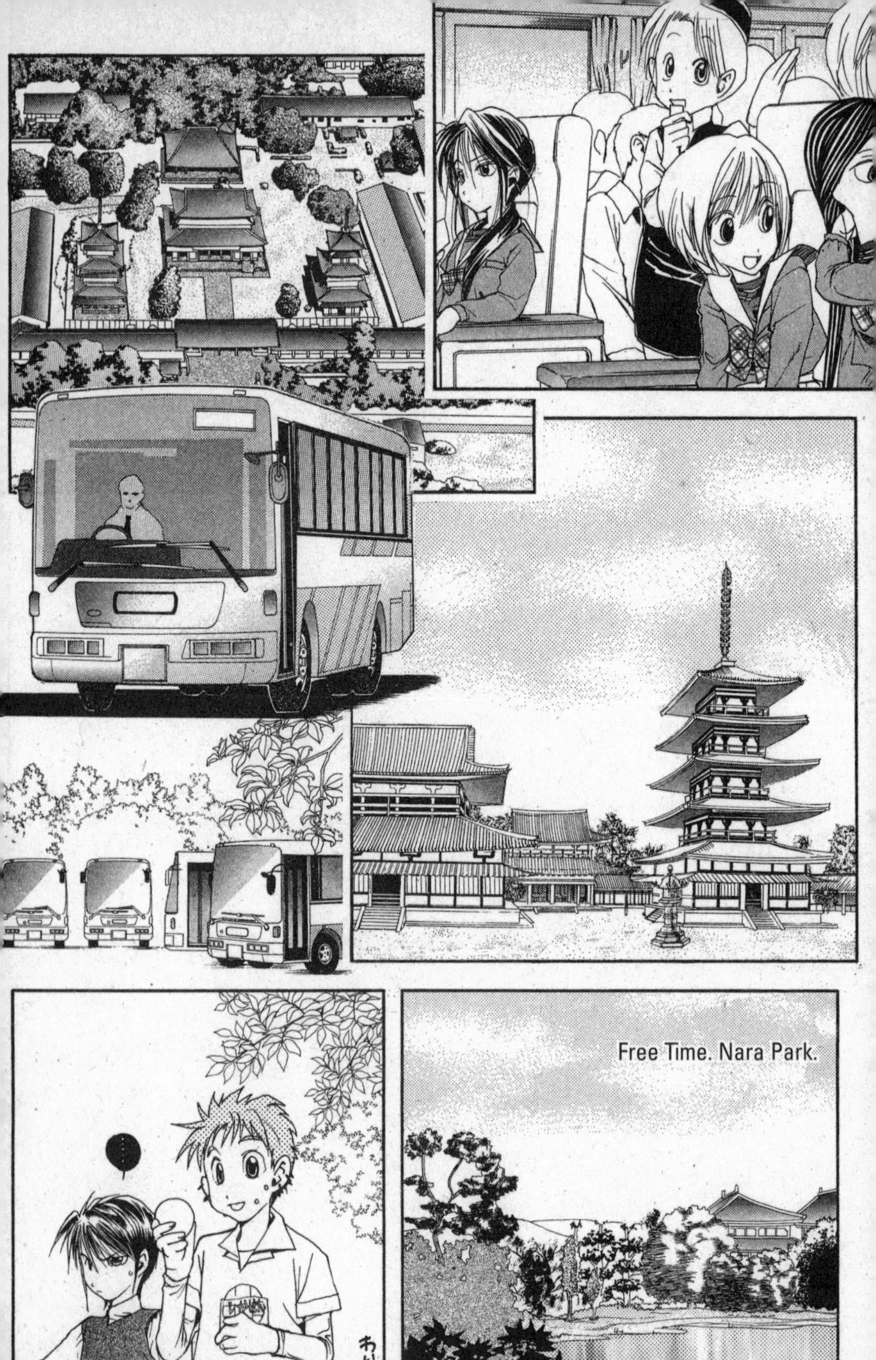
Free Time. Nara Park.
…
わい
わい

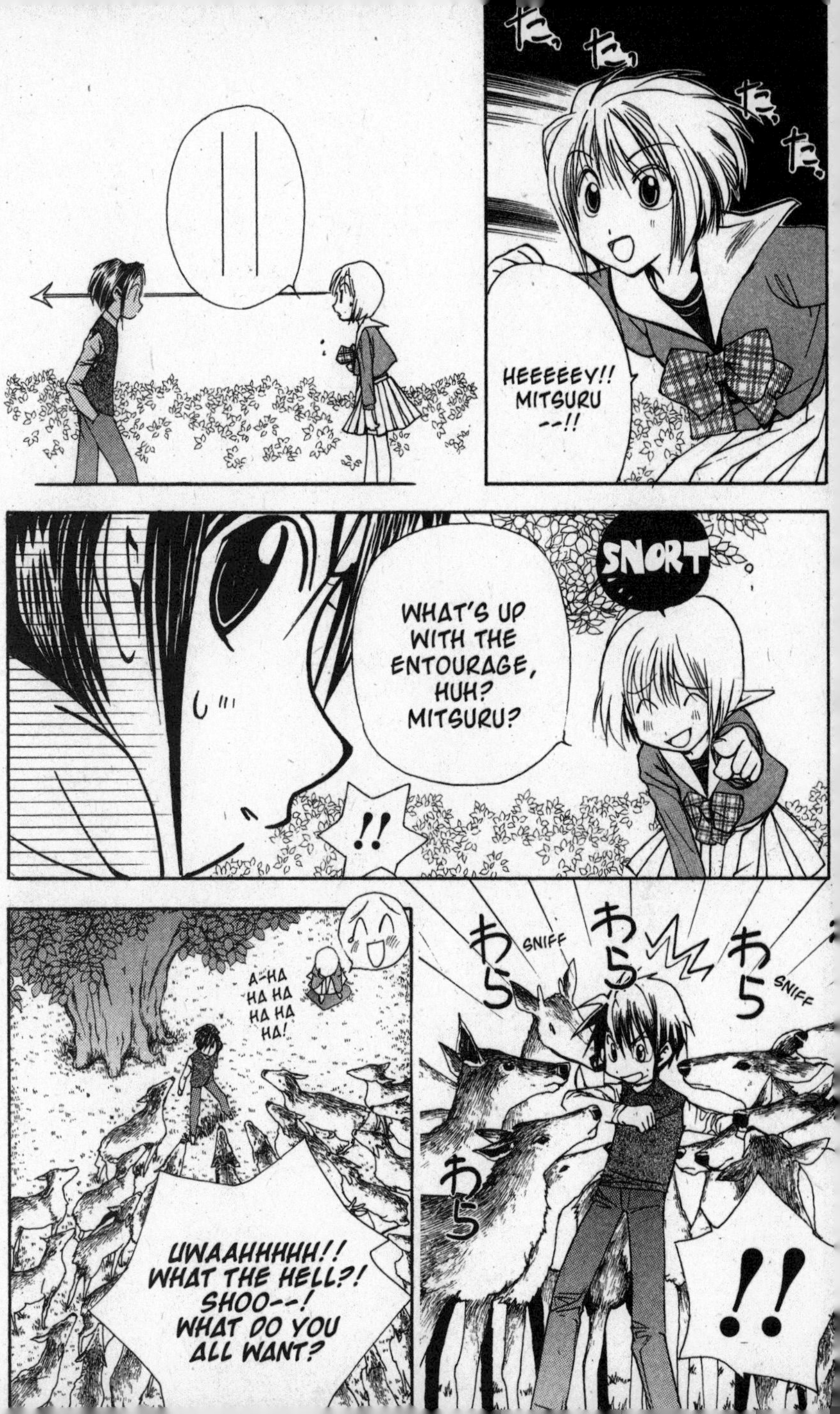

たたたた
HEEEEEY!! MITSURU --!!
SNORT
WHAT'S UP WITH THE ENTOURAGE, HUH? MITSURU?
!!
わら
SNIFF
わら
わら
SNIFF
わら
!!
A-HA HA HA HA HA HA!
UWAAHHHHH!! WHAT THE HELL?! SHOO--! WHAT DO YOU ALL WANT?

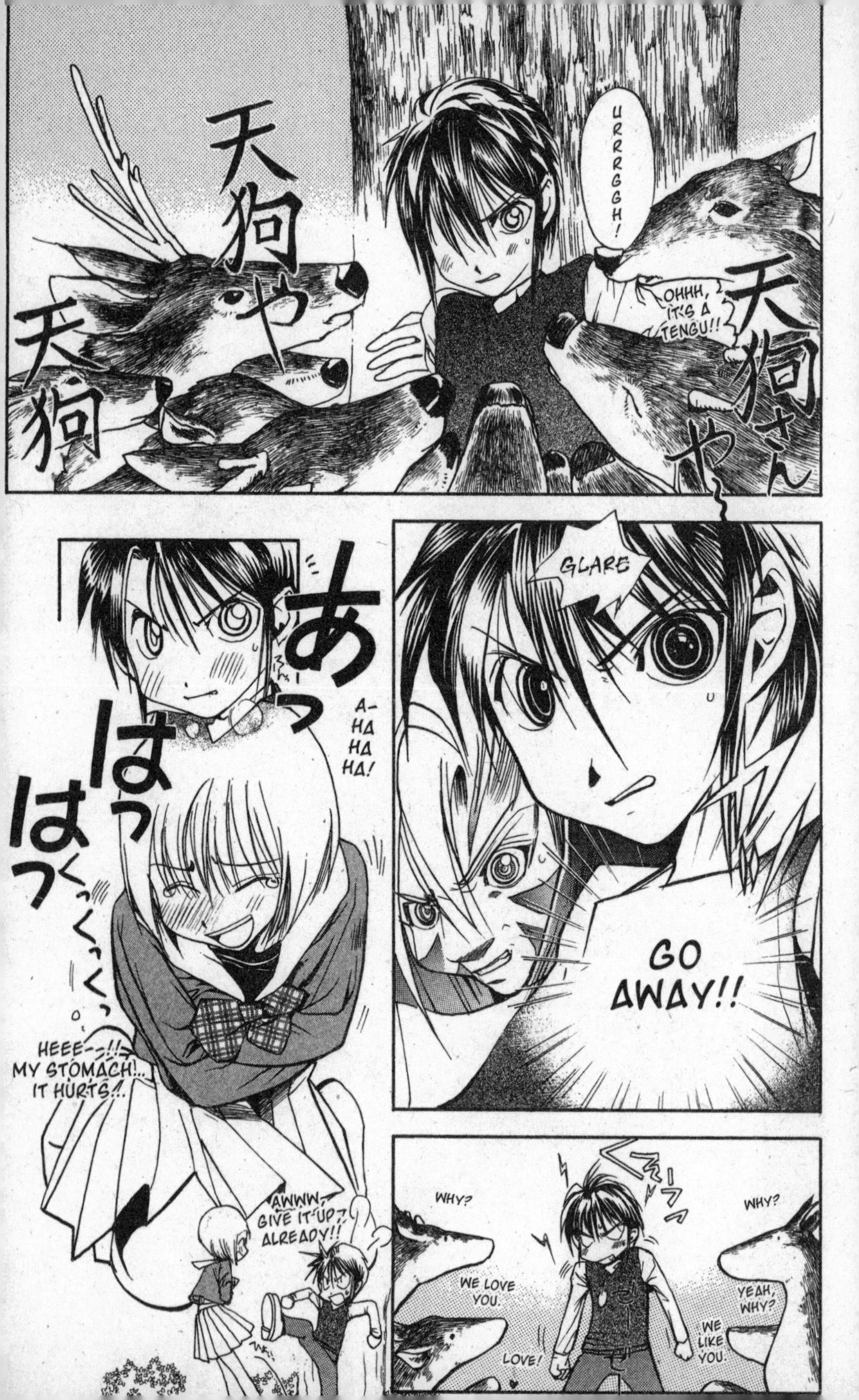

天狗さんや~
OHHH, IT'S A TENGU!!
URRRGGH!
天狗や
天狗
GLARE
GO AWAY!!
WHY?
WHY?
YEAH, WHY?
WE LIKE YOU.
WE LOVE YOU.
LOVE!
あっはっはっ
A-HA HA HA HA!
くっくっくっ
HEEE--!! MY STOMACH!.. IT HURTS!..
AWWW, GIVE IT UP ALREADY!!

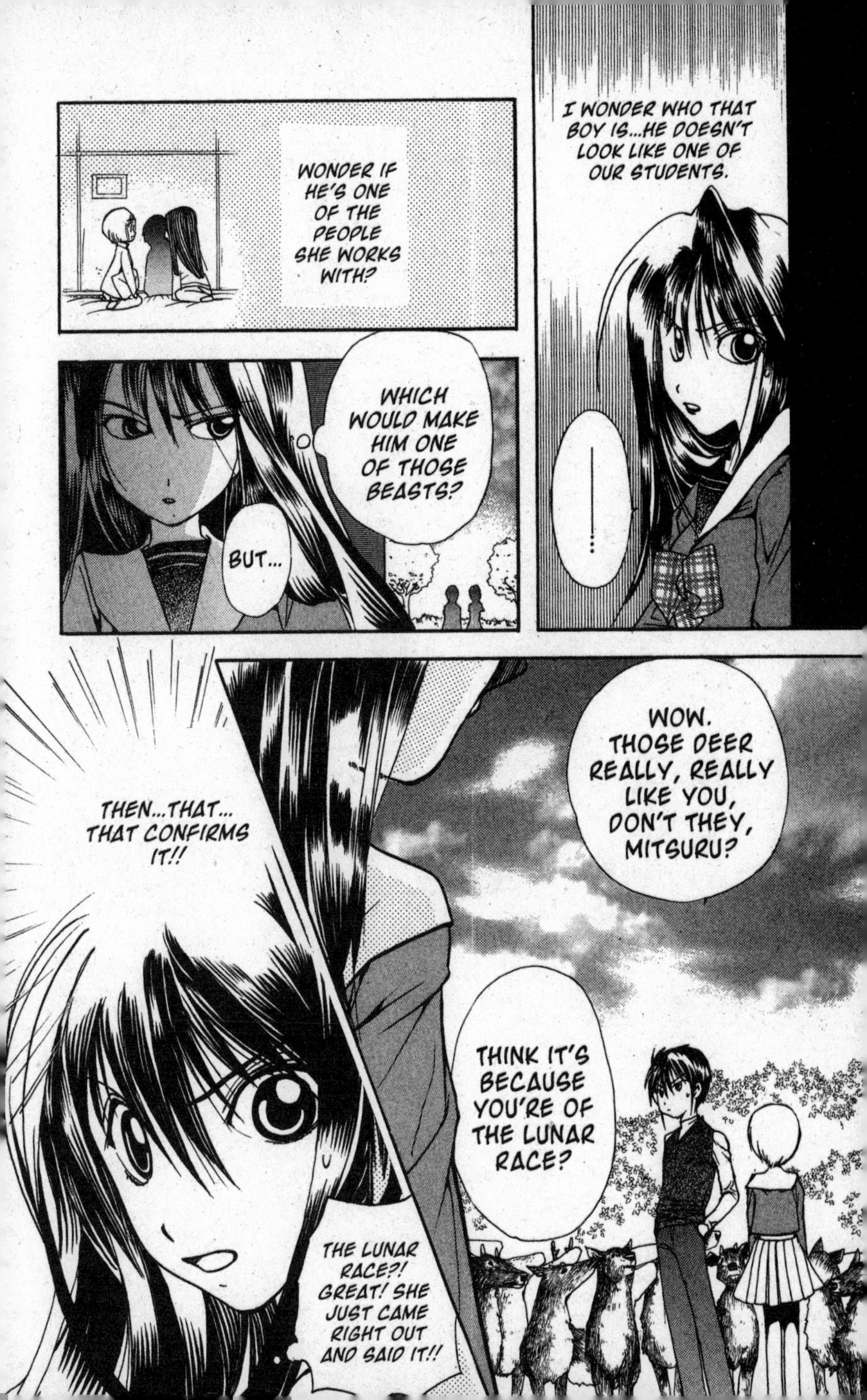
I WONDER WHO THAT BOY IS...HE DOESN'T LOOK LIKE ONE OF OUR STUDENTS.
...!
WONDER IF HE'S ONE OF THE PEOPLE SHE WORKS WITH?
WHICH WOULD MAKE HIM ONE OF THOSE BEASTS?
BUT...
WOW. THOSE DEER REALLY, REALLY LIKE YOU, DON'T THEY, MITSURU?
THINK IT'S BECAUSE YOU'RE OF THE LUNAR RACE?
THE LUNAR RACE?! GREAT! SHE JUST CAME RIGHT OUT AND SAID IT!!
THEN...THAT... THAT CONFIRMS IT!!

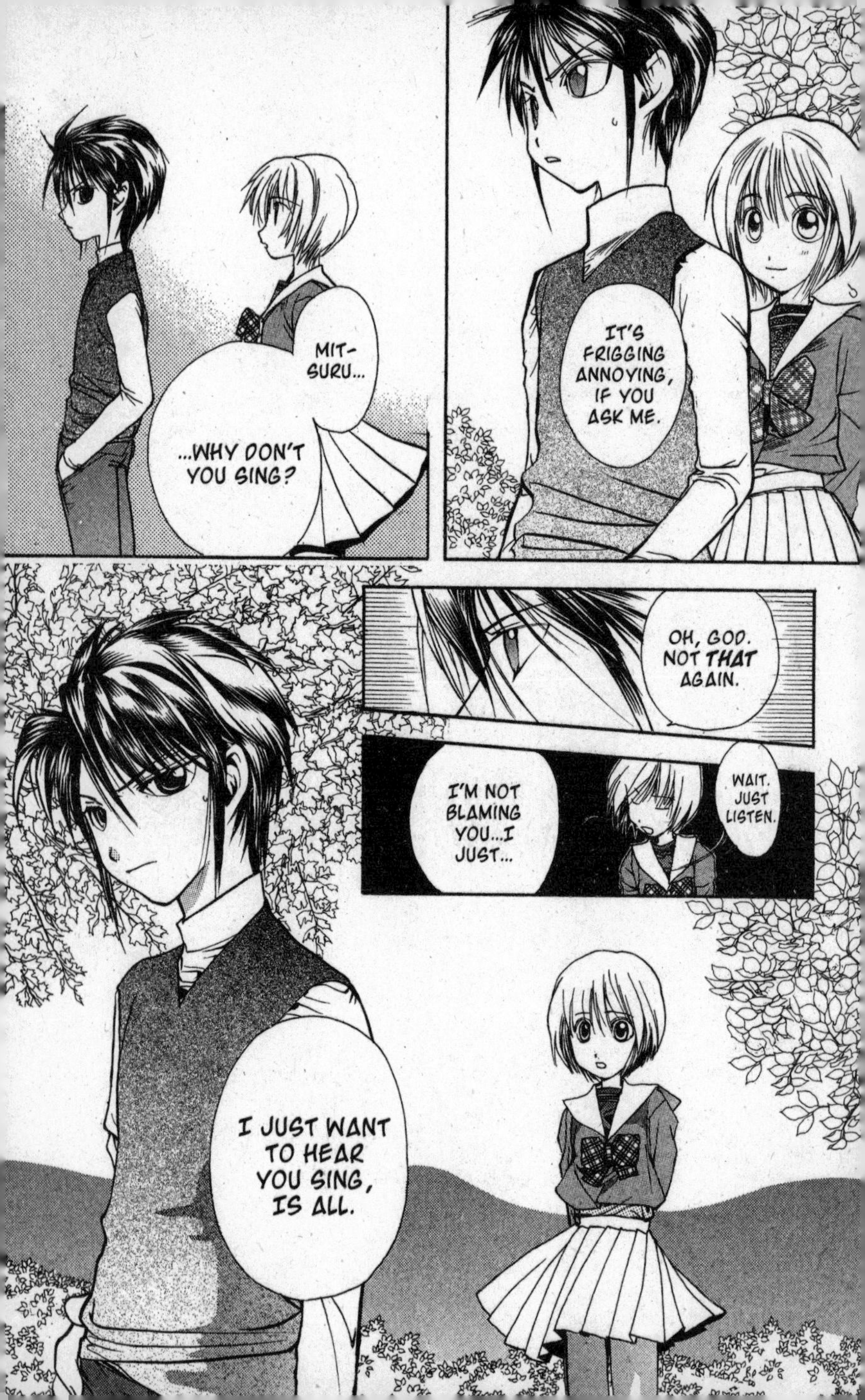
IT'S FRIGGING ANNOYING, IF YOU ASK ME.
MIT-SURU...
...WHY DON'T YOU SING?
OH, GOD. NOT **THAT** AGAIN.
WAIT. JUST LISTEN.
I'M NOT BLAMING YOU...I JUST...
I JUST WANT TO HEAR YOU SING, IS ALL.

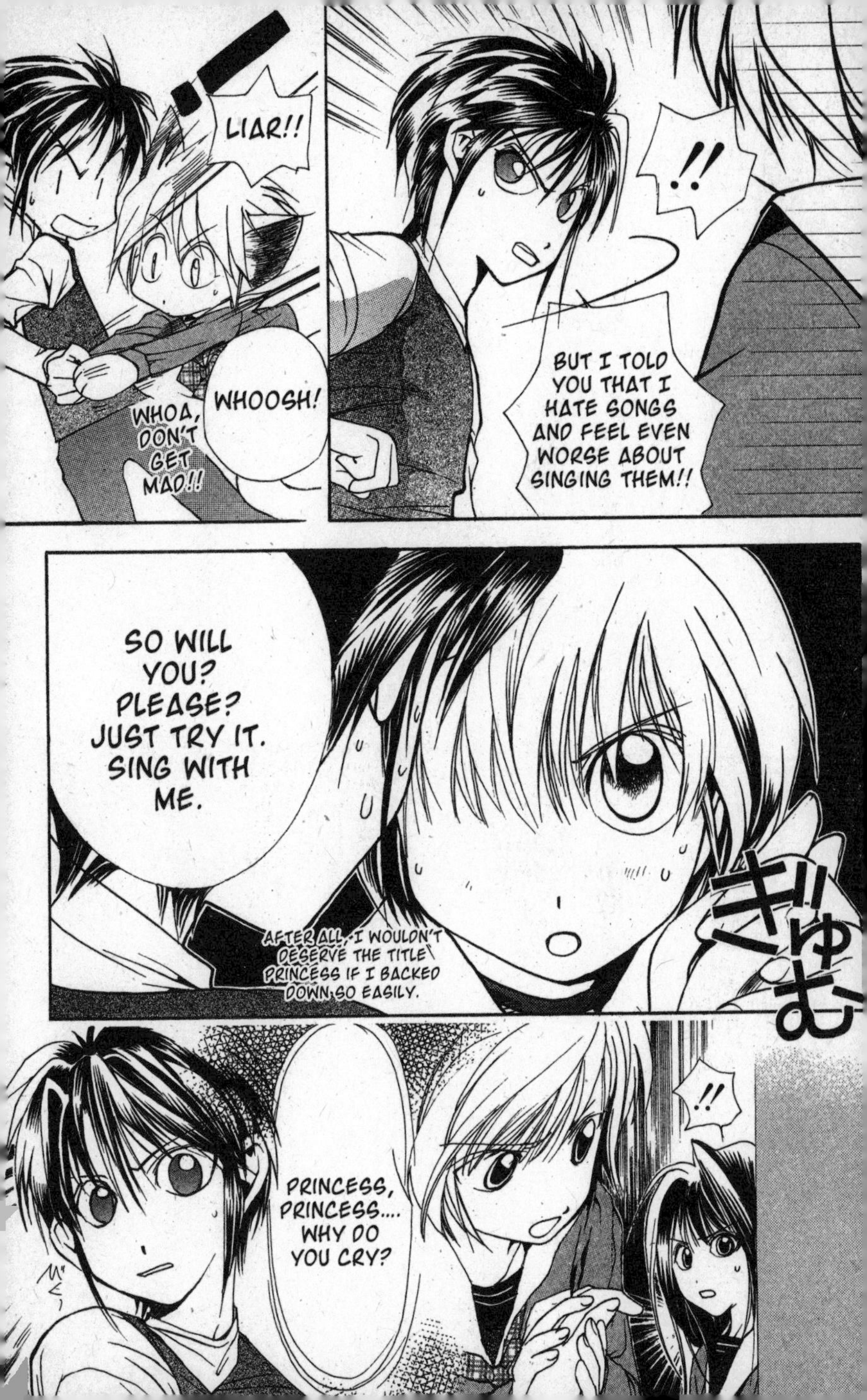
!!
BUT I TOLD YOU THAT I HATE SONGS AND FEEL EVEN WORSE ABOUT SINGING THEM!!
LIAR!!
WHOOSH!
WHOA, DON'T GET MAD!!
ぎゅむ
SO WILL YOU? PLEASE? JUST TRY IT. SING WITH ME.
AFTER ALL, I WOULDN'T DESERVE THE TITLE PRINCESS IF I BACKED DOWN SO EASILY.
!!
PRINCESS, PRINCESS.... WHY DO YOU CRY?

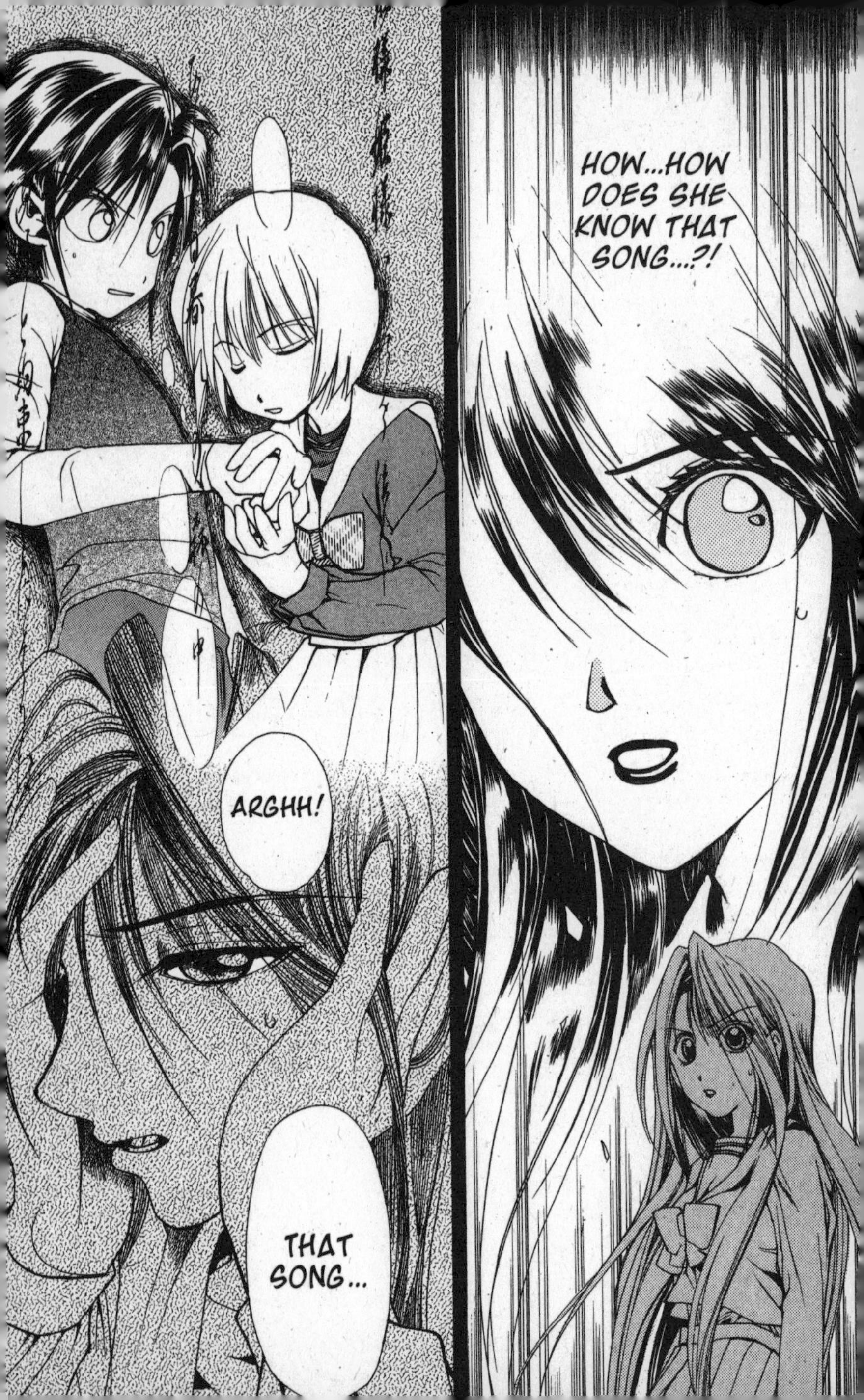
HOW...HOW DOES SHE KNOW THAT SONG...?!
ARGHH!
THAT SONG...

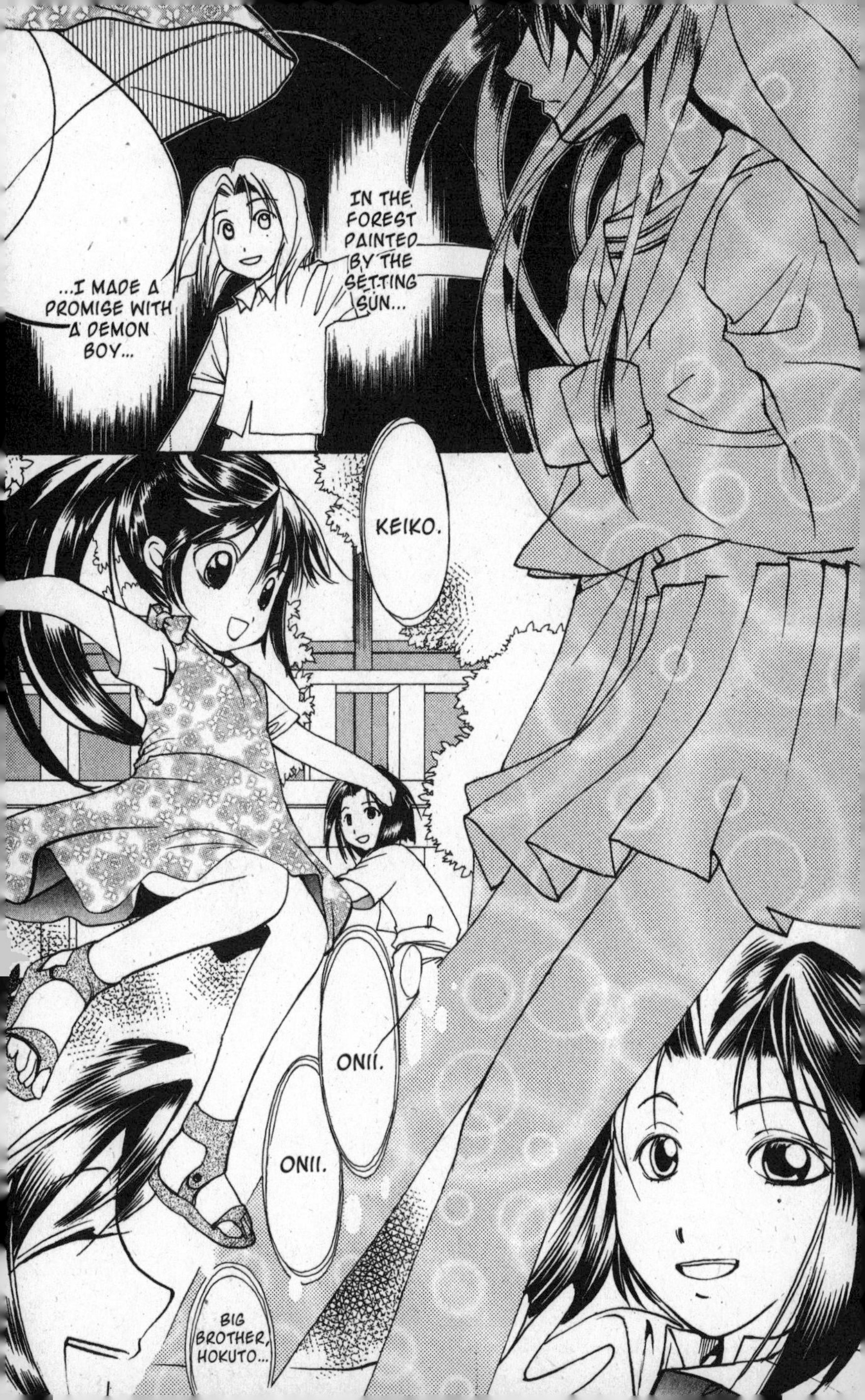
IN THE FOREST PAINTED BY THE SETTING SUN...
...I MADE A PROMISE WITH A DEMON BOY...
KEIKO.
ONII.
ONII.
BIG BROTHER, HOKUTO...

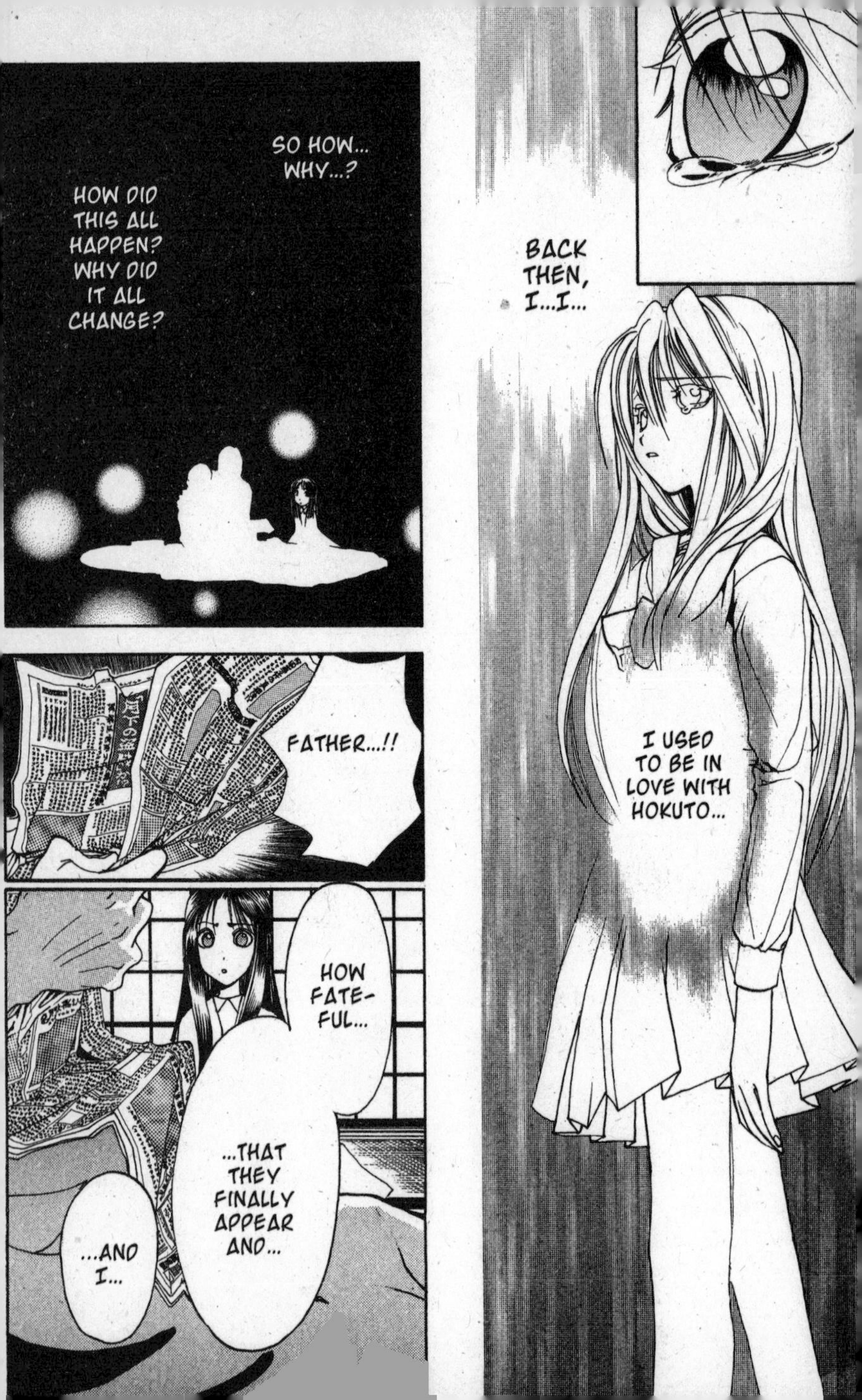
BACK THEN, I...I...
I USED TO BE IN LOVE WITH HOKUTO...
SO HOW... WHY...?
HOW DID THIS ALL HAPPEN? WHY DID IT ALL CHANGE?
FATHER...!!
HOW FATE-FUL...
...THAT THEY FINALLY APPEAR AND...
...AND I...

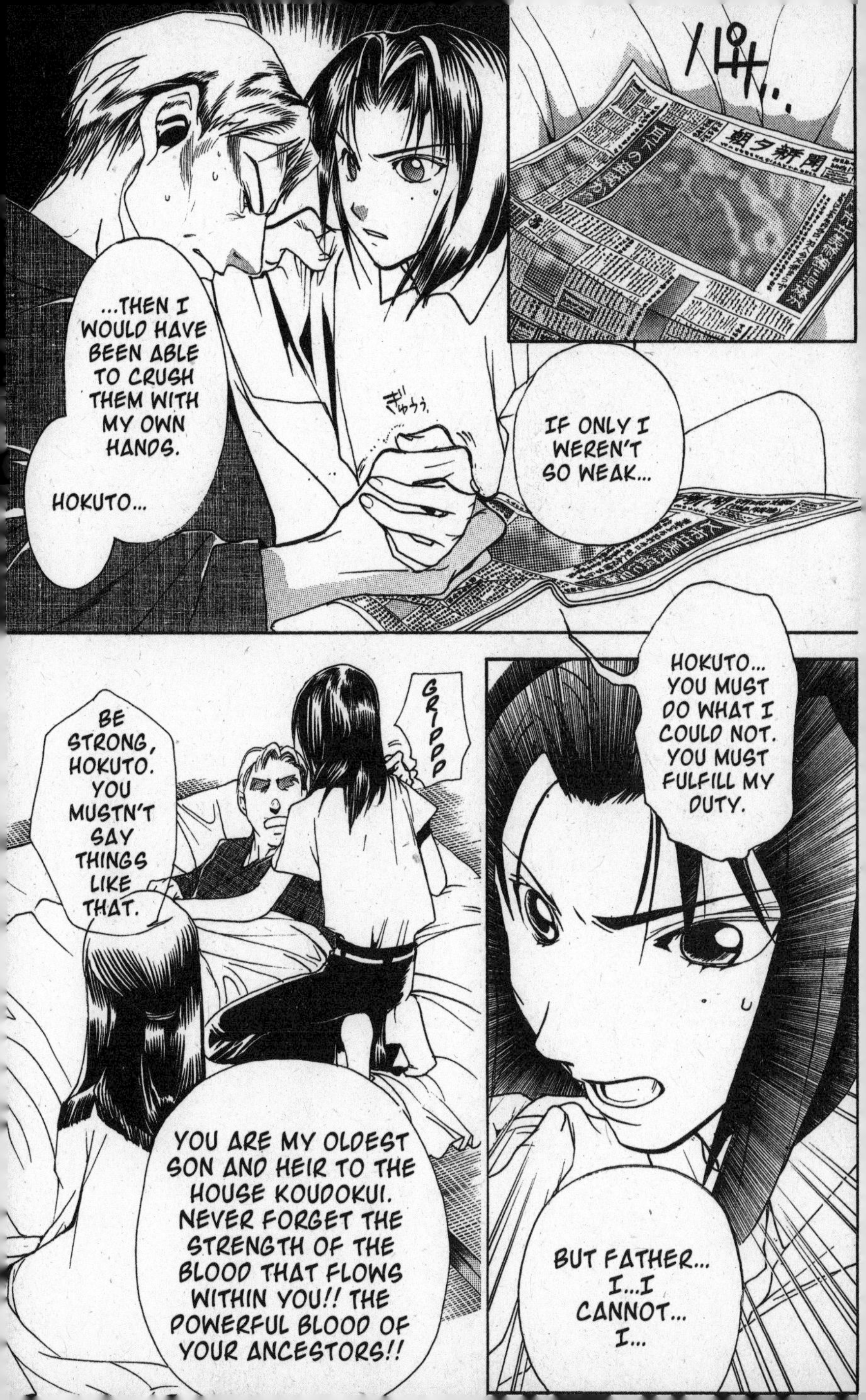
朝夕新聞
IF ONLY I WEREN'T SO WEAK...
...THEN I WOULD HAVE BEEN ABLE TO CRUSH THEM WITH MY OWN HANDS.
HOKUTO...
HOKUTO... YOU MUST DO WHAT I COULD NOT. YOU MUST FULFILL MY DUTY.
BUT FATHER... I...I CANNOT... I...
GRIPPP
BE STRONG, HOKUTO. YOU MUSTN'T SAY THINGS LIKE THAT.
YOU ARE MY OLDEST SON AND HEIR TO THE HOUSE KOUDOKUI. NEVER FORGET THE STRENGTH OF THE BLOOD THAT FLOWS WITHIN YOU!! THE POWERFUL BLOOD OF YOUR ANCESTORS!!

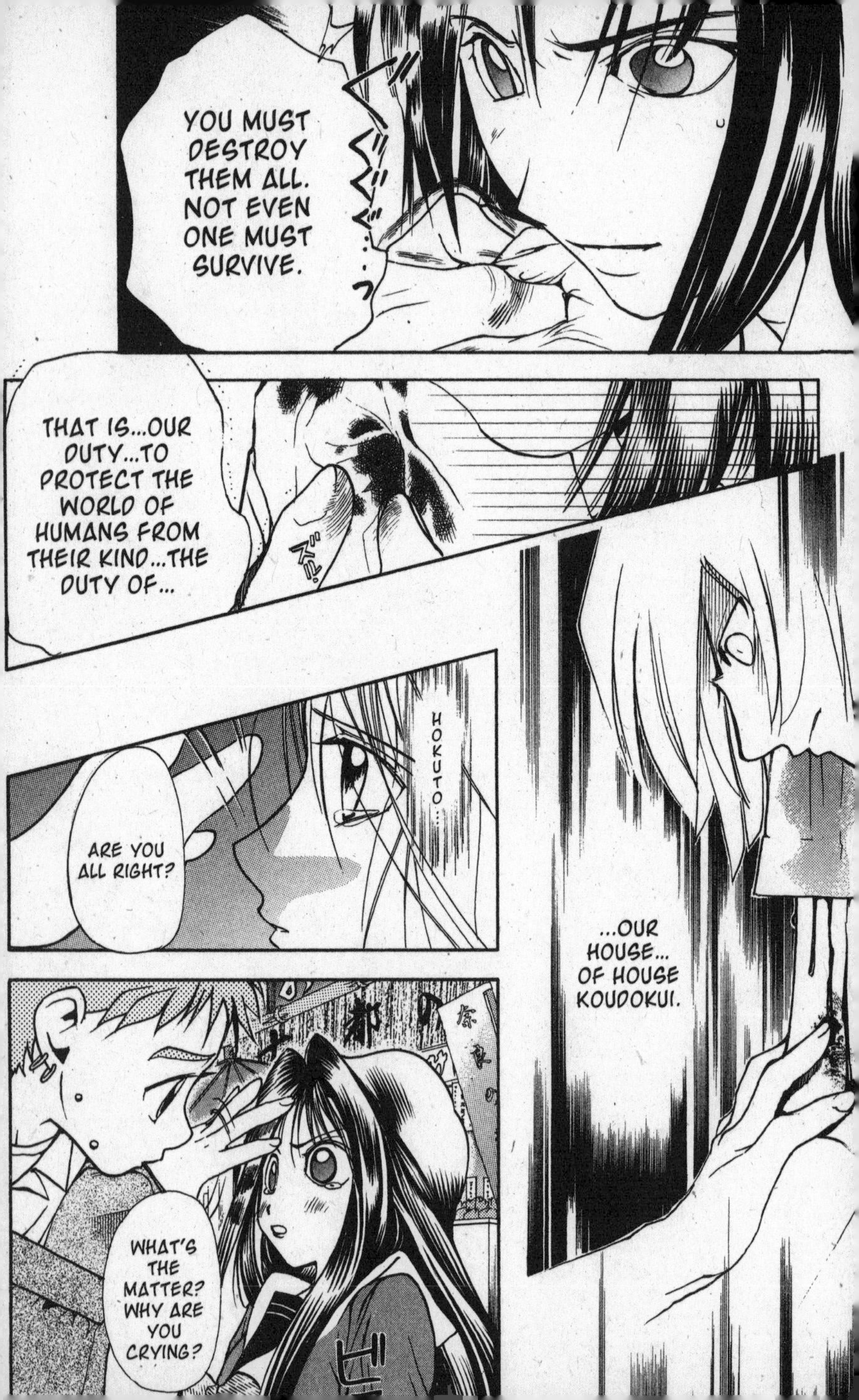

YOU MUST DESTROY THEM ALL. NOT EVEN ONE MUST SURVIVE.
THAT IS...OUR DUTY...TO PROTECT THE WORLD OF HUMANS FROM THEIR KIND...THE DUTY OF...
...OUR HOUSE... OF HOUSE KOUDOKUI.
HOKUTO...
ARE YOU ALL RIGHT?
WHAT'S THE MATTER? WHY ARE YOU CRYING?

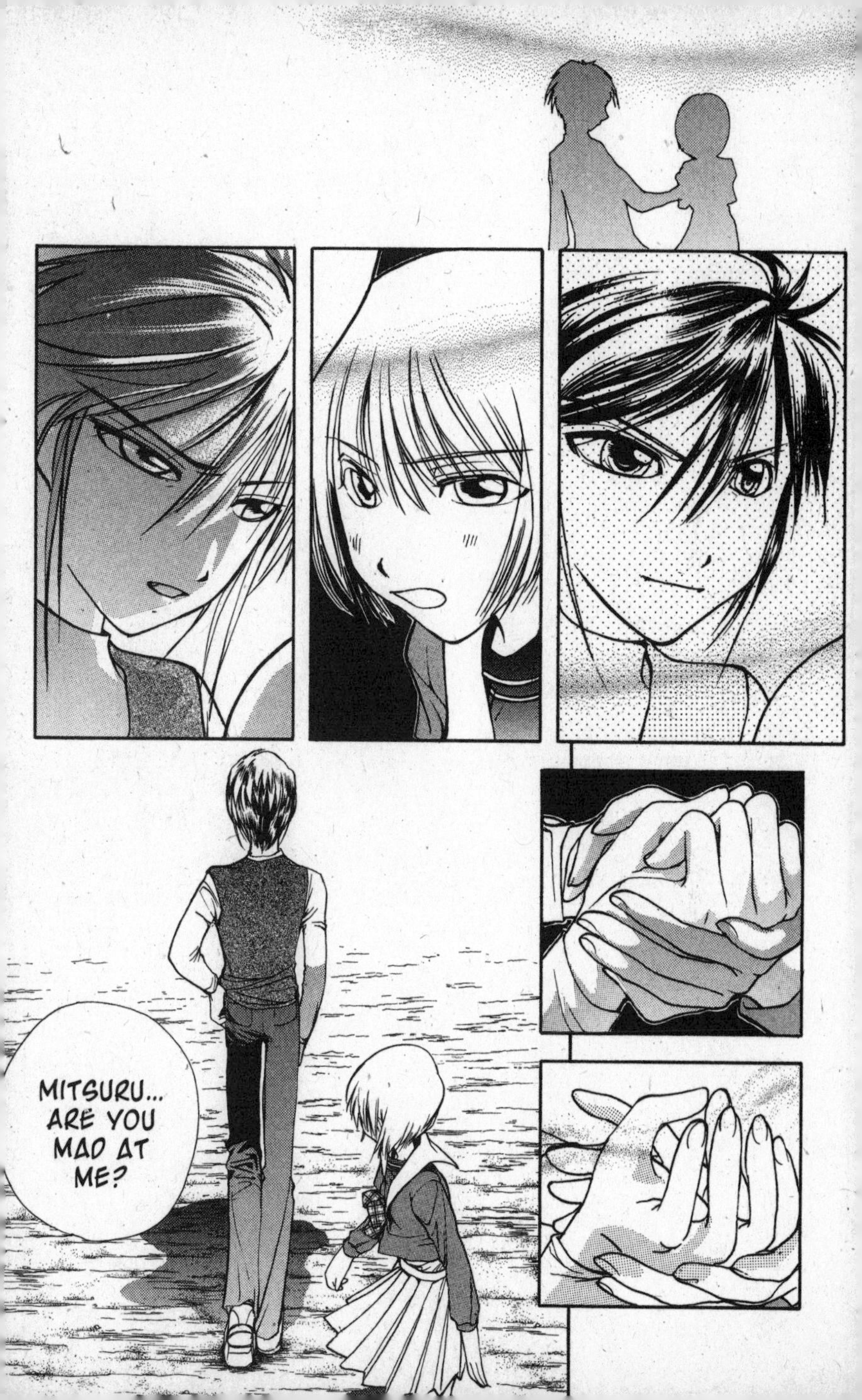
MITSURU... ARE YOU MAD AT ME?

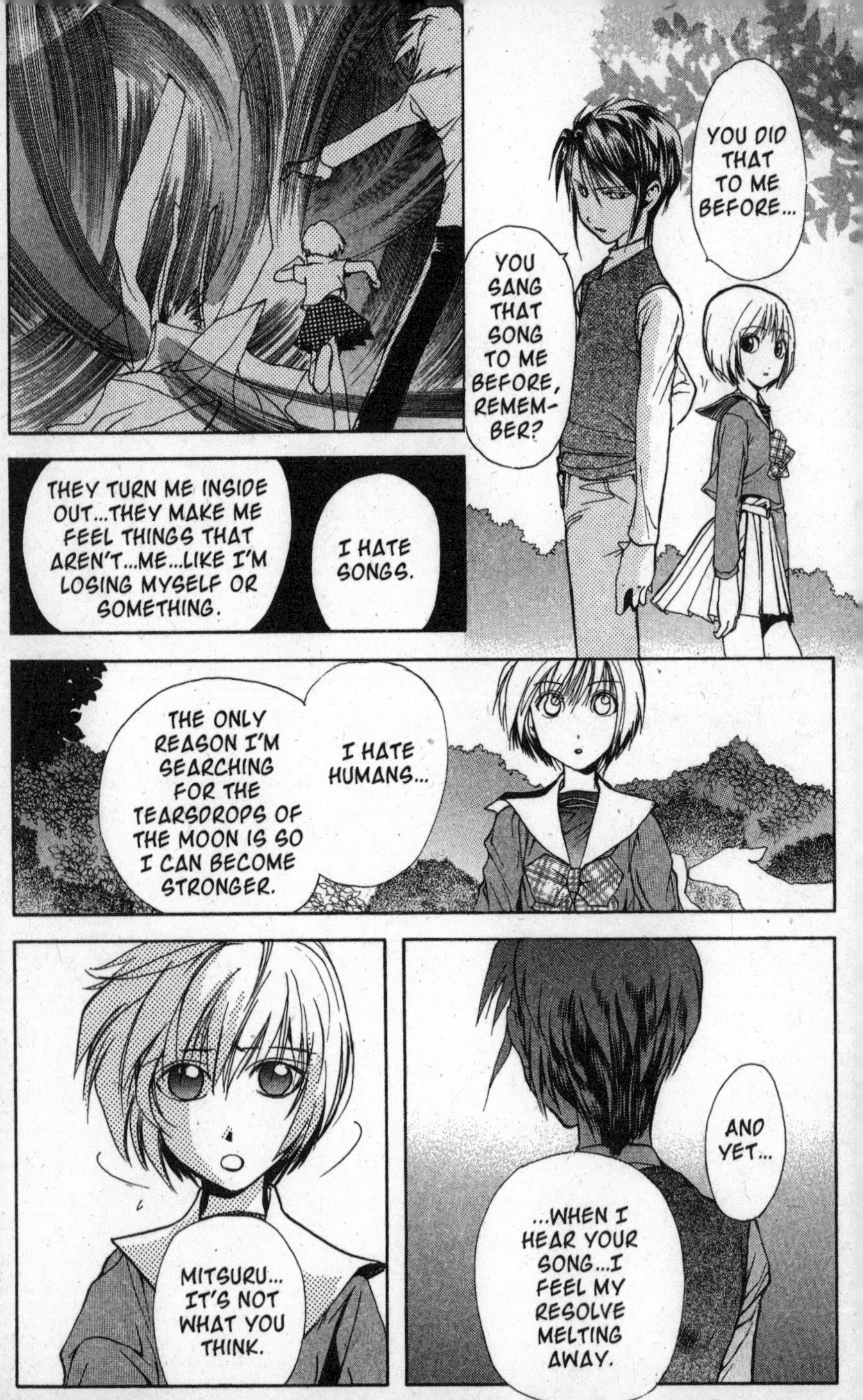
YOU DID THAT TO ME BEFORE...
YOU SANG THAT SONG TO ME BEFORE, REMEMBER?
I HATE SONGS.
THEY TURN ME INSIDE OUT...THEY MAKE ME FEEL THINGS THAT AREN'T...ME...LIKE I'M LOSING MYSELF OR SOMETHING.
I HATE HUMANS...
THE ONLY REASON I'M SEARCHING FOR THE TEARSDROPS OF THE MOON IS SO I CAN BECOME STRONGER.
AND YET...
...WHEN I HEAR YOUR SONG...I FEEL MY RESOLVE MELTING AWAY.
MITSURU... IT'S NOT WHAT YOU THINK.

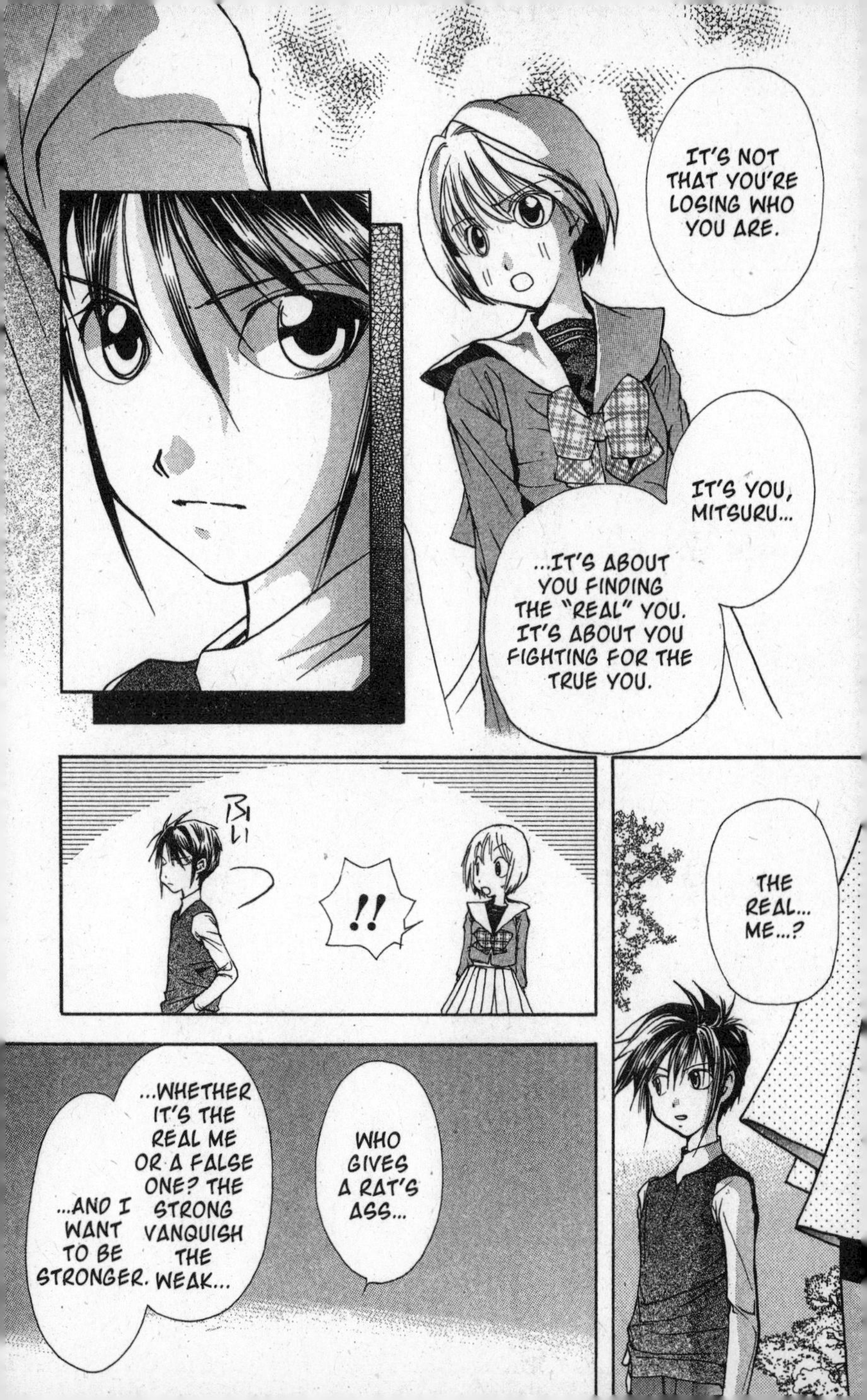
IT'S NOT THAT YOU'RE LOSING WHO YOU ARE.
IT'S YOU, MITSURU...
...IT'S ABOUT YOU FINDING THE "REAL" YOU. IT'S ABOUT YOU FIGHTING FOR THE TRUE YOU.
THE REAL... ME...?
!!
WHO GIVES A RAT'S ASS...
...WHETHER IT'S THE REAL ME OR A FALSE ONE? THE STRONG VANQUISH THE WEAK...
...AND I WANT TO BE STRONGER.

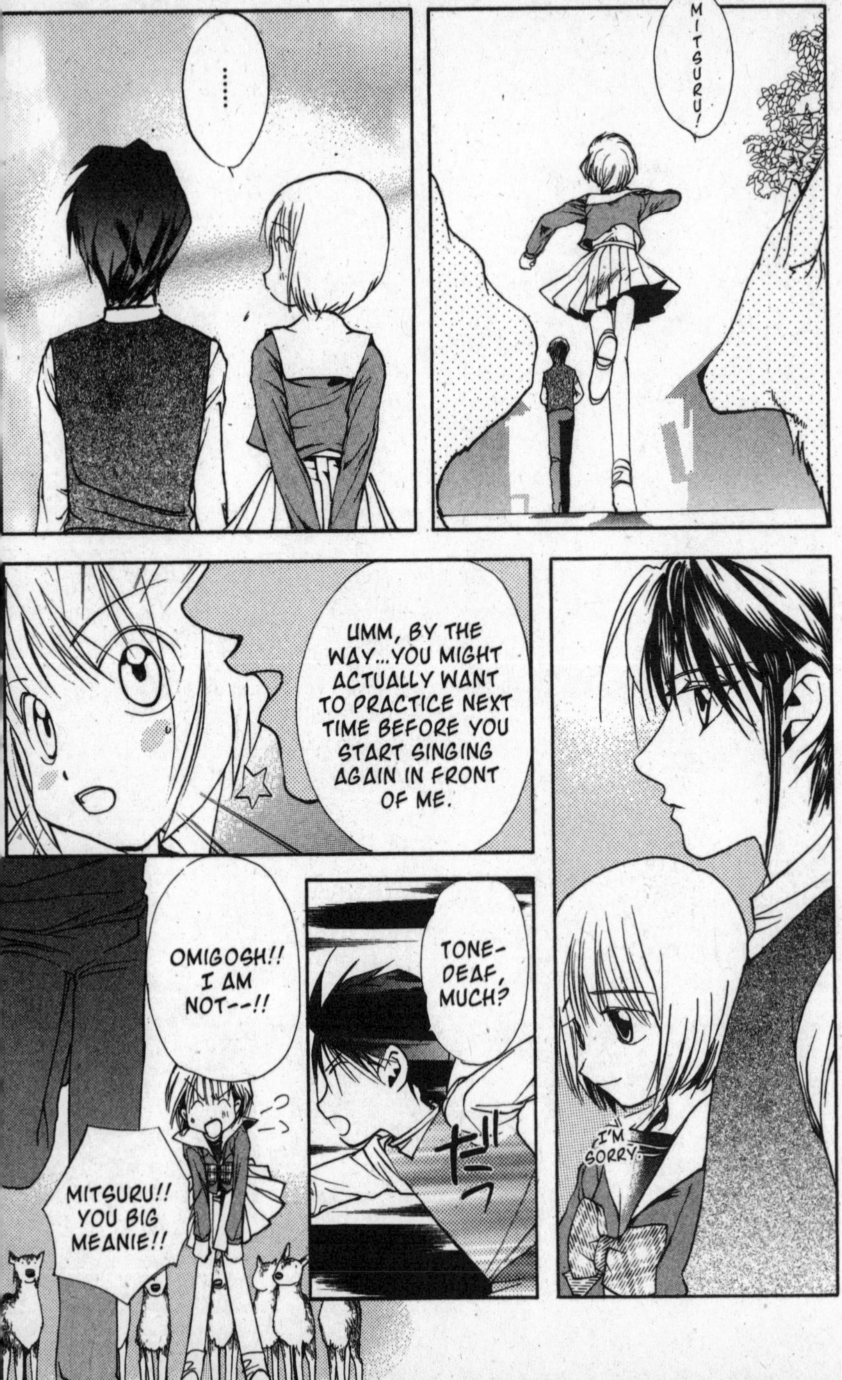
MITSURU!
......
I'M SORRY.
UMM, BY THE WAY...YOU MIGHT ACTUALLY WANT TO PRACTICE NEXT TIME BEFORE YOU START SINGING AGAIN IN FRONT OF ME.
TONE-DEAF, MUCH?
OMIGOSH!! I AM NOT--!!
MITSURU!! YOU BIG MEANIE!!

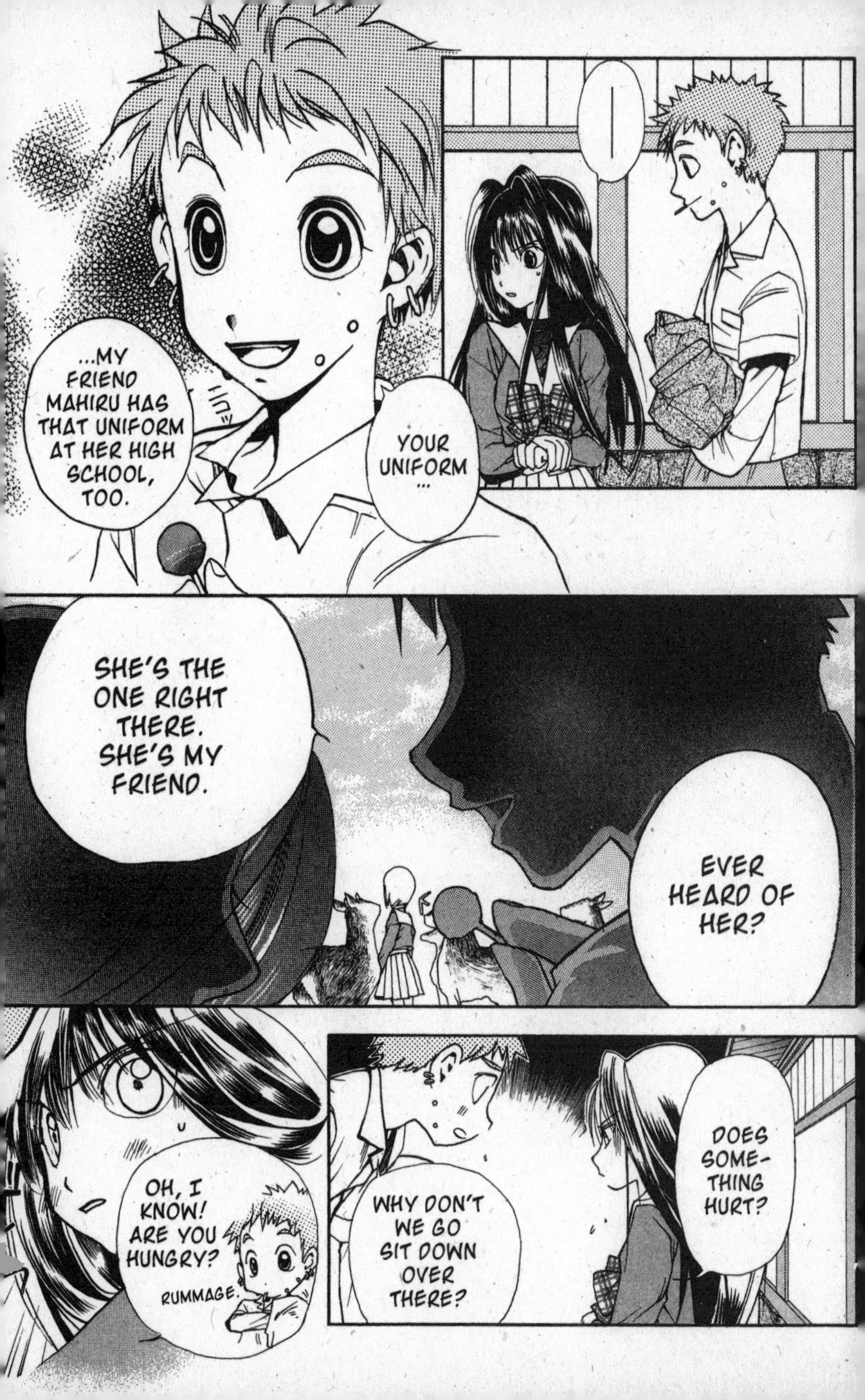
YOUR UNIFORM ...
...MY FRIEND MAHIRU HAS THAT UNIFORM AT HER HIGH SCHOOL, TOO.
SHE'S THE ONE RIGHT THERE. SHE'S MY FRIEND.
EVER HEARD OF HER?
DOES SOME-THING HURT?
WHY DON'T WE GO SIT DOWN OVER THERE?
OH, I KNOW! ARE YOU HUNGRY?
RUMMAGE.

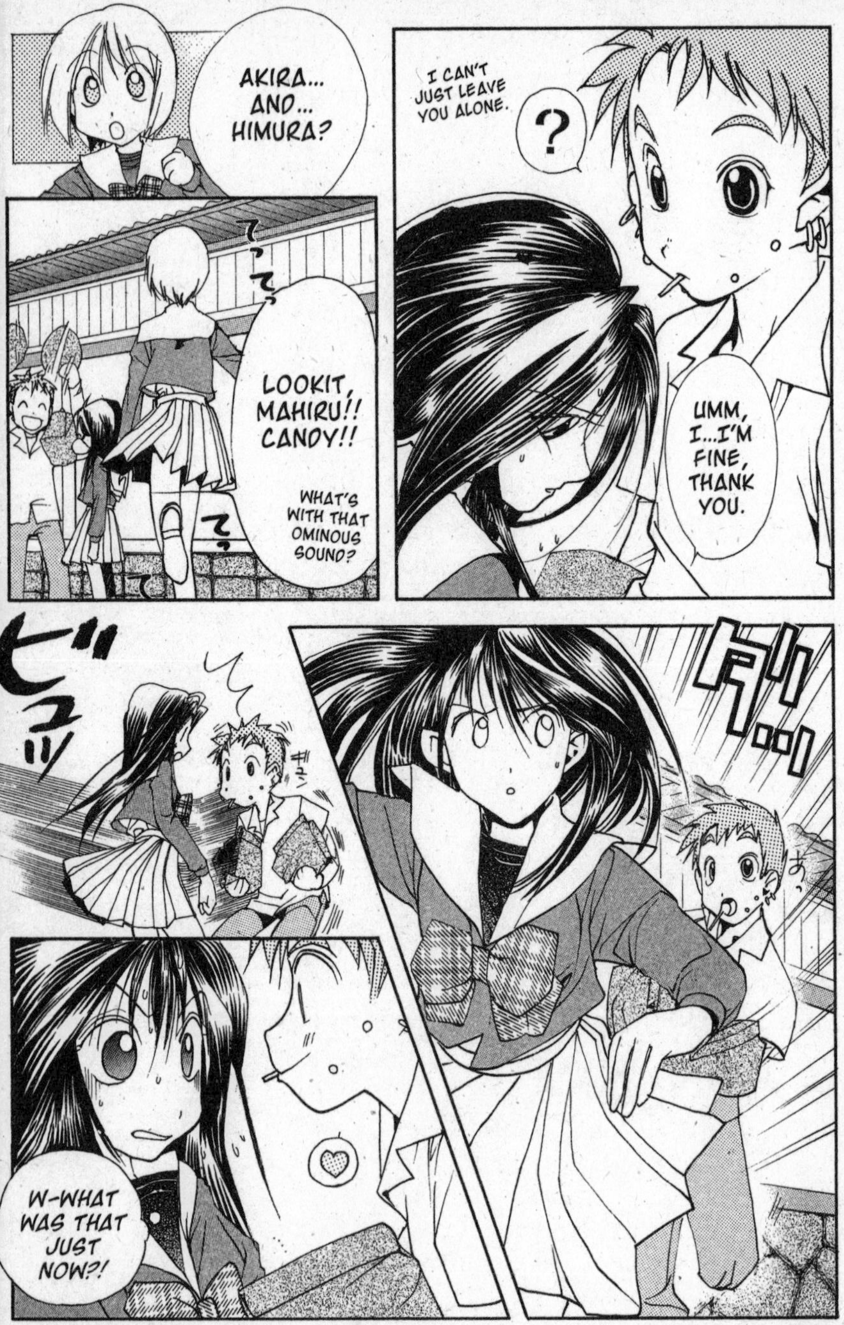
I CAN'T JUST LEAVE YOU ALONE.
?
UMM, I...I'M FINE, THANK YOU.
AKIRA... AND... HIMURA?
LOOKIT, MAHIRU!! CANDY!!
WHAT'S WITH THAT OMINOUS SOUND?
W-WHAT WAS THAT JUST NOW?!

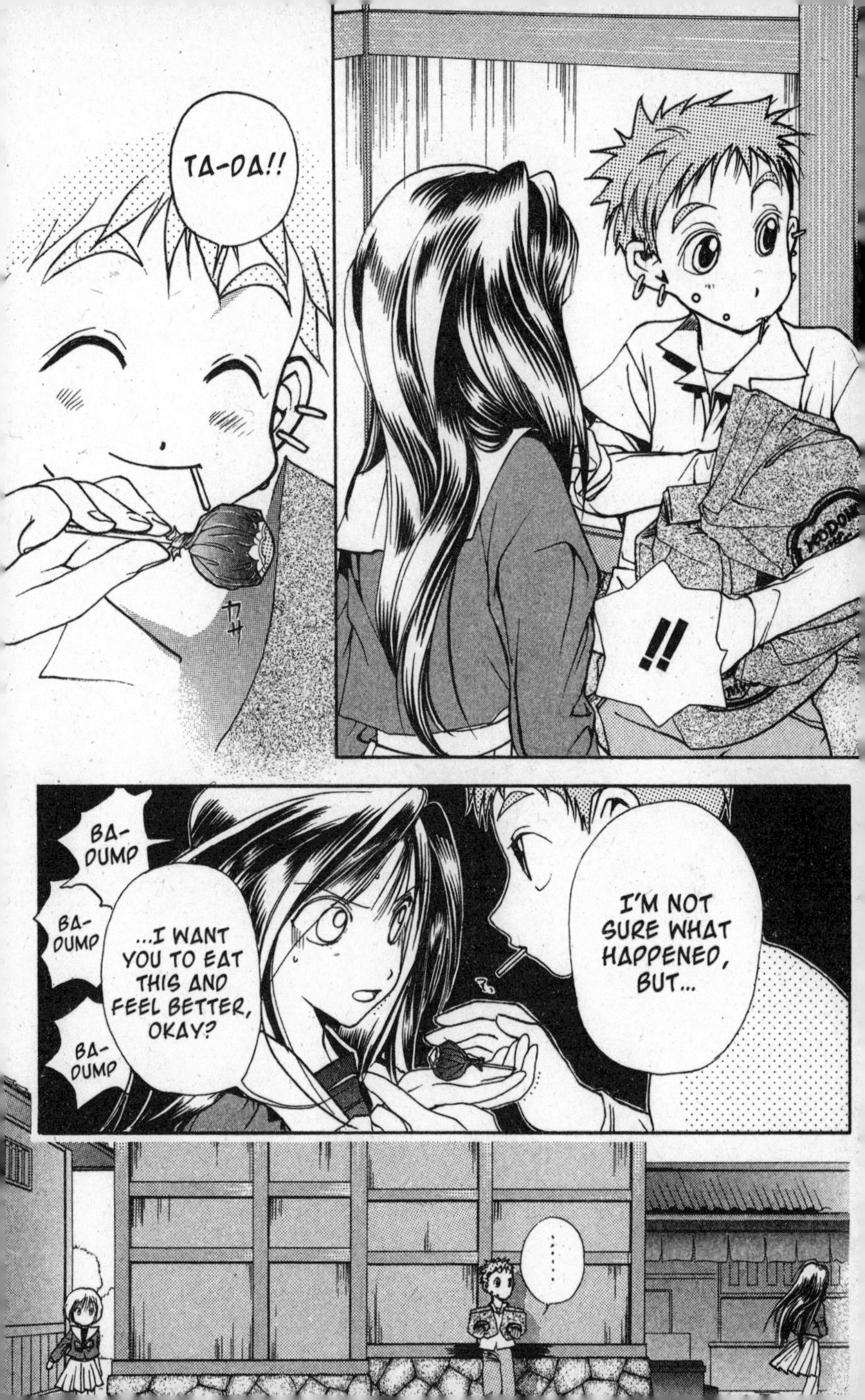
!!
TA-DA!!
I'M NOT SURE WHAT HAPPENED, BUT...
...I WANT YOU TO EAT THIS AND FEEL BETTER, OKAY?
BA-DUMP
BA-DUMP
BA-DUMP
......

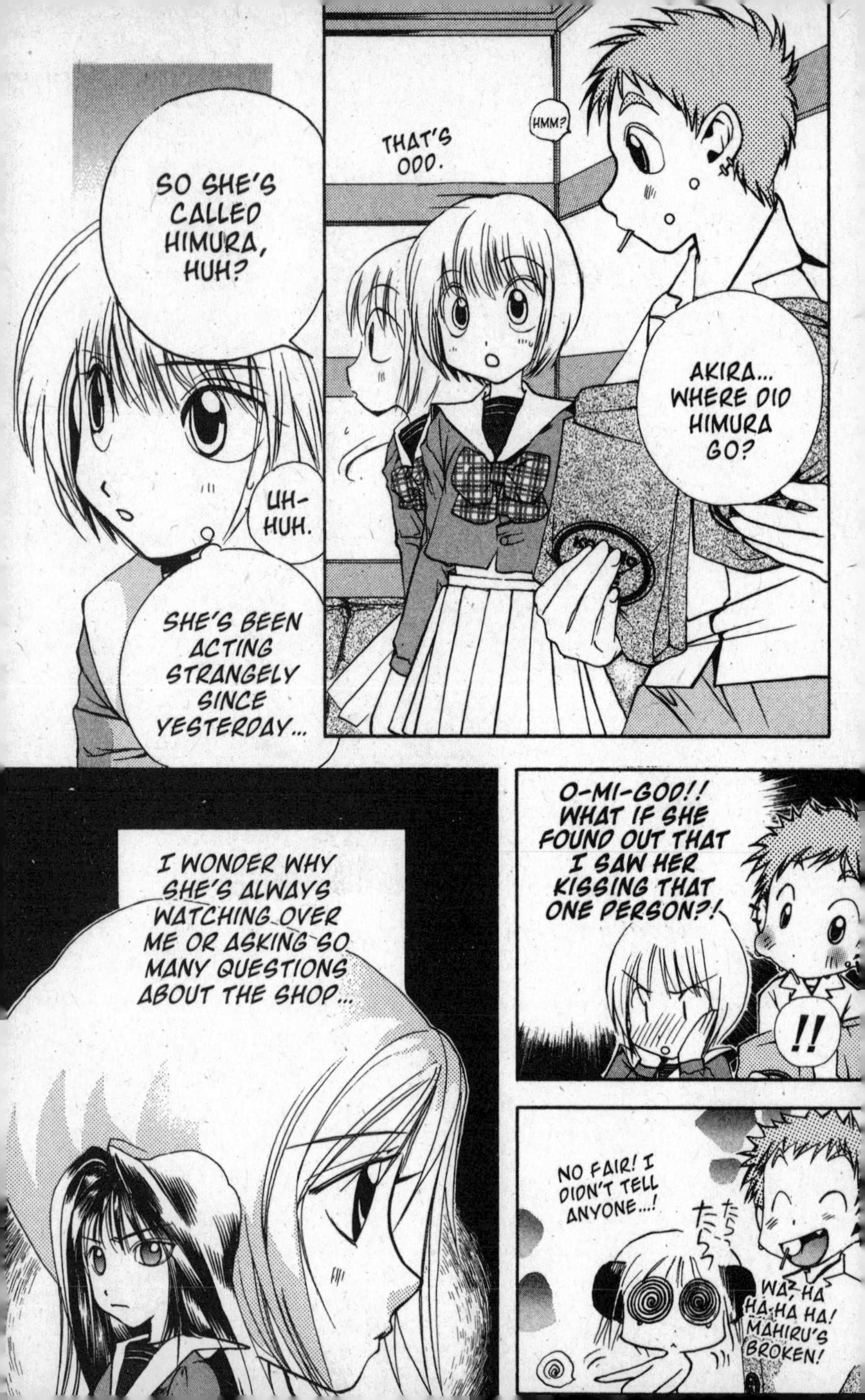
HMM?
THAT'S ODD.
AKIRA... WHERE DID HIMURA GO?
SO SHE'S CALLED HIMURA, HUH?
UH-HUH.
SHE'S BEEN ACTING STRANGELY SINCE YESTERDAY...
O-MI-GOD!! WHAT IF SHE FOUND OUT THAT I SAW HER KISSING THAT ONE PERSON?!
!!
NO FAIR! I DIDN'T TELL ANYONE...!
WA HA HA HA HA! MAHIRU'S BROKEN!
I WONDER WHY SHE'S ALWAYS WATCHING OVER ME OR ASKING SO MANY QUESTIONS ABOUT THE SHOP...

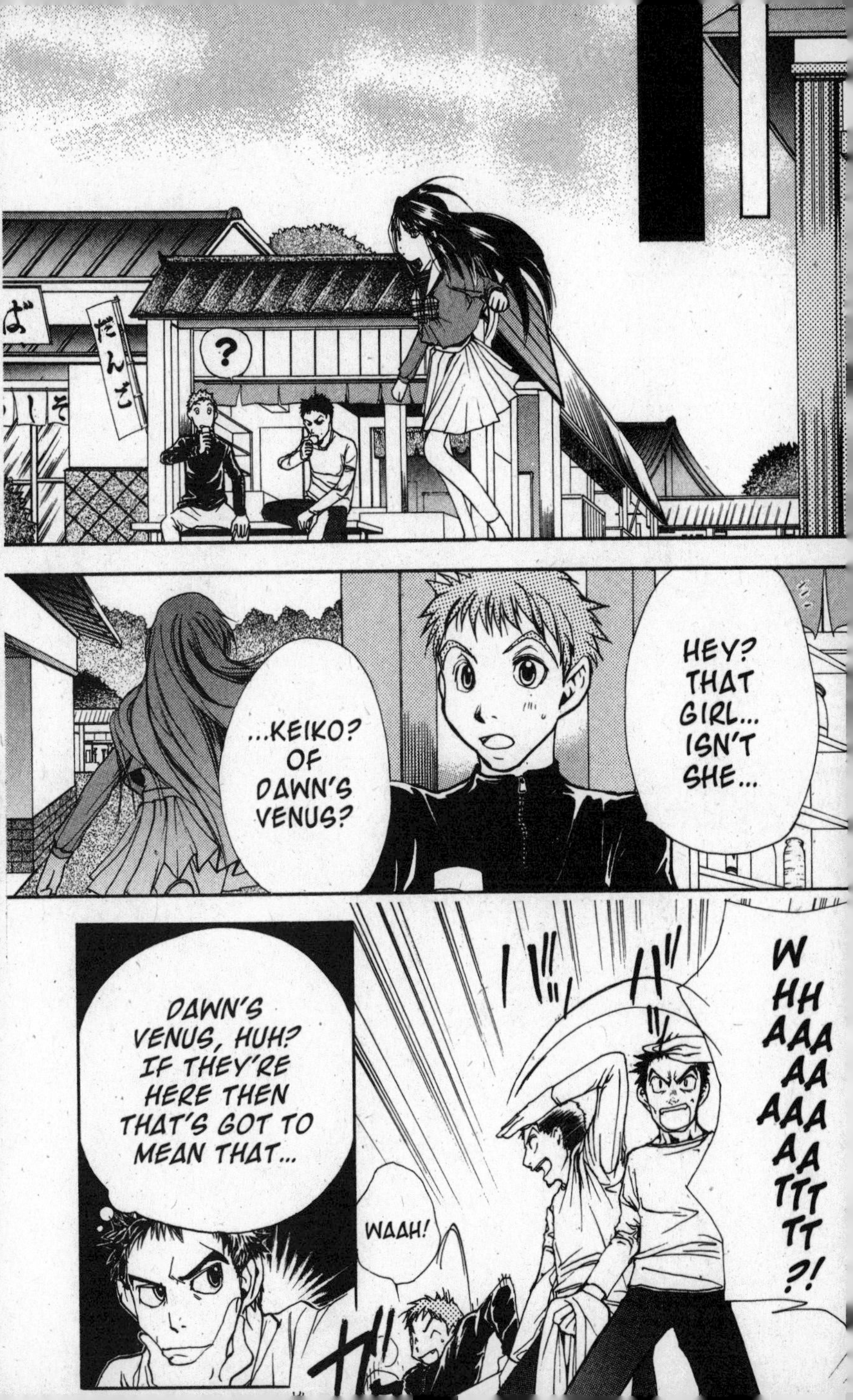
?
HEY? THAT GIRL... ISN'T SHE...
...KEIKO? OF DAWN'S VENUS?
WHHAAAAAAAAAAATTTTT?!
WAAH!
DAWN'S VENUS, HUH? IF THEY'RE HERE THEN THAT'S GOT TO MEAN THAT...

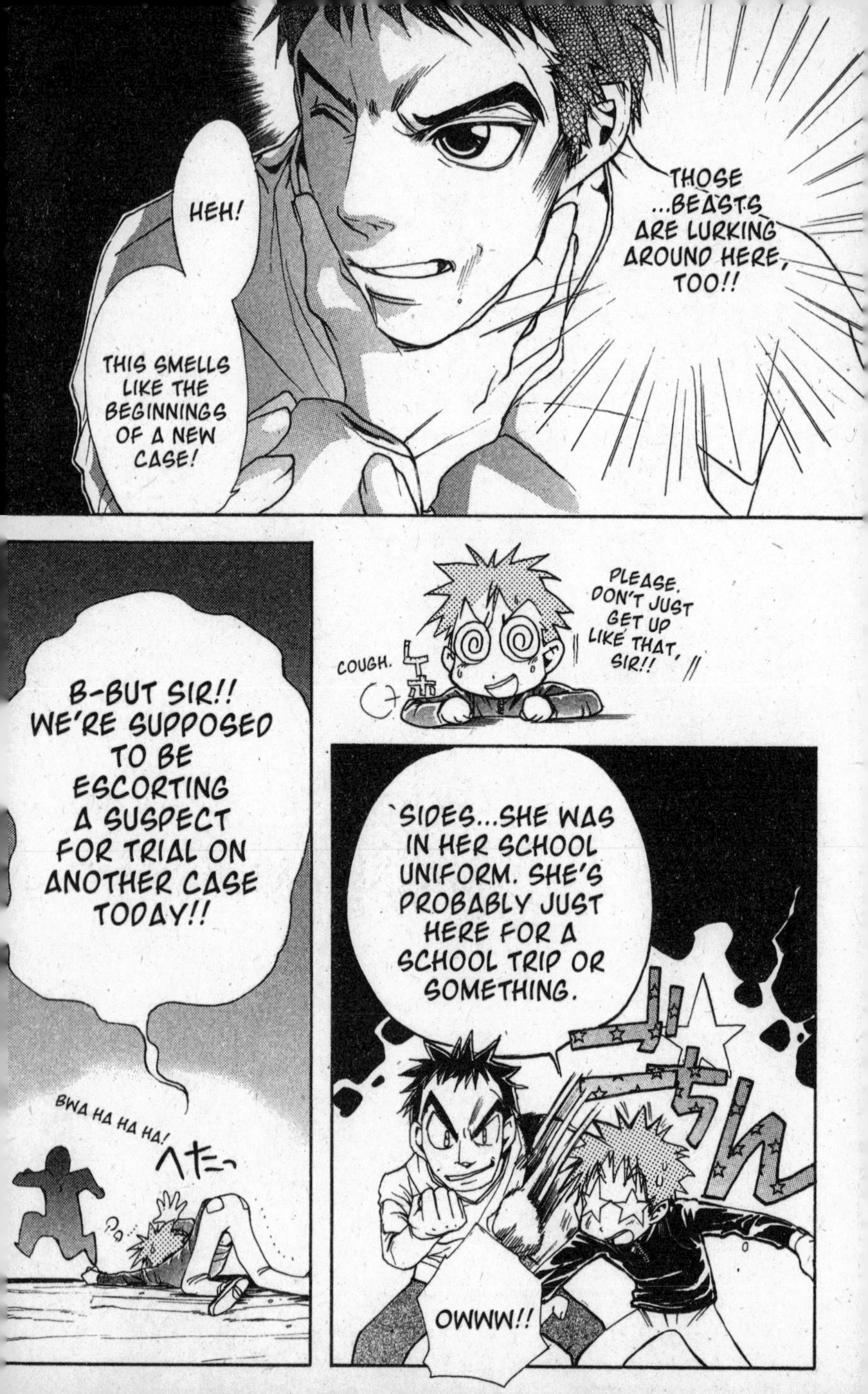
THOSE ...BEASTS ARE LURKING AROUND HERE, TOO!!
HEH!
THIS SMELLS LIKE THE BEGINNINGS OF A NEW CASE!
PLEASE. DON'T JUST GET UP LIKE THAT, SIR!!
COUGH.
`SIDES...SHE WAS IN HER SCHOOL UNIFORM. SHE'S PROBABLY JUST HERE FOR A SCHOOL TRIP OR SOMETHING.
OWWW!!
B-BUT SIR!! WE'RE SUPPOSED TO BE ESCORTING A SUSPECT FOR TRIAL ON ANOTHER CASE TODAY!!
BWA HA HA HA!

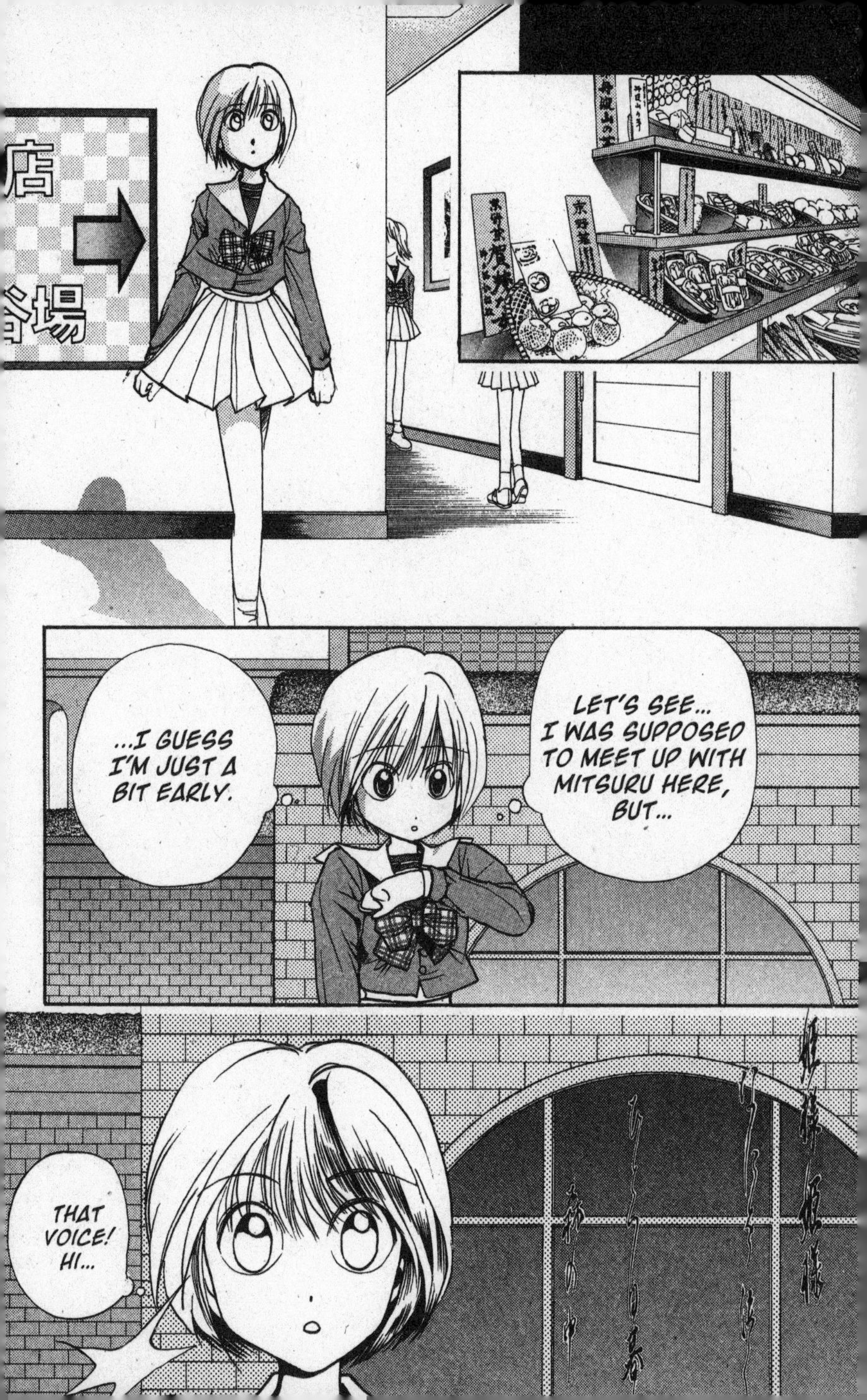
店
LET'S SEE... I WAS SUPPOSED TO MEET UP WITH MITSURU HERE, BUT...
...I GUESS I'M JUST A BIT EARLY.
THAT VOICE! HI...

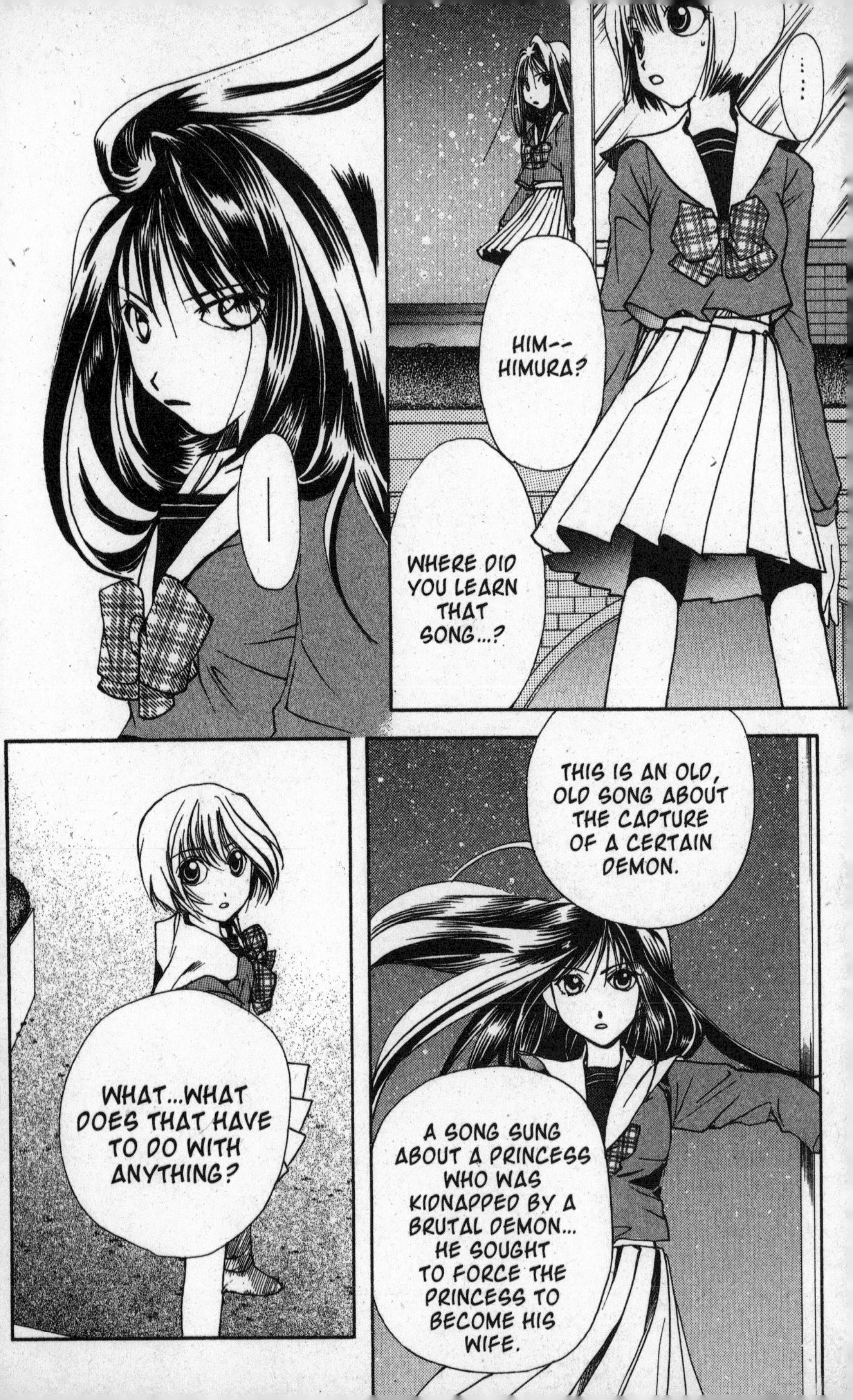
......
HIM--HIMURA?
WHERE DID YOU LEARN THAT SONG...?
—
THIS IS AN OLD, OLD SONG ABOUT THE CAPTURE OF A CERTAIN DEMON.
A SONG SUNG ABOUT A PRINCESS WHO WAS KIDNAPPED BY A BRUTAL DEMON... HE SOUGHT TO FORCE THE PRINCESS TO BECOME HIS WIFE.
WHAT...WHAT DOES THAT HAVE TO DO WITH ANYTHING?

WELL,
I CAN'T HELP
BUT THINK THAT
YOU'RE THE
"PRINCESS"
AND THOSE
BOYS ARE THE
"DEMONS"!

!!

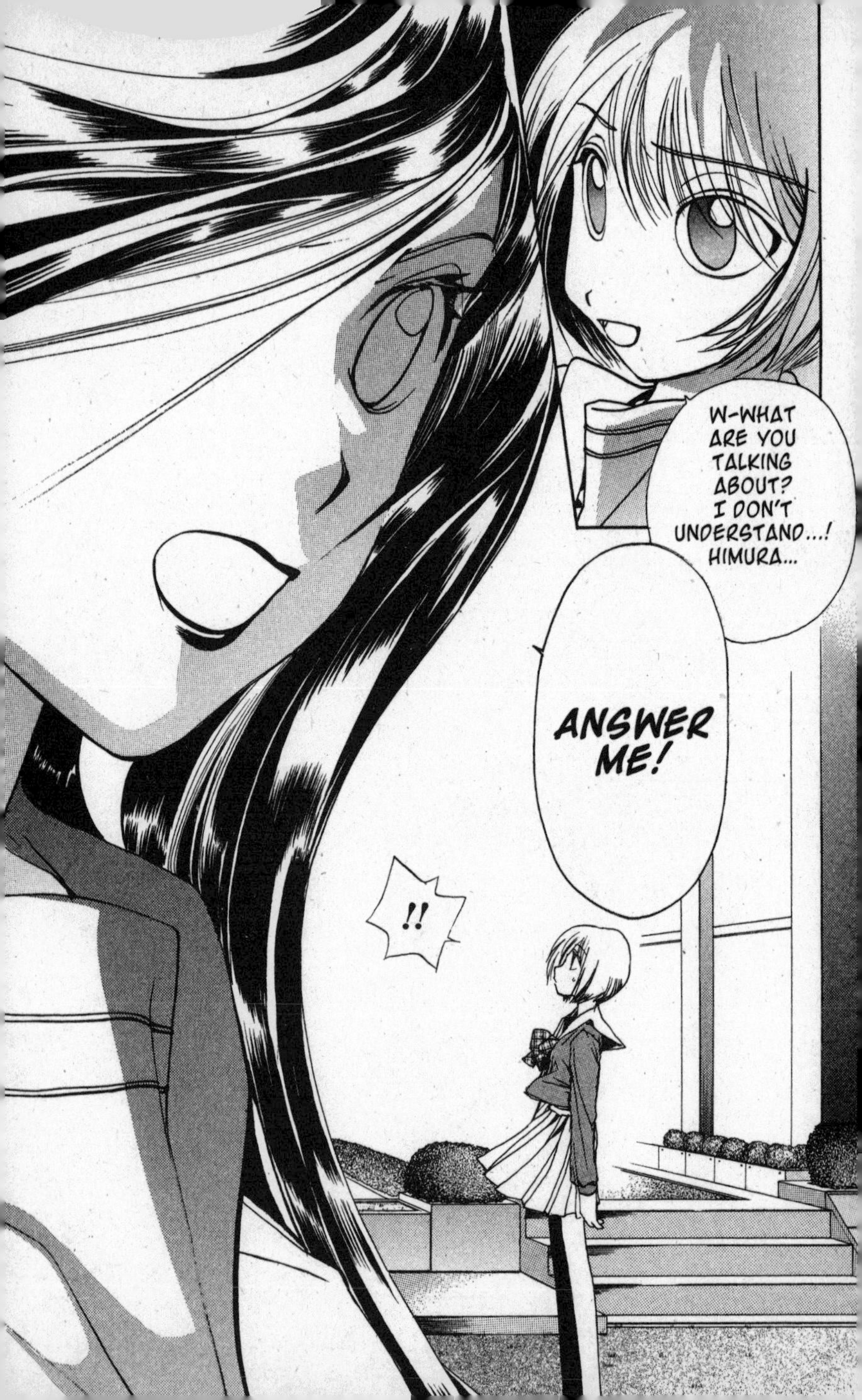
W-WHAT ARE YOU TALKING ABOUT? I DON'T UNDERSTAND...! HIMURA...
ANSWER ME!
!!

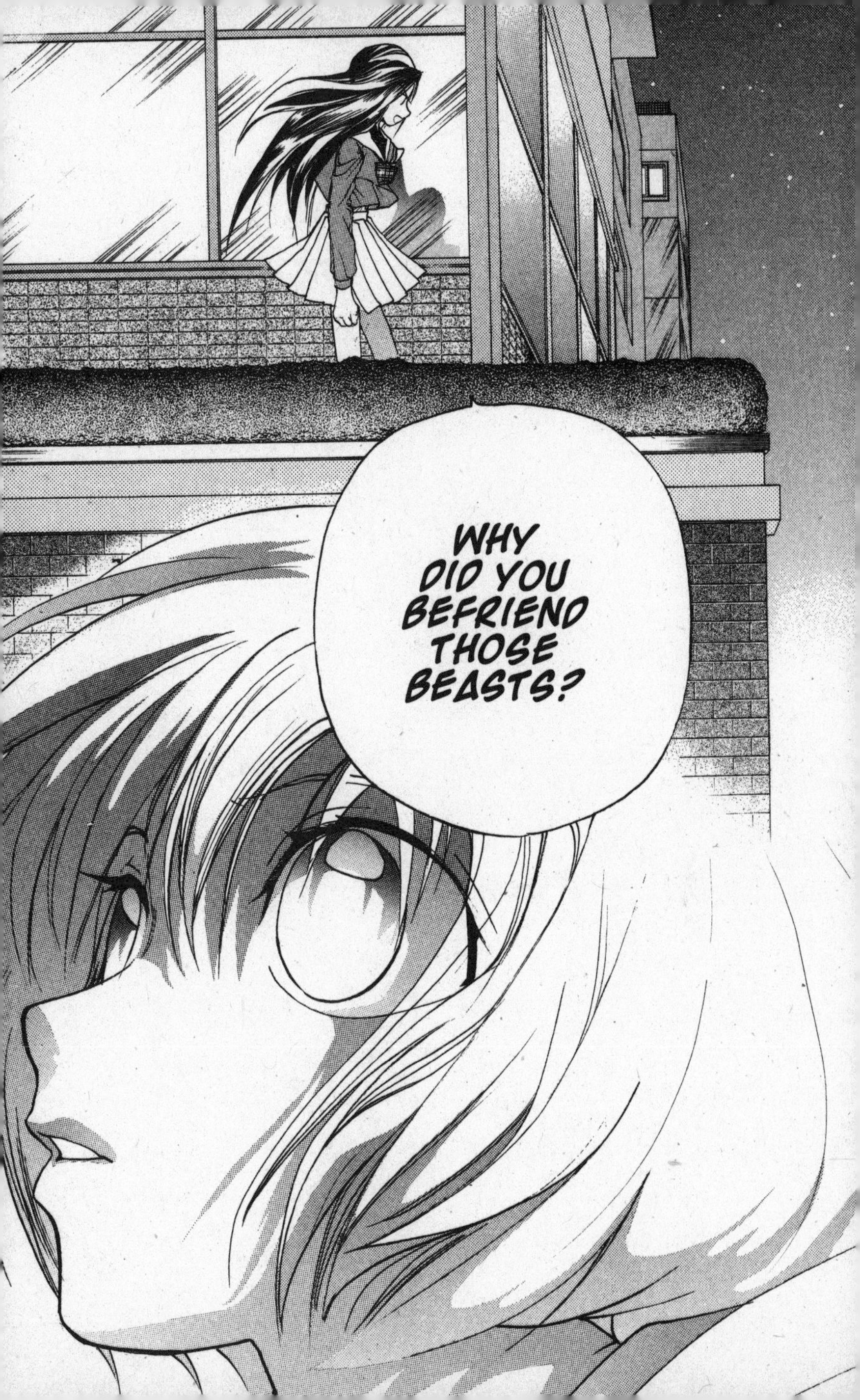
WHY DID YOU BEFRIEND THOSE BEASTS?

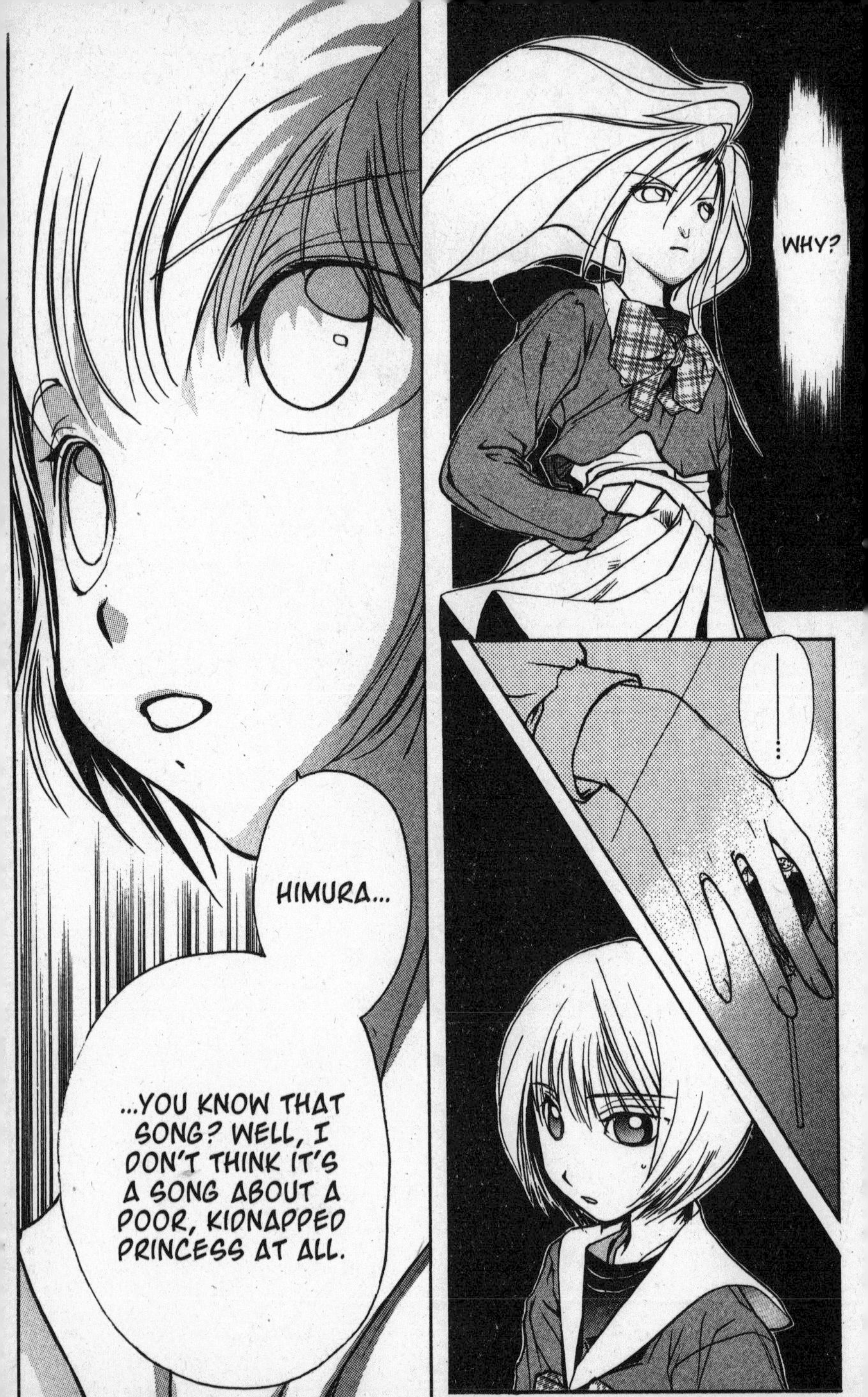
WHY?
HIMURA...
...YOU KNOW THAT SONG? WELL, I DON'T THINK IT'S A SONG ABOUT A POOR, KIDNAPPED PRINCESS AT ALL.

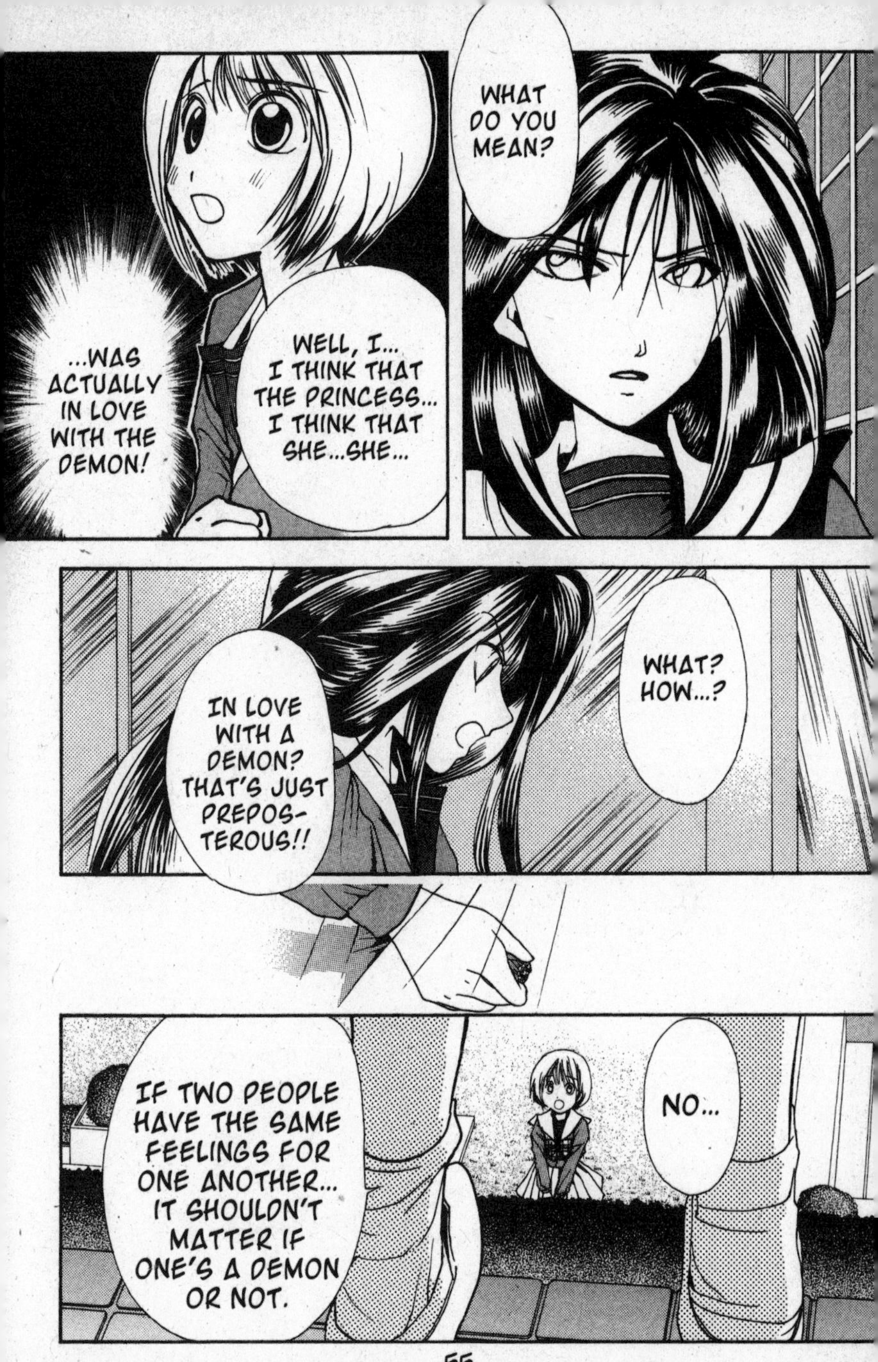
WHAT DO YOU MEAN?
WELL, I... I THINK THAT THE PRINCESS... I THINK THAT SHE...SHE...
...WAS ACTUALLY IN LOVE WITH THE DEMON!
WHAT? HOW...?
IN LOVE WITH A DEMON? THAT'S JUST PREPOS-TEROUS!!
NO...
IF TWO PEOPLE HAVE THE SAME FEELINGS FOR ONE ANOTHER... IT SHOULDN'T MATTER IF ONE'S A DEMON OR NOT.

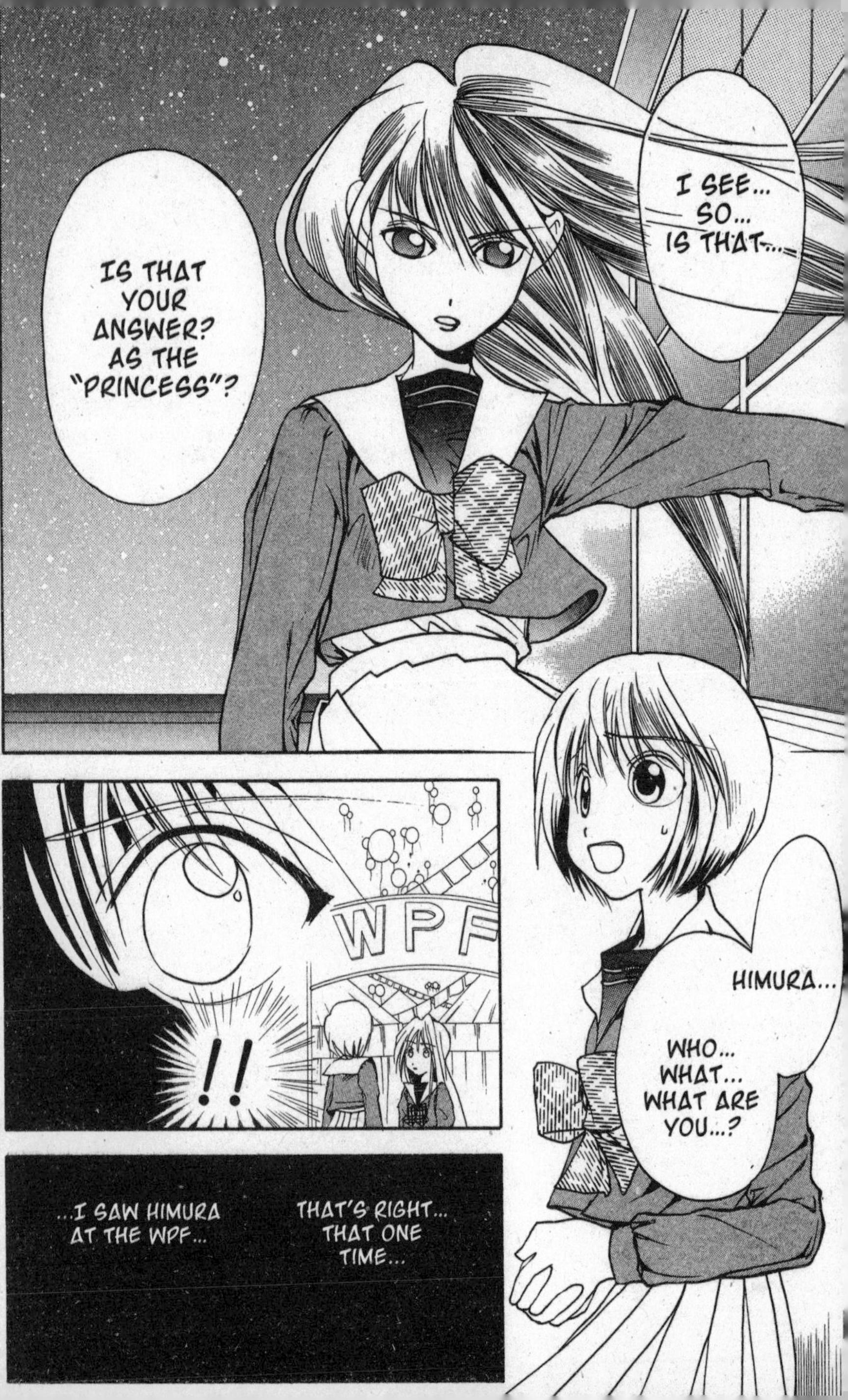
I SEE... SO... IS THAT...
IS THAT YOUR ANSWER? AS THE "PRINCESS"?
HIMURA...
WHO... WHAT... WHAT ARE YOU...?
WPF
!!
THAT'S RIGHT... THAT ONE TIME...
...I SAW HIMURA AT THE WPF...

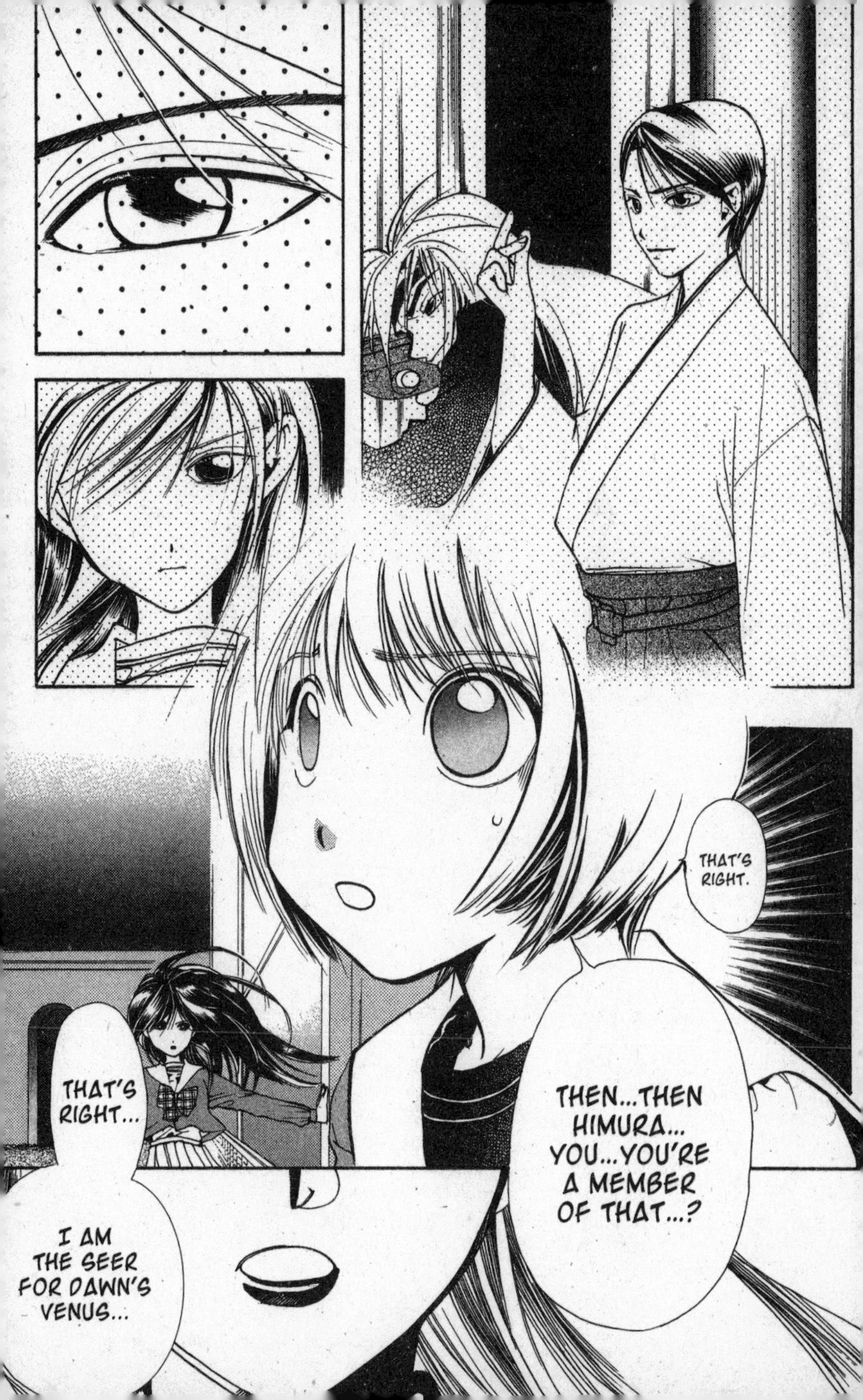
THAT'S RIGHT.
THEN...THEN HIMURA... YOU...YOU'RE A MEMBER OF THAT...?
THAT'S RIGHT...
I AM THE SEER FOR DAWN'S VENUS...

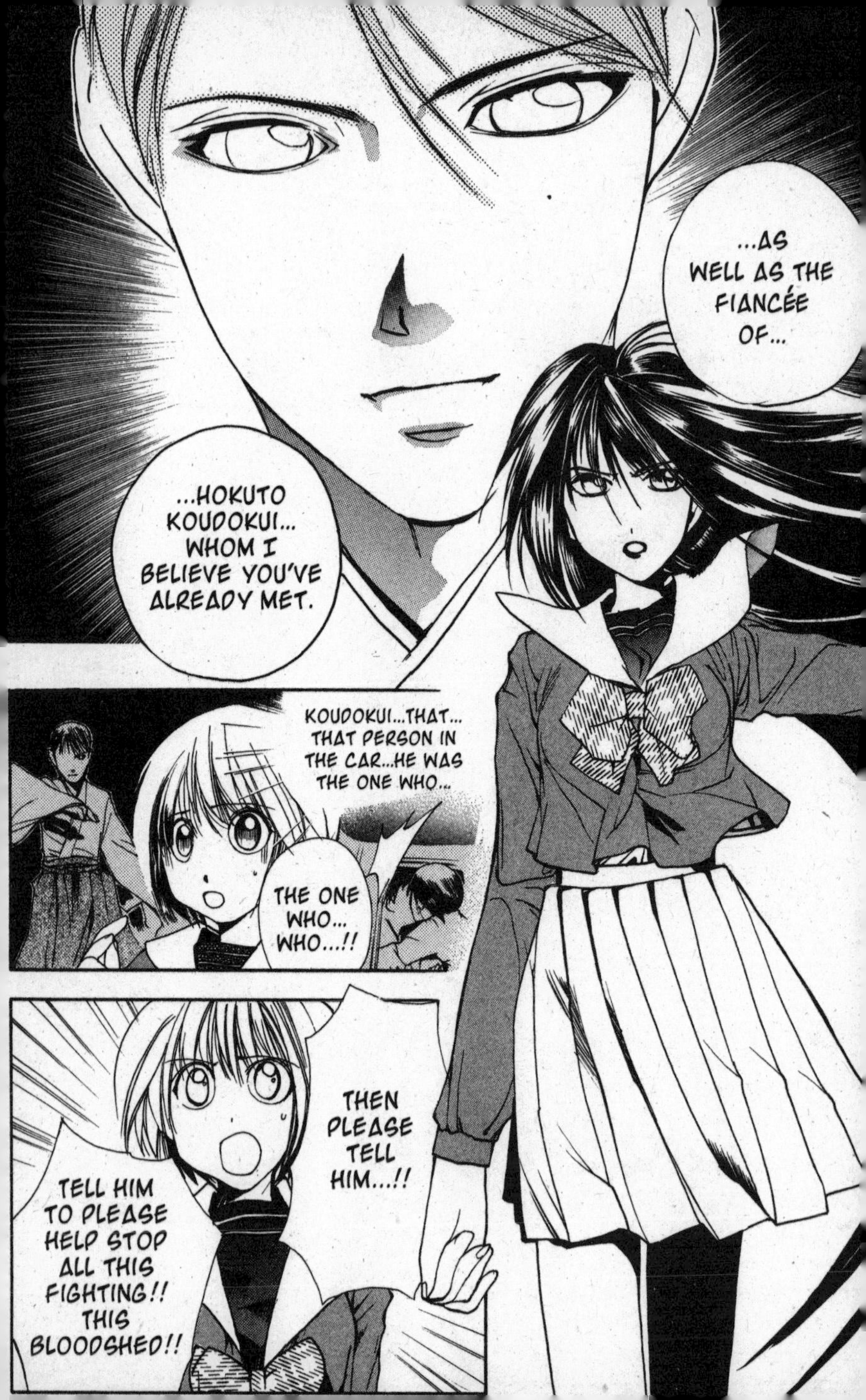
...AS WELL AS THE FIANCÉE OF...
...HOKUTO KOUDOKUI... WHOM I BELIEVE YOU'VE ALREADY MET.
KOUDOKUI...THAT... THAT PERSON IN THE CAR...HE WAS THE ONE WHO...
THE ONE WHO... WHO...!!
THEN PLEASE TELL HIM...!!
TELL HIM TO PLEASE HELP STOP ALL THIS FIGHTING!! THIS BLOODSHED!!

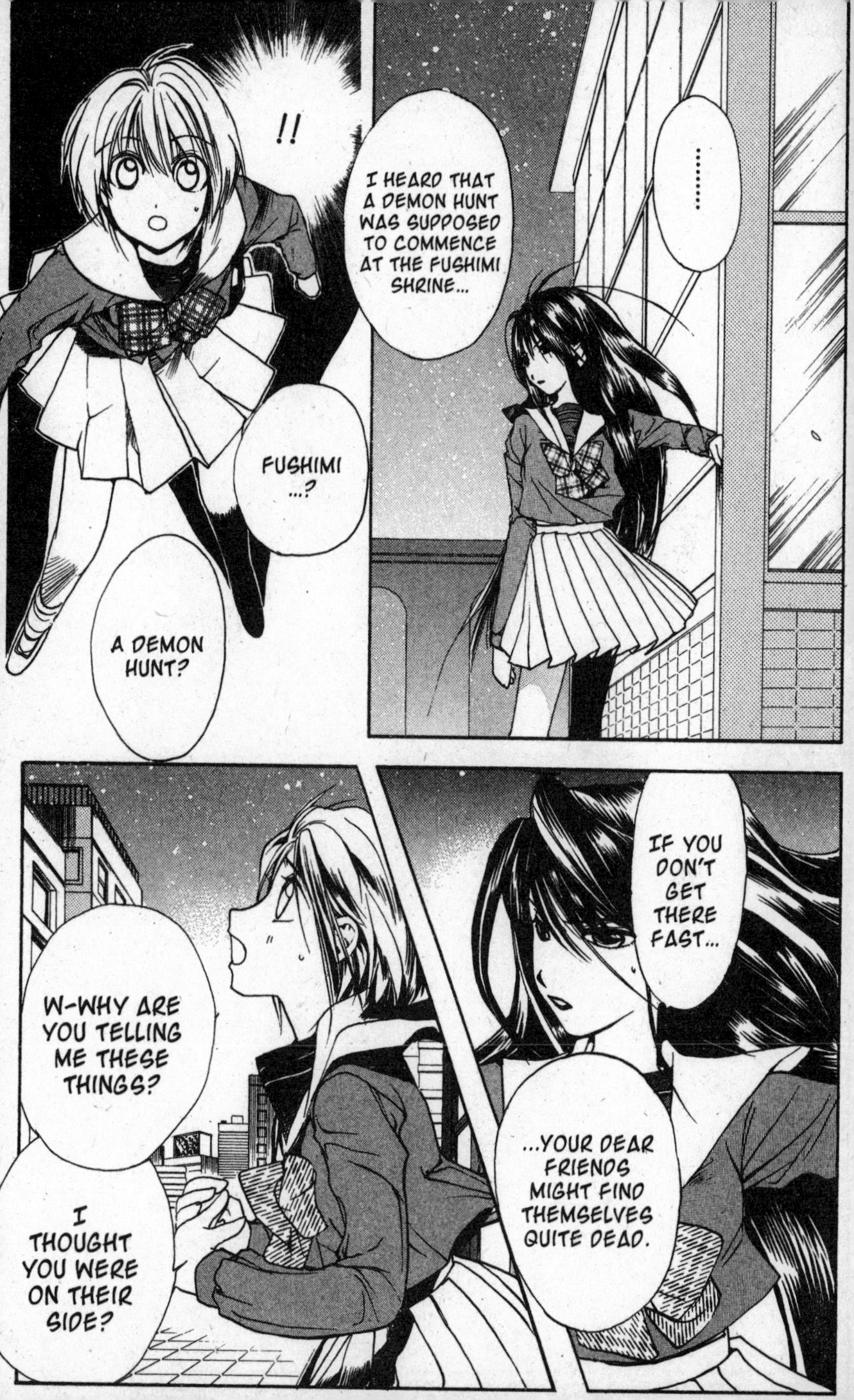

......
I HEARD THAT A DEMON HUNT WAS SUPPOSED TO COMMENCE AT THE FUSHIMI SHRINE...
!!
FUSHIMI ...?
A DEMON HUNT?
IF YOU DON'T GET THERE FAST...
...YOUR DEAR FRIENDS MIGHT FIND THEMSELVES QUITE DEAD.
W-WHY ARE YOU TELLING ME THESE THINGS?
I THOUGHT YOU WERE ON THEIR SIDE?

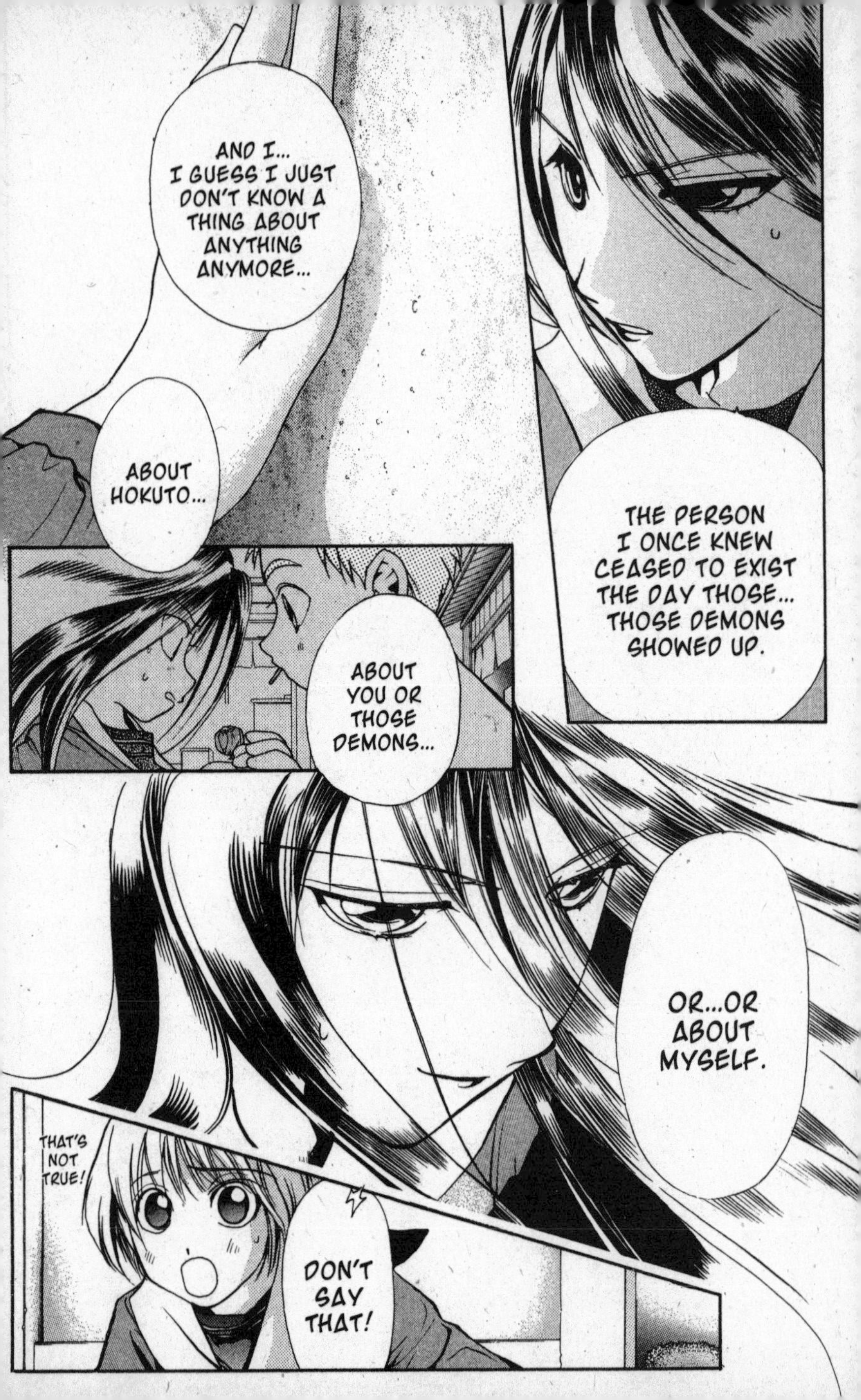
THE PERSON I ONCE KNEW CEASED TO EXIST THE DAY THOSE... THOSE DEMONS SHOWED UP.
AND I... I GUESS I JUST DON'T KNOW A THING ABOUT ANYTHING ANYMORE...
ABOUT HOKUTO...
ABOUT YOU OR THOSE DEMONS...
OR...OR ABOUT MYSELF.
THAT'S NOT TRUE!
DON'T SAY THAT!

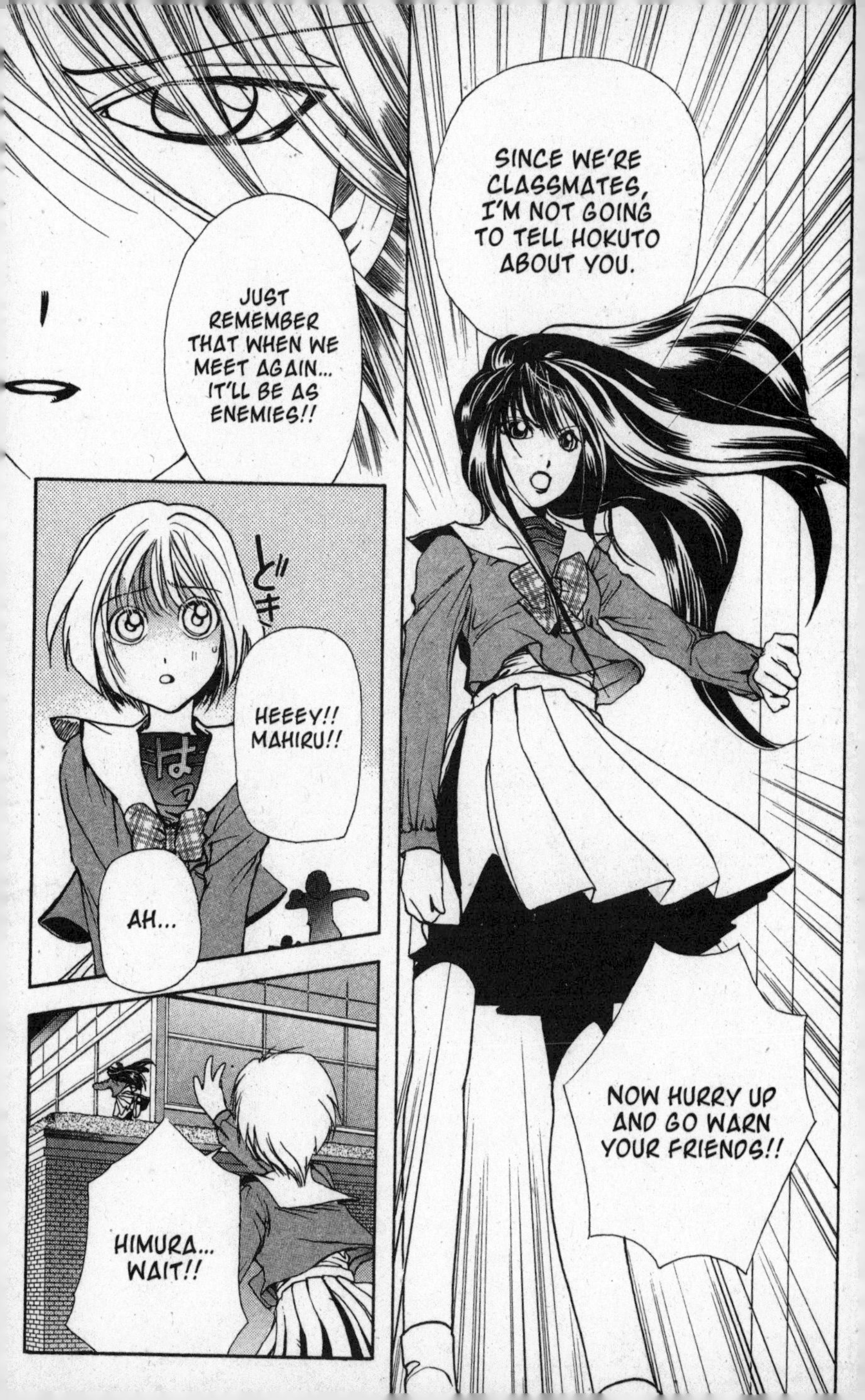
SINCE WE'RE CLASSMATES, I'M NOT GOING TO TELL HOKUTO ABOUT YOU.
NOW HURRY UP AND GO WARN YOUR FRIENDS!!
JUST REMEMBER THAT WHEN WE MEET AGAIN... IT'LL BE AS ENEMIES!!
どキ
HEEEY!! MAHIRU!!
はっ
AH...
HIMURA... WAIT!!

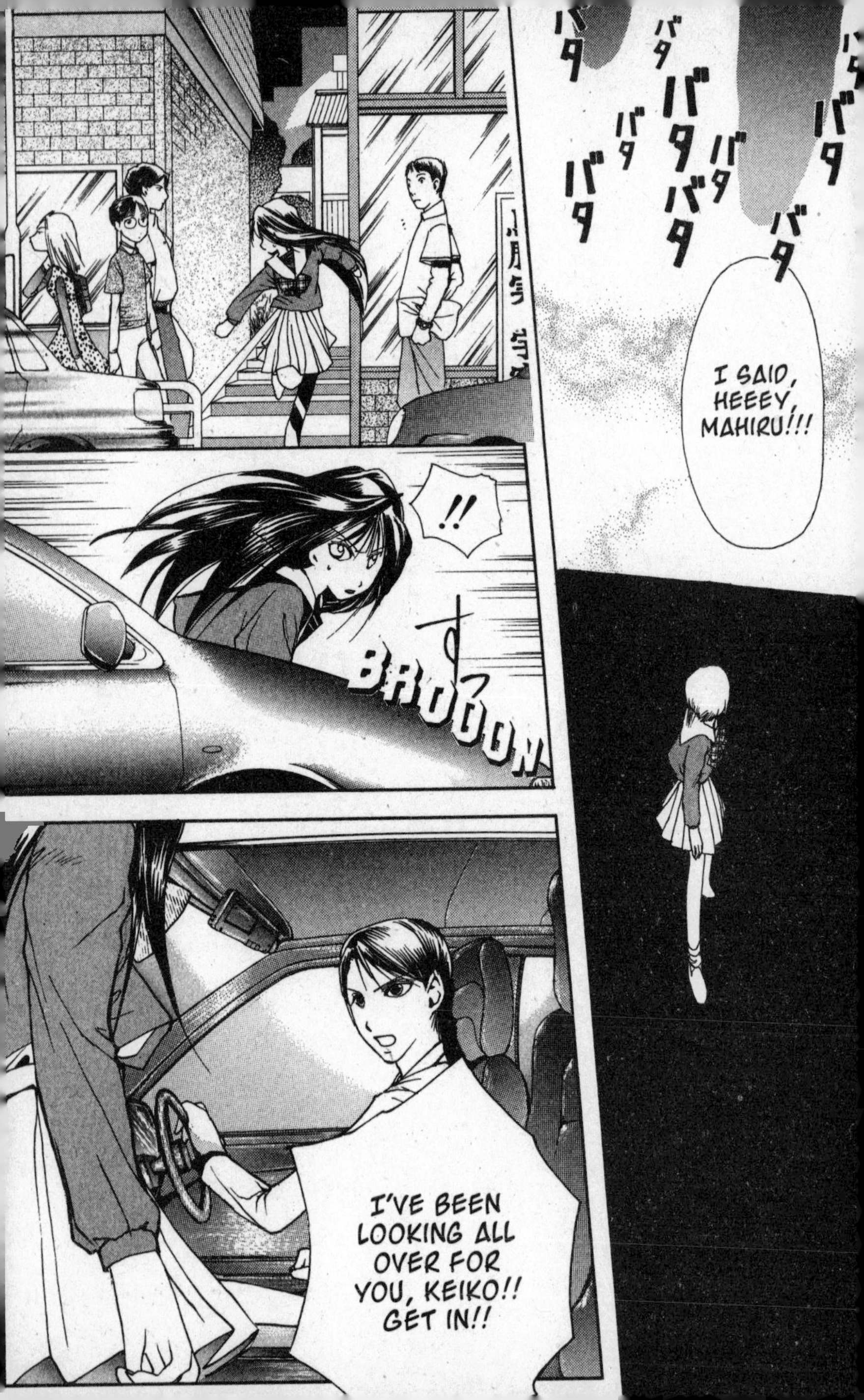
バタバタ
バタ
バタ
バタバタ
バタ
バタ
バタ
I SAID, HEEEY, MAHIRU!!!
!!
BROOOON
I'VE BEEN LOOKING ALL OVER FOR YOU, KEIKO!! GET IN!!

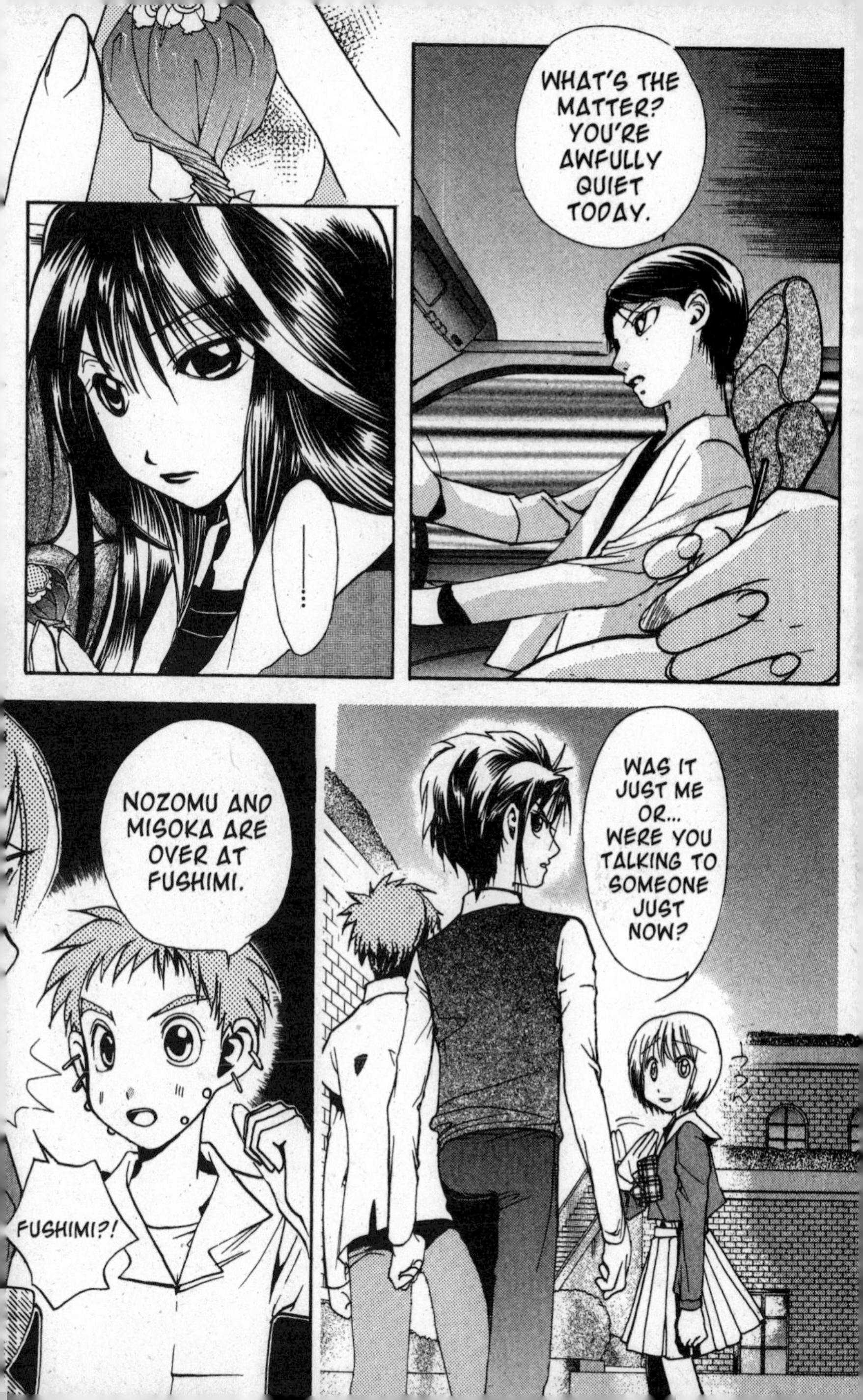
WHAT'S THE MATTER? YOU'RE AWFULLY QUIET TODAY.
......
WAS IT JUST ME OR... WERE YOU TALKING TO SOMEONE JUST NOW?
NOZOMU AND MISOKA ARE OVER AT FUSHIMI.
FUSHIMI?!

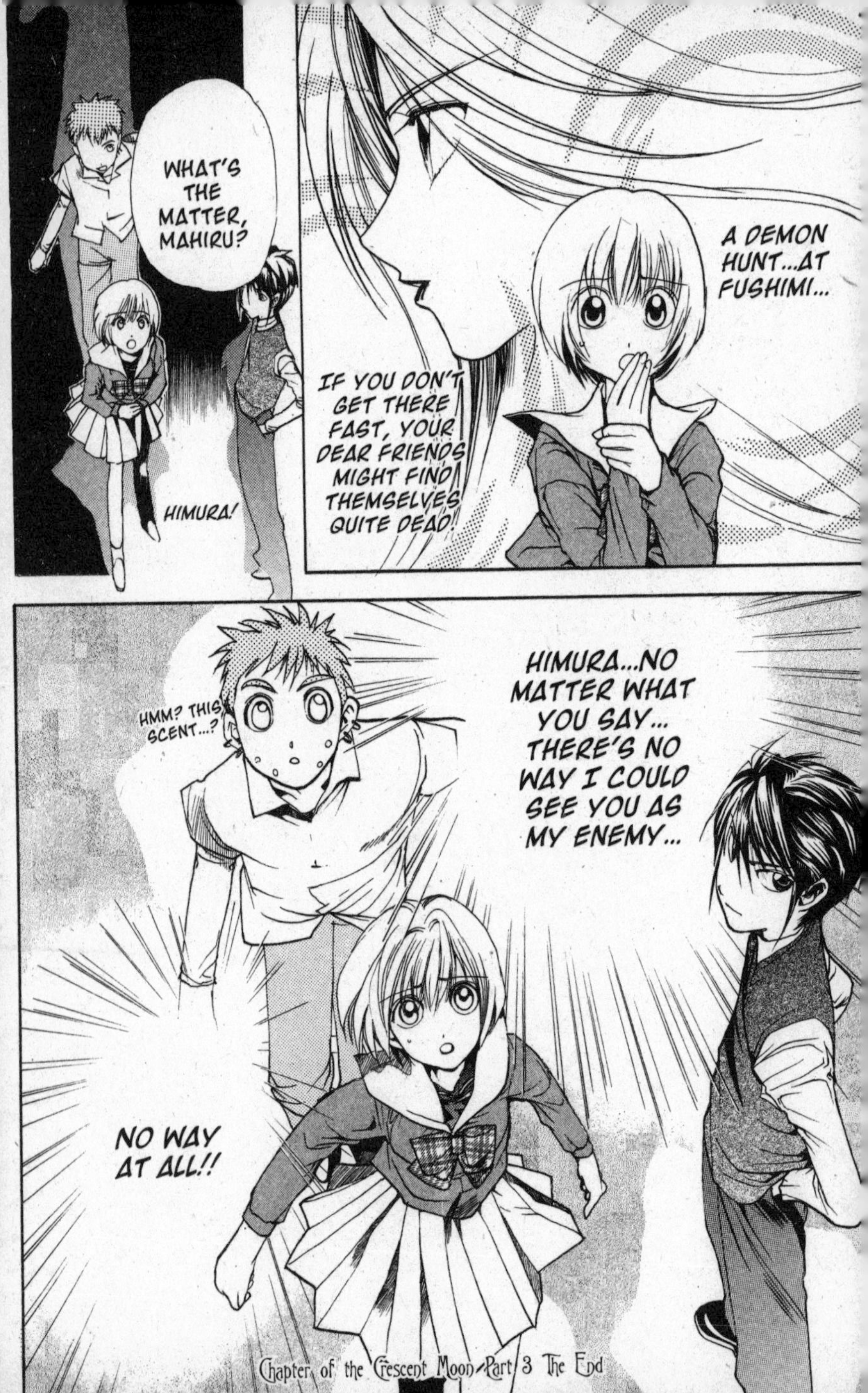
A DEMON HUNT...AT FUSHIMI...
IF YOU DON'T GET THERE FAST, YOUR DEAR FRIENDS MIGHT FIND THEMSELVES QUITE DEAD!
WHAT'S THE MATTER, MAHIRU?
HIMURA!
HIMURA...NO MATTER WHAT YOU SAY... THERE'S NO WAY I COULD SEE YOU AS MY ENEMY...
HMM? THIS SCENT...?
NO WAY AT ALL!!
Chapter of the Crescent Moon Part 3 The End

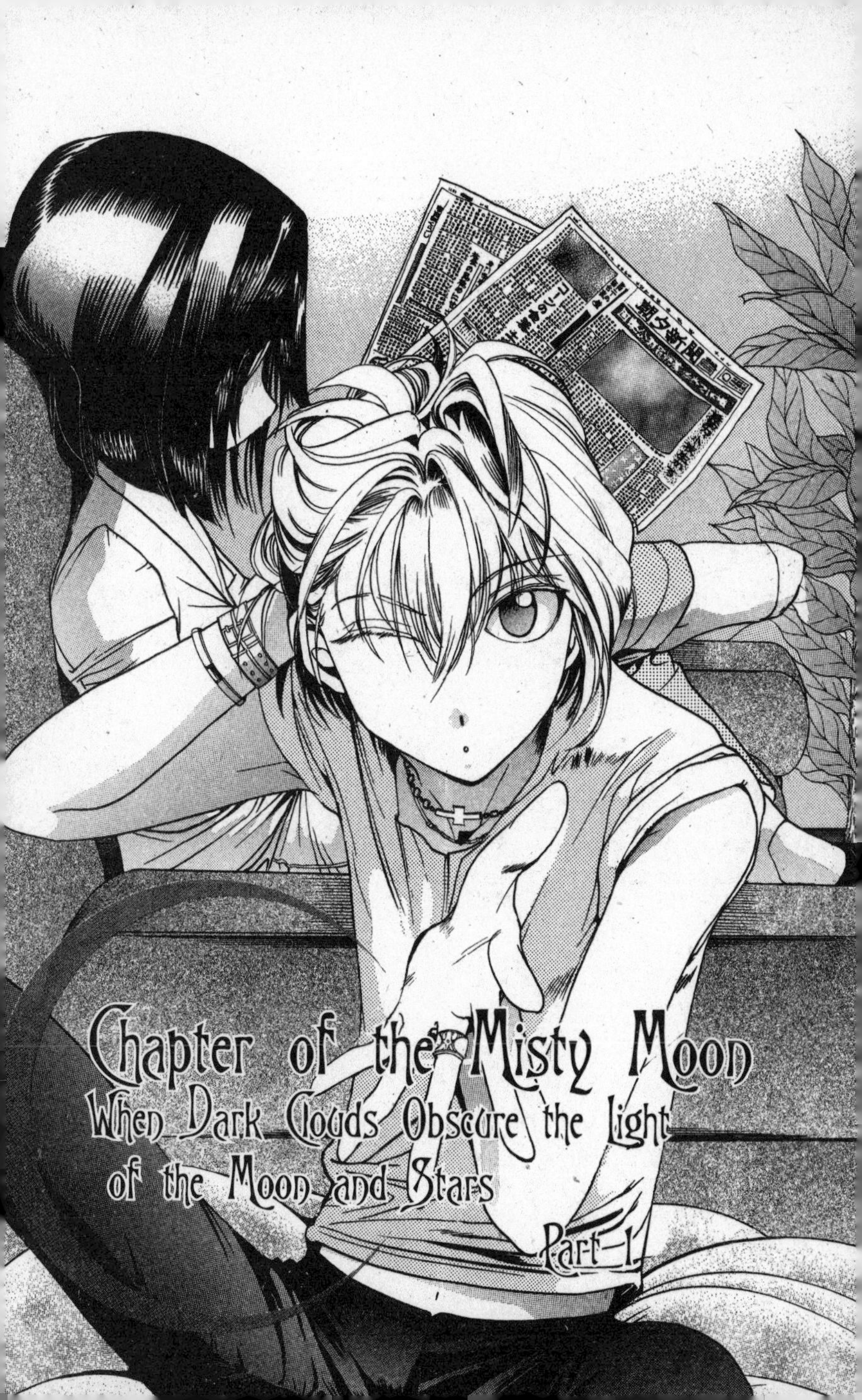
Chapter of the Misty Moon
When Dark Clouds Obscure the Light of the Moon and Stars
Part 1

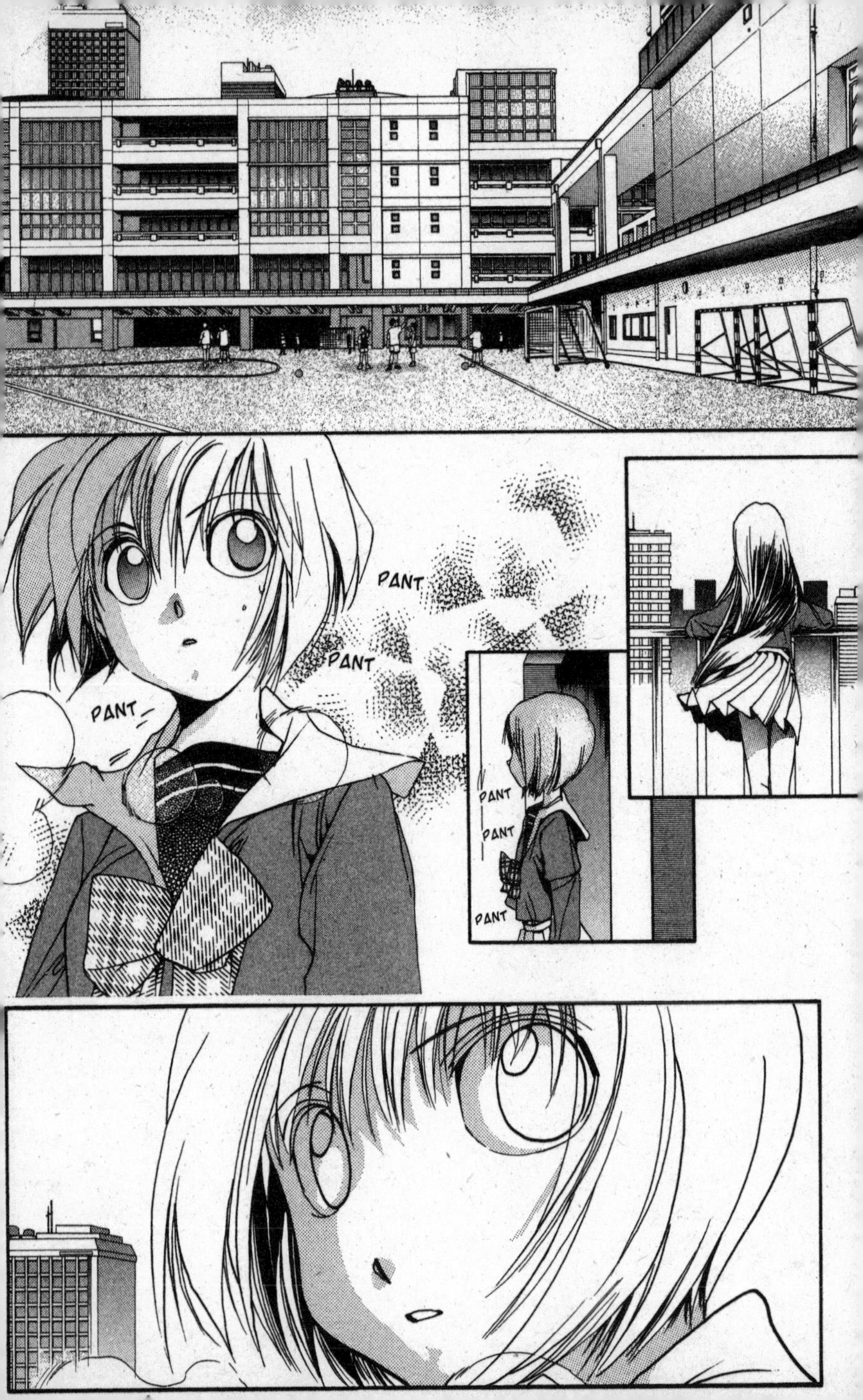
PANT
PANT
PANT
PANT
PANT
PANT

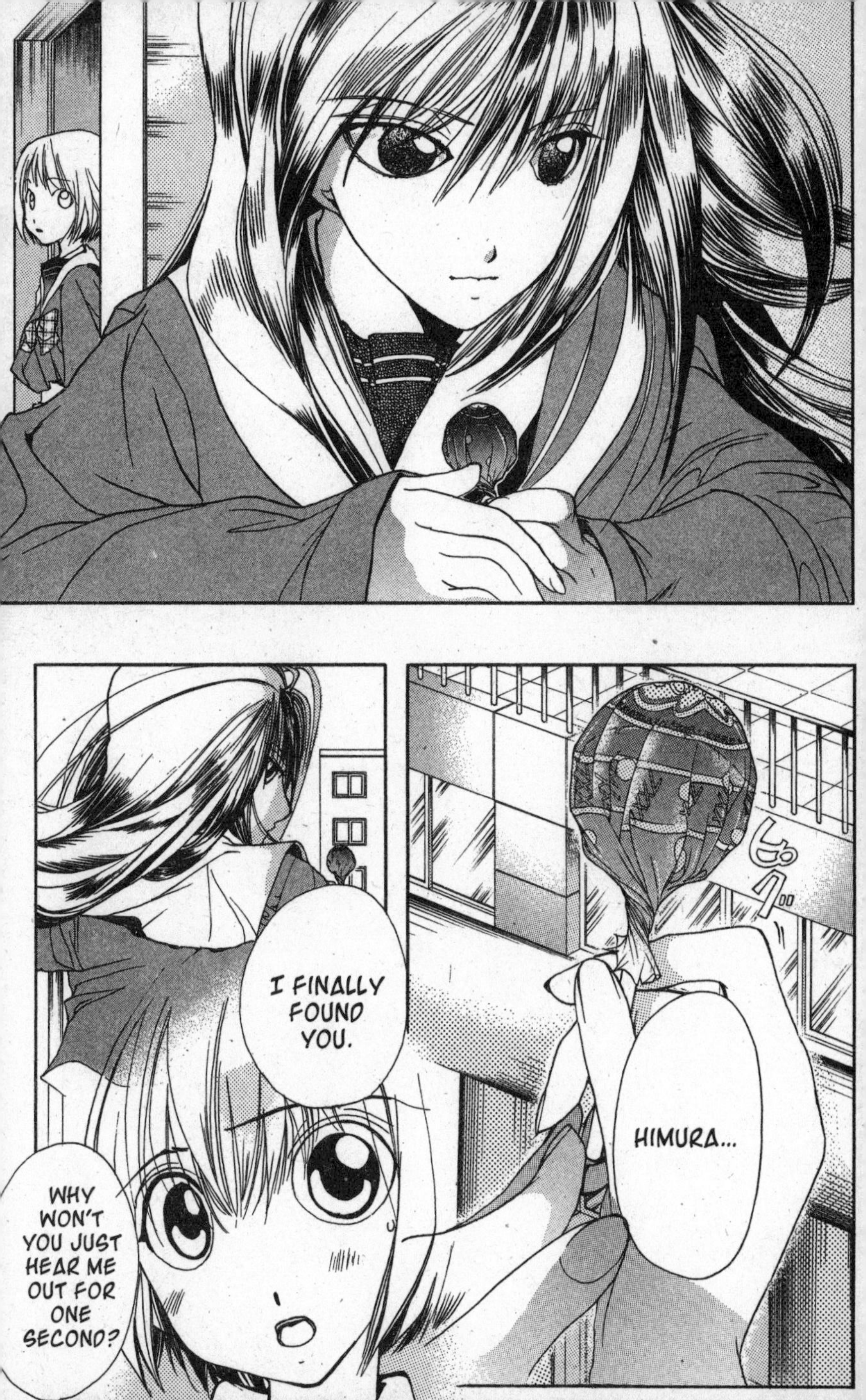
HIMURA...
I FINALLY FOUND YOU.
WHY WON'T YOU JUST HEAR ME OUT FOR ONE SECOND?

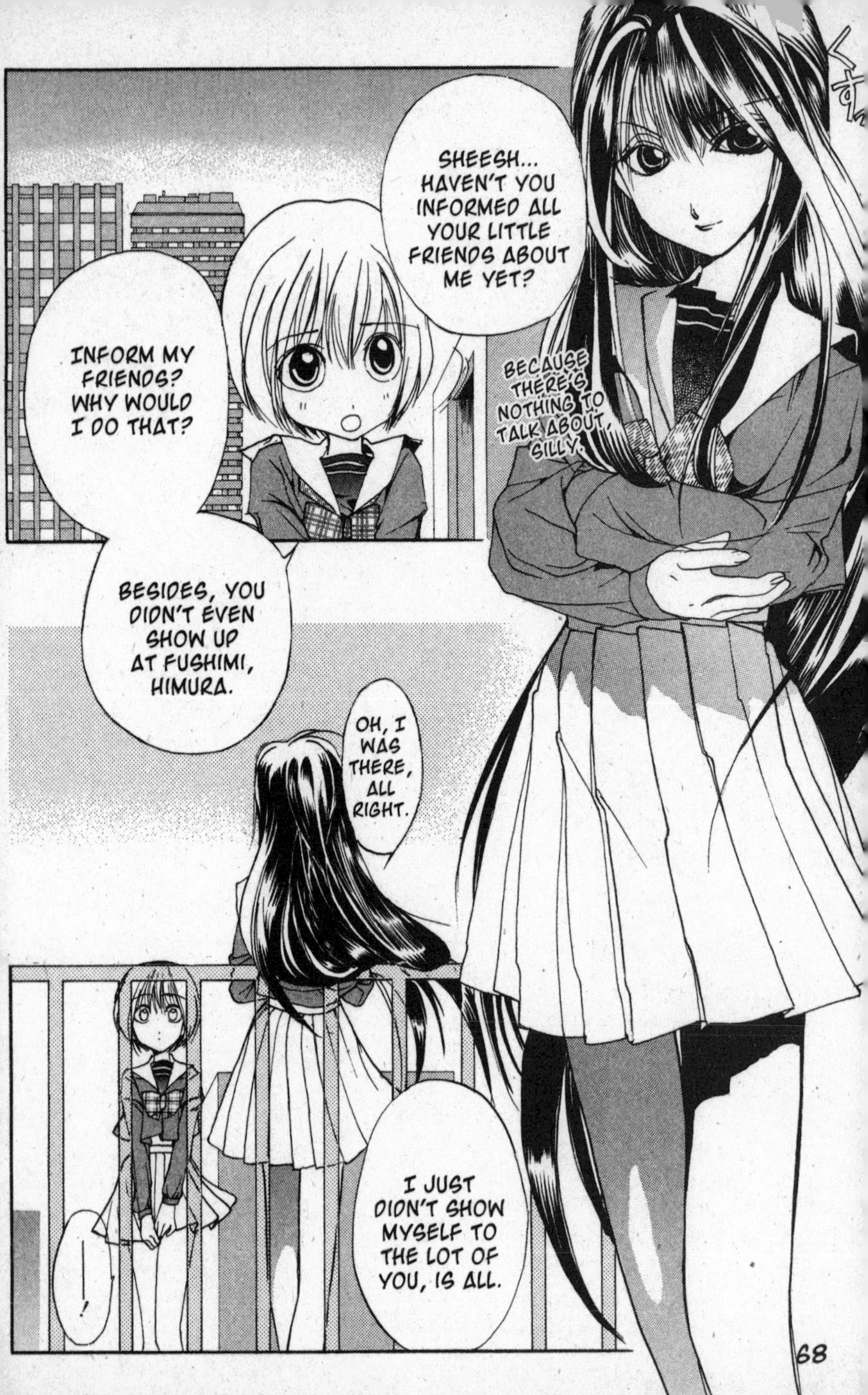
SHEESH... HAVEN'T YOU INFORMED ALL YOUR LITTLE FRIENDS ABOUT ME YET?
BECAUSE THERE'S NOTHING TO TALK ABOUT, SILLY.
INFORM MY FRIENDS? WHY WOULD I DO THAT?
BESIDES, YOU DIDN'T EVEN SHOW UP AT FUSHIMI, HIMURA.
OH, I WAS THERE, ALL RIGHT.
I JUST DIDN'T SHOW MYSELF TO THE LOT OF YOU, IS ALL.
...!

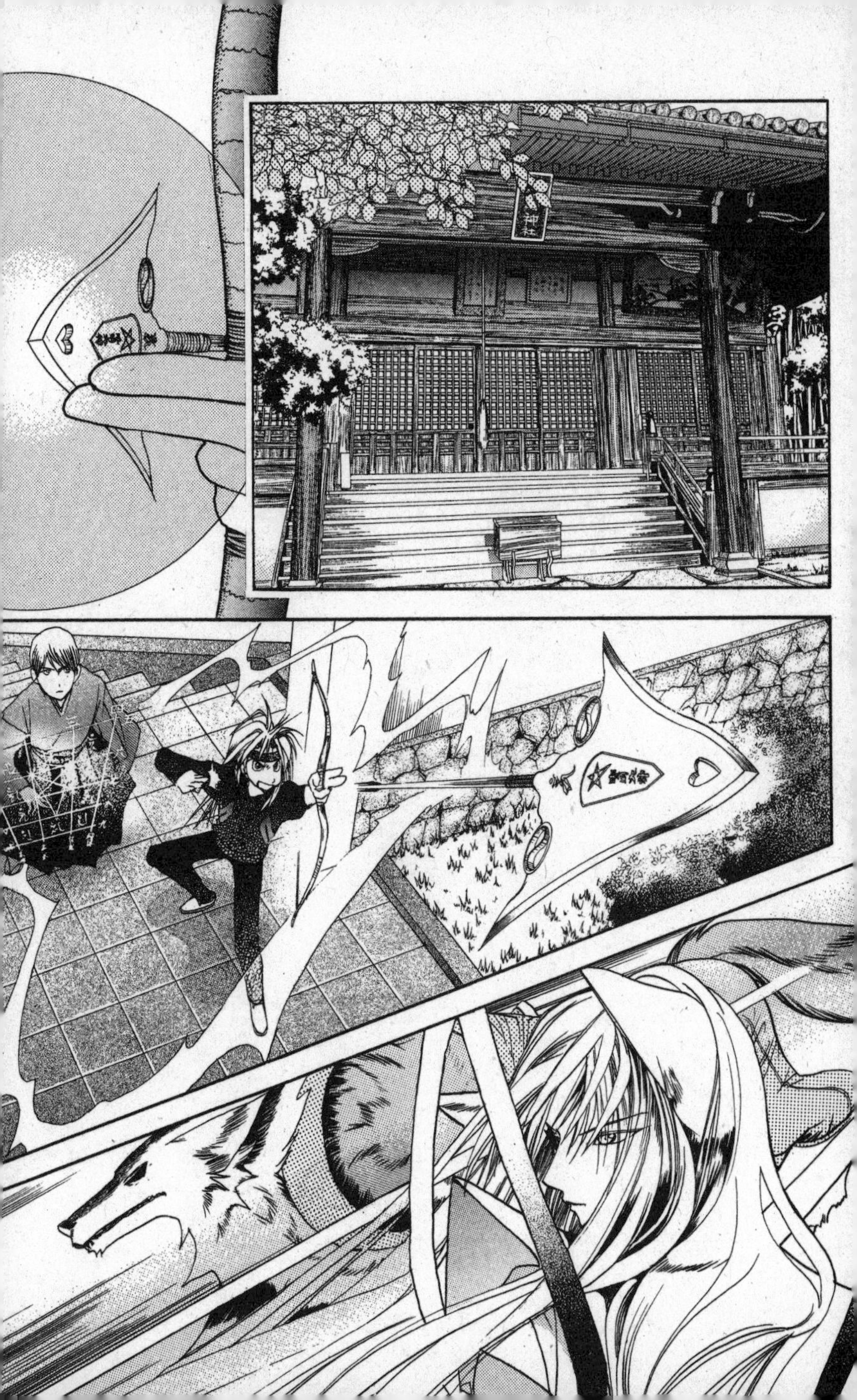
神社

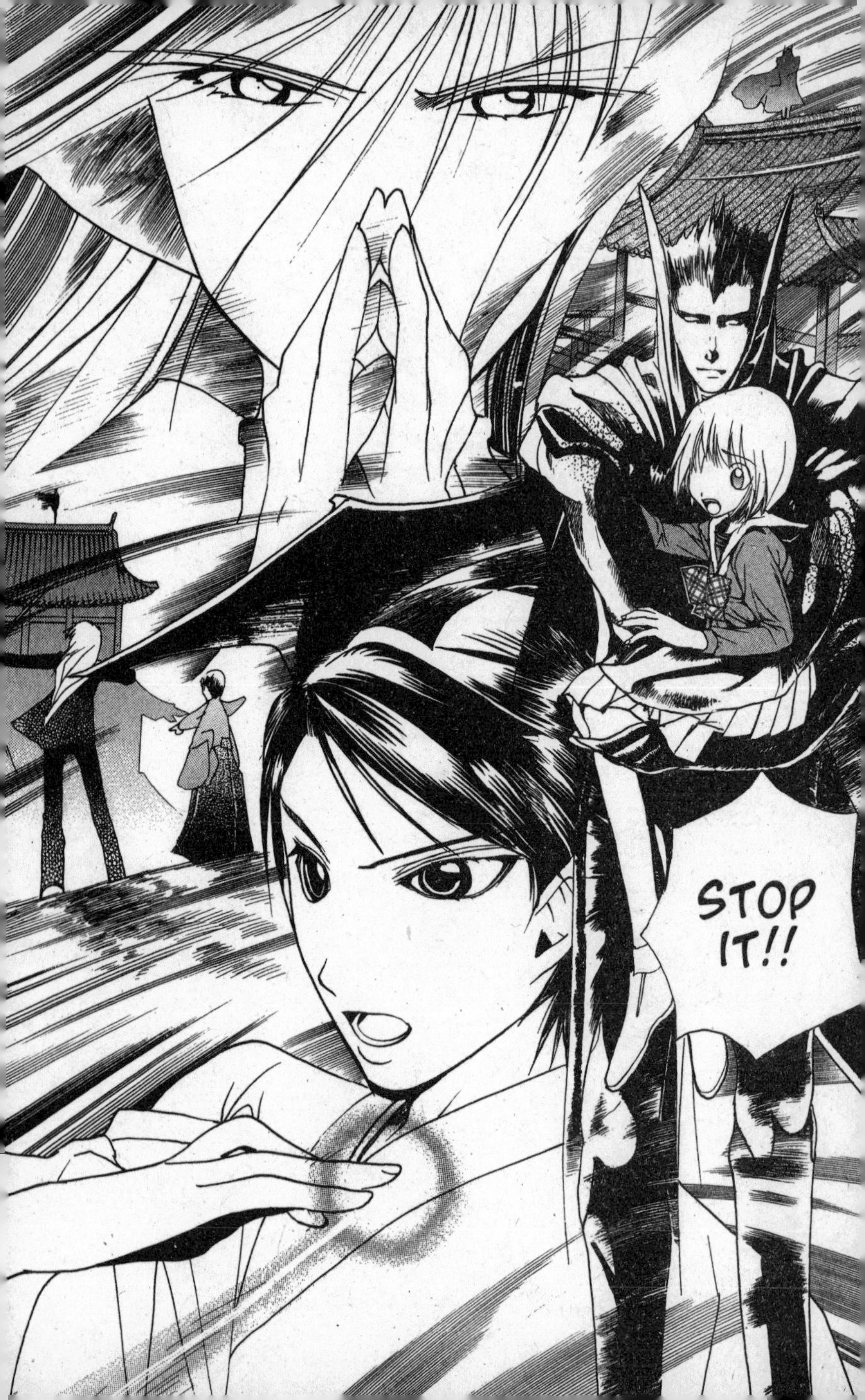
STOP IT!!

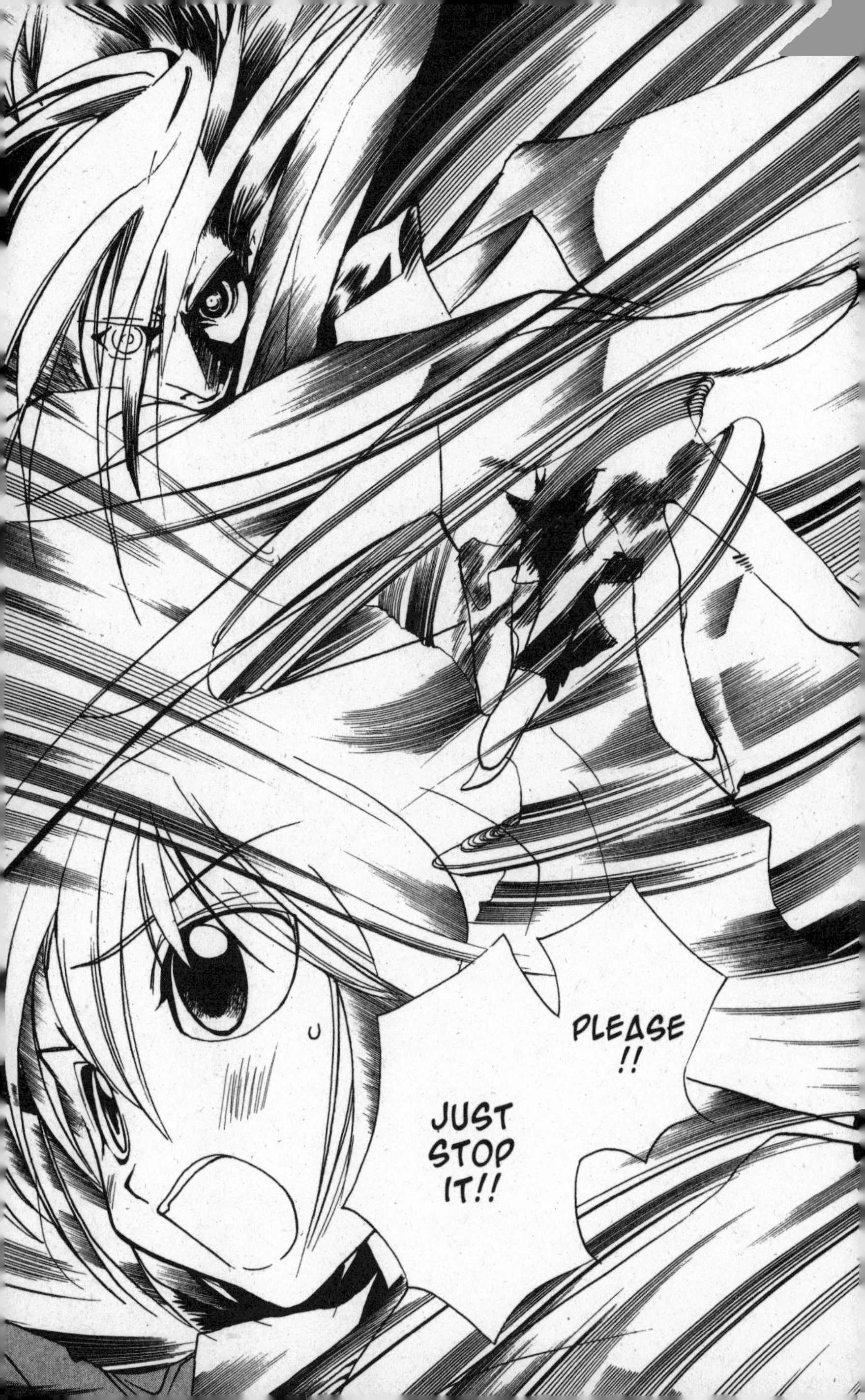
PLEASE !!
JUST STOP IT!!

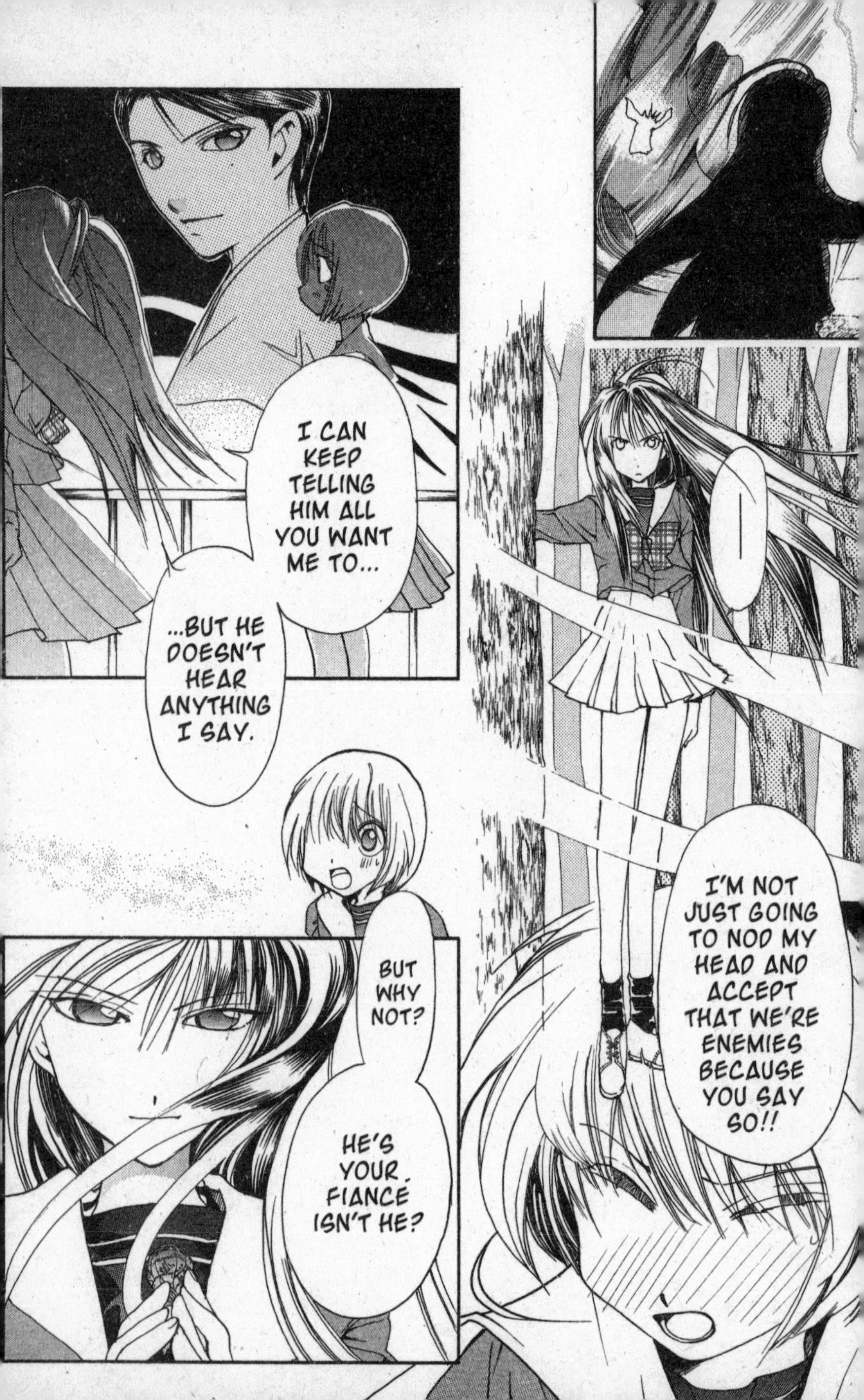
I'M NOT JUST GOING TO NOD MY HEAD AND ACCEPT THAT WE'RE ENEMIES BECAUSE YOU SAY SO!!
I CAN KEEP TELLING HIM ALL YOU WANT ME TO...
...BUT HE DOESN'T HEAR ANYTHING I SAY.
BUT WHY NOT?
HE'S YOUR FIANCE ISN'T HE?

ALL HE SEES ME AS ANYMORE... IS A PAWN IN THIS WAR.
THAT'S TERRIBLE...
BUT MORE IMPORTANT... SHOULD YOU REALLY BE HERE WITH THE LIKES OF ME? IF YOUR FRIENDS FIND OUT...THEY'RE SURE TO BRAND YOU A TRAITOR.
HIMURA, WAIT!!

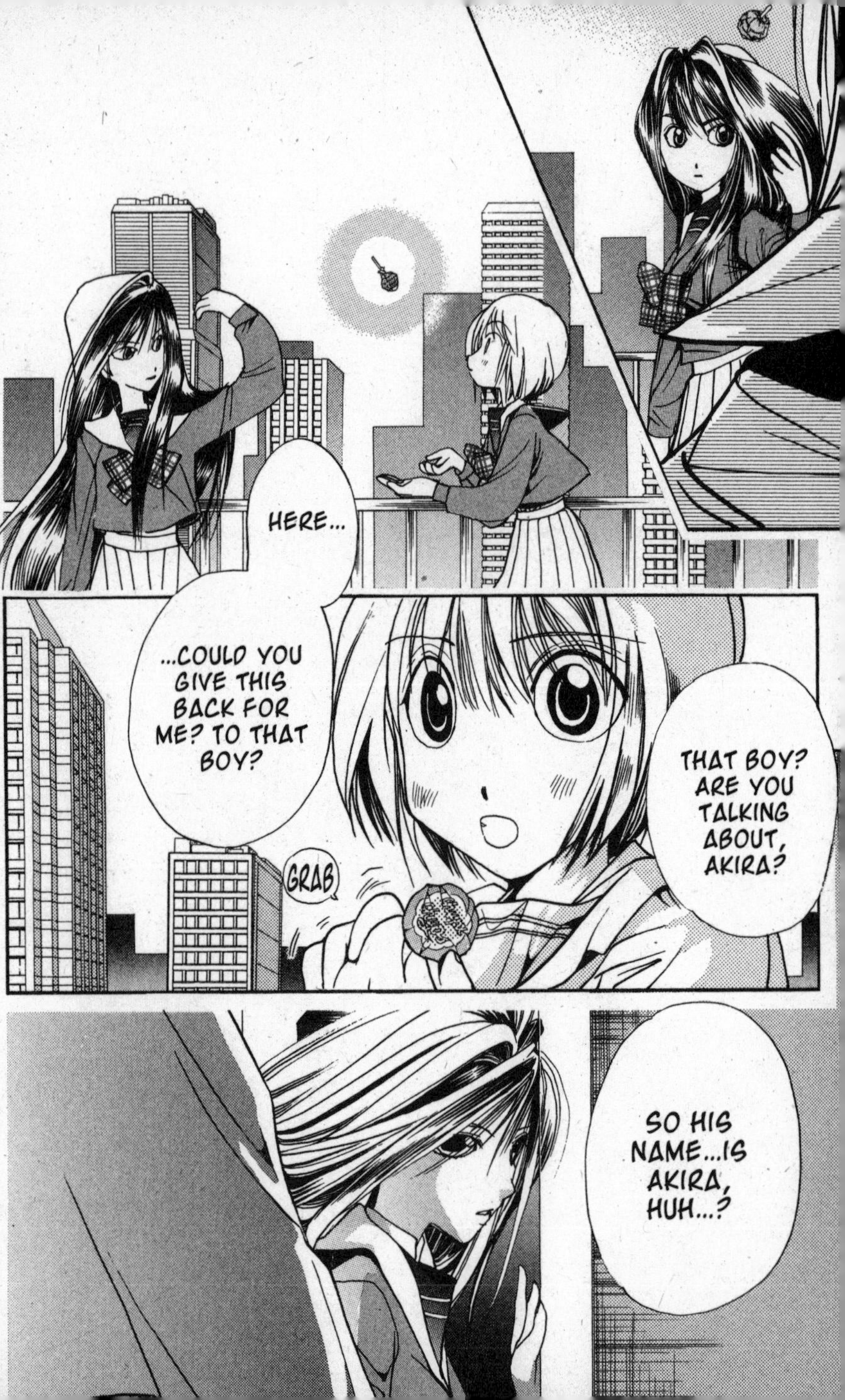
HERE...
...COULD YOU GIVE THIS BACK FOR ME? TO THAT BOY?
THAT BOY? ARE YOU TALKING ABOUT, AKIRA?
GRAB
SO HIS NAME...IS AKIRA, HUH...?

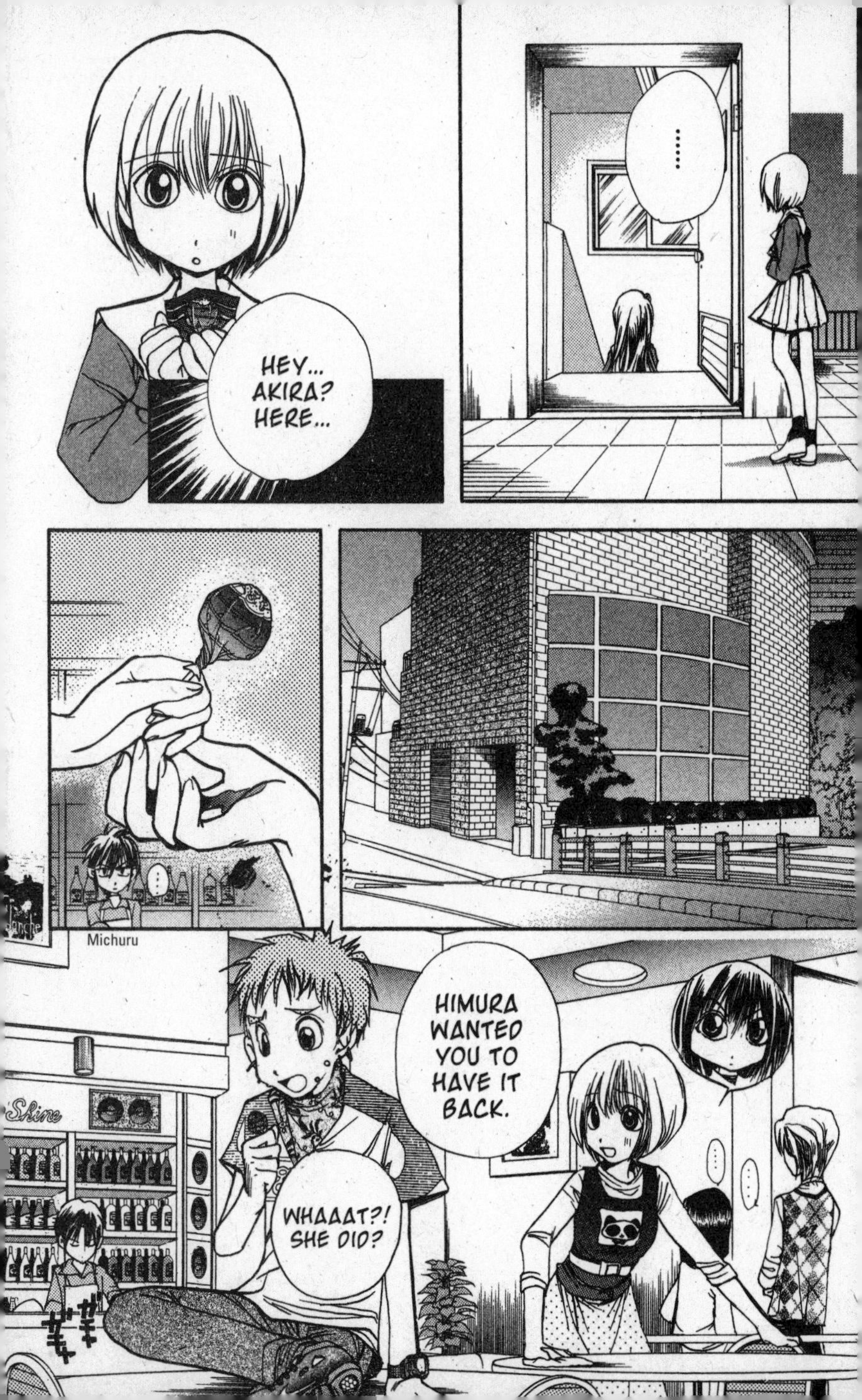
……
HEY... AKIRA? HERE...
Michuru
HIMURA WANTED YOU TO HAVE IT BACK.
Shine
WHAAAT?! SHE DID?

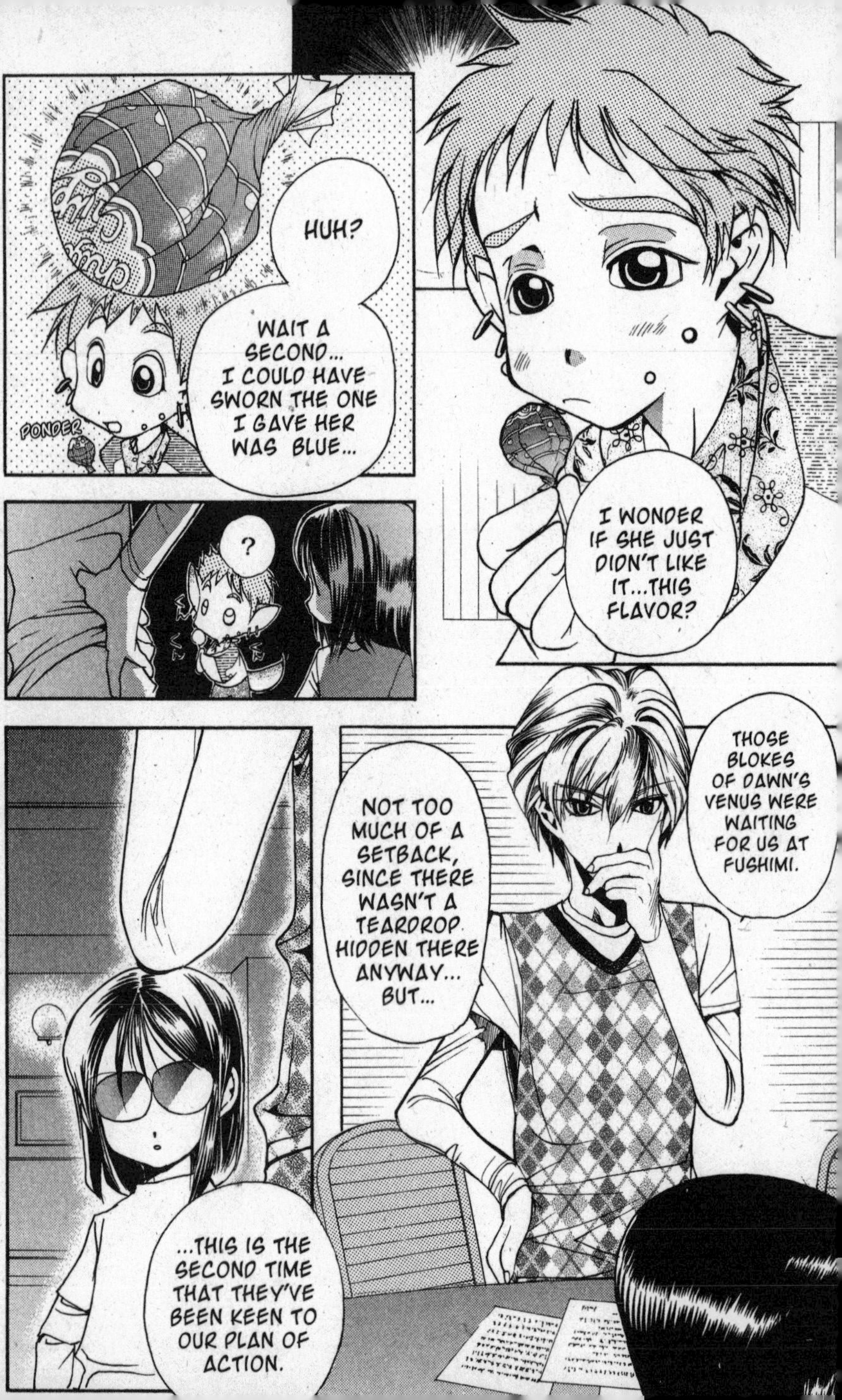
I WONDER IF SHE JUST DIDN'T LIKE IT...THIS FLAVOR?
HUH?
WAIT A SECOND... I COULD HAVE SWORN THE ONE I GAVE HER WAS BLUE...
PONDER
?
THOSE BLOKES OF DAWN'S VENUS WERE WAITING FOR US AT FUSHIMI.
NOT TOO MUCH OF A SETBACK, SINCE THERE WASN'T A TEARDROP HIDDEN THERE ANYWAY... BUT...
...THIS IS THE SECOND TIME THAT THEY'VE BEEN KEEN TO OUR PLAN OF ACTION.

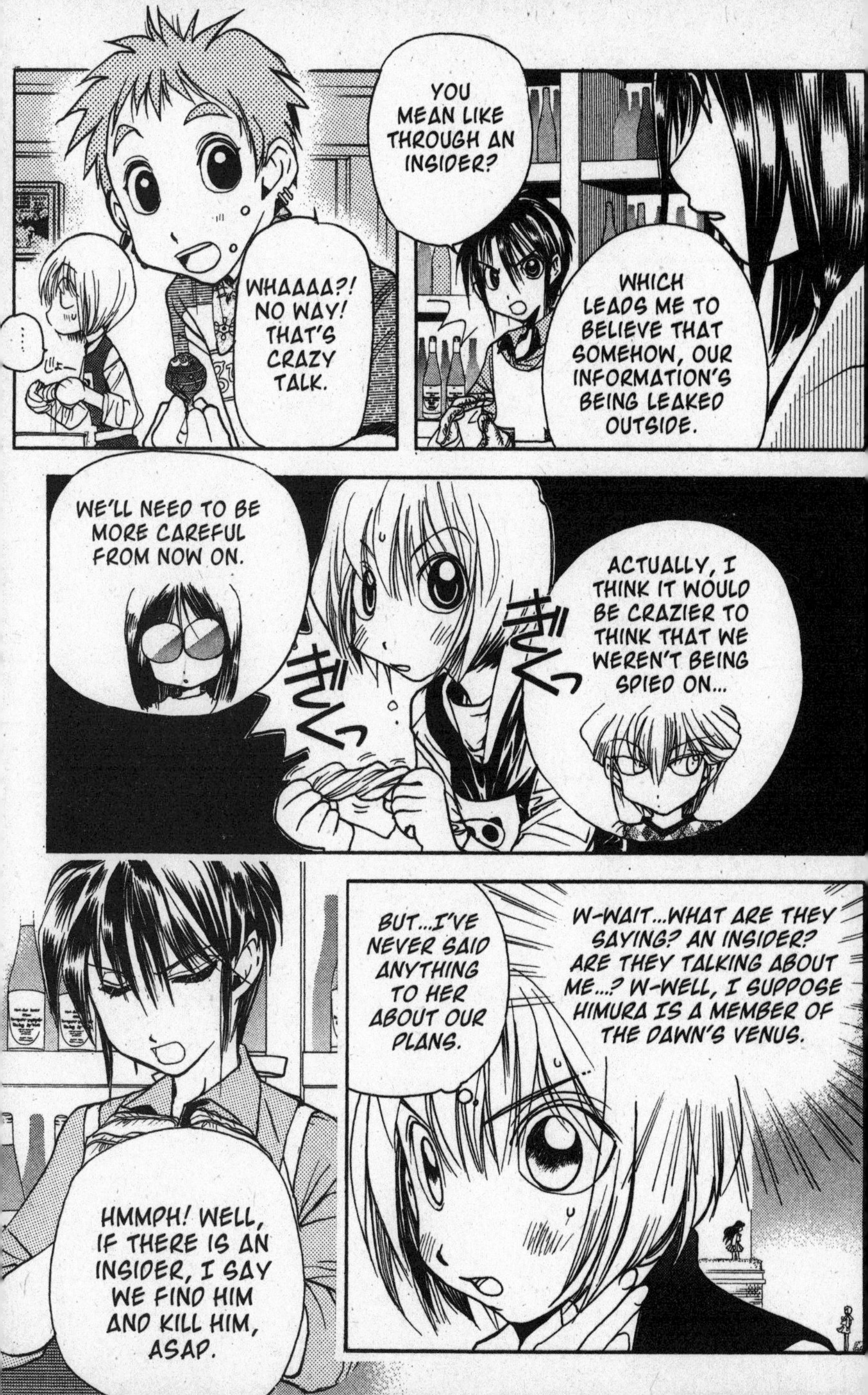
WHICH LEADS ME TO BELIEVE THAT SOMEHOW, OUR INFORMATION'S BEING LEAKED OUTSIDE.
YOU MEAN LIKE THROUGH AN INSIDER?
WHAAAA?! NO WAY! THAT'S CRAZY TALK.
...
ACTUALLY, I THINK IT WOULD BE CRAZIER TO THINK THAT WE WEREN'T BEING SPIED ON...
ぎくっ
ぎくっ
WE'LL NEED TO BE MORE CAREFUL FROM NOW ON.
W-WAIT...WHAT ARE THEY SAYING? AN INSIDER? ARE THEY TALKING ABOUT ME...? W-WELL, I SUPPOSE HIMURA IS A MEMBER OF THE DAWN'S VENUS.
BUT...I'VE NEVER SAID ANYTHING TO HER ABOUT OUR PLANS.
HMMPH! WELL, IF THERE IS AN INSIDER, I SAY WE FIND HIM AND KILL HIM, ASAP.

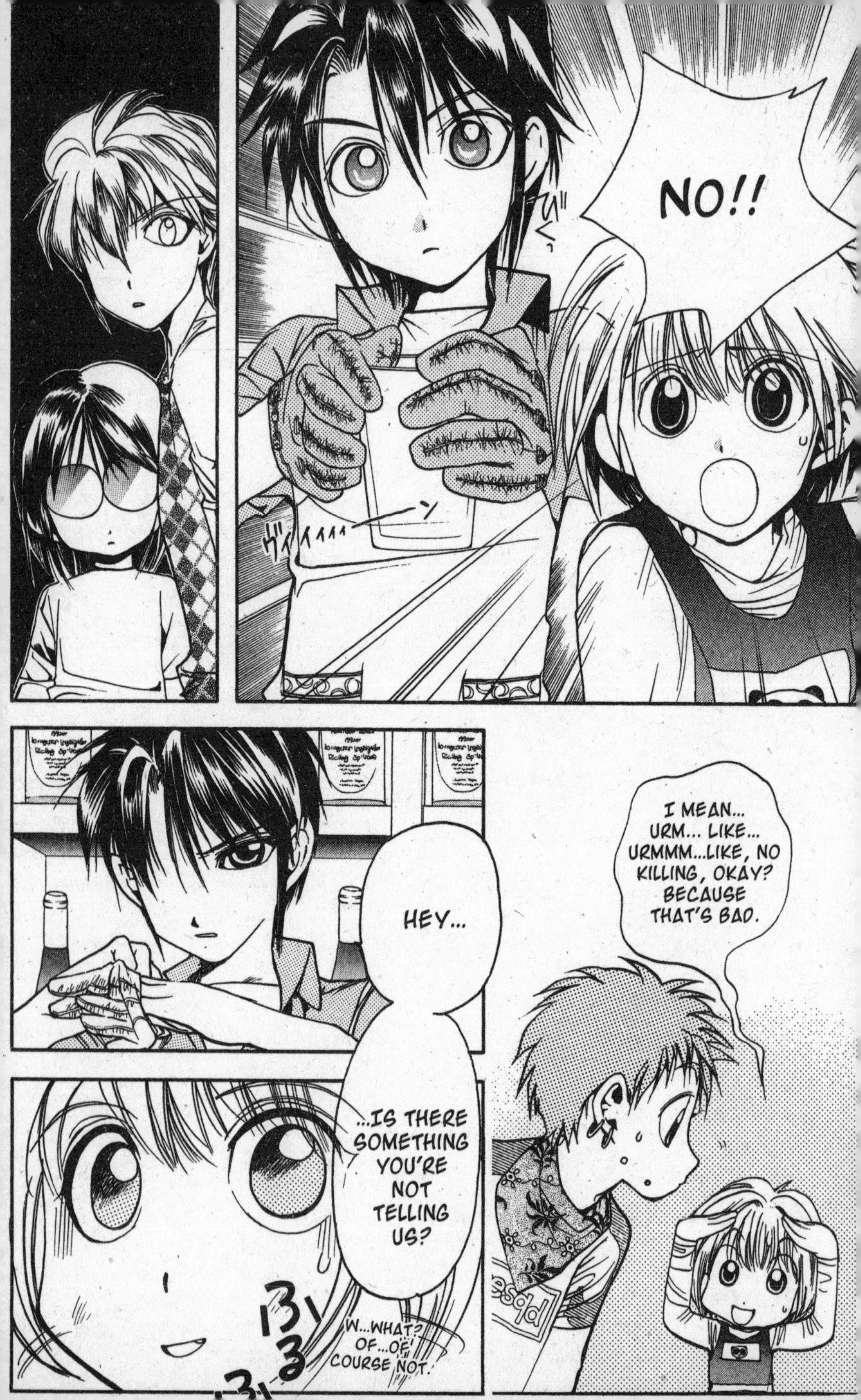
NO!!
I MEAN... URM... LIKE... URMMM...LIKE, NO KILLING, OKAY? BECAUSE THAT'S BAD.
HEY...
...IS THERE SOMETHING YOU'RE NOT TELLING US?
W...WHAT? OF...OF COURSE NOT.

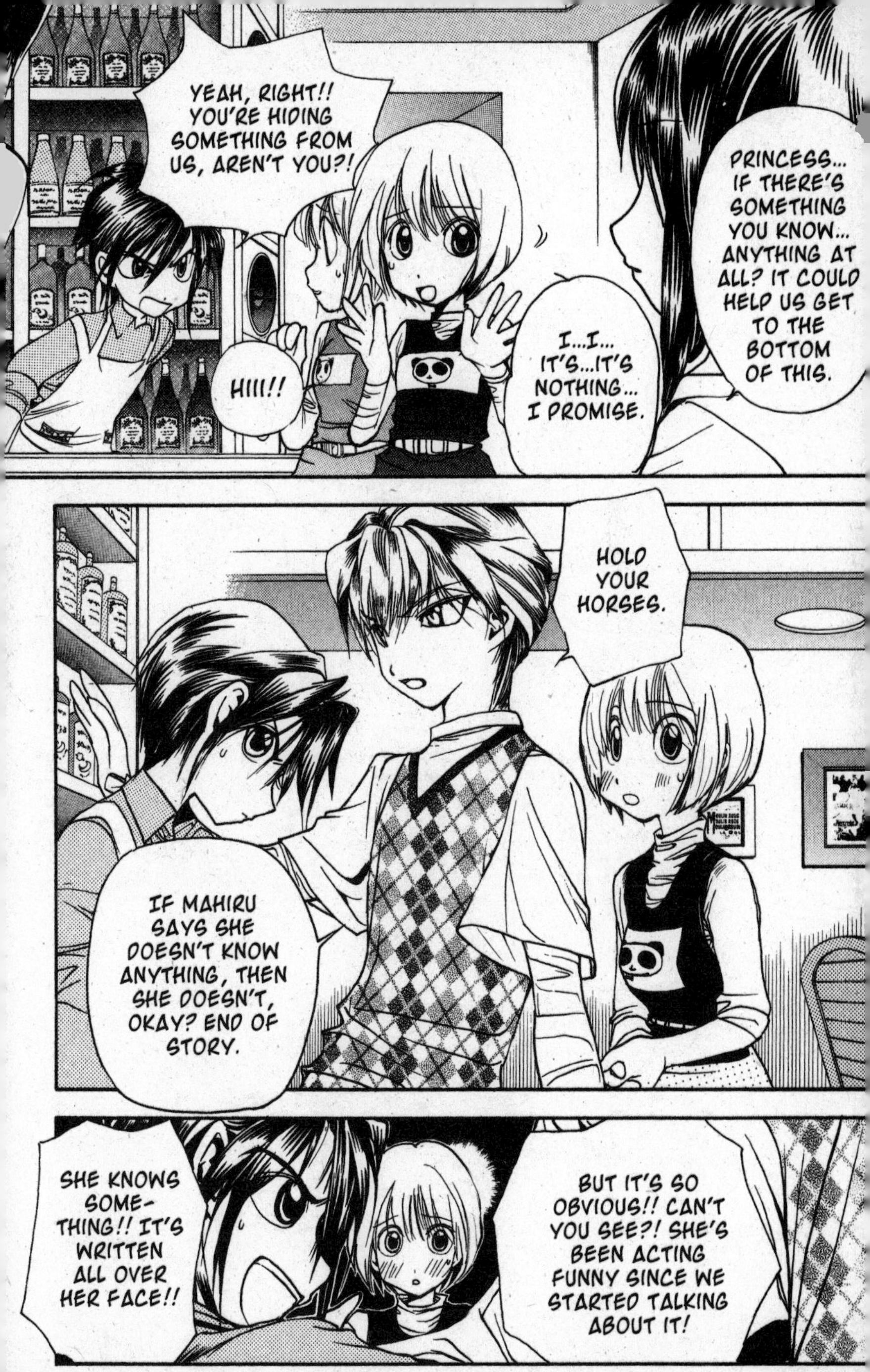
PRINCESS... IF THERE'S SOMETHING YOU KNOW... ANYTHING AT ALL? IT COULD HELP US GET TO THE BOTTOM OF THIS.
YEAH, RIGHT!! YOU'RE HIDING SOMETHING FROM US, AREN'T YOU?!
I...I... IT'S...IT'S NOTHING... I PROMISE.
HIII!!
HOLD YOUR HORSES.
IF MAHIRU SAYS SHE DOESN'T KNOW ANYTHING, THEN SHE DOESN'T, OKAY? END OF STORY.
BUT IT'S SO OBVIOUS!! CAN'T YOU SEE?! SHE'S BEEN ACTING FUNNY SINCE WE STARTED TALKING ABOUT IT!
SHE KNOWS SOME-THING!! IT'S WRITTEN ALL OVER HER FACE!!

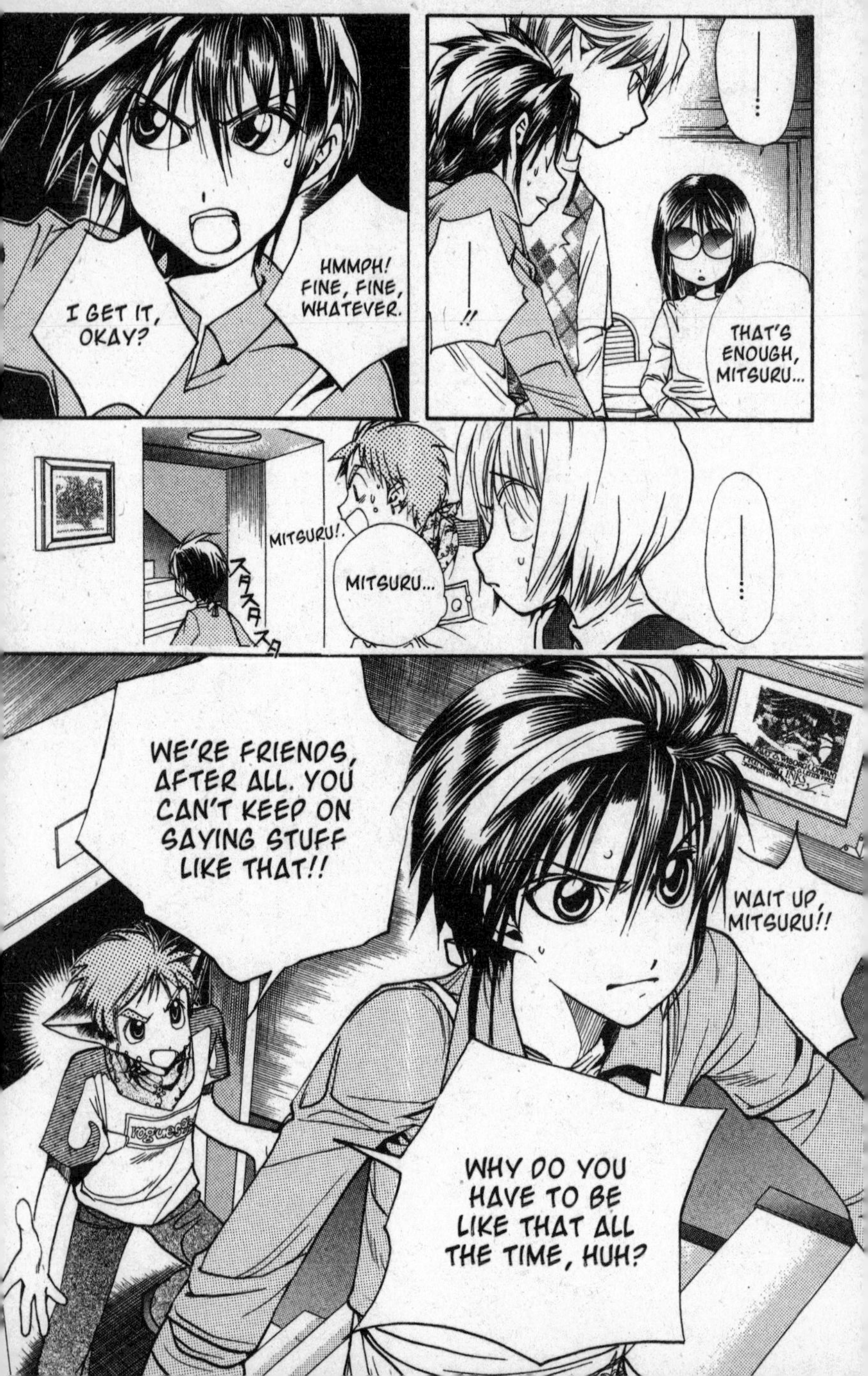
……
……!!
THAT'S ENOUGH, MITSURU...
HMMPH! FINE, FINE, WHATEVER.
I GET IT, OKAY?
……
MITSURU...
MITSURU!
スタスタスタ
WAIT UP, MITSURU!!
WE'RE FRIENDS, AFTER ALL. YOU CAN'T KEEP ON SAYING STUFF LIKE THAT!!
WHY DO YOU HAVE TO BE LIKE THAT ALL THE TIME, HUH?

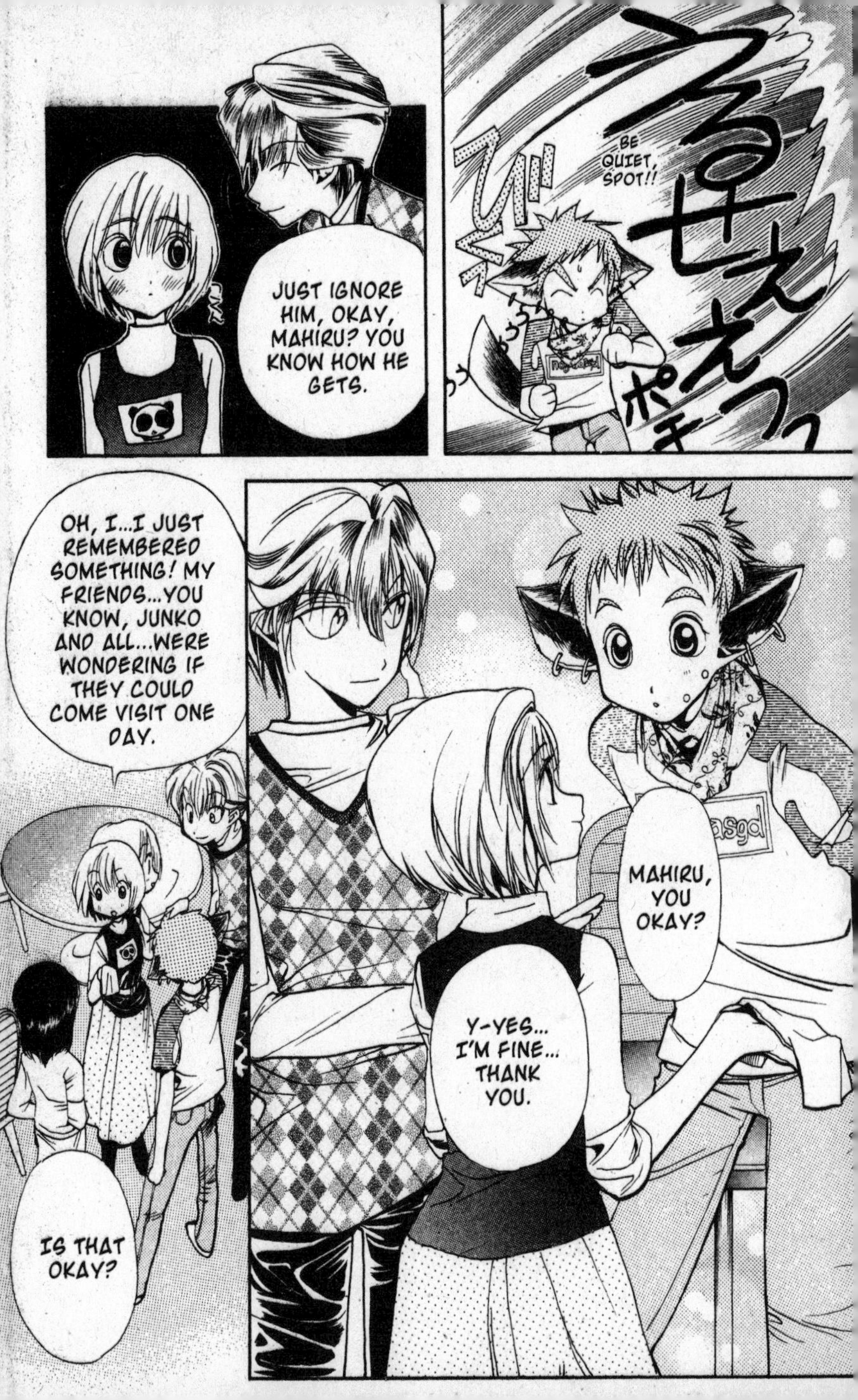
うるせえっ
BE QUIET, SPOT!!
ポキ
JUST IGNORE HIM, OKAY, MAHIRU? YOU KNOW HOW HE GETS.
MAHIRU, YOU OKAY?
Y-YES... I'M FINE... THANK YOU.
OH, I...I JUST REMEMBERED SOMETHING! MY FRIENDS...YOU KNOW, JUNKO AND ALL...WERE WONDERING IF THEY COULD COME VISIT ONE DAY.
IS THAT OKAY?

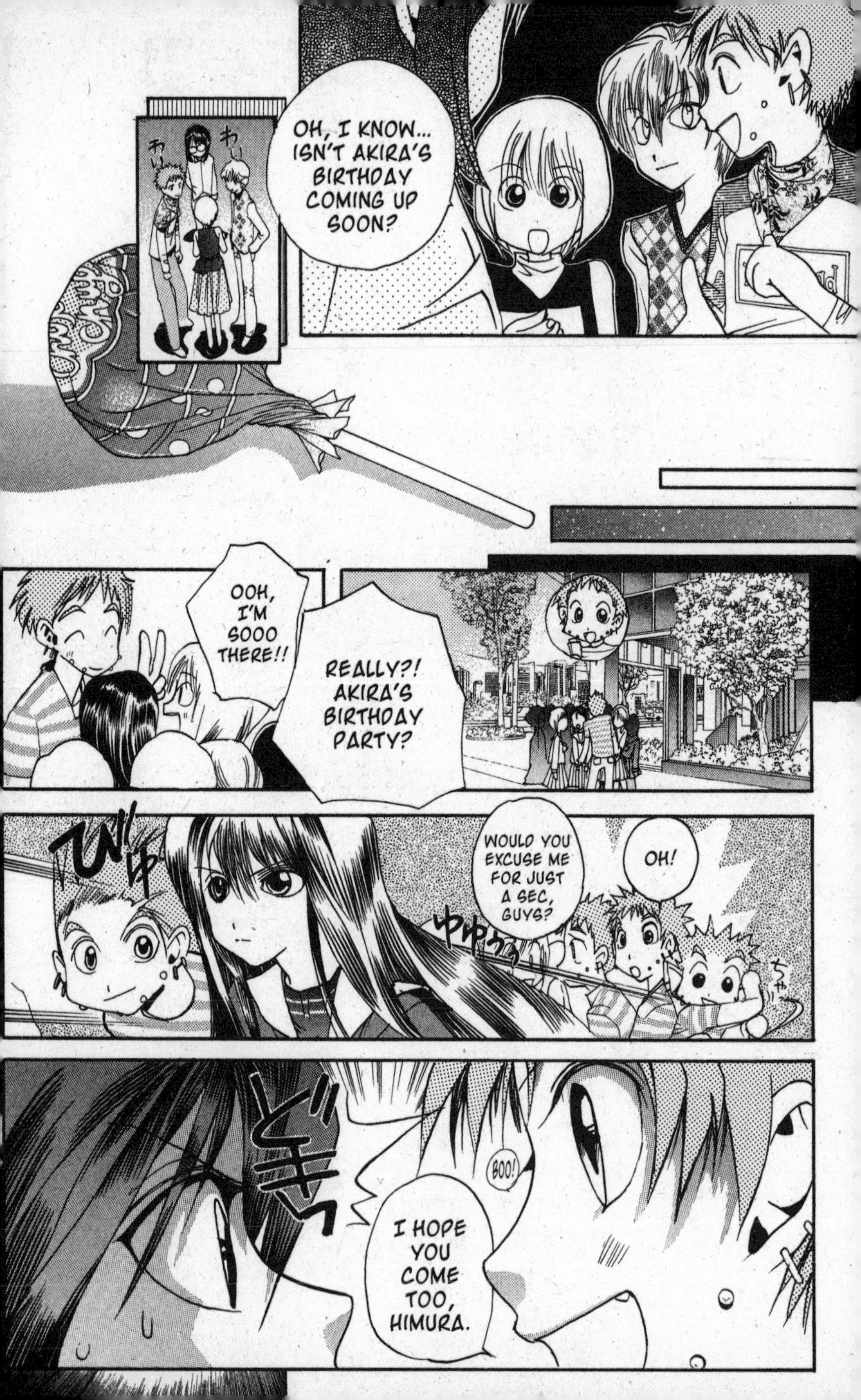
OH, I KNOW... ISN'T AKIRA'S BIRTHDAY COMING UP SOON?
REALLY?! AKIRA'S BIRTHDAY PARTY?
OOH, I'M SOOO THERE!!
OH!
WOULD YOU EXCUSE ME FOR JUST A SEC, GUYS?
BOO!
I HOPE YOU COME TOO, HIMURA.

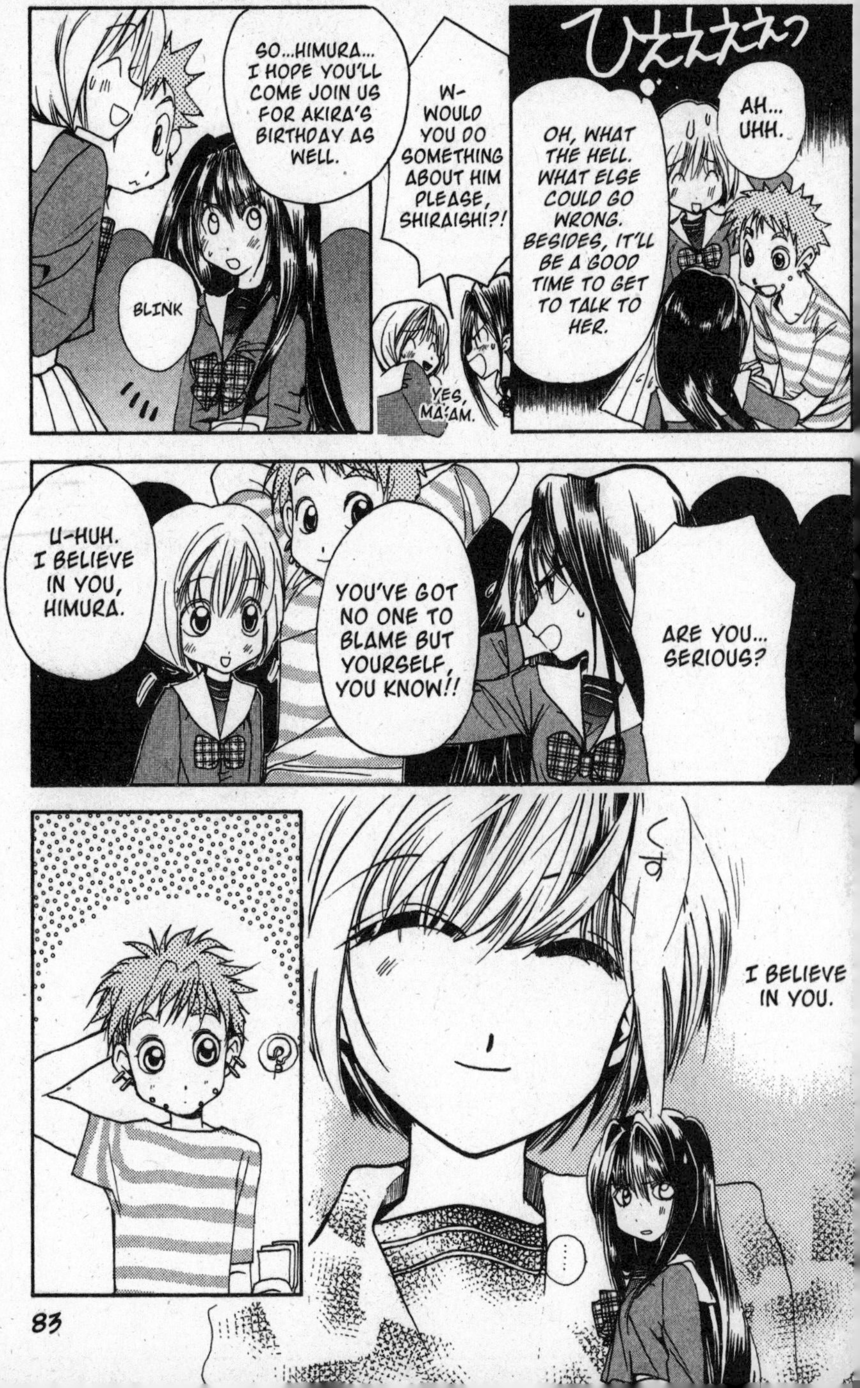
ひえええぇっ
AH... UHH.
OH, WHAT THE HELL. WHAT ELSE COULD GO WRONG. BESIDES, IT'LL BE A GOOD TIME TO GET TO TALK TO HER.
W-WOULD YOU DO SOMETHING ABOUT HIM PLEASE, SHIRAISHI?!
YES, MA'AM.
SO...HIMURA... I HOPE YOU'LL COME JOIN US FOR AKIRA'S BIRTHDAY AS WELL.
BLINK
ARE YOU... SERIOUS?
YOU'VE GOT NO ONE TO BLAME BUT YOURSELF, YOU KNOW!!
U-HUH. I BELIEVE IN YOU, HIMURA.
くす
I BELIEVE IN YOU.
...

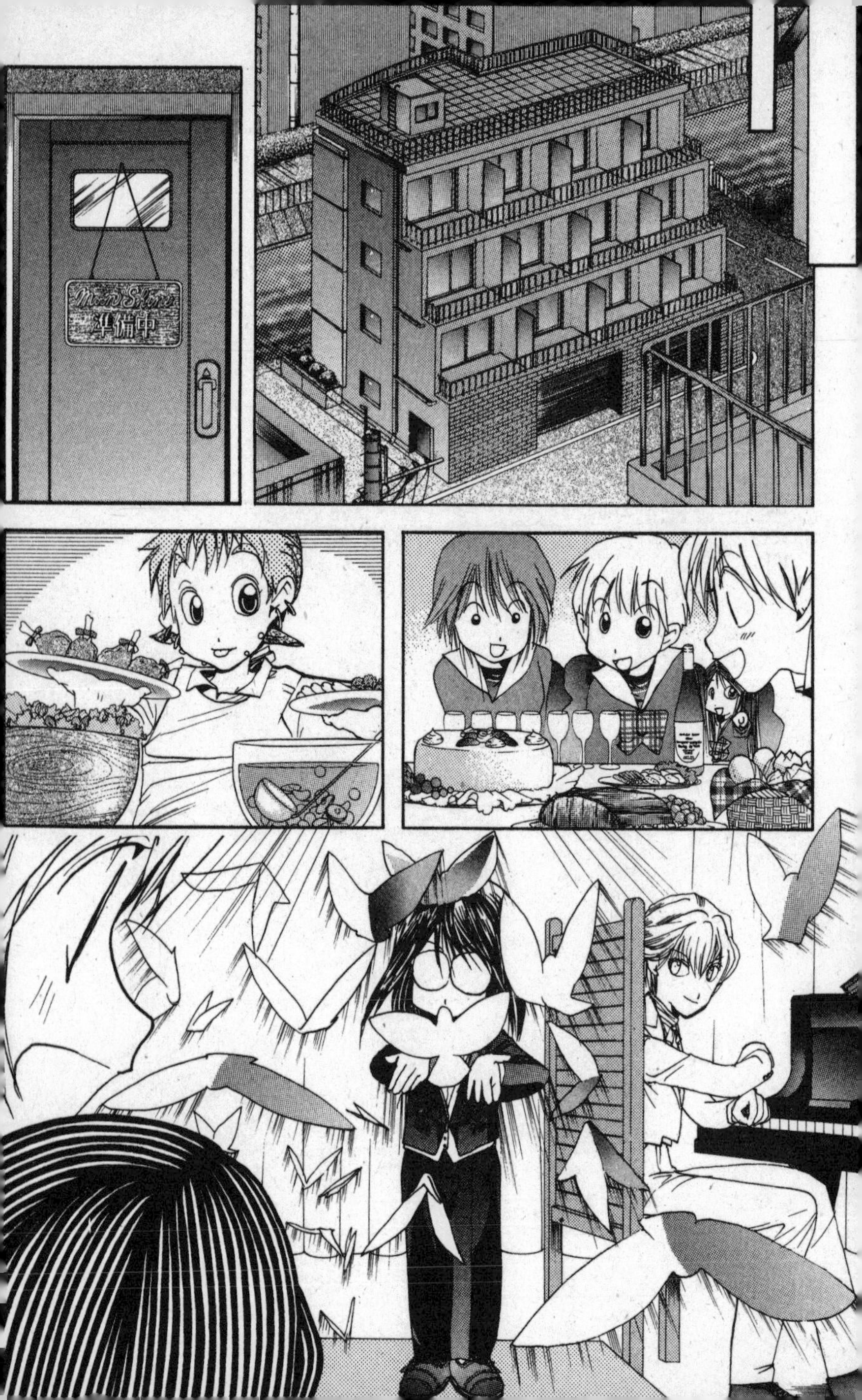
Moon Shine
準備中

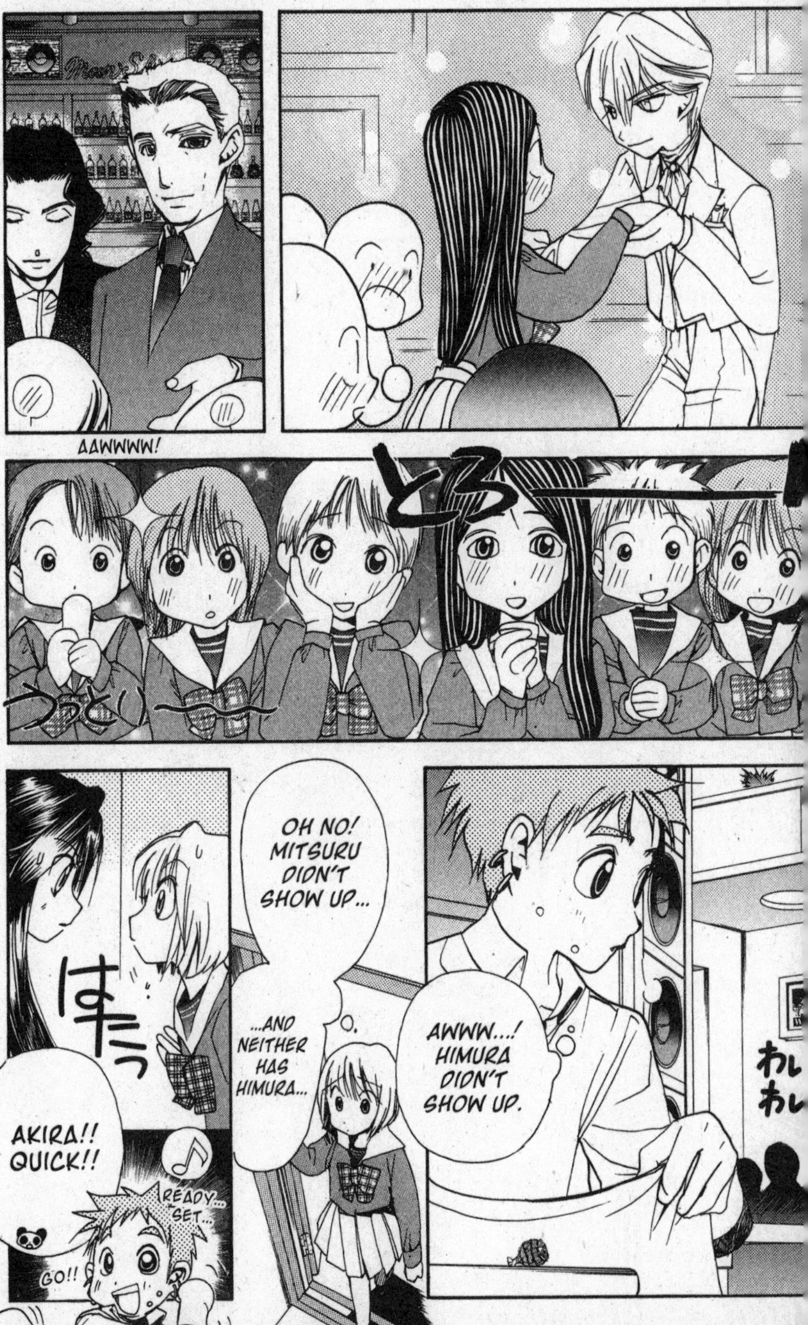
AAWWWW!
とろ——
うっとり——
AWWW...! HIMURA DIDN'T SHOW UP.
OH NO! MITSURU DIDN'T SHOW UP...
...AND NEITHER HAS HIMURA...
ほっ
AKIRA!! QUICK!!
READY... SET...
GO!!
TAP

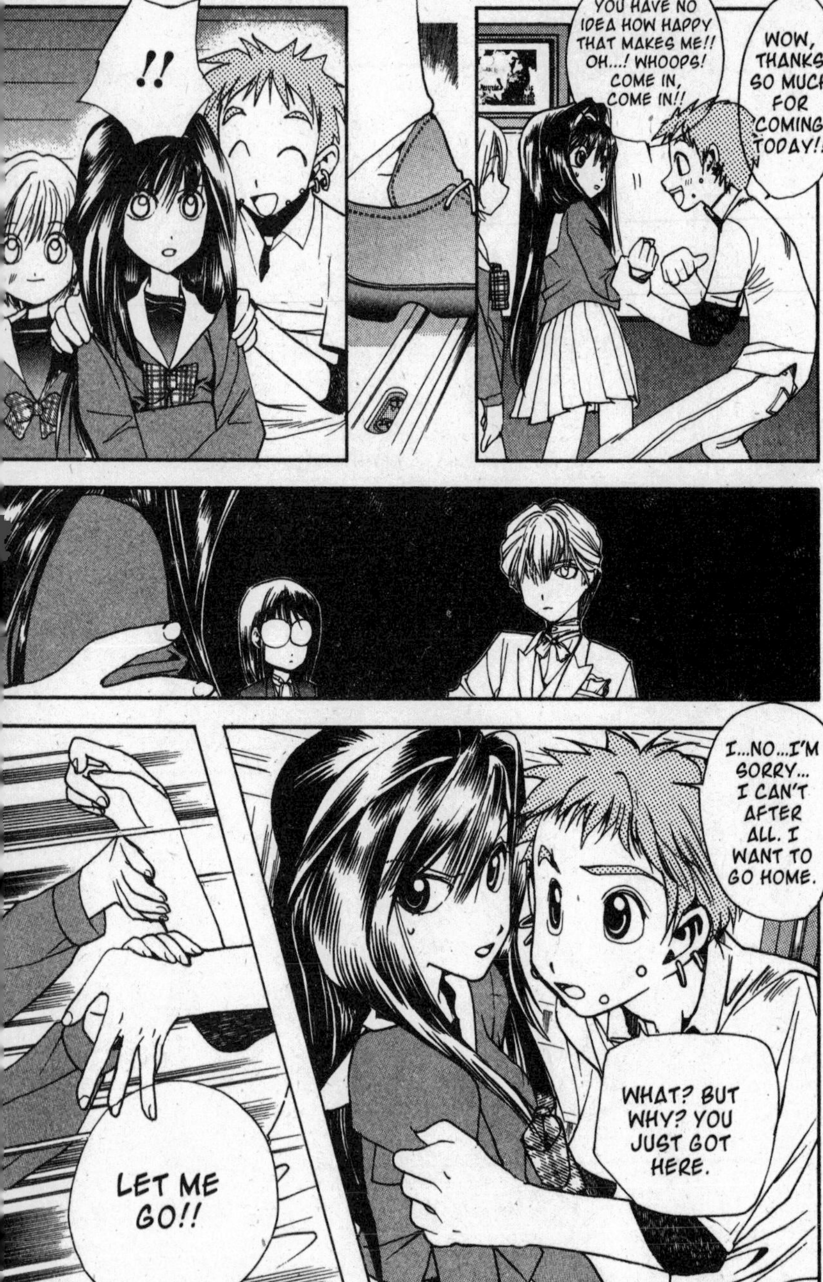
WOW, THANKS SO MUCH FOR COMING TODAY!!
YOU HAVE NO IDEA HOW HAPPY THAT MAKES ME!! OH...! WHOOPS! COME IN, COME IN!!
!!
I...NO...I'M SORRY... I CAN'T AFTER ALL. I WANT TO GO HOME.
WHAT? BUT WHY? YOU JUST GOT HERE.
LET ME GO!!

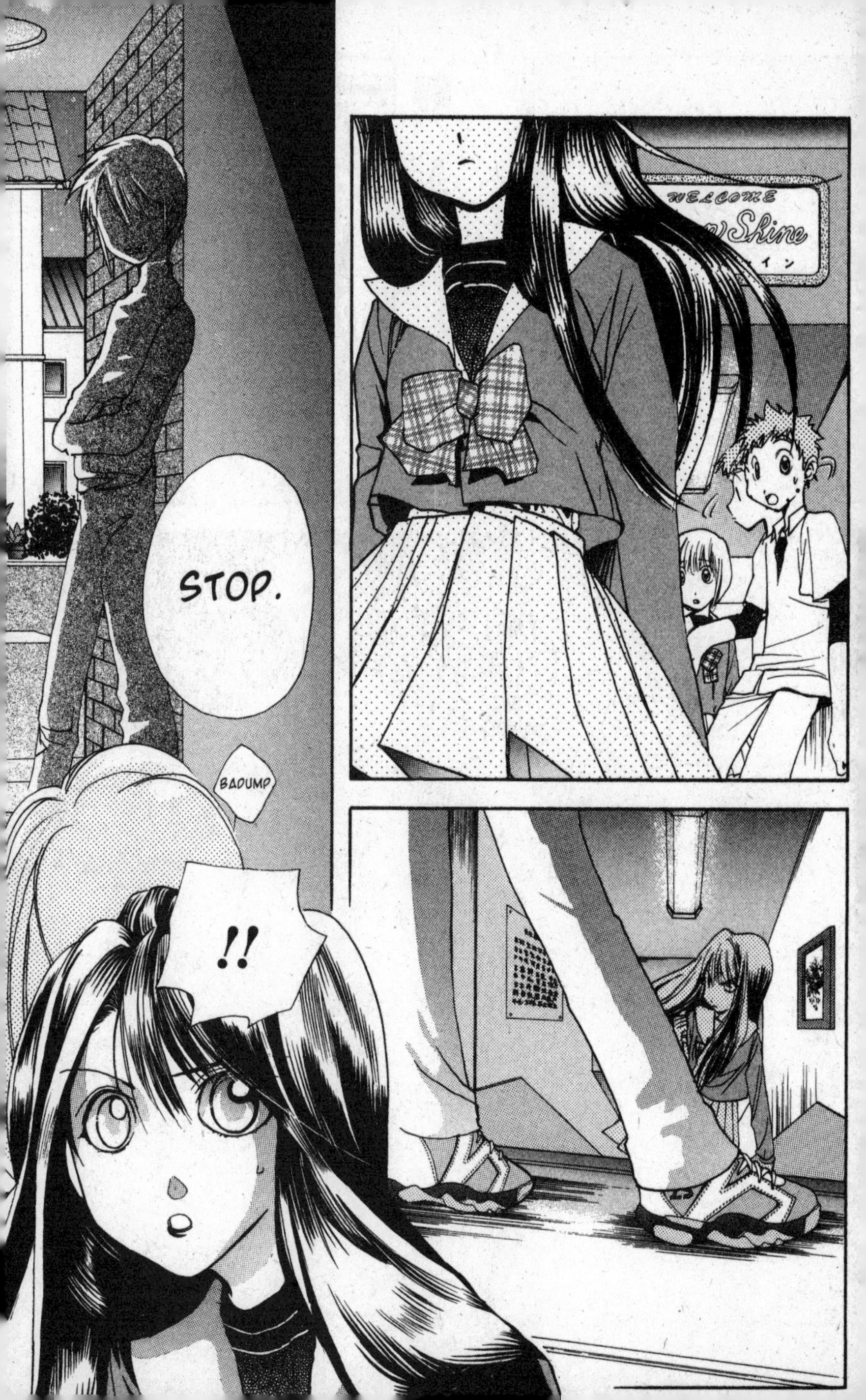
WELCOME
STOP.
BADUMP
!!

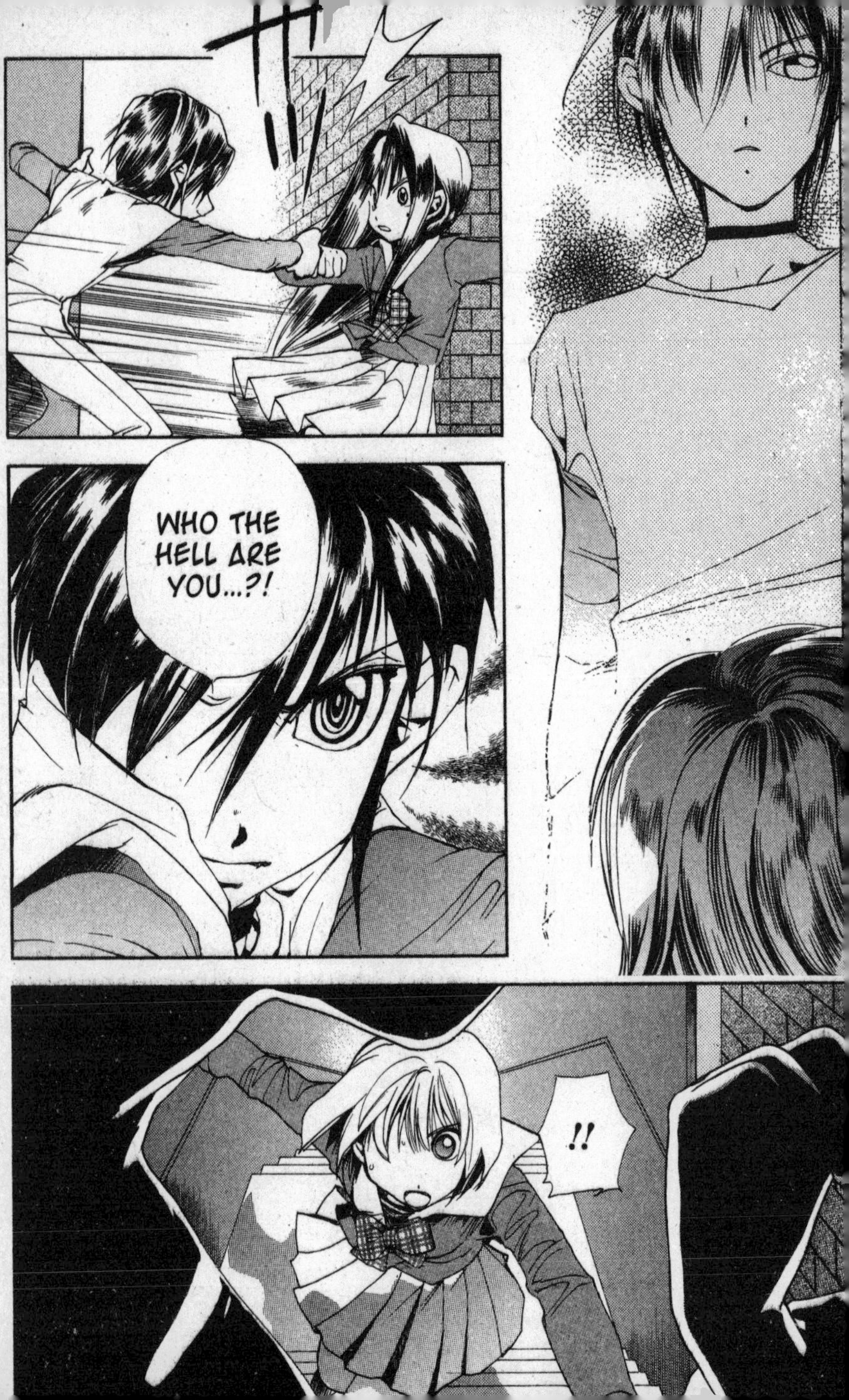
WHO THE HELL ARE YOU...?!
!!

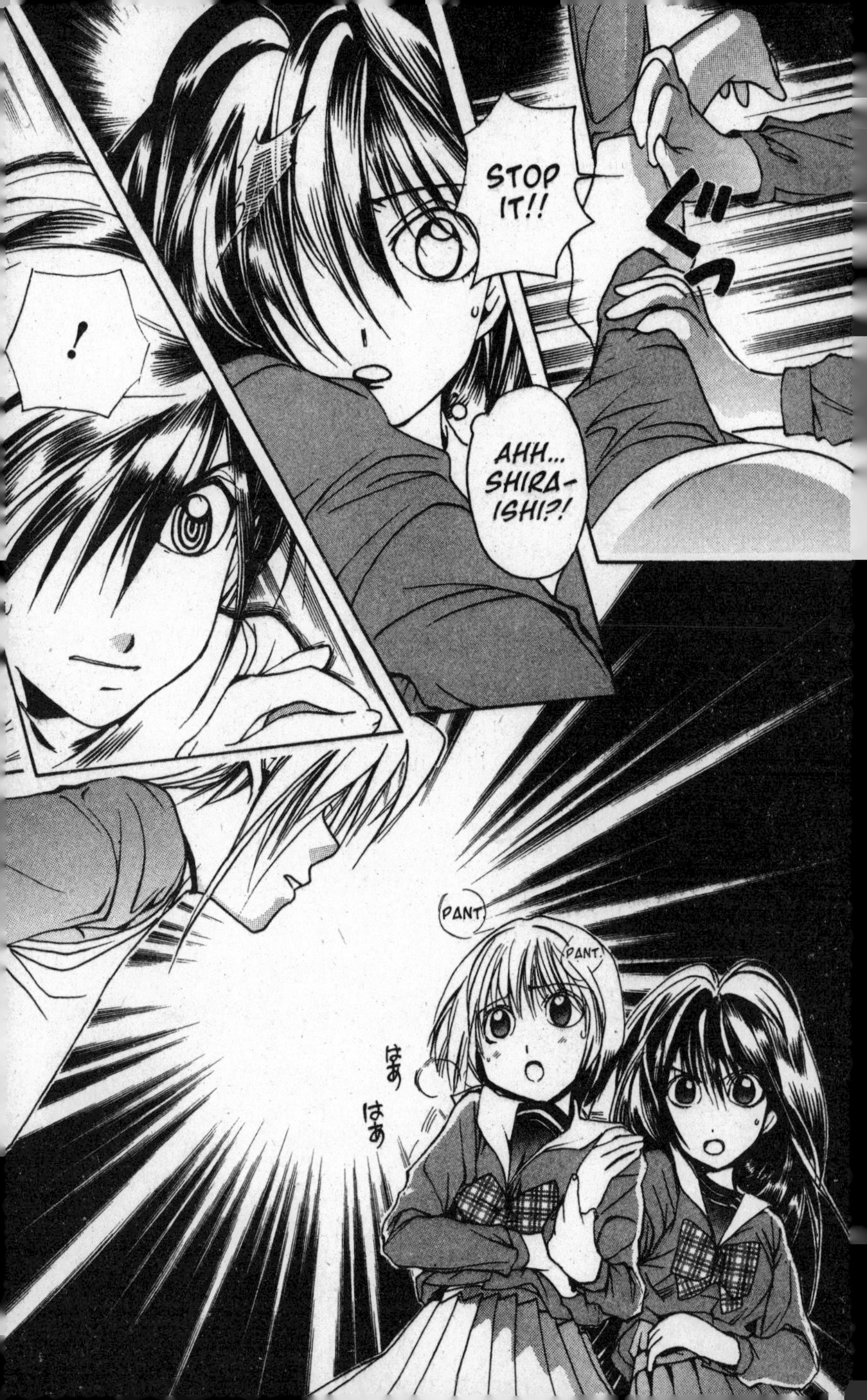
STOP IT!!
ぐっ
AHH... SHIRA-ISHI?!
!
PANT.
PANT.
はあ
はあ

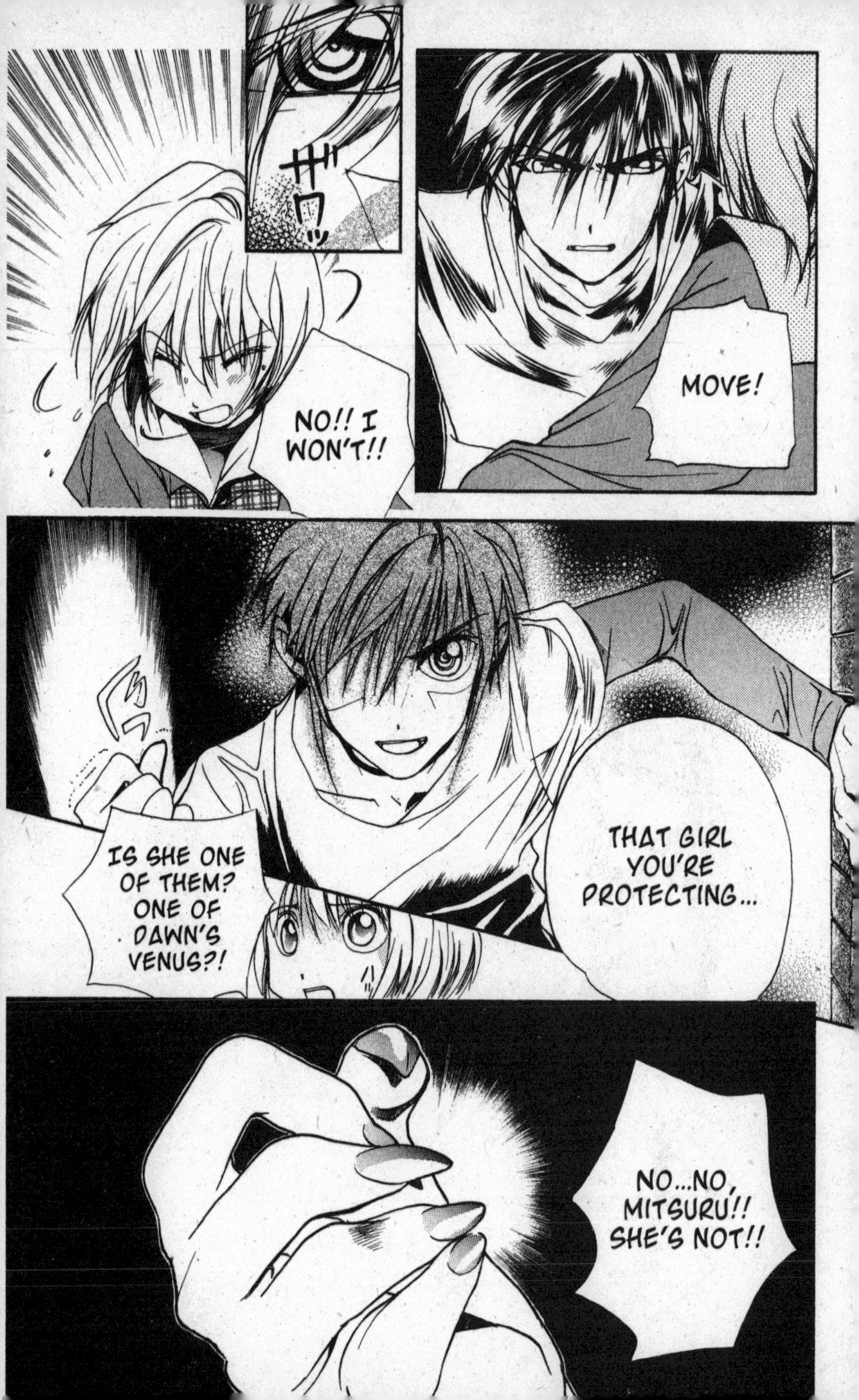
MOVE!
NO!! I WON'T!!
THAT GIRL YOU'RE PROTECTING...
IS SHE ONE OF THEM? ONE OF DAWN'S VENUS?!
NO...NO, MITSURU!! SHE'S NOT!!

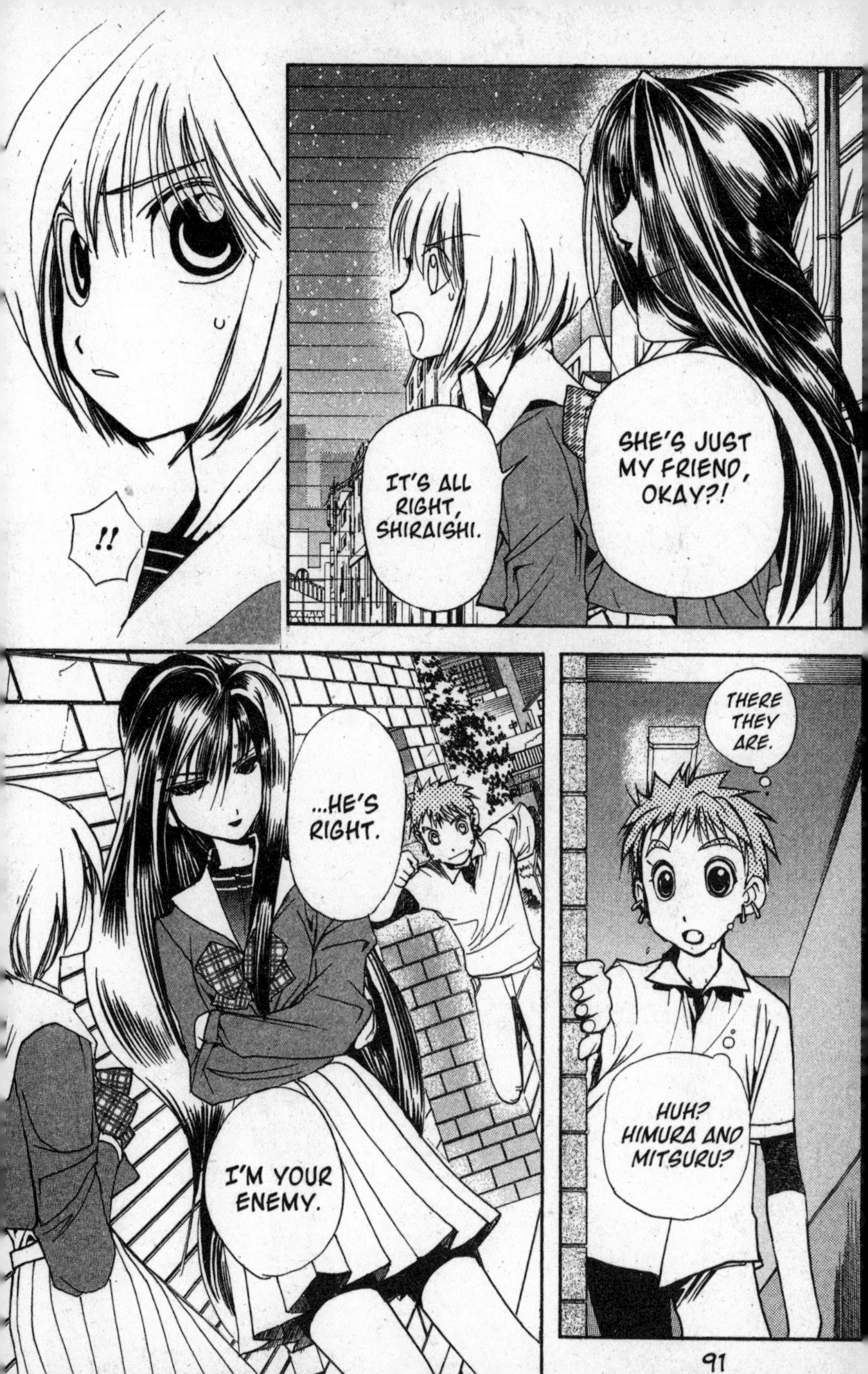
SHE'S JUST MY FRIEND, OKAY?!
IT'S ALL RIGHT, SHIRAISHI.
!!
THERE THEY ARE.
HUH? HIMURA AND MITSURU?
...HE'S RIGHT.
I'M YOUR ENEMY.

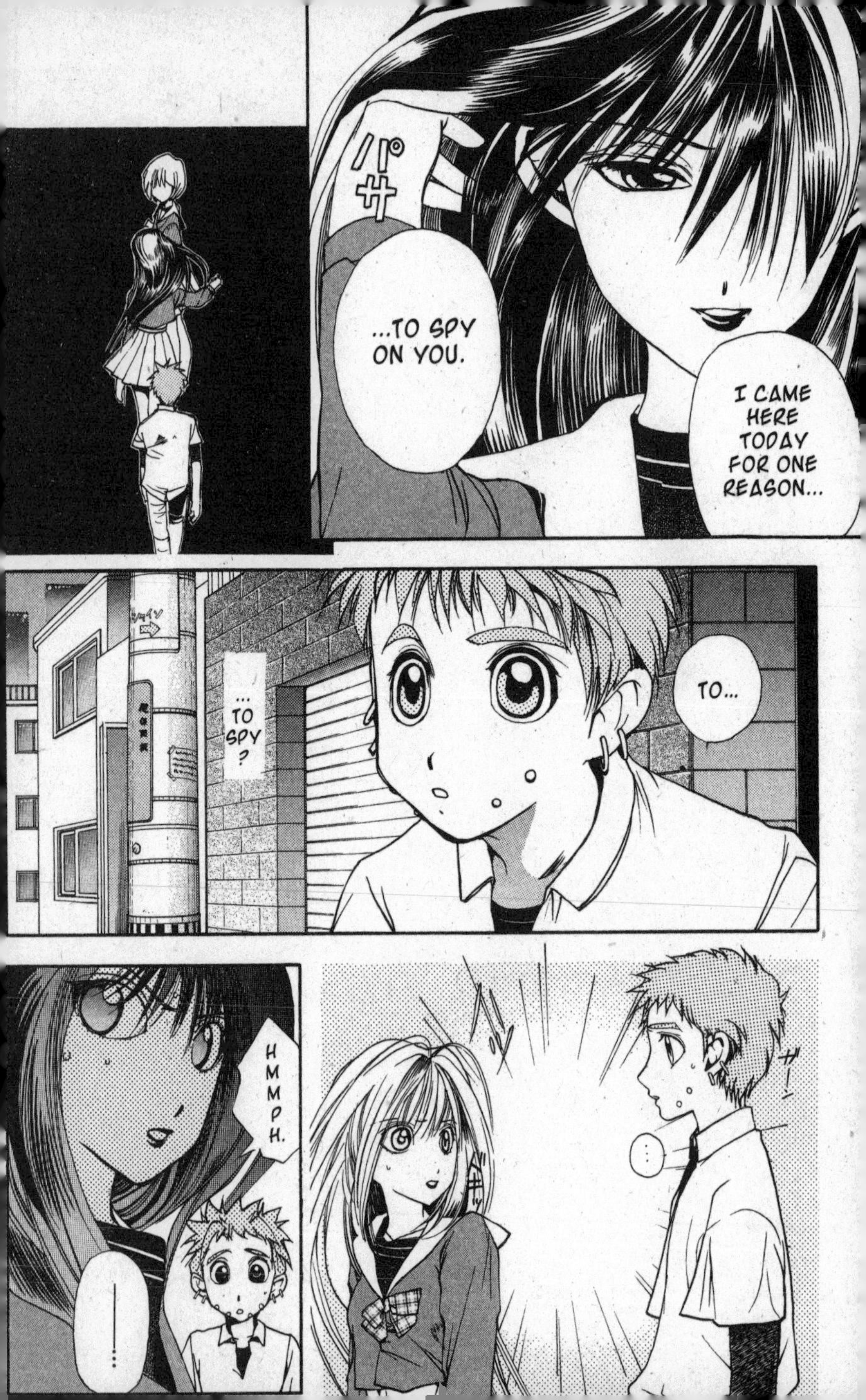
パサ
I CAME HERE TODAY FOR ONE REASON...
...TO SPY ON YOU.
TO...
...TO SPY?
...
ガ!
HMMPH.
......

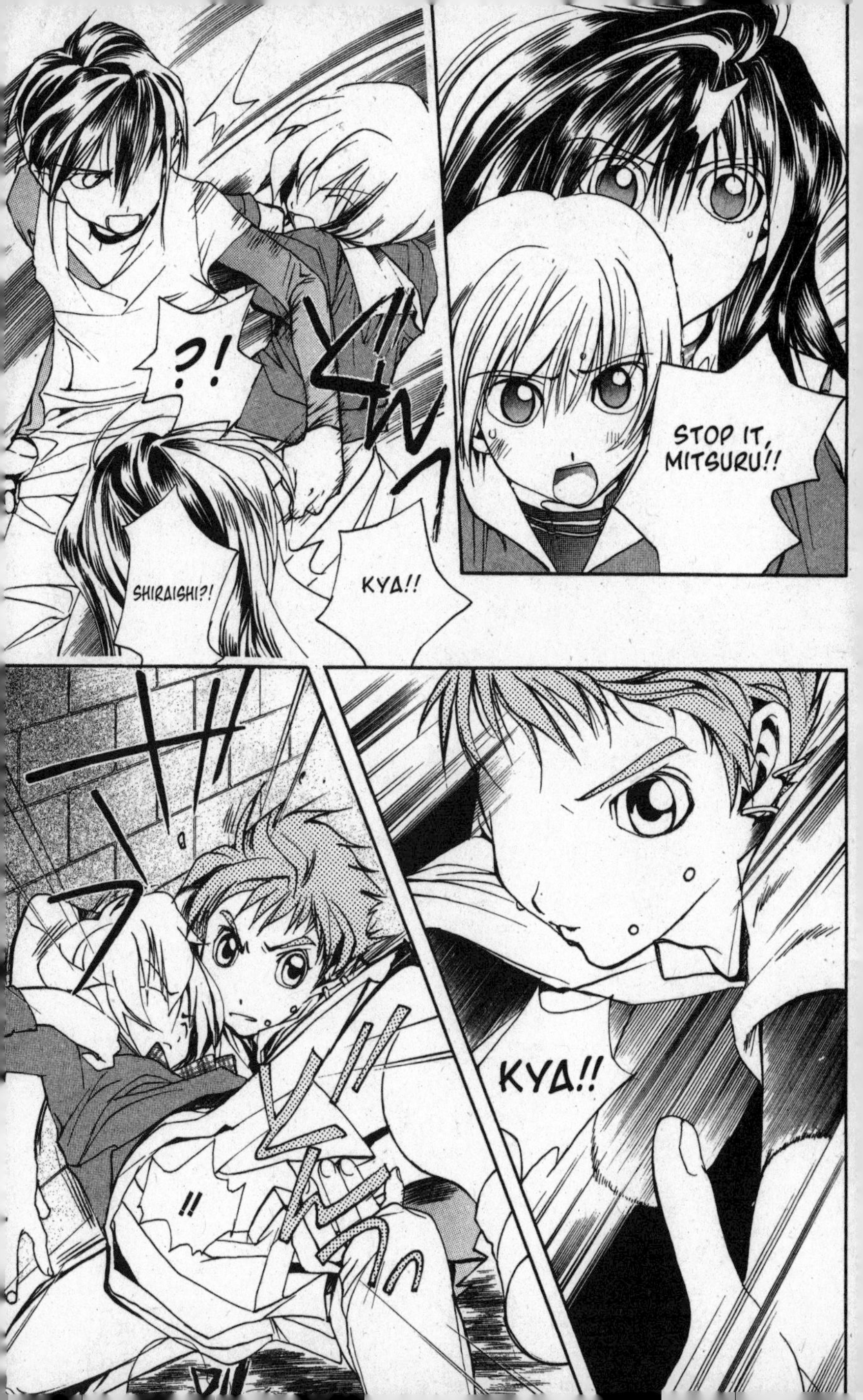
STOP IT, MITSURU!!
?!
KYA!!
SHIRAISHI?!
KYA!!
!!

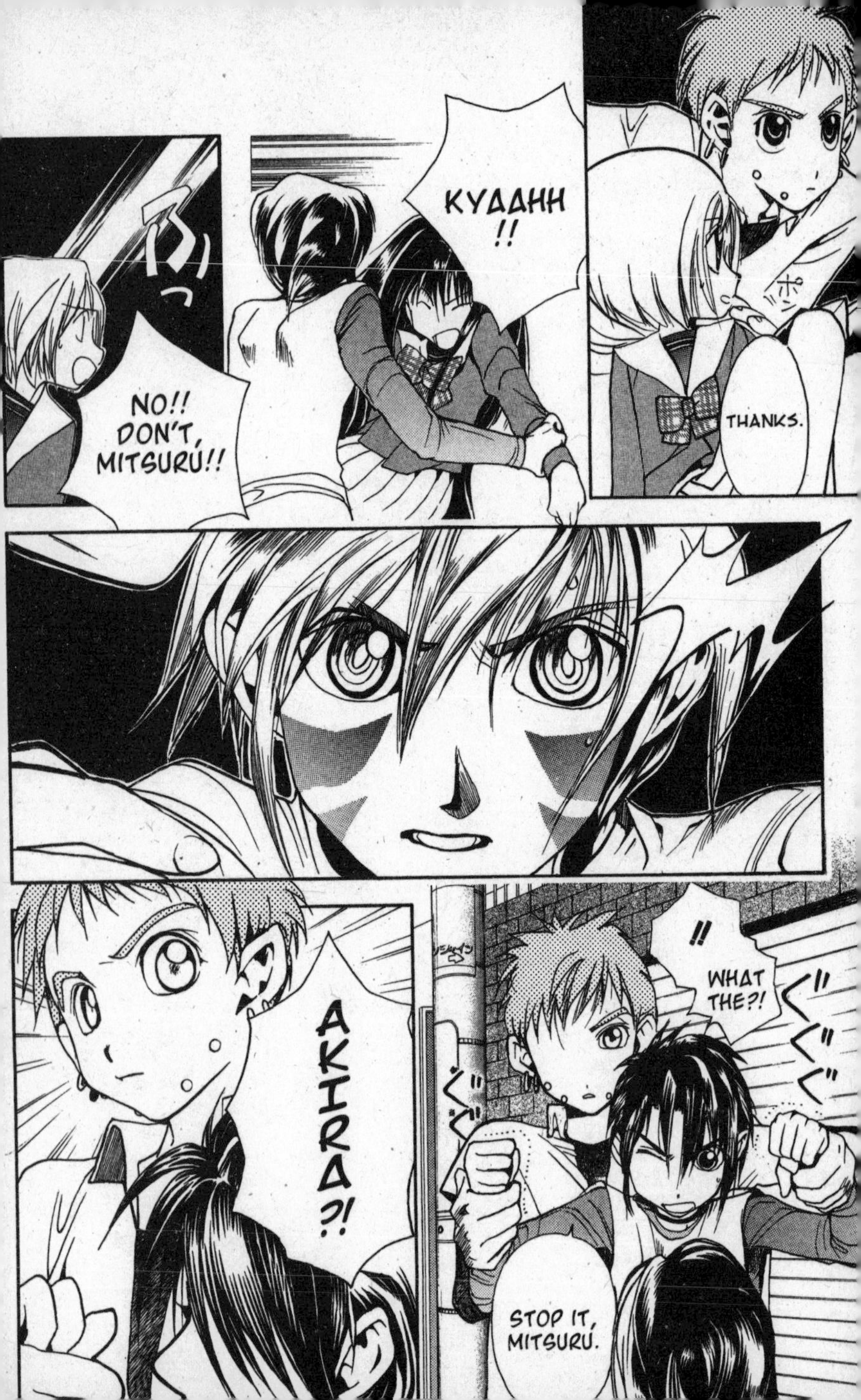
THANKS.
KYAAHH !!
NO!! DON'T, MITSURU!!
!!
WHAT THE?!
STOP IT, MITSURU.
AKIRA?!

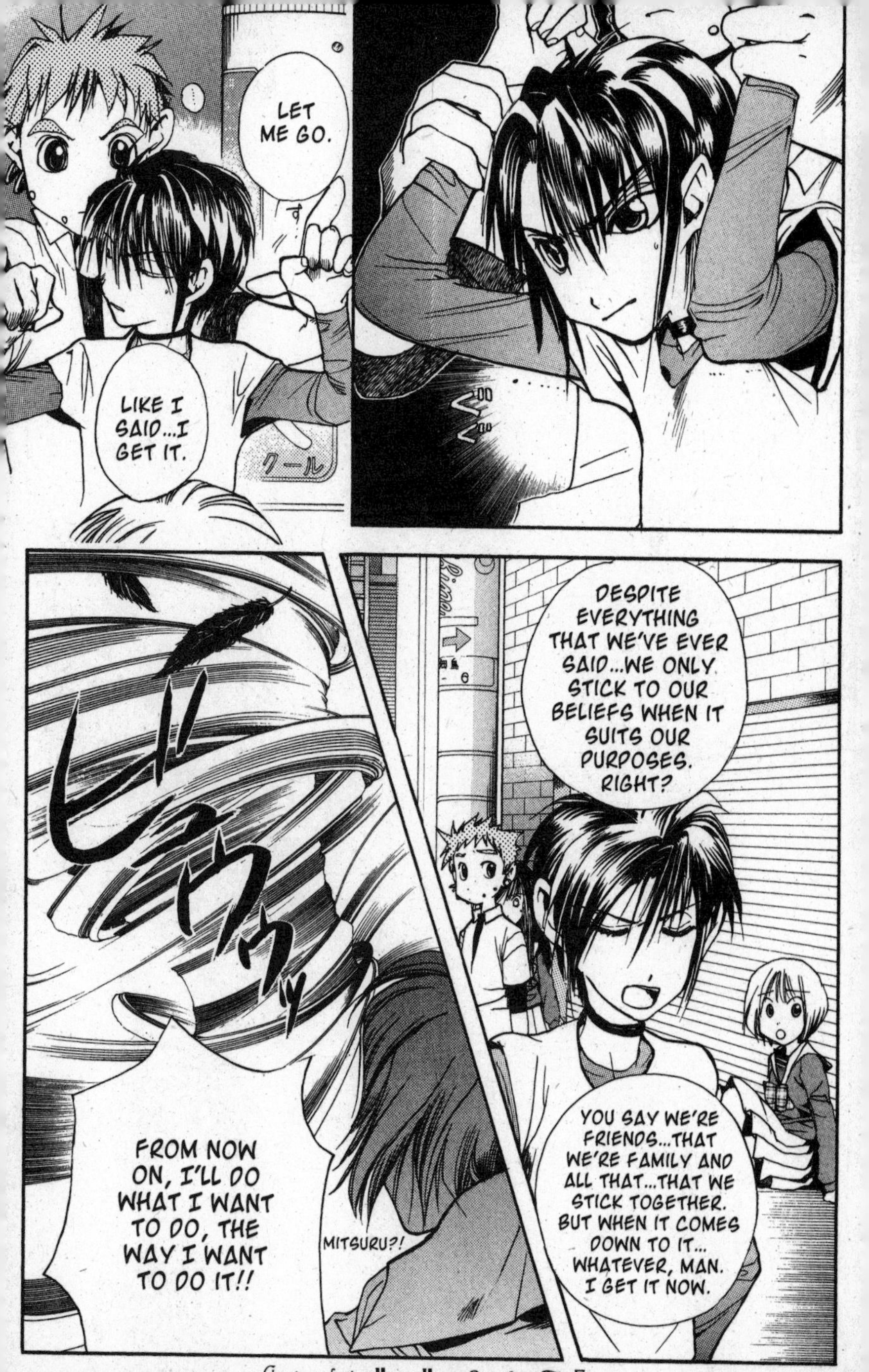
LET ME GO.
LIKE I SAID...I GET IT.
クール
DESPITE EVERYTHING THAT WE'VE EVER SAID...WE ONLY STICK TO OUR BELIEFS WHEN IT SUITS OUR PURPOSES. RIGHT?
YOU SAY WE'RE FRIENDS...THAT WE'RE FAMILY AND ALL THAT...THAT WE STICK TOGETHER. BUT WHEN IT COMES DOWN TO IT... WHATEVER, MAN. I GET IT NOW.
FROM NOW ON, I'LL DO WHAT I WANT TO DO, THE WAY I WANT TO DO IT!!
MITSURU?!

Chapter of the Misty Moon Part One The End

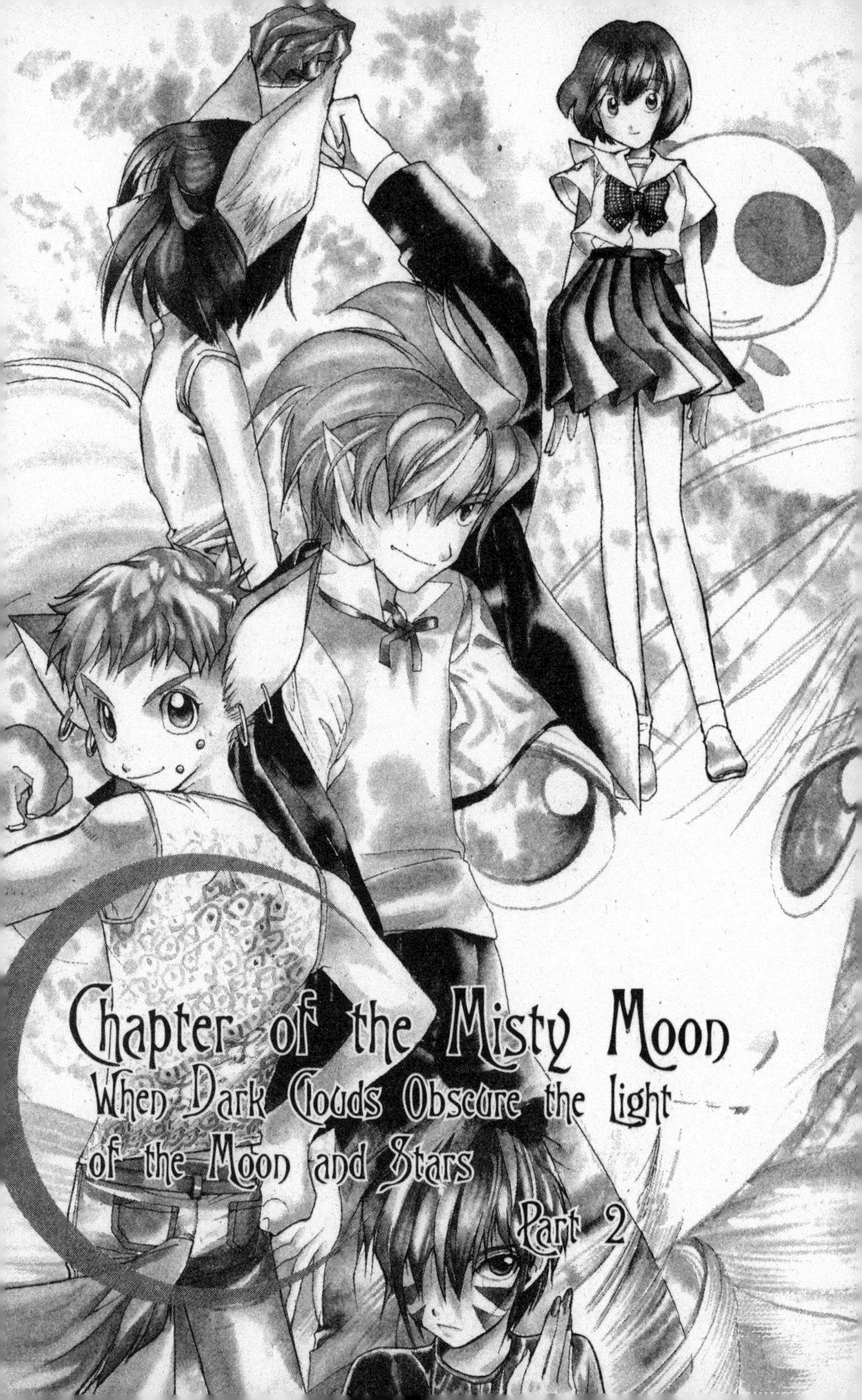
Chapter of the Misty Moon
When Dark Clouds Obscure the Light of the Moon and Stars
Part 2

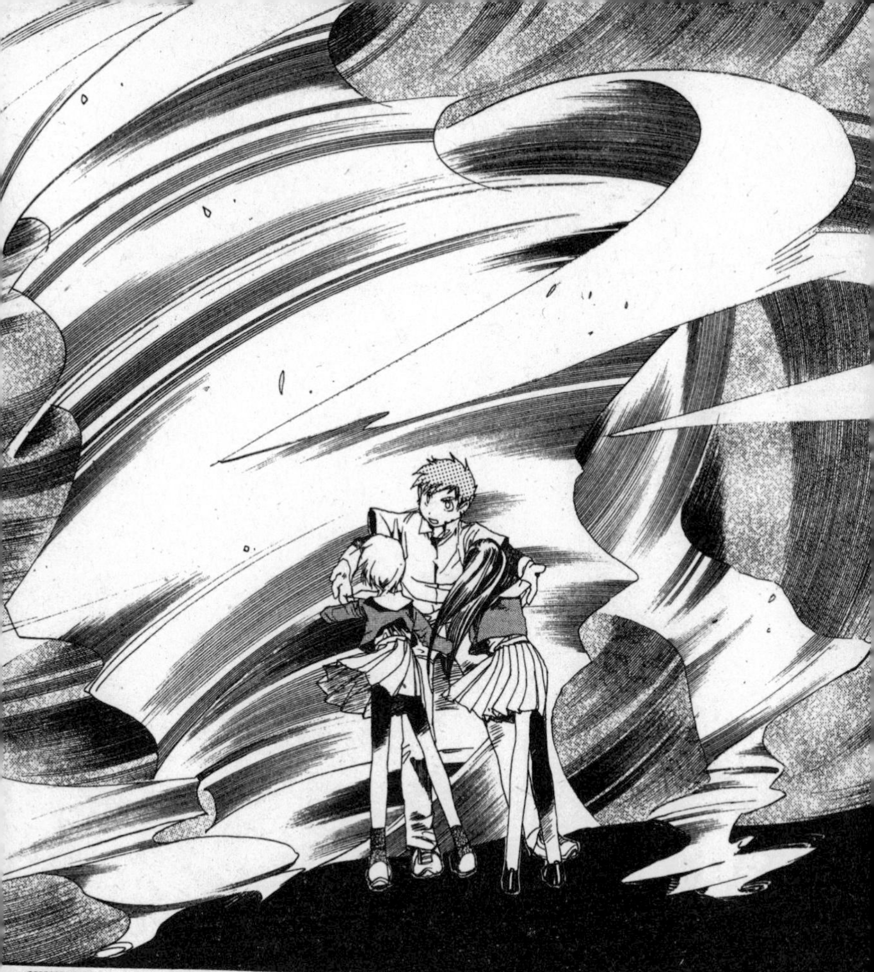

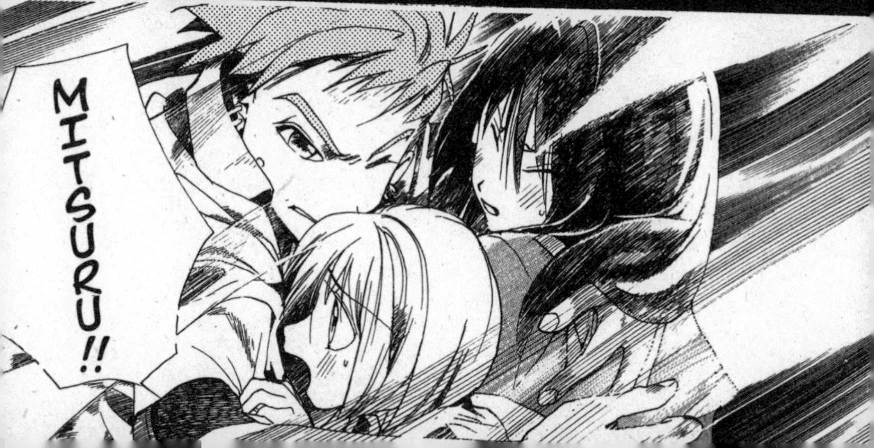
MITSURU!!

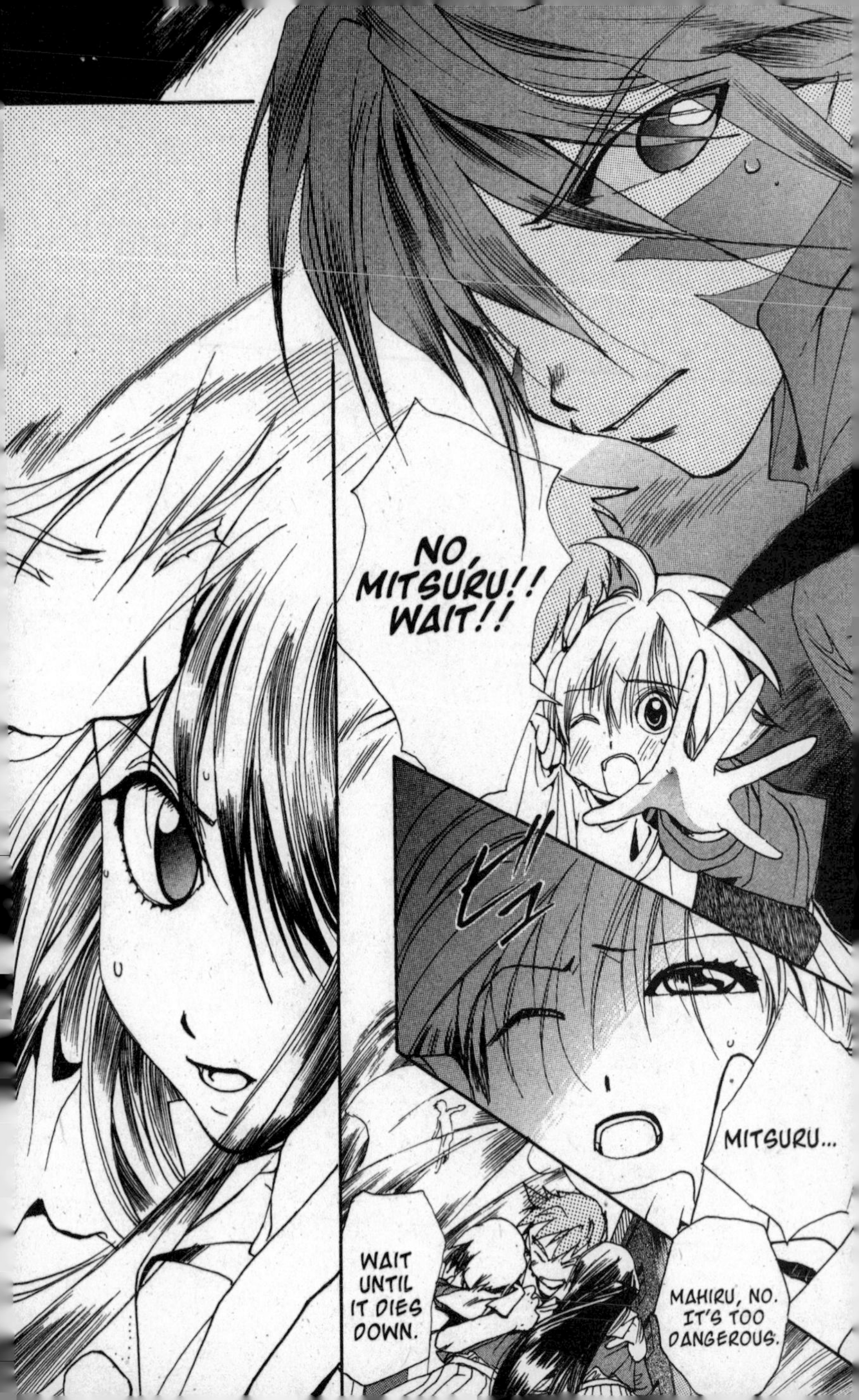
NO, MITSURU!! WAIT!!
MITSURU...
MAHIRU, NO. IT'S TOO DANGEROUS.
WAIT UNTIL IT DIES DOWN.

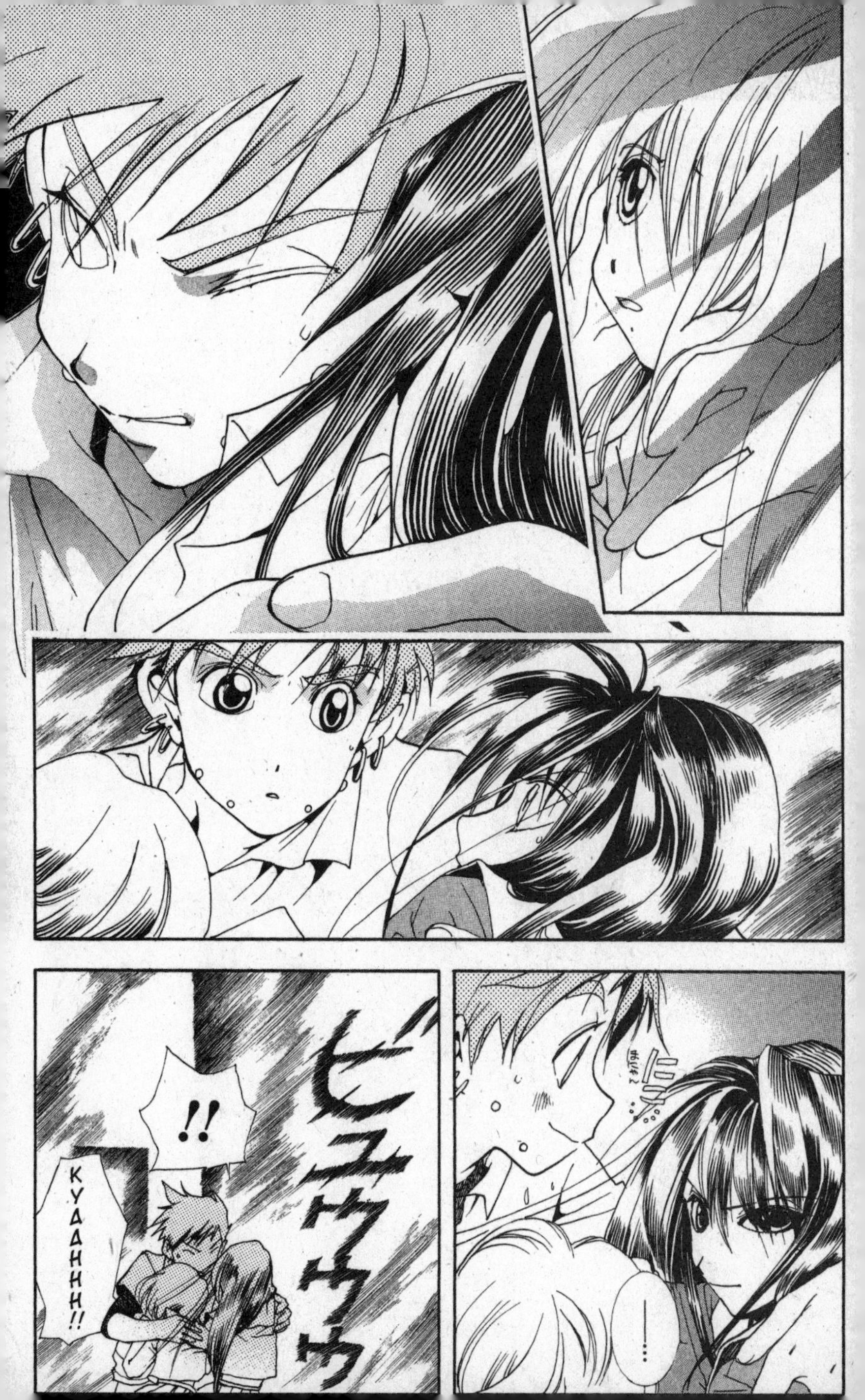
...!
ビュウウウ
!!
KYAAHHH!!

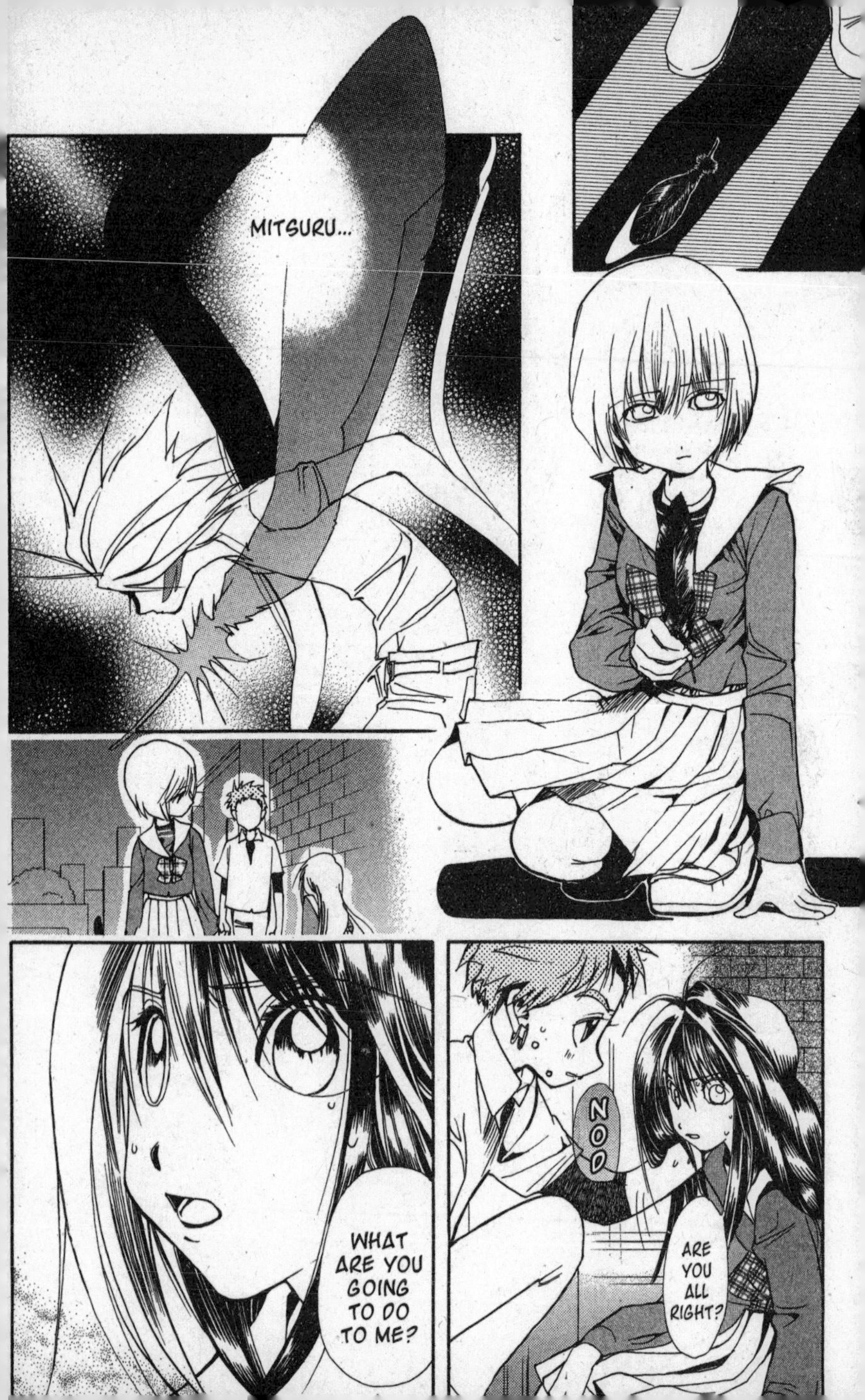
MITSURU...
NOD
ARE YOU ALL RIGHT?
WHAT ARE YOU GOING TO DO TO ME?

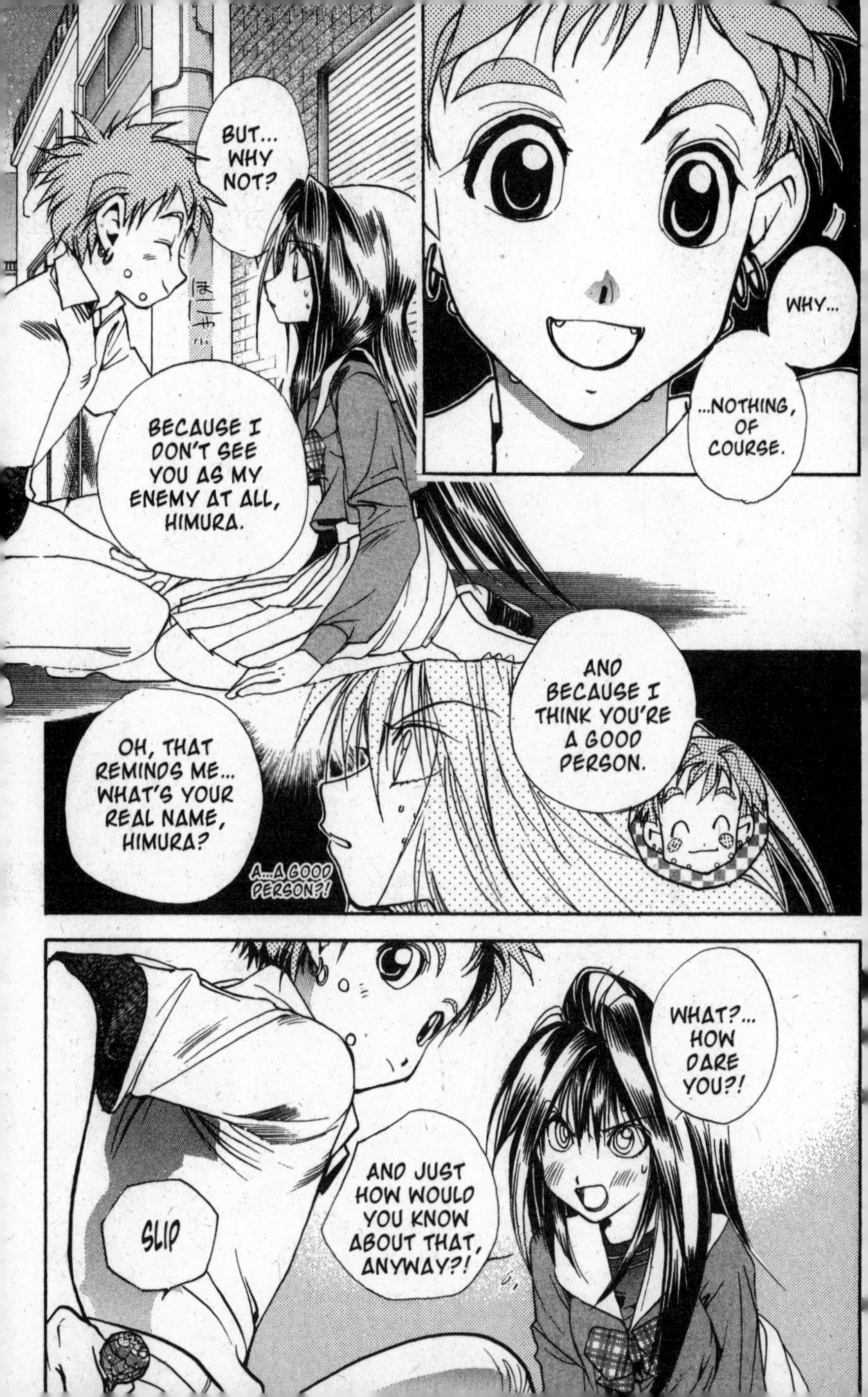
WHY...
...NOTHING, OF COURSE.
BUT... WHY NOT?
BECAUSE I DON'T SEE YOU AS MY ENEMY AT ALL, HIMURA.
AND BECAUSE I THINK YOU'RE A GOOD PERSON.
A...A GOOD PERSON?!
OH, THAT REMINDS ME... WHAT'S YOUR REAL NAME, HIMURA?
WHAT?... HOW DARE YOU?!
AND JUST HOW WOULD YOU KNOW ABOUT THAT, ANYWAY?!
SLIP

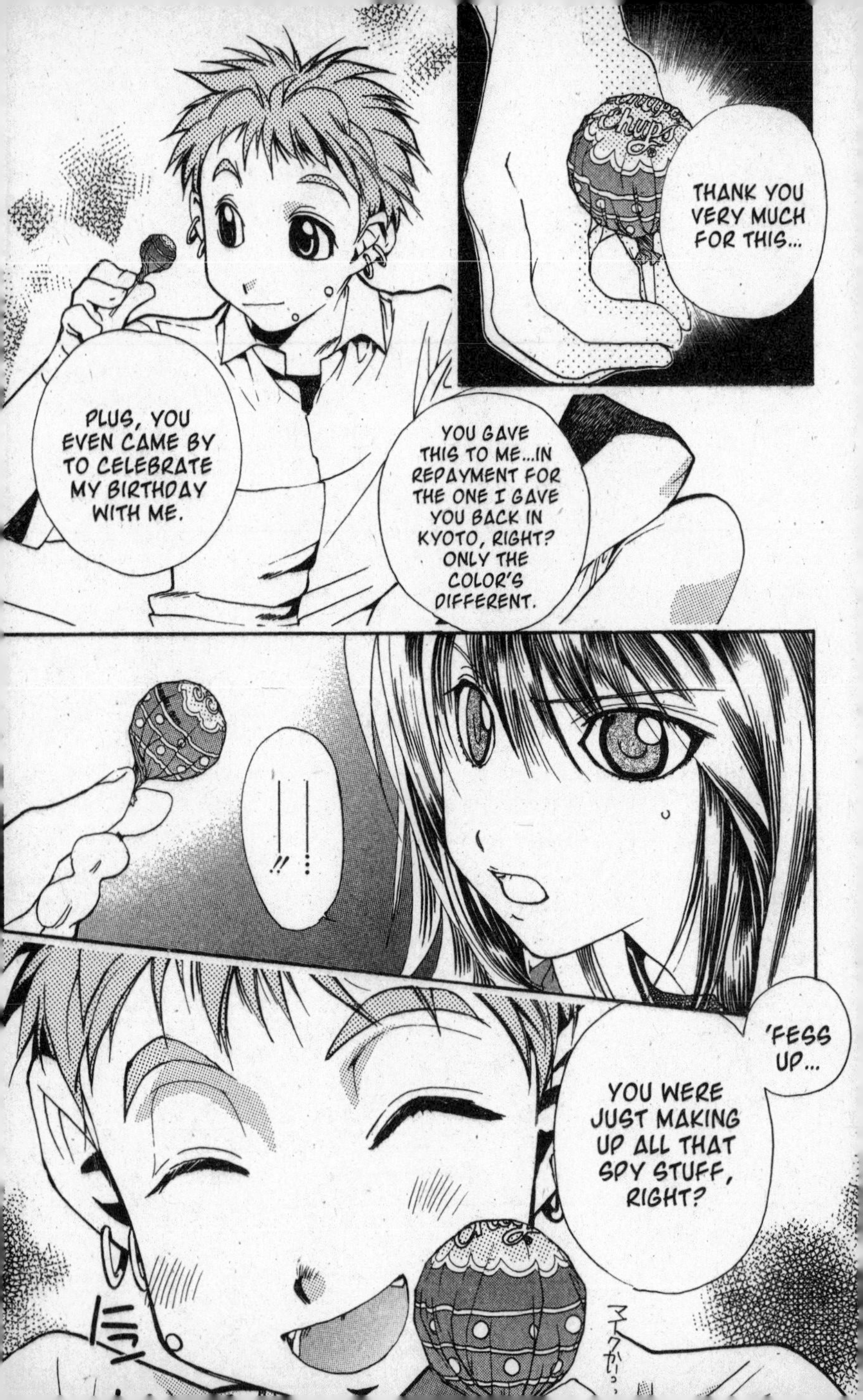
THANK YOU VERY MUCH FOR THIS...
PLUS, YOU EVEN CAME BY TO CELEBRATE MY BIRTHDAY WITH ME.
YOU GAVE THIS TO ME...IN REPAYMENT FOR THE ONE I GAVE YOU BACK IN KYOTO, RIGHT? ONLY THE COLOR'S DIFFERENT.
!!...
'FESS UP...
YOU WERE JUST MAKING UP ALL THAT SPY STUFF, RIGHT?

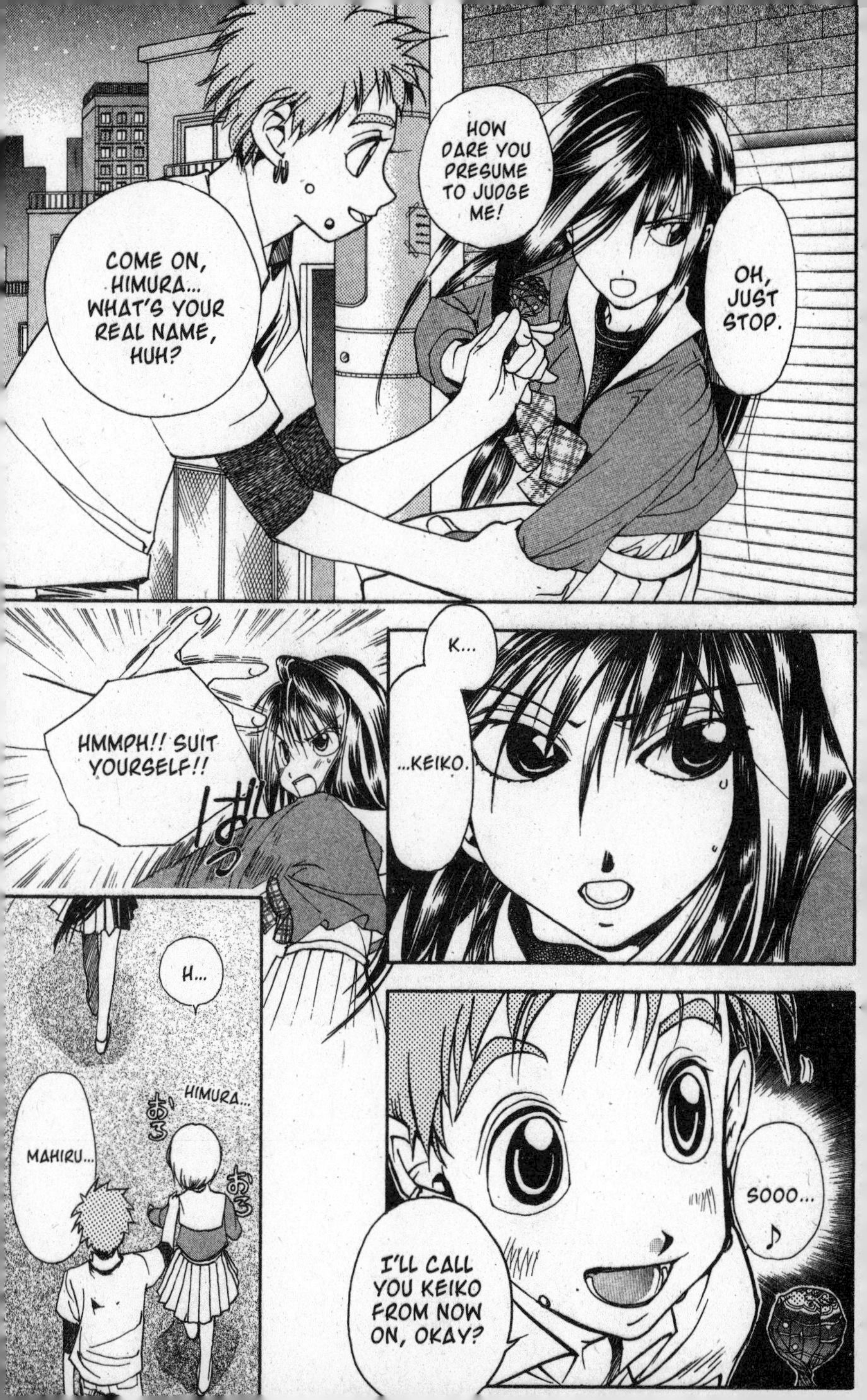
HOW DARE YOU PRESUME TO JUDGE ME!
OH, JUST STOP.
COME ON, HIMURA... WHAT'S YOUR REAL NAME, HUH?
K...
...KEIKO.
HMMPH!! SUIT YOURSELF!!
ぱっ
SOOO... ♪
I'LL CALL YOU KEIKO FROM NOW ON, OKAY?
H...
HIMURA...
MAHIRU...

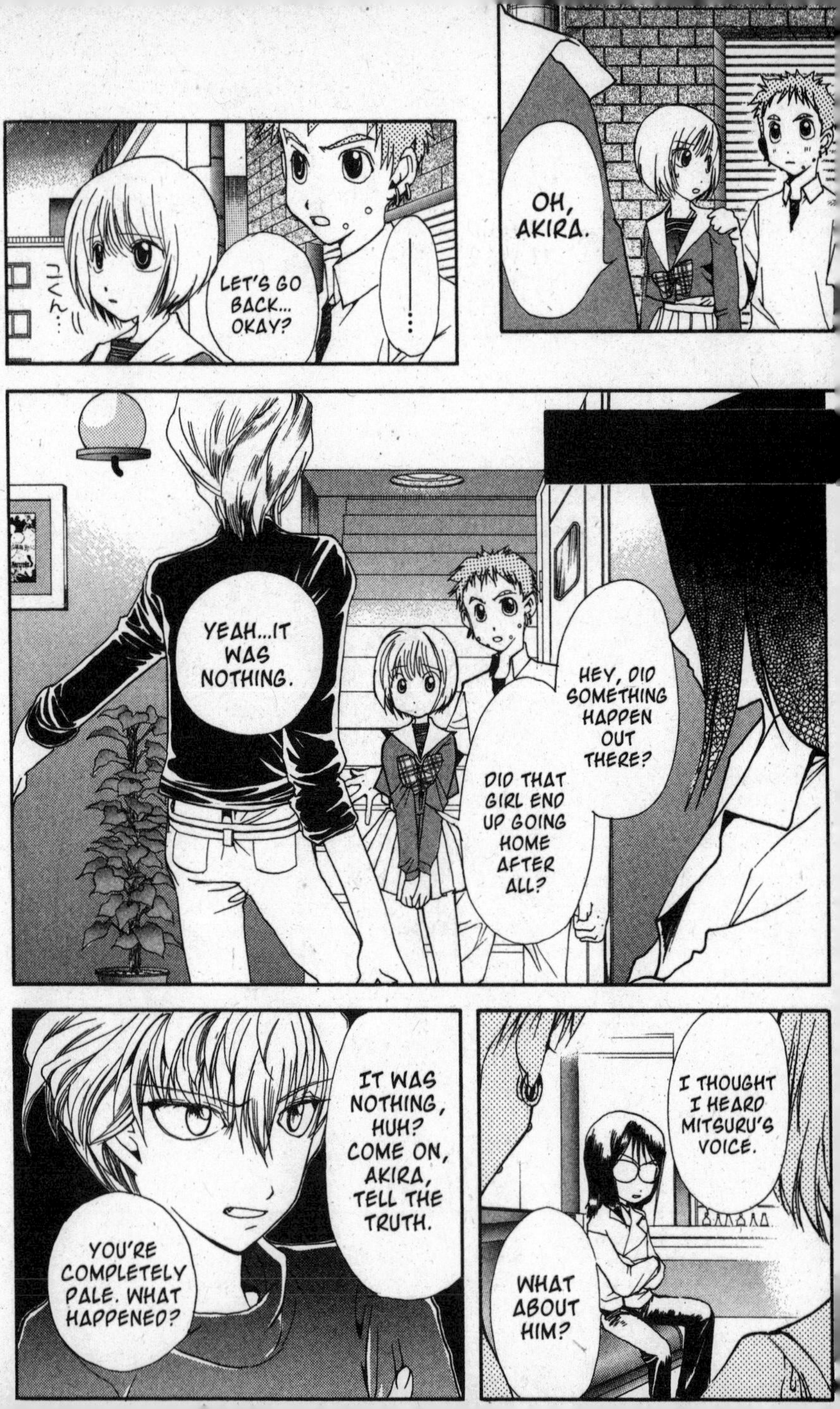
OH, AKIRA.
......
LET'S GO BACK... OKAY?
コくん…
HEY, DID SOMETHING HAPPEN OUT THERE?
DID THAT GIRL END UP GOING HOME AFTER ALL?
YEAH...IT WAS NOTHING.
I THOUGHT I HEARD MITSURU'S VOICE.
WHAT ABOUT HIM?
IT WAS NOTHING, HUH? COME ON, AKIRA, TELL THE TRUTH.
YOU'RE COMPLETELY PALE. WHAT HAPPENED?

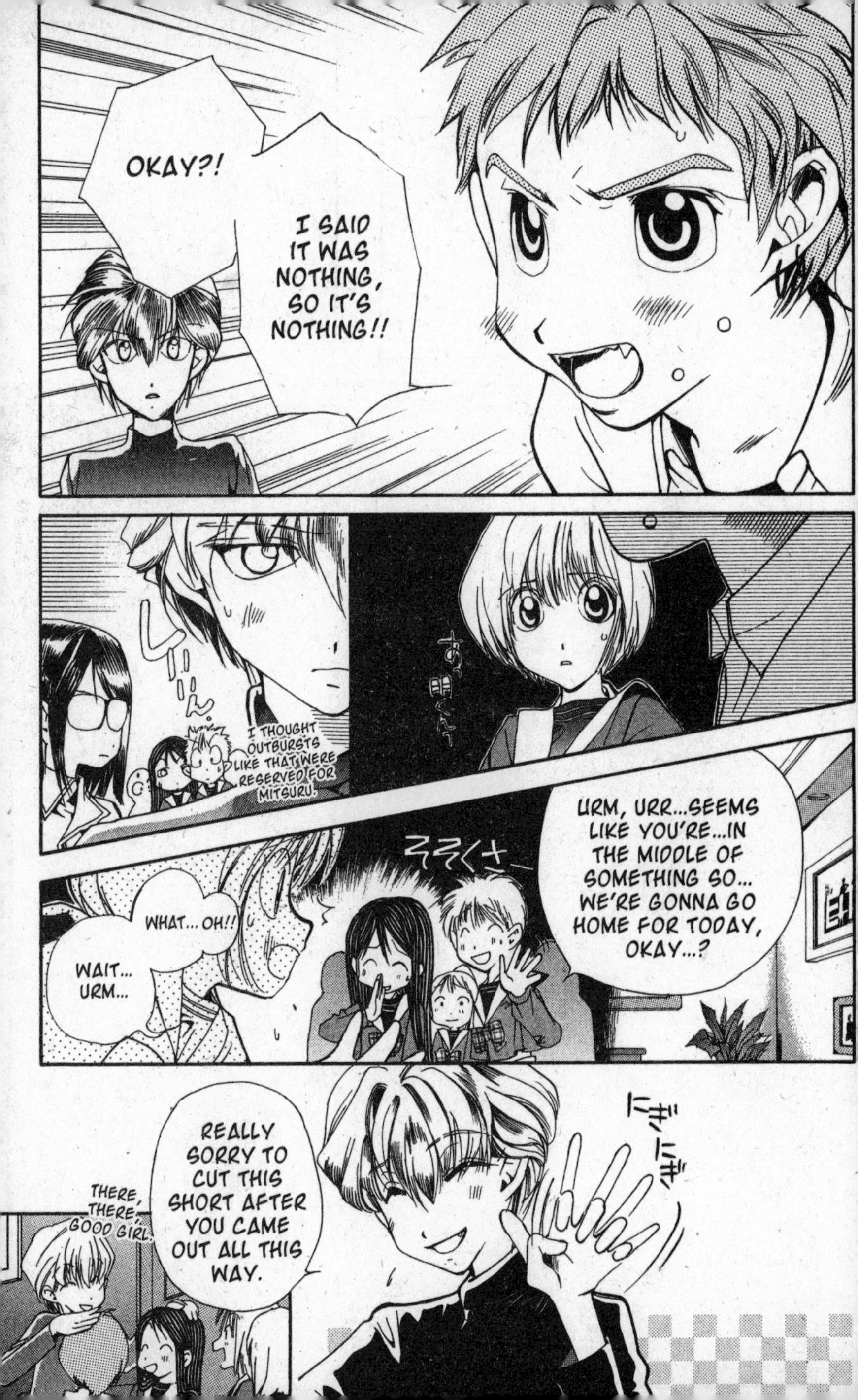
I SAID IT WAS NOTHING, SO IT'S NOTHING!!
OKAY?!
I THOUGHT OUTBURSTS LIKE THAT WERE RESERVED FOR MITSURU.
URM, URR...SEEMS LIKE YOU'RE...IN THE MIDDLE OF SOMETHING SO... WE'RE GONNA GO HOME FOR TODAY, OKAY...?
そそくさ
WHAT... OH!!
WAIT... URM...
にぎにぎ
REALLY SORRY TO CUT THIS SHORT AFTER YOU CAME OUT ALL THIS WAY.
THERE, THERE, GOOD GIRL.

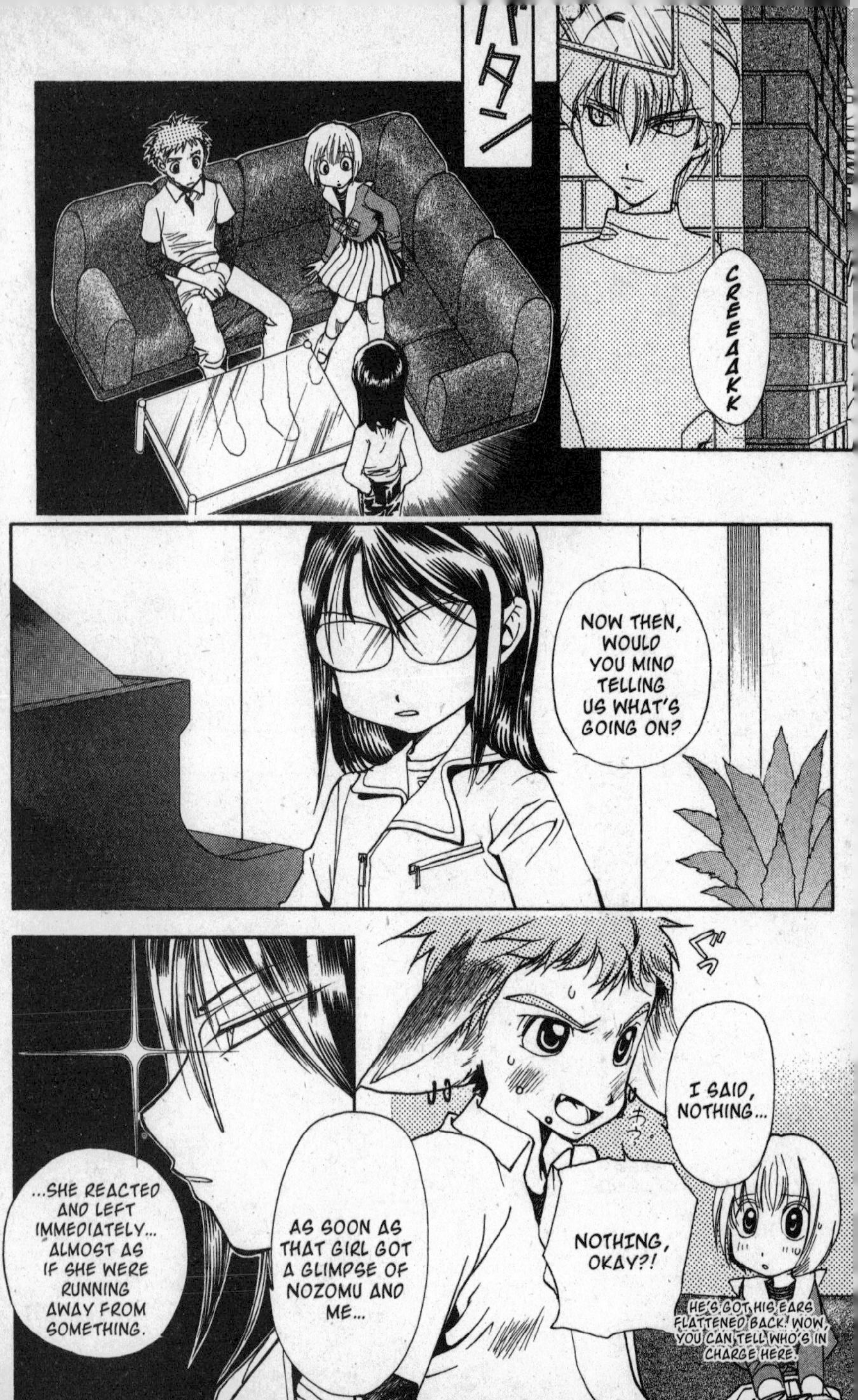
CREEAAKK
バタン
NOW THEN, WOULD YOU MIND TELLING US WHAT'S GOING ON?
I SAID, NOTHING...
NOTHING, OKAY?!
HE'S GOT HIS EARS FLATTENED BACK. WOW, YOU CAN TELL WHO'S IN CHARGE HERE.
AS SOON AS THAT GIRL GOT A GLIMPSE OF NOZOMU AND ME...
...SHE REACTED AND LEFT IMMEDIATELY... ALMOST AS IF SHE WERE RUNNING AWAY FROM SOMETHING.

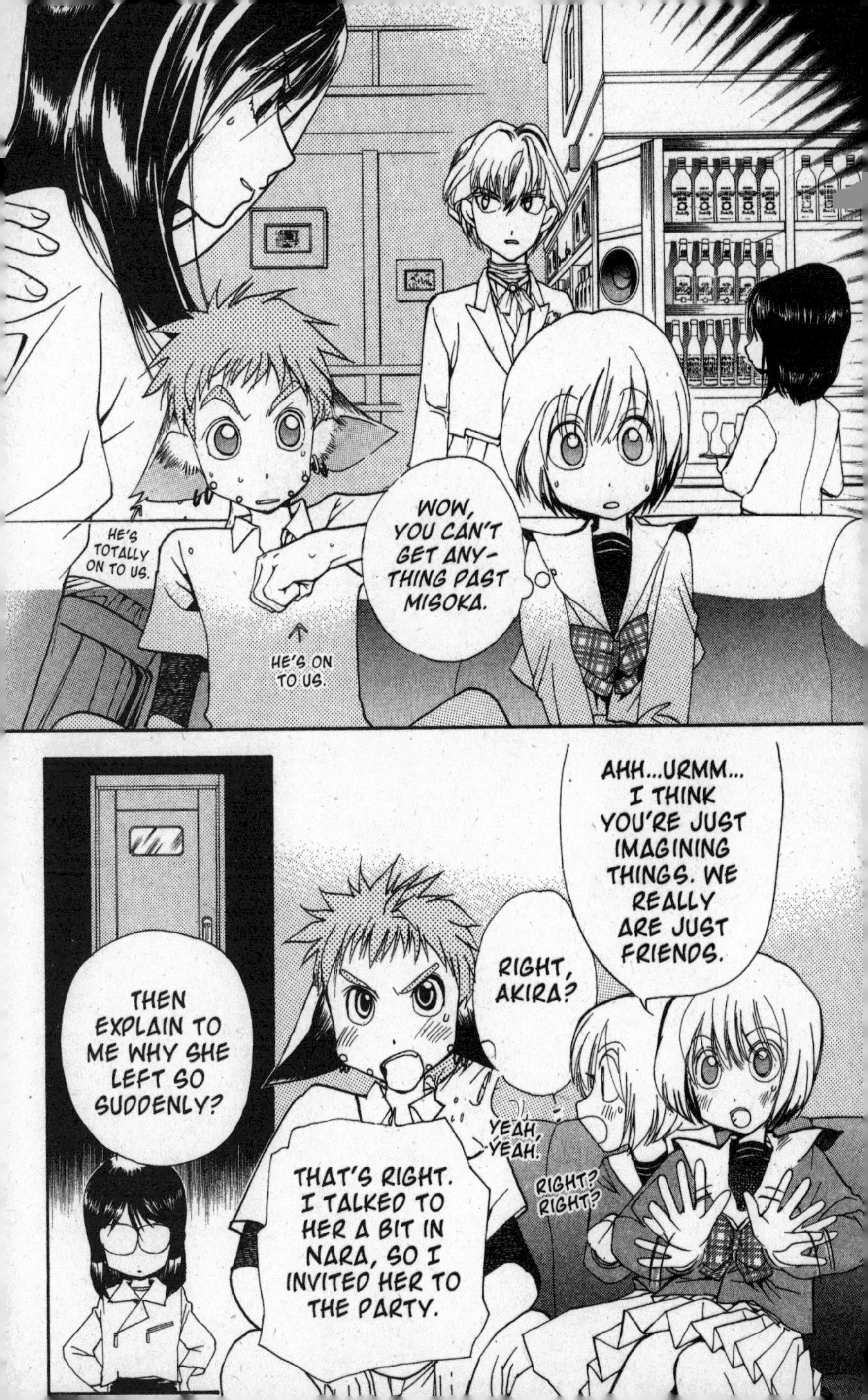
WOW, YOU CAN'T GET ANY-THING PAST MISOKA.
HE'S TOTALLY ON TO US.
HE'S ON TO US.
AHH...URMM... I THINK YOU'RE JUST IMAGINING THINGS. WE REALLY ARE JUST FRIENDS.
RIGHT, AKIRA?
YEAH, YEAH.
RIGHT? RIGHT?
THEN EXPLAIN TO ME WHY SHE LEFT SO SUDDENLY?
THAT'S RIGHT. I TALKED TO HER A BIT IN NARA, SO I INVITED HER TO THE PARTY.

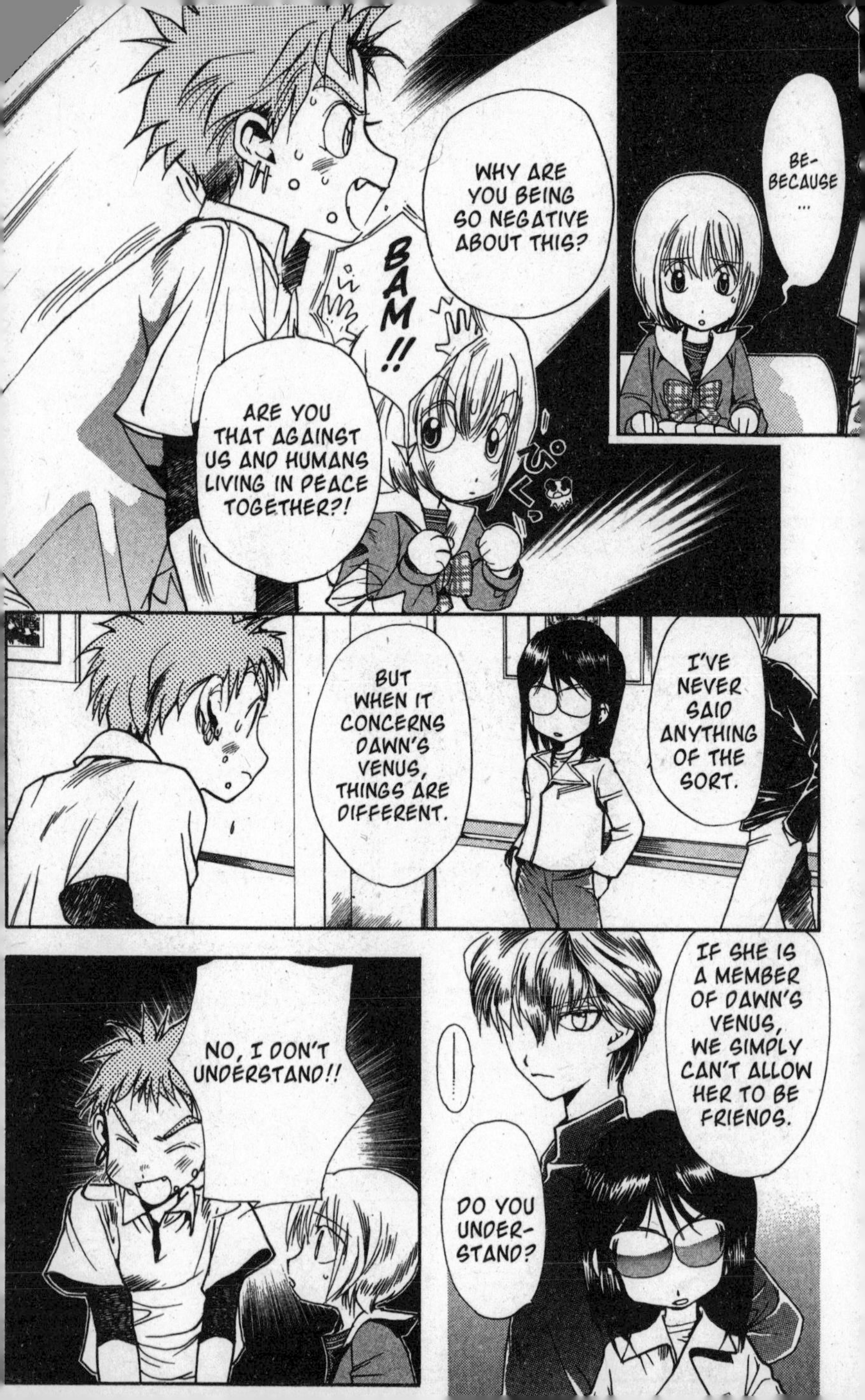
BE-BECAUSE...
WHY ARE YOU BEING SO NEGATIVE ABOUT THIS?
BAM!!
ARE YOU THAT AGAINST US AND HUMANS LIVING IN PEACE TOGETHER?!
I'VE NEVER SAID ANYTHING OF THE SORT.
BUT WHEN IT CONCERNS DAWN'S VENUS, THINGS ARE DIFFERENT.
IF SHE IS A MEMBER OF DAWN'S VENUS, WE SIMPLY CAN'T ALLOW HER TO BE FRIENDS.
!
DO YOU UNDERSTAND?
NO, I DON'T UNDERSTAND!!

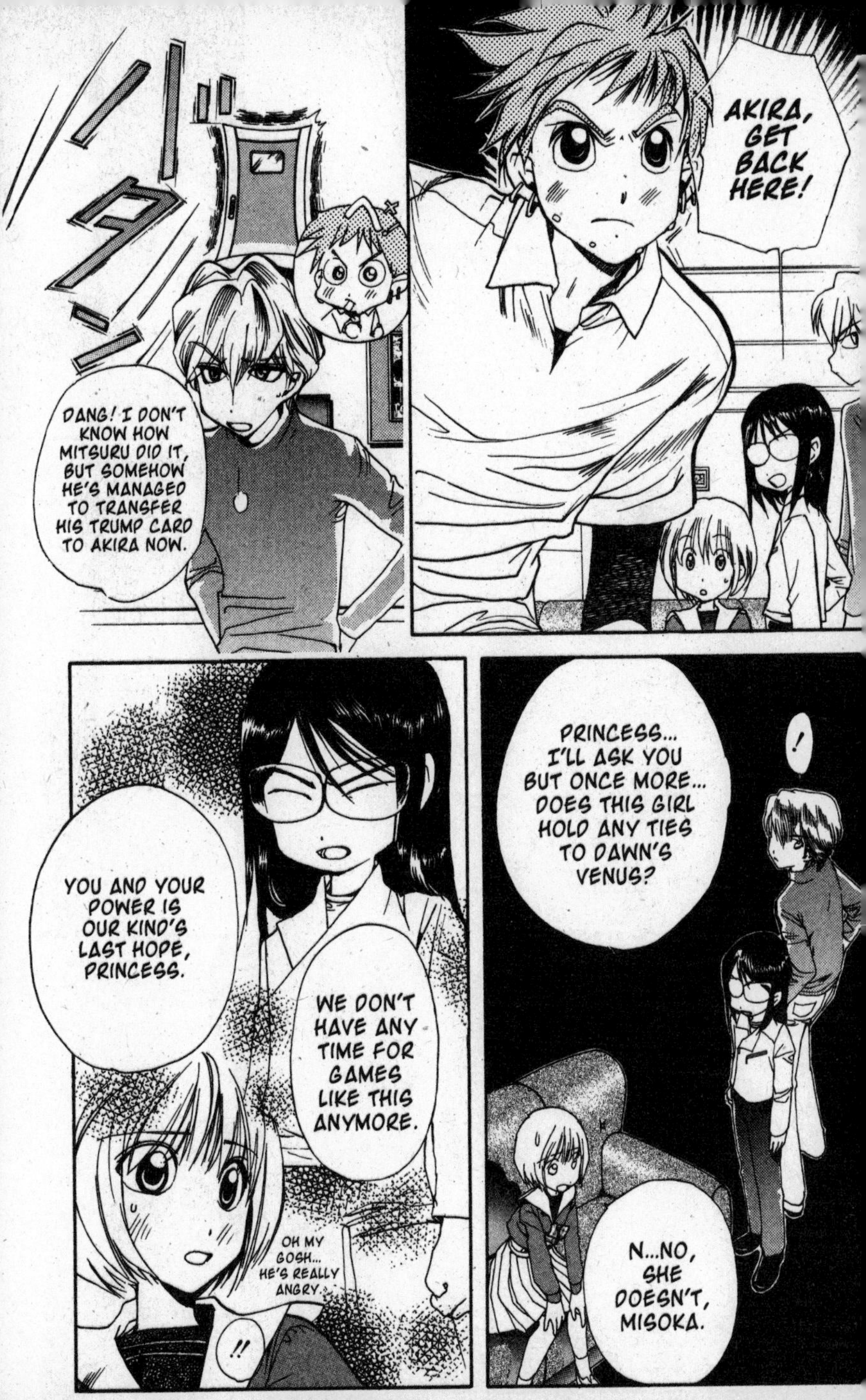
AKIRA, GET BACK HERE!
バタン
DANG! I DON'T KNOW HOW MITSURU DID IT, BUT SOMEHOW HE'S MANAGED TO TRANSFER HIS TRUMP CARD TO AKIRA NOW.
PRINCESS... I'LL ASK YOU BUT ONCE MORE... DOES THIS GIRL HOLD ANY TIES TO DAWN'S VENUS?
!
N...NO, SHE DOESN'T, MISOKA.
YOU AND YOUR POWER IS OUR KIND'S LAST HOPE, PRINCESS.
WE DON'T HAVE ANY TIME FOR GAMES LIKE THIS ANYMORE.
OH MY GOSH... HE'S REALLY ANGRY.
!!

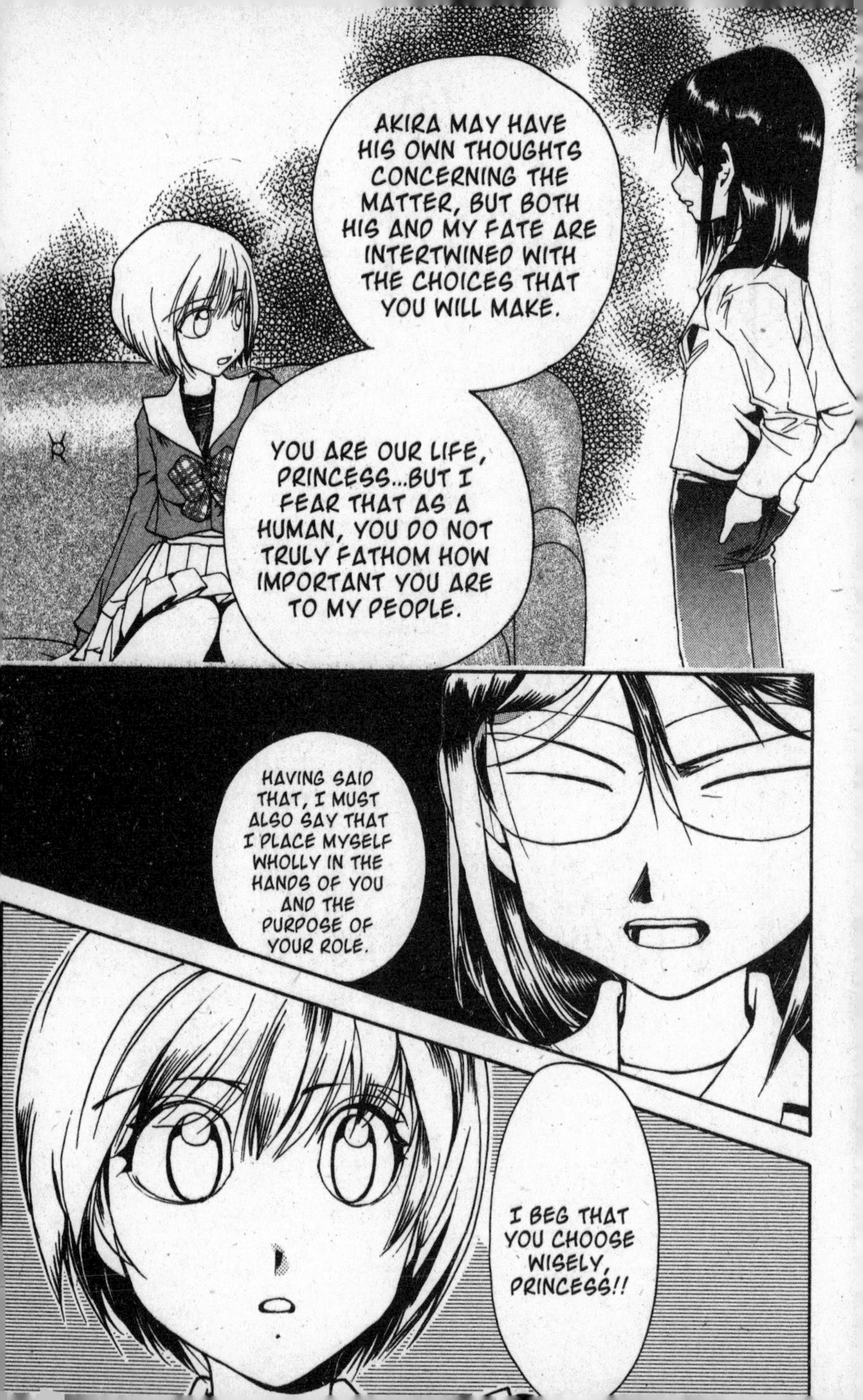
AKIRA MAY HAVE HIS OWN THOUGHTS CONCERNING THE MATTER, BUT BOTH HIS AND MY FATE ARE INTERTWINED WITH THE CHOICES THAT YOU WILL MAKE.
YOU ARE OUR LIFE, PRINCESS...BUT I FEAR THAT AS A HUMAN, YOU DO NOT TRULY FATHOM HOW IMPORTANT YOU ARE TO MY PEOPLE.
HAVING SAID THAT, I MUST ALSO SAY THAT I PLACE MYSELF WHOLLY IN THE HANDS OF YOU AND THE PURPOSE OF YOUR ROLE.
I BEG THAT YOU CHOOSE WISELY, PRINCESS!!

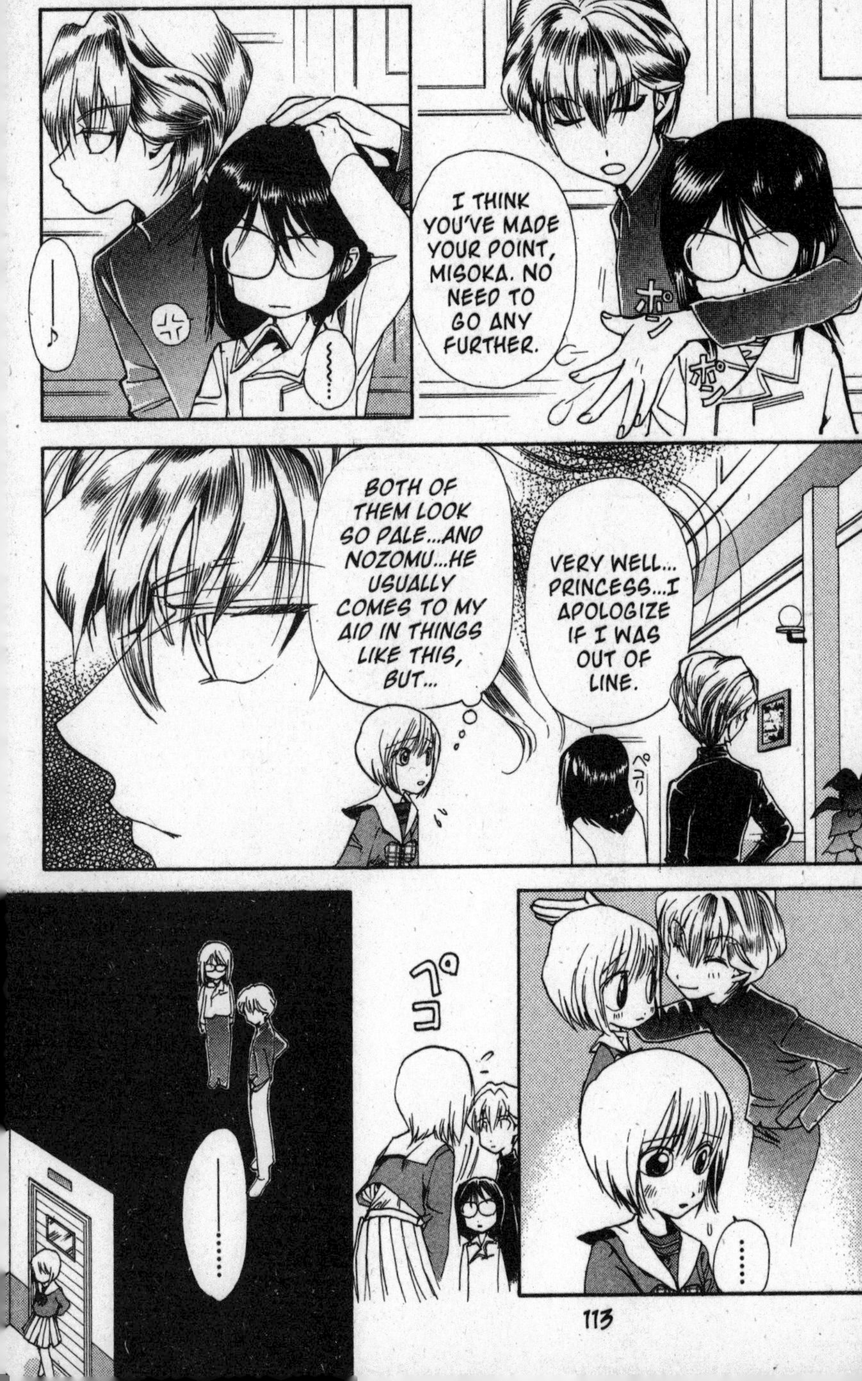
I THINK YOU'VE MADE YOUR POINT, MISOKA. NO NEED TO GO ANY FURTHER.
ポン
ポン
......
--- ♪
VERY WELL... PRINCESS...I APOLOGIZE IF I WAS OUT OF LINE.
BOTH OF THEM LOOK SO PALE...AND NOZOMU...HE USUALLY COMES TO MY AID IN THINGS LIKE THIS, BUT...
ペコ
......
--......

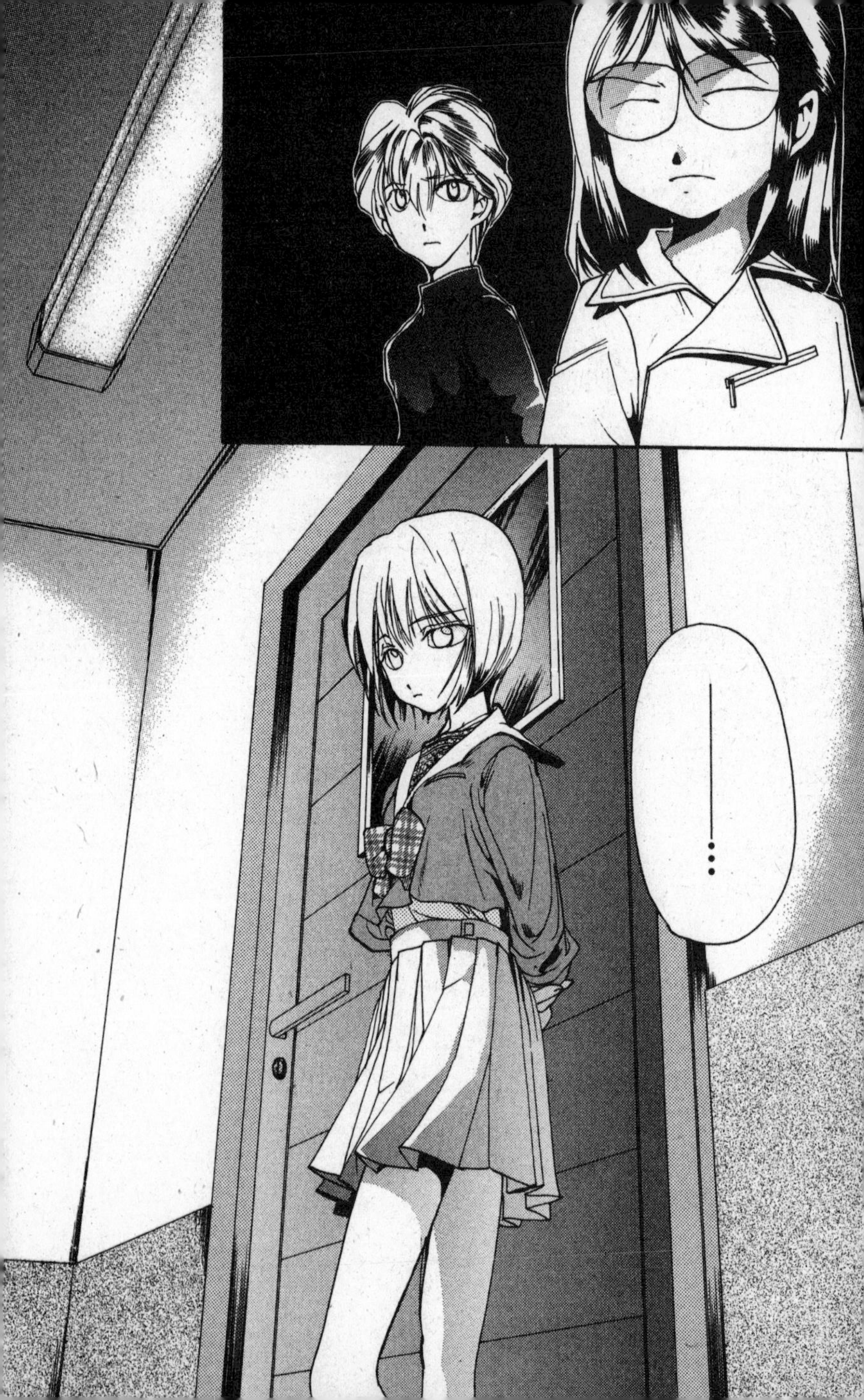
――…

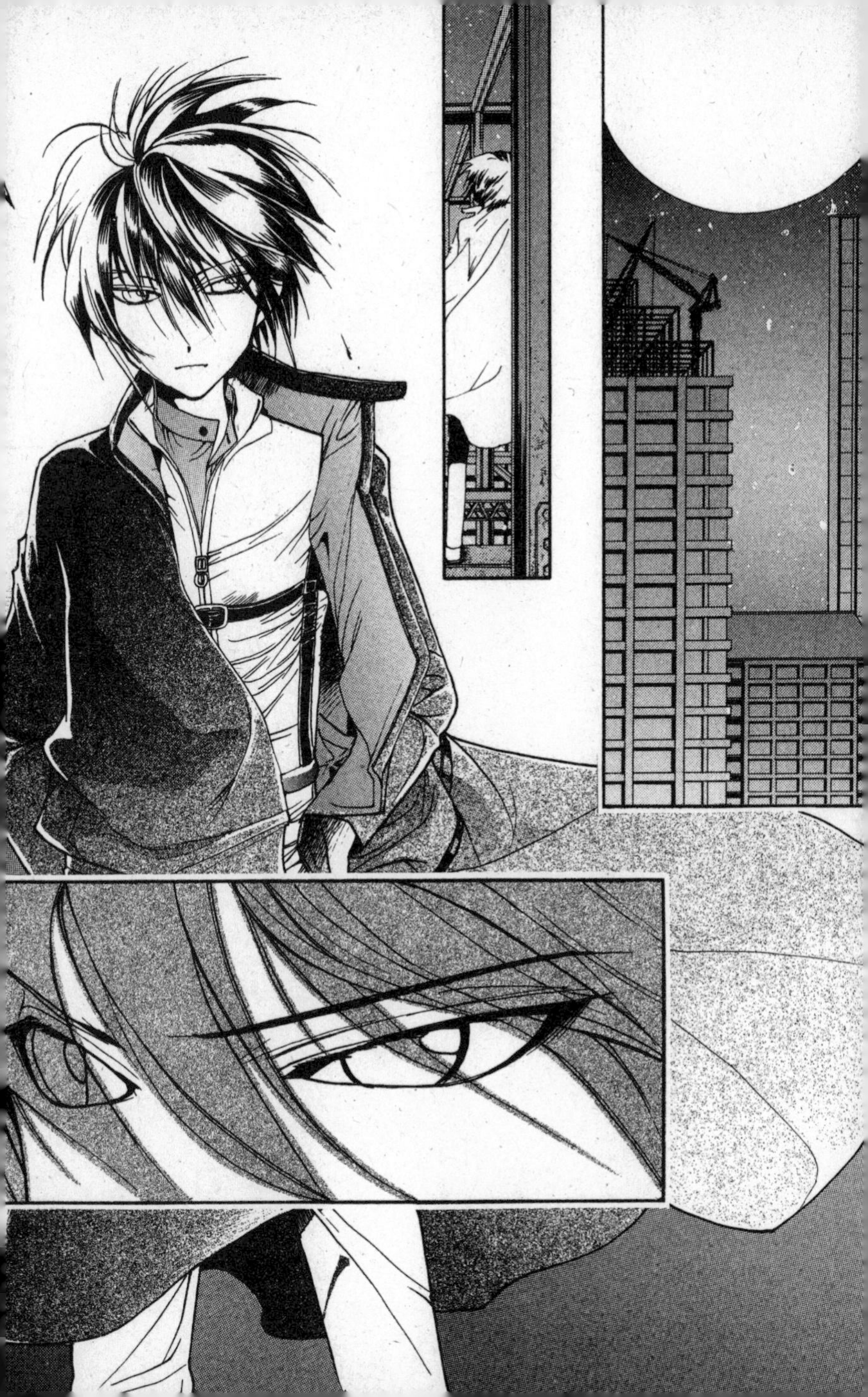

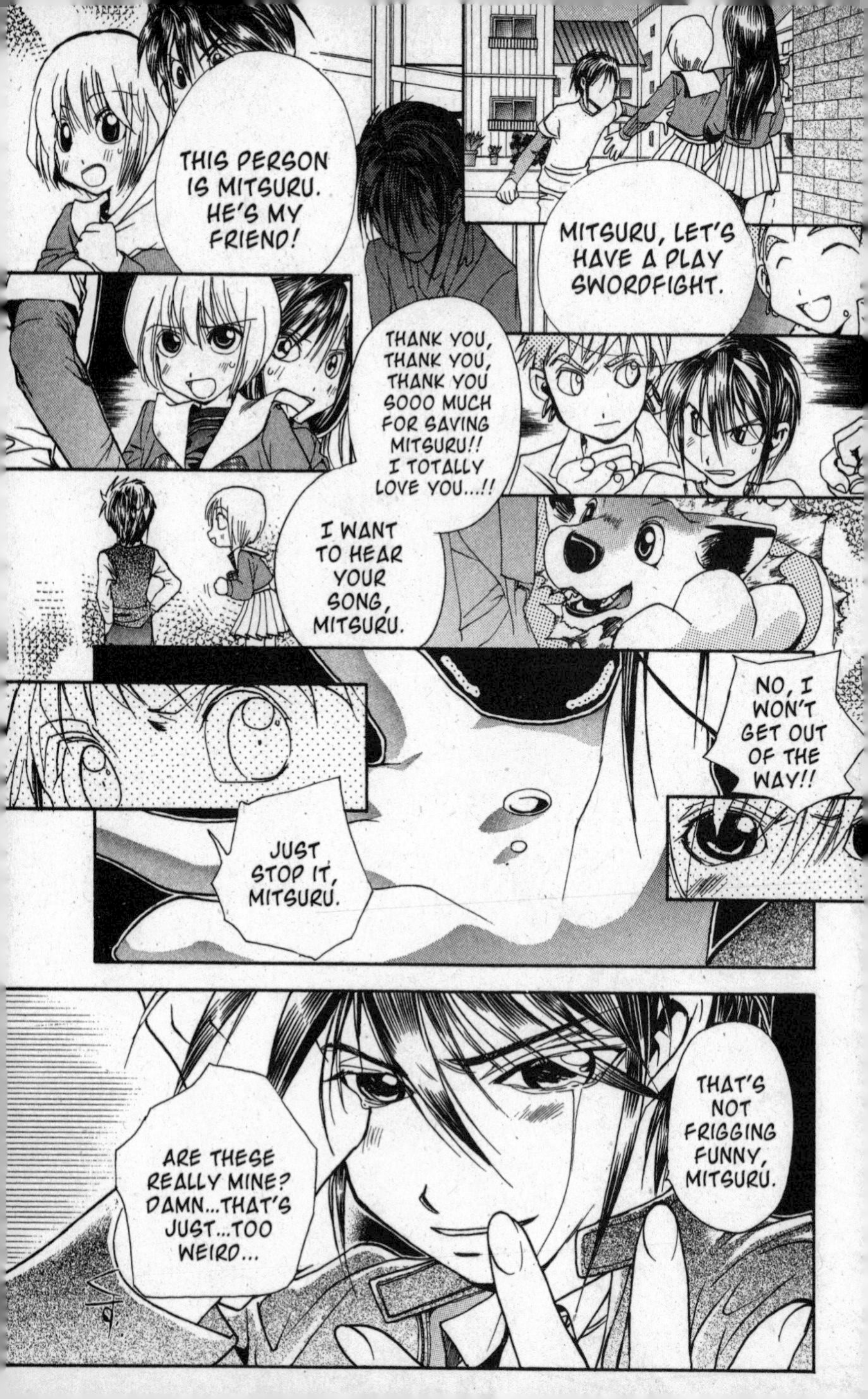
MITSURU, LET'S HAVE A PLAY SWORDFIGHT.
THIS PERSON IS MITSURU. HE'S MY FRIEND!
THANK YOU, THANK YOU, THANK YOU SOOO MUCH FOR SAVING MITSURU!! I TOTALLY LOVE YOU...!!
I WANT TO HEAR YOUR SONG, MITSURU.
NO, I WON'T GET OUT OF THE WAY!!
JUST STOP IT, MITSURU.
THAT'S NOT FRIGGING FUNNY, MITSURU.
ARE THESE REALLY MINE? DAMN...THAT'S JUST...TOO WEIRD...

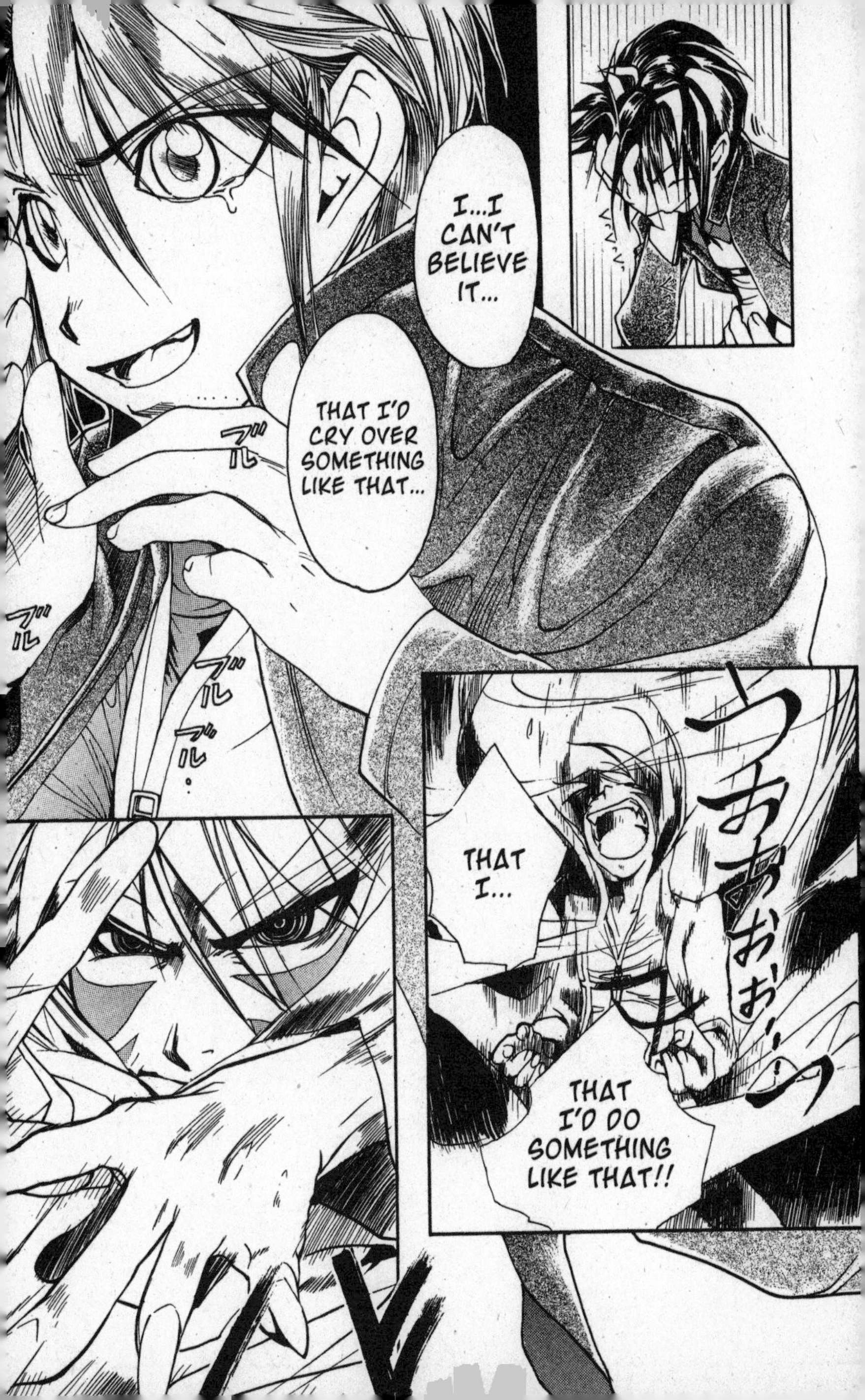
I...I CAN'T BELIEVE IT...
THAT I'D CRY OVER SOMETHING LIKE THAT...
ブル
ブル
ブル
ブル
THAT I...
THAT I'D DO SOMETHING LIKE THAT!!

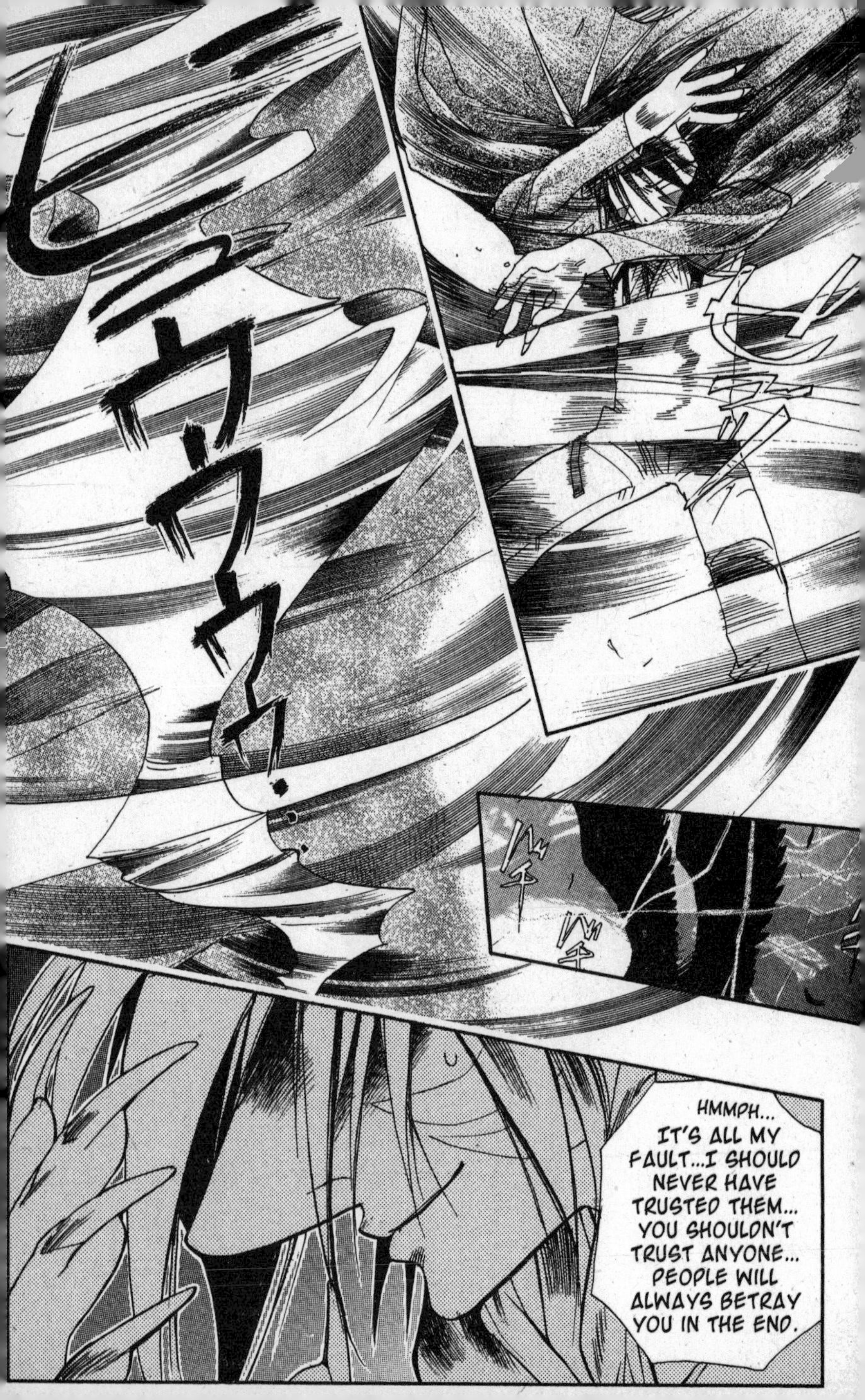
HMMPH... IT'S ALL MY FAULT...I SHOULD NEVER HAVE TRUSTED THEM... YOU SHOULDN'T TRUST ANYONE... PEOPLE WILL ALWAYS BETRAY YOU IN THE END.

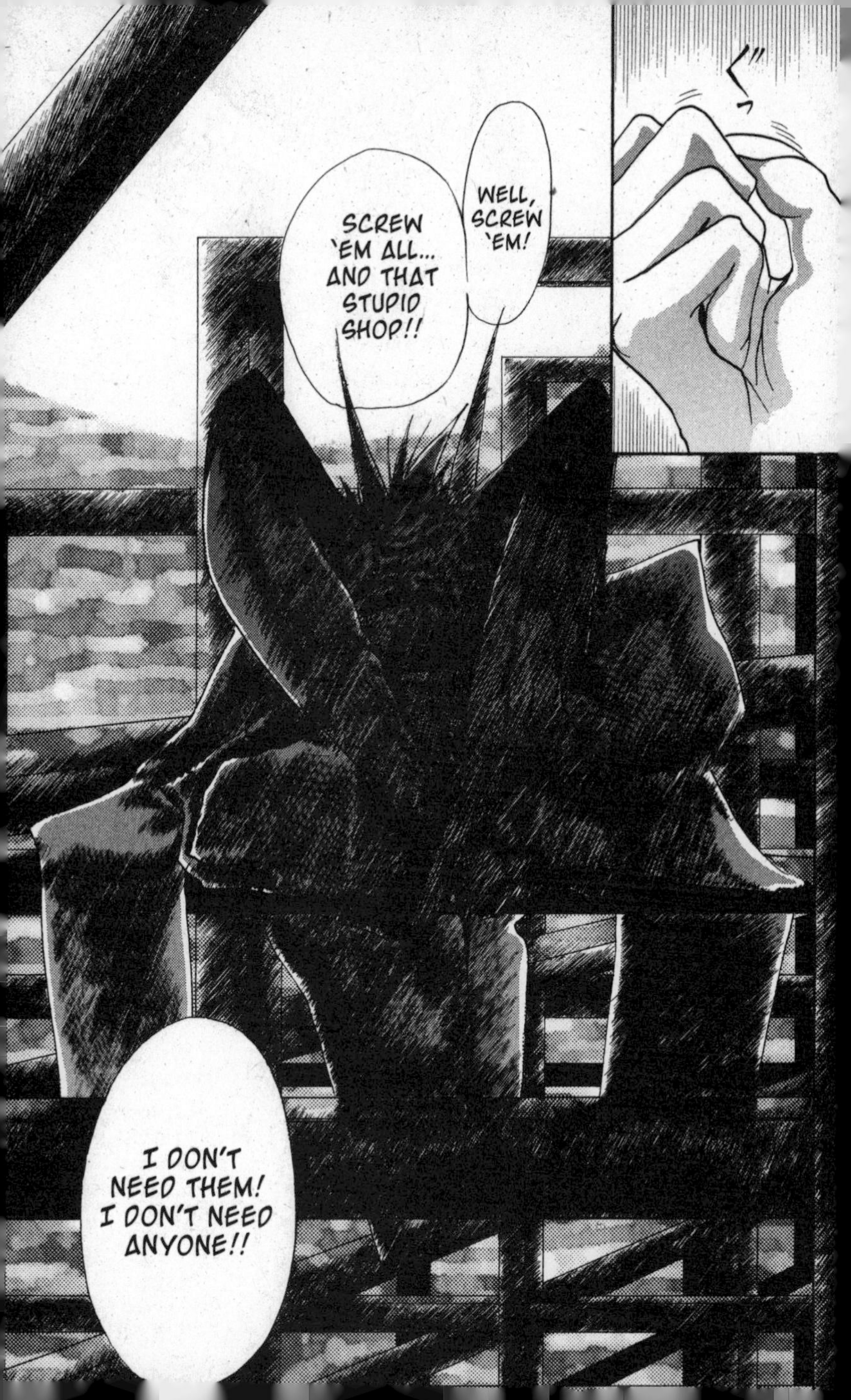
WELL, SCREW 'EM!
SCREW 'EM ALL... AND THAT STUPID SHOP!!
I DON'T NEED THEM! I DON'T NEED ANYONE!!

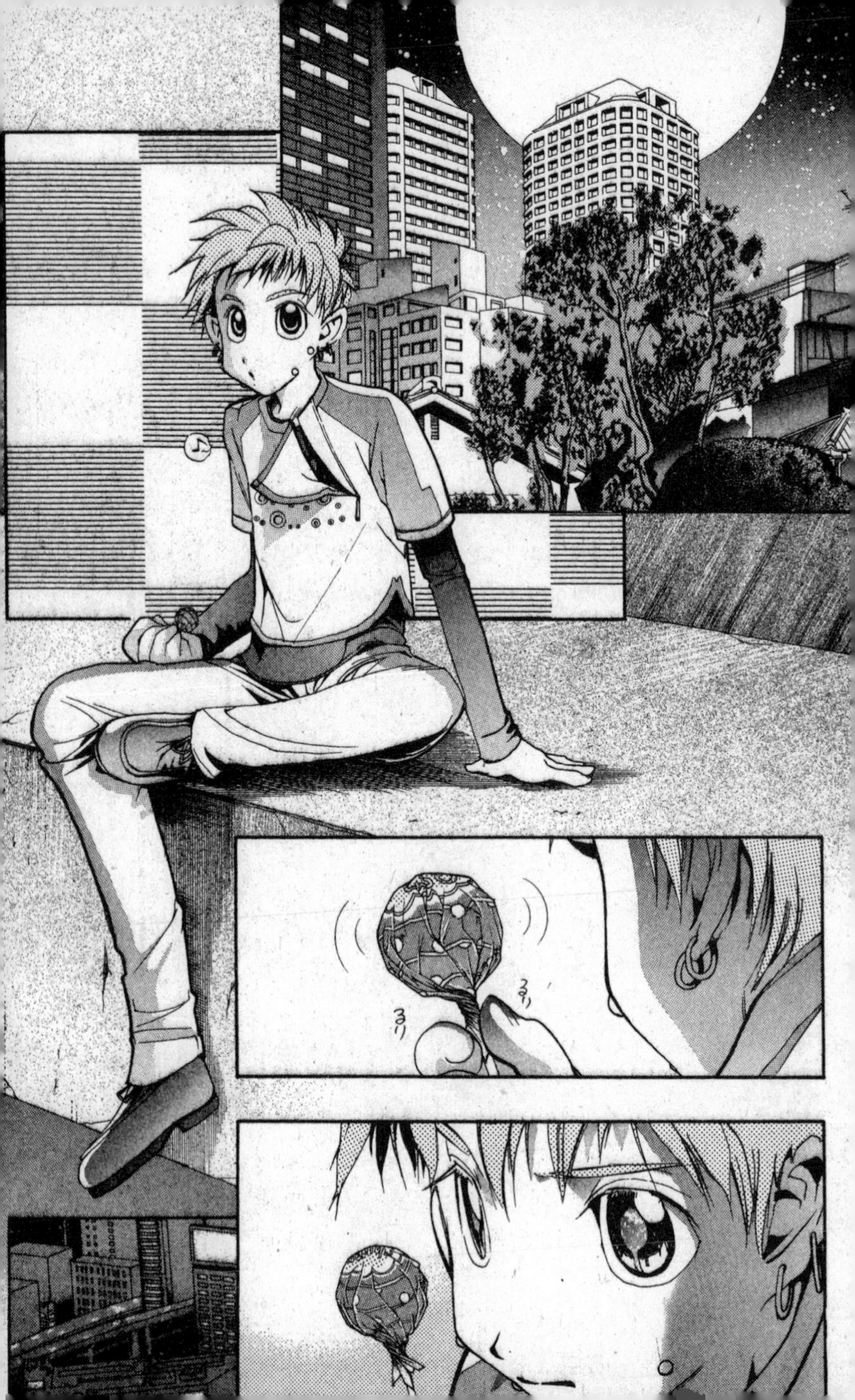
ふり
ふり

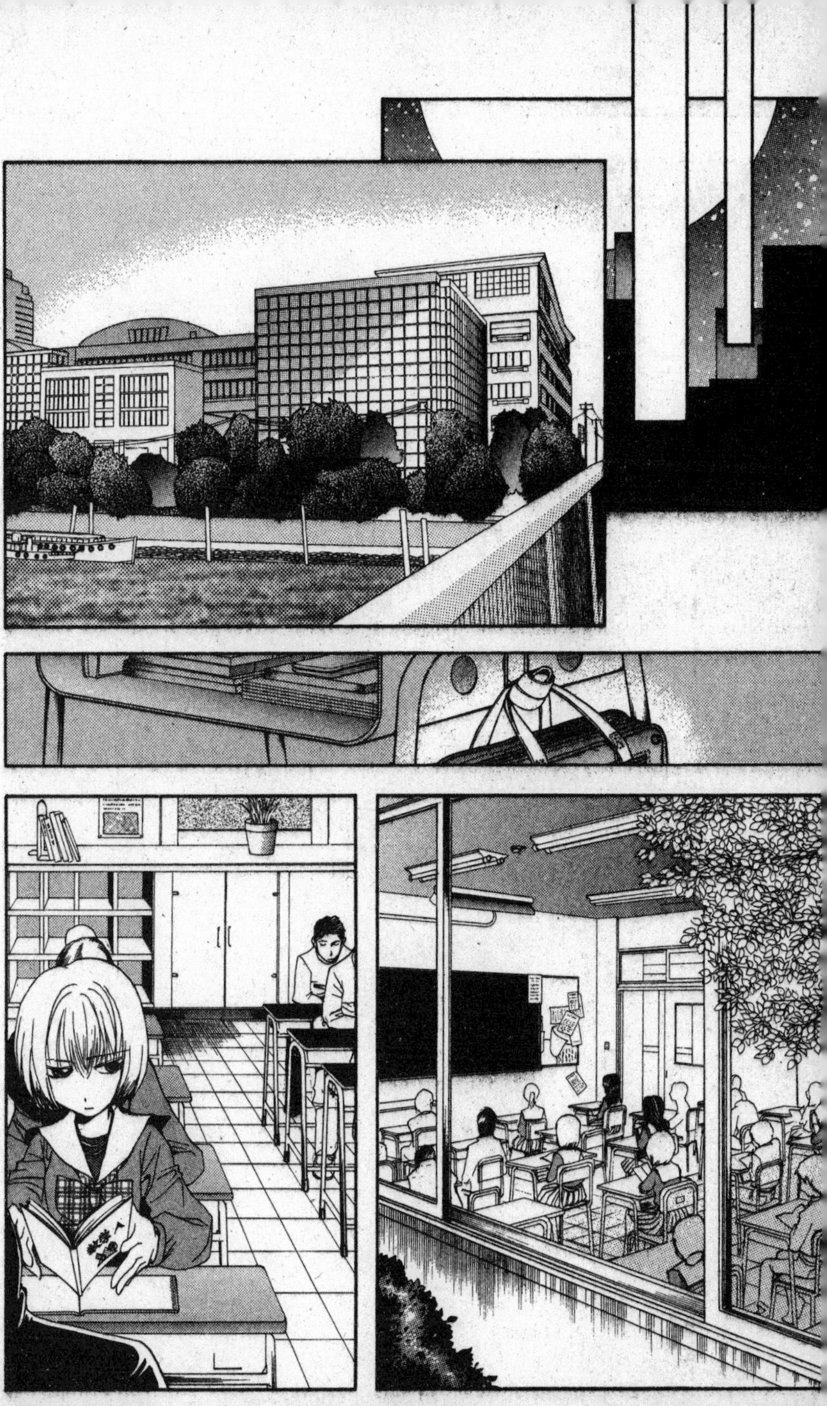

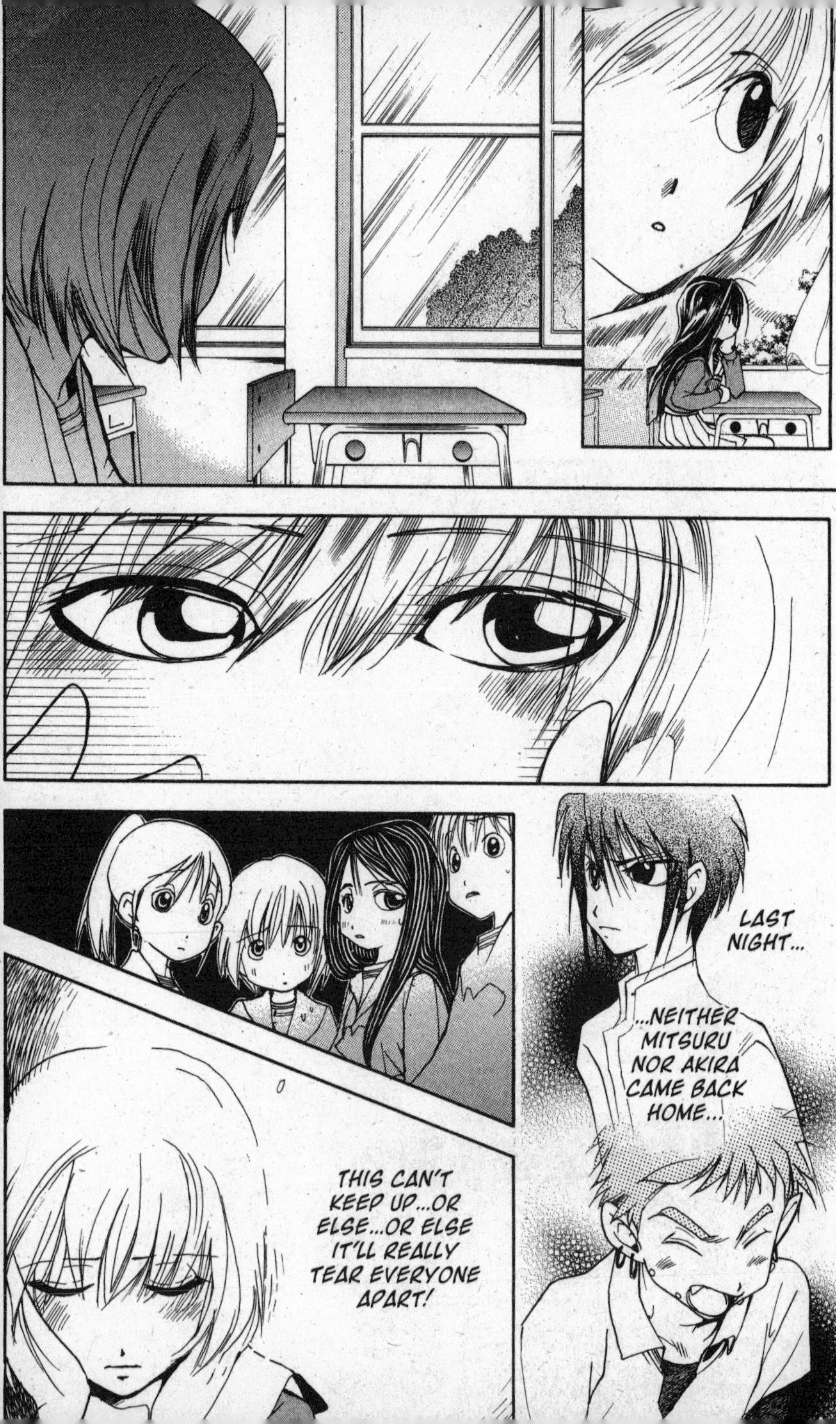
LAST NIGHT...
...NEITHER MITSURU NOR AKIRA CAME BACK HOME...
THIS CAN'T KEEP UP...OR ELSE...OR ELSE IT'LL REALLY TEAR EVERYONE APART!

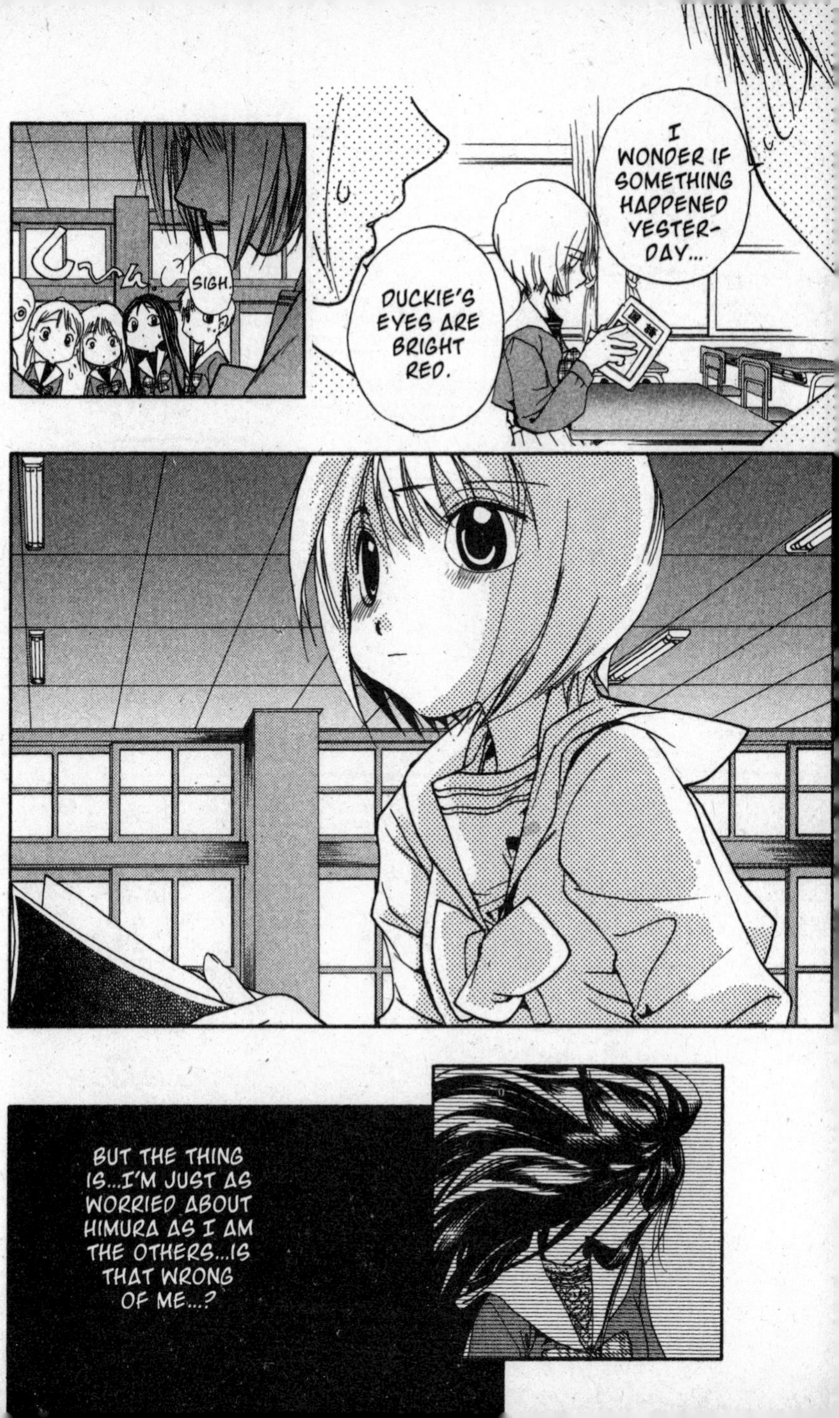
I WONDER IF SOMETHING HAPPENED YESTER-DAY...
DUCKIE'S EYES ARE BRIGHT RED.
SIGH.
BUT THE THING IS...I'M JUST AS WORRIED ABOUT HIMURA AS I AM THE OTHERS...IS THAT WRONG OF ME...?

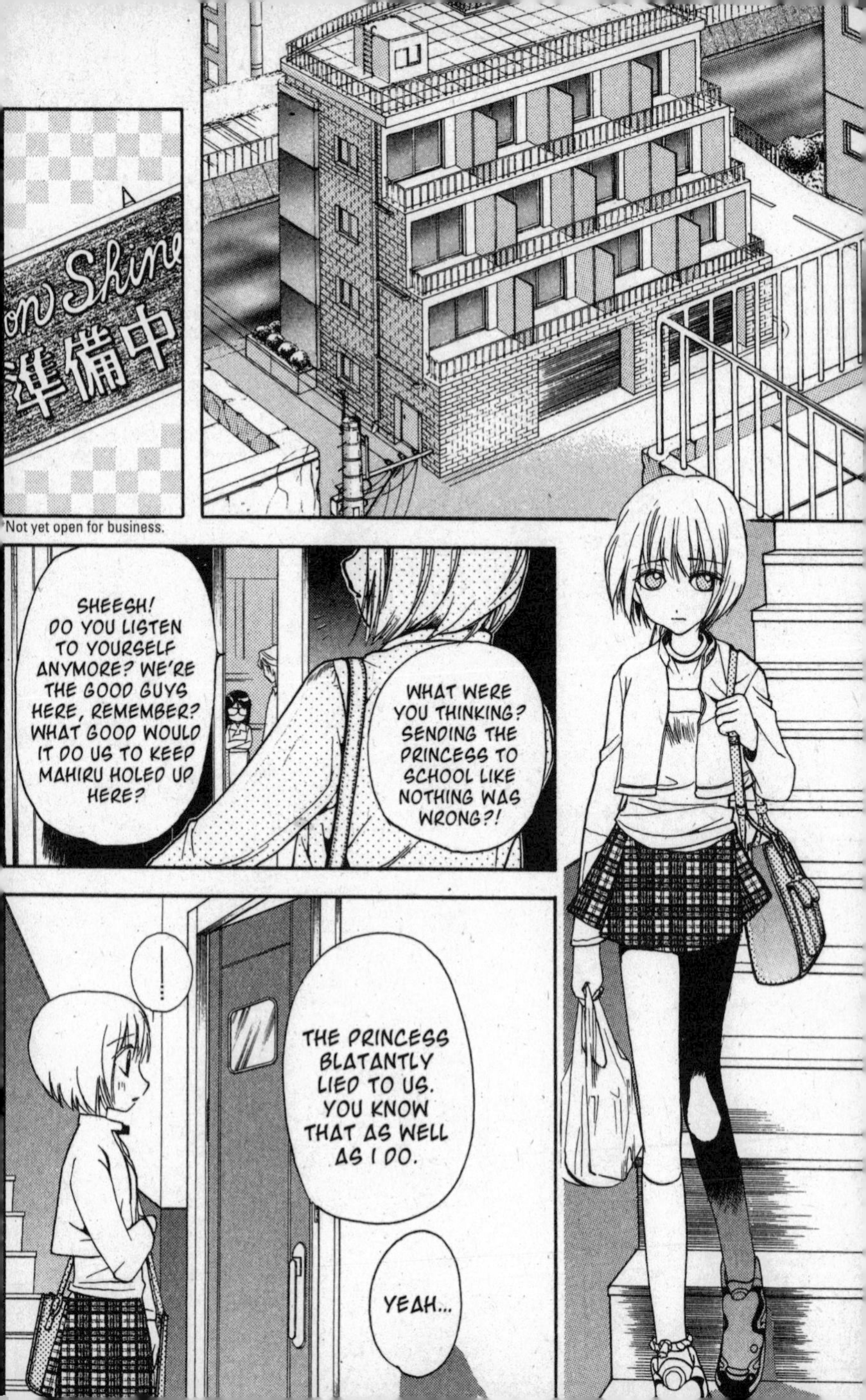
on Shine
準備中
WHAT WERE YOU THINKING? SENDING THE PRINCESS TO SCHOOL LIKE NOTHING WAS WRONG?!
SHEESH! DO YOU LISTEN TO YOURSELF ANYMORE? WE'RE THE GOOD GUYS HERE, REMEMBER? WHAT GOOD WOULD IT DO US TO KEEP MAHIRU HOLED UP HERE?
THE PRINCESS BLATANTLY LIED TO US. YOU KNOW THAT AS WELL AS I DO.
!
YEAH...
*Not yet open for business.

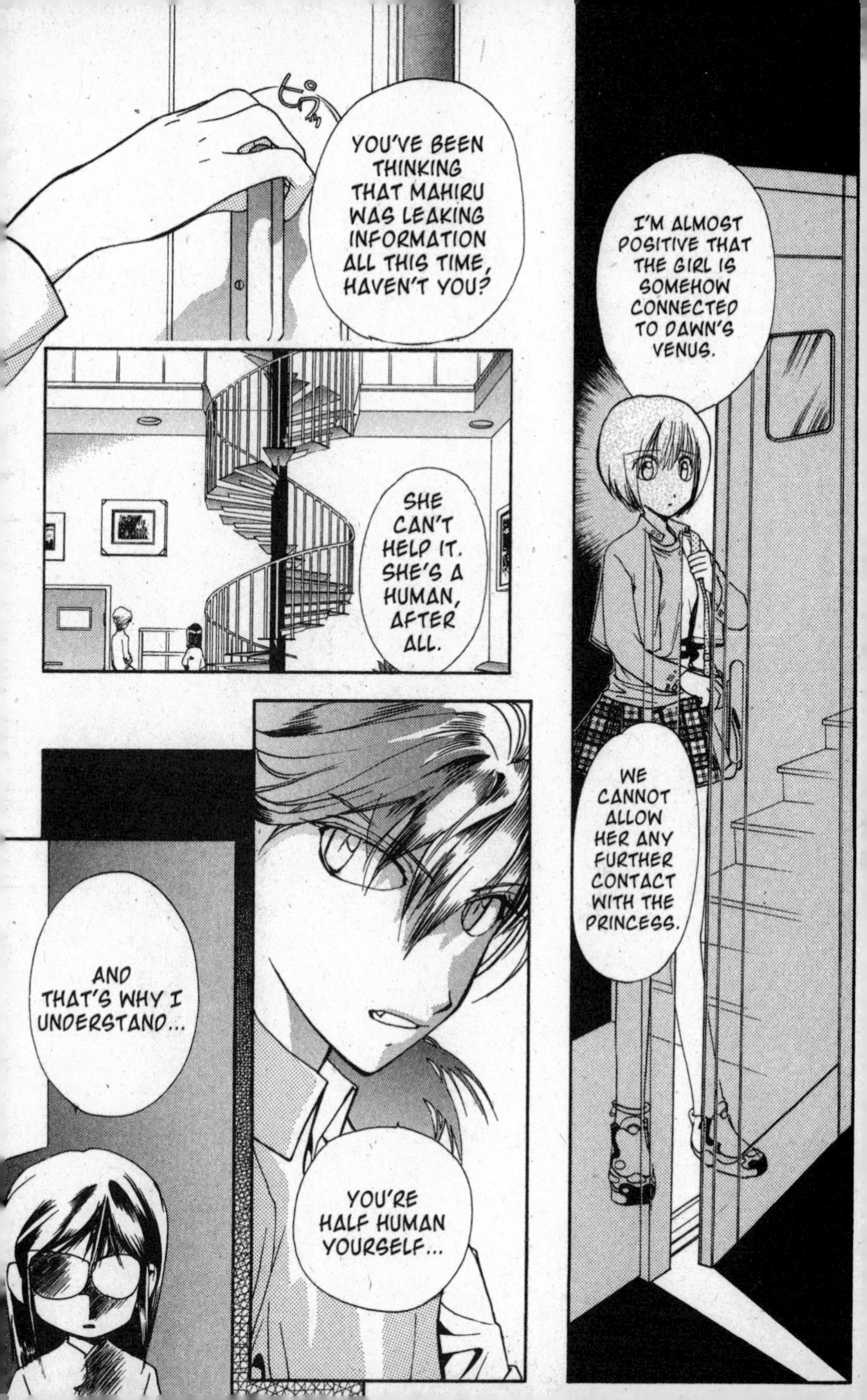
I'M ALMOST POSITIVE THAT THE GIRL IS SOMEHOW CONNECTED TO DAWN'S VENUS.
WE CANNOT ALLOW HER ANY FURTHER CONTACT WITH THE PRINCESS.
YOU'VE BEEN THINKING THAT MAHIRU WAS LEAKING INFORMATION ALL THIS TIME, HAVEN'T YOU?
SHE CAN'T HELP IT. SHE'S A HUMAN, AFTER ALL.
AND THAT'S WHY I UNDERSTAND...
YOU'RE HALF HUMAN YOURSELF...

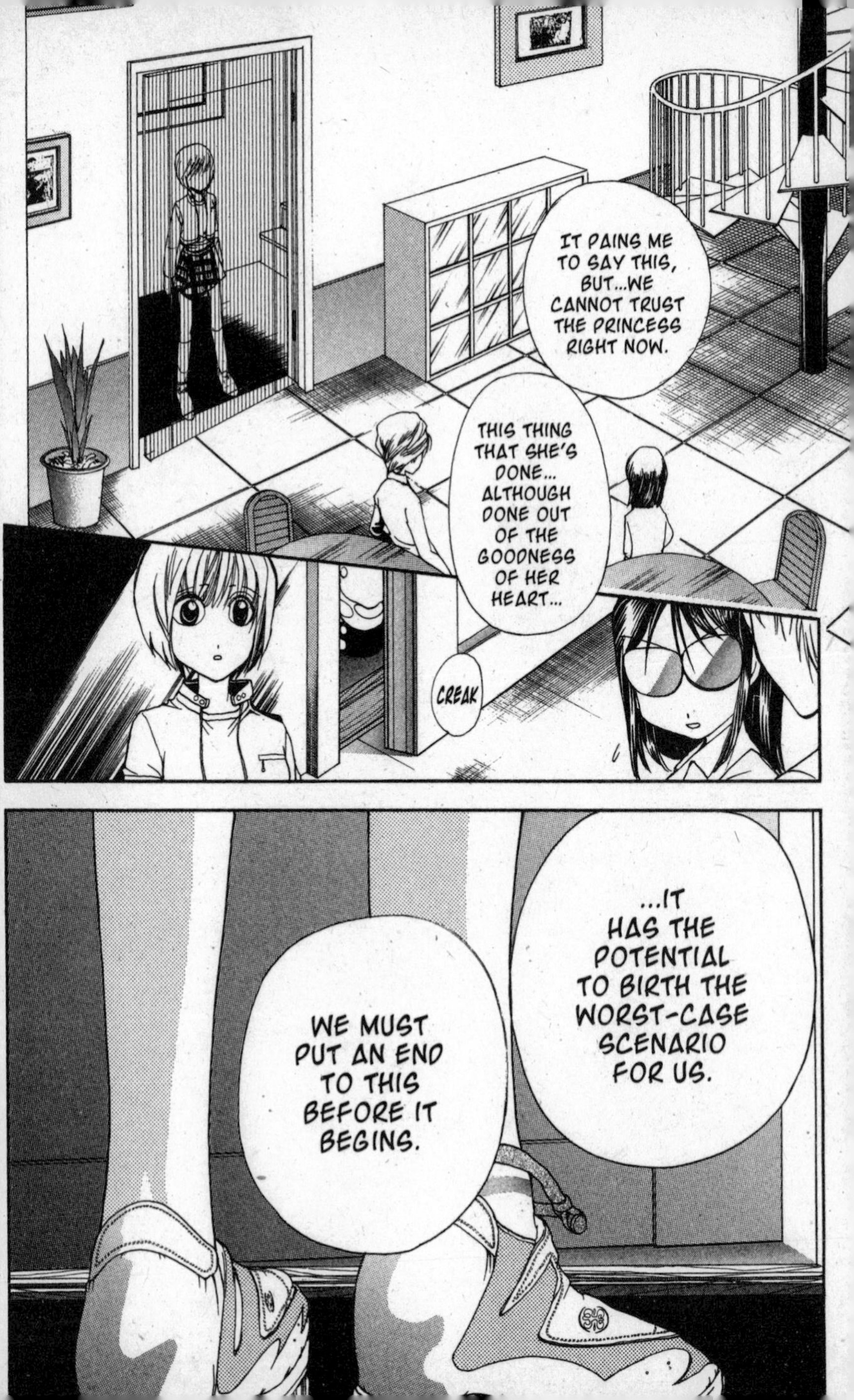
IT PAINS ME TO SAY THIS, BUT...WE CANNOT TRUST THE PRINCESS RIGHT NOW.
THIS THING THAT SHE'S DONE... ALTHOUGH DONE OUT OF THE GOODNESS OF HER HEART...
CREAK
...IT HAS THE POTENTIAL TO BIRTH THE WORST-CASE SCENARIO FOR US.
WE MUST PUT AN END TO THIS BEFORE IT BEGINS.

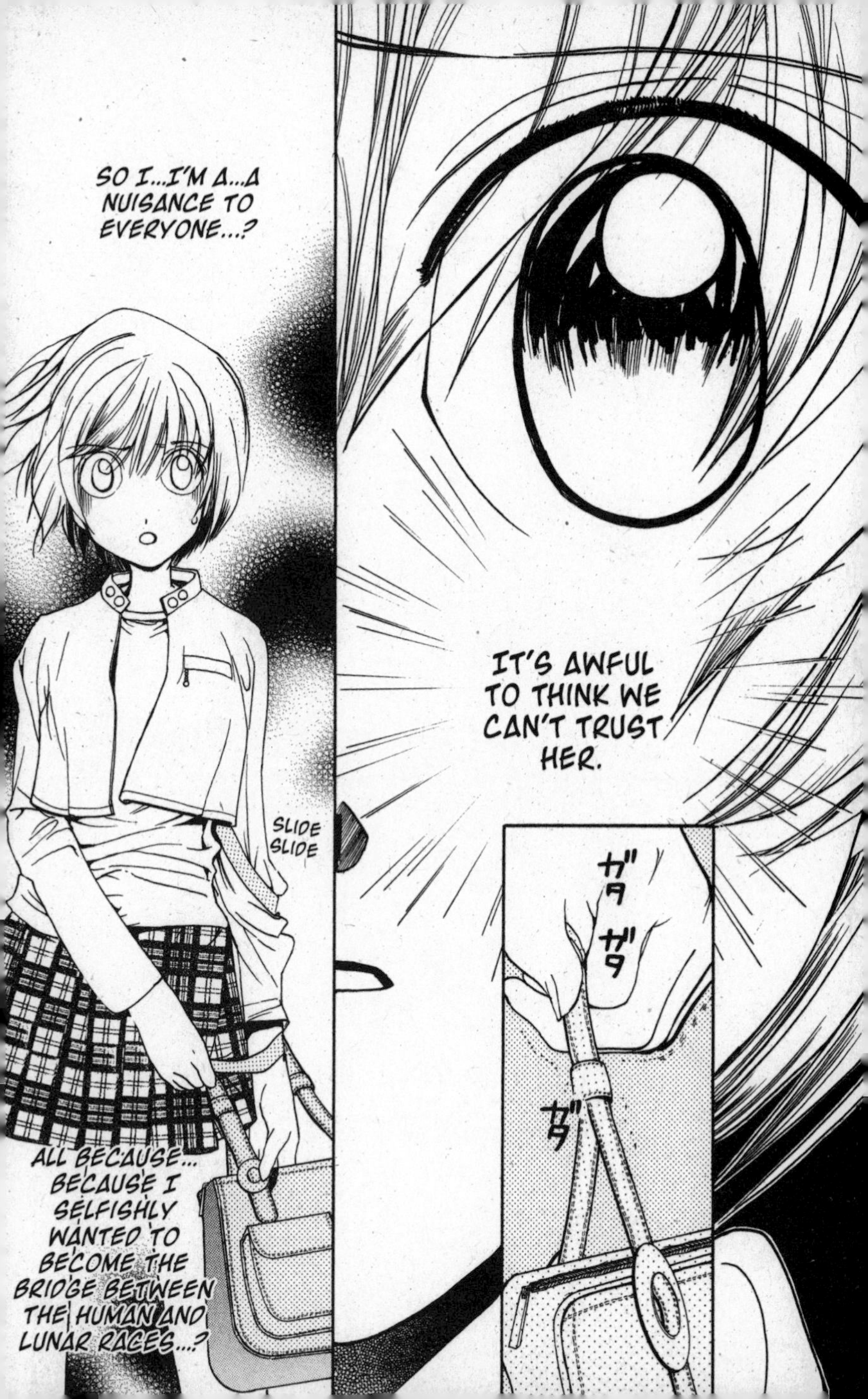
IT'S AWFUL TO THINK WE CAN'T TRUST HER.
ガタ
ガタ
ガタ
SO I...I'M A...A NUISANCE TO EVERYONE...?
SLIDE SLIDE
ALL BECAUSE... BECAUSE I SELFISHLY WANTED TO BECOME THE BRIDGE BETWEEN THE HUMAN AND LUNAR RACES...?

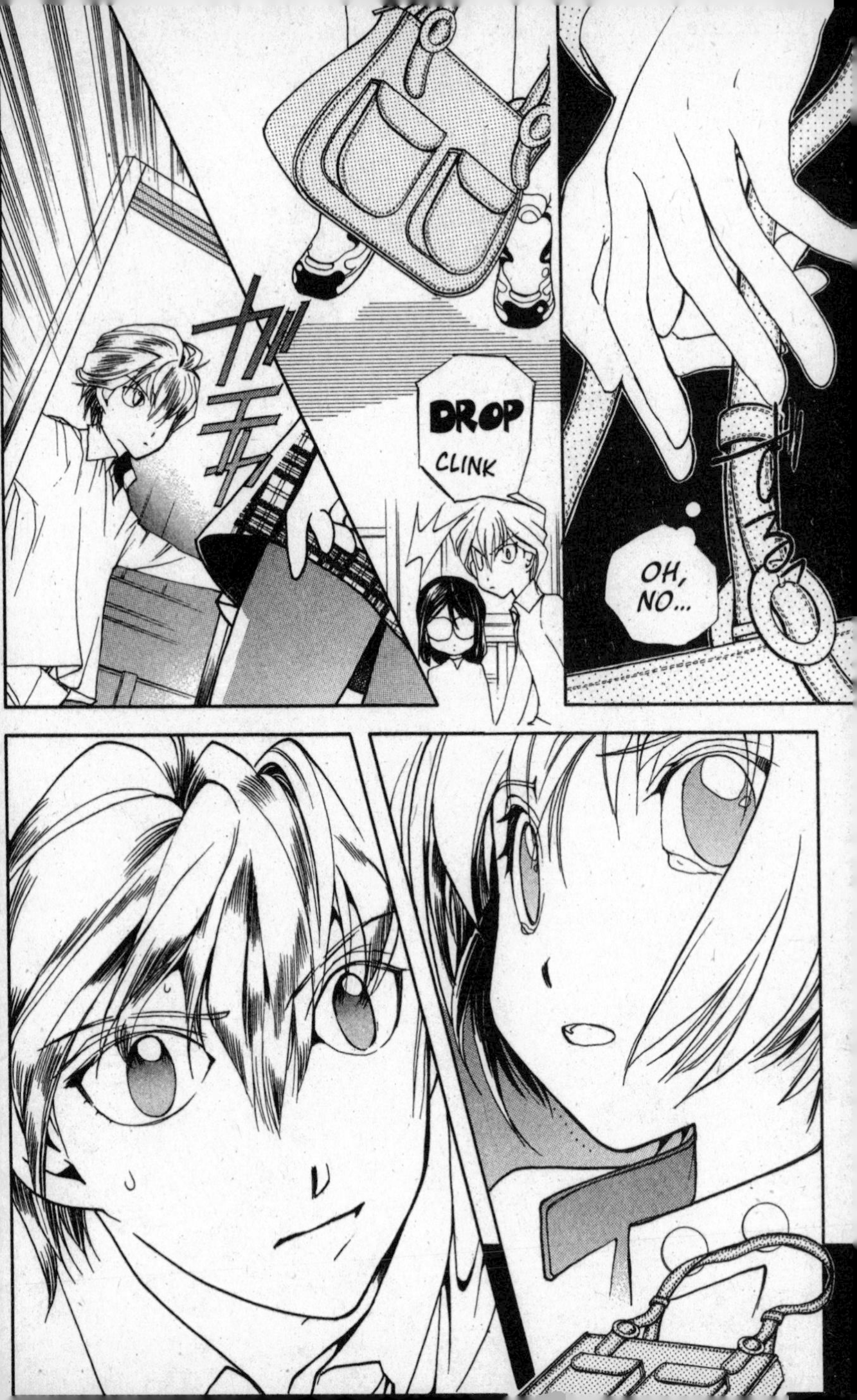
OH, NO...
DROP
CLINK

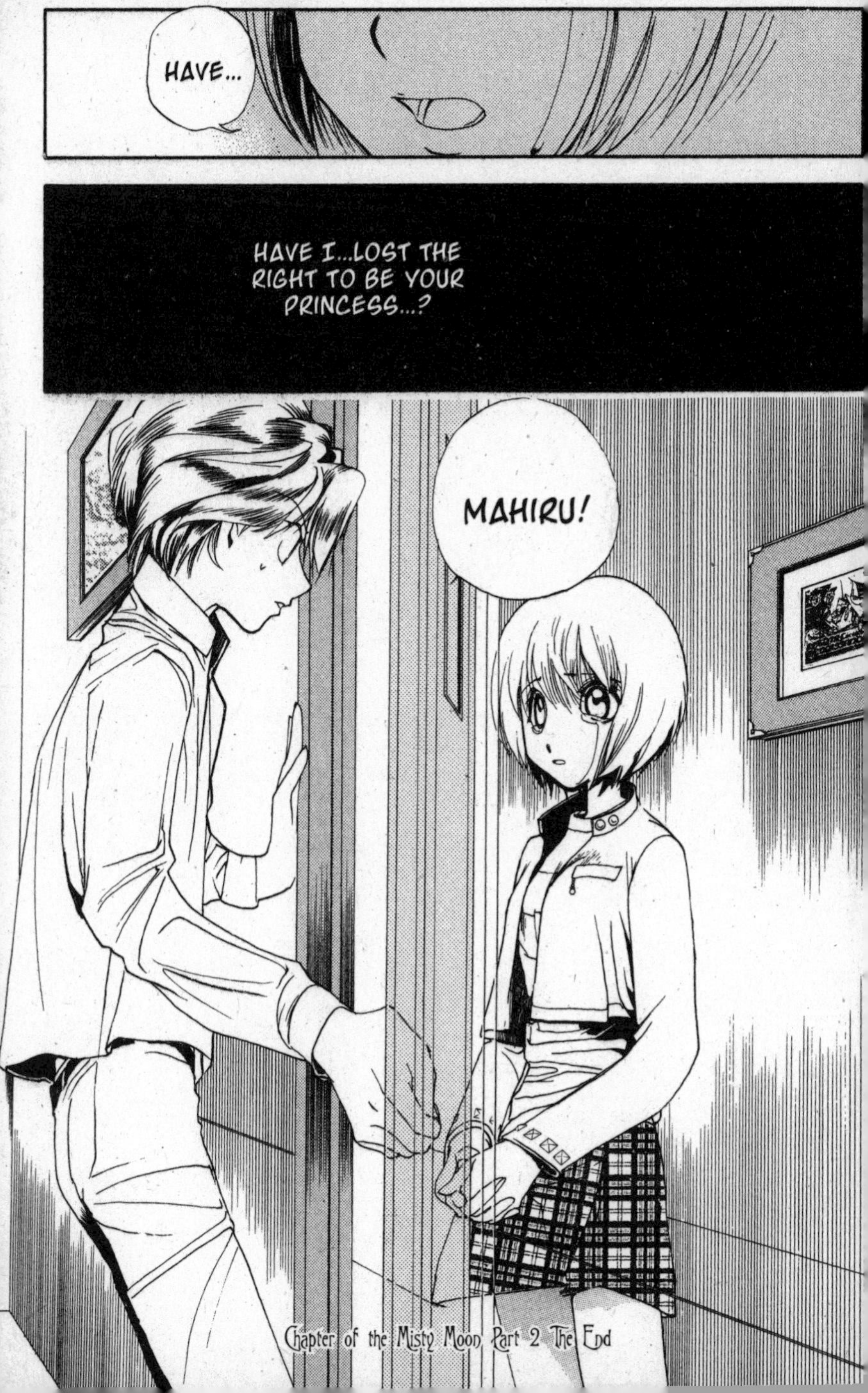
HAVE...
HAVE I...LOST THE RIGHT TO BE YOUR PRINCESS...?
MAHIRU!
Chapter of the Misty Moon Part 2 The End

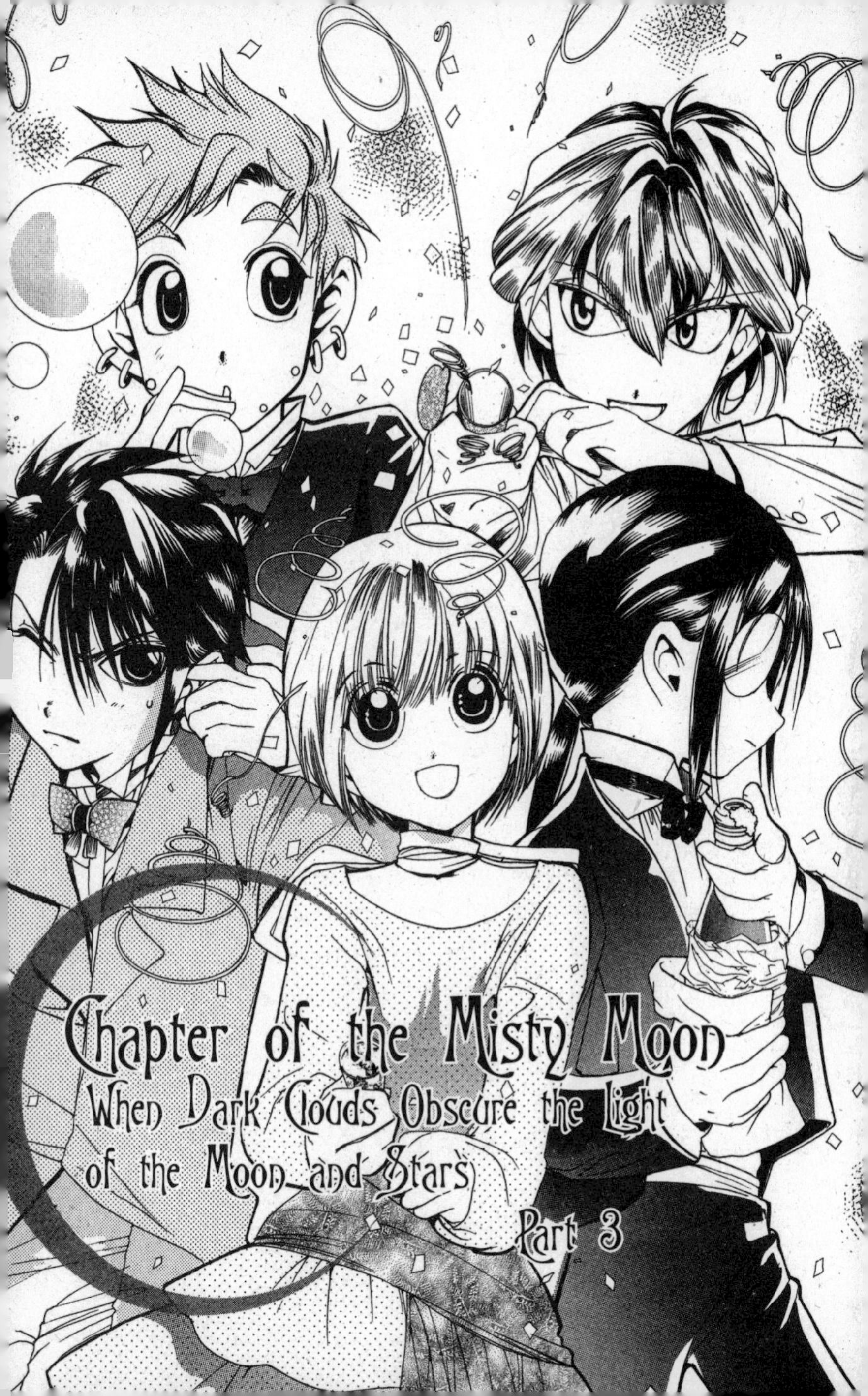
Chapter of the Misty Moon
When Dark Clouds Obscure the Light of the Moon and Stars
Part 3

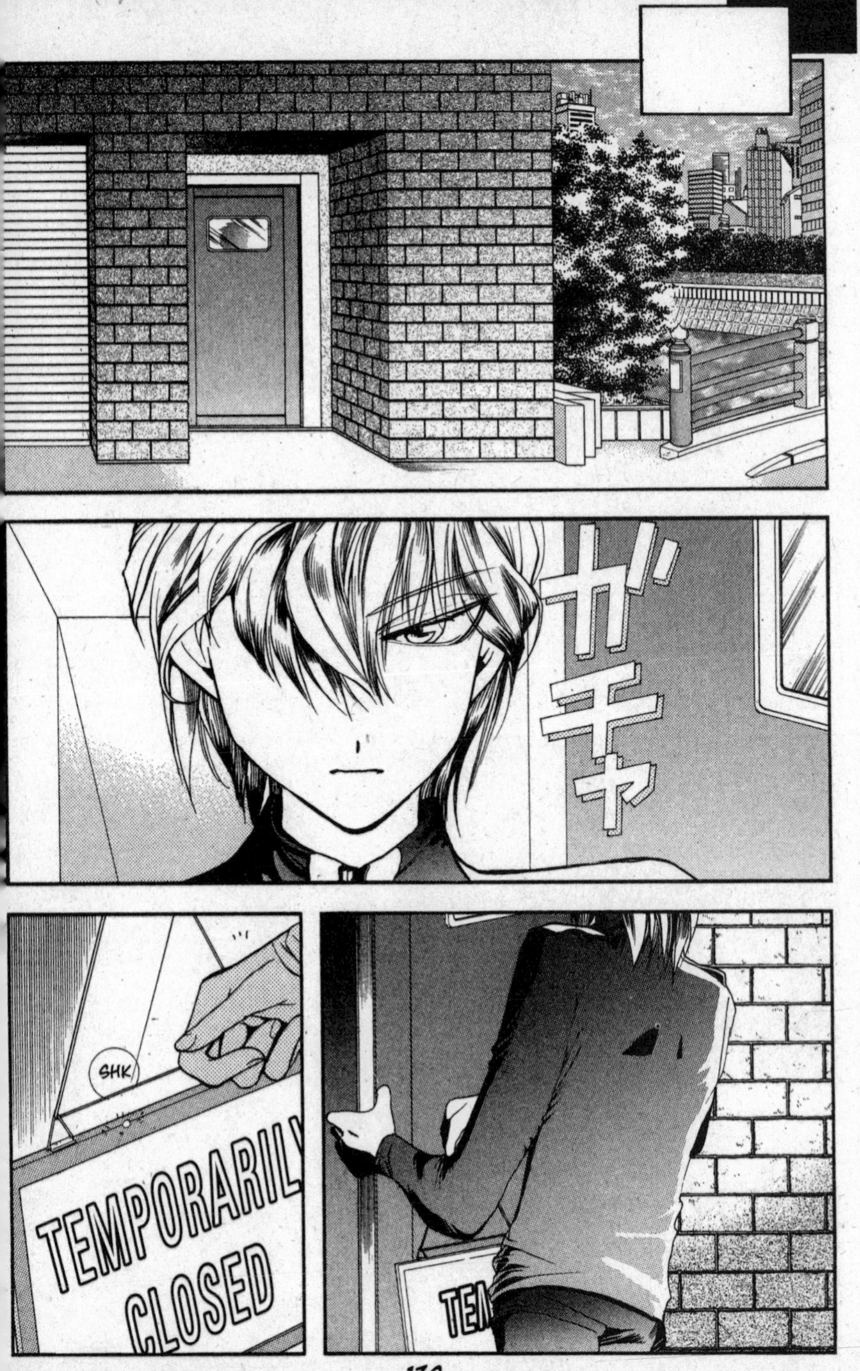
ガチャ
TEM
SHK
TEMPORARILY
CLOSED

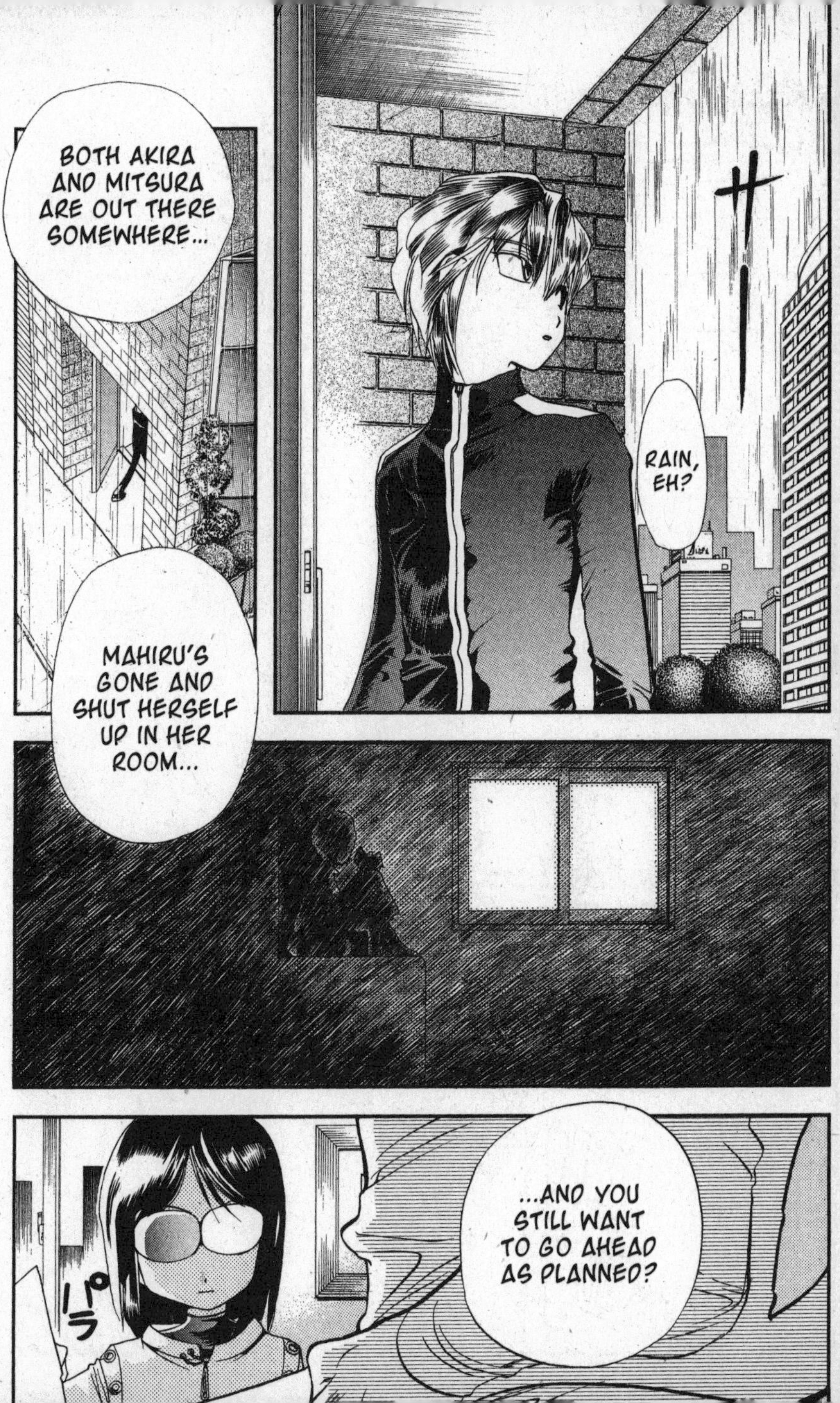
サー
RAIN, EH?
BOTH AKIRA AND MITSURA ARE OUT THERE SOMEWHERE...
MAHIRU'S GONE AND SHUT HERSELF UP IN HER ROOM...
...AND YOU STILL WANT TO GO AHEAD AS PLANNED?
パラ

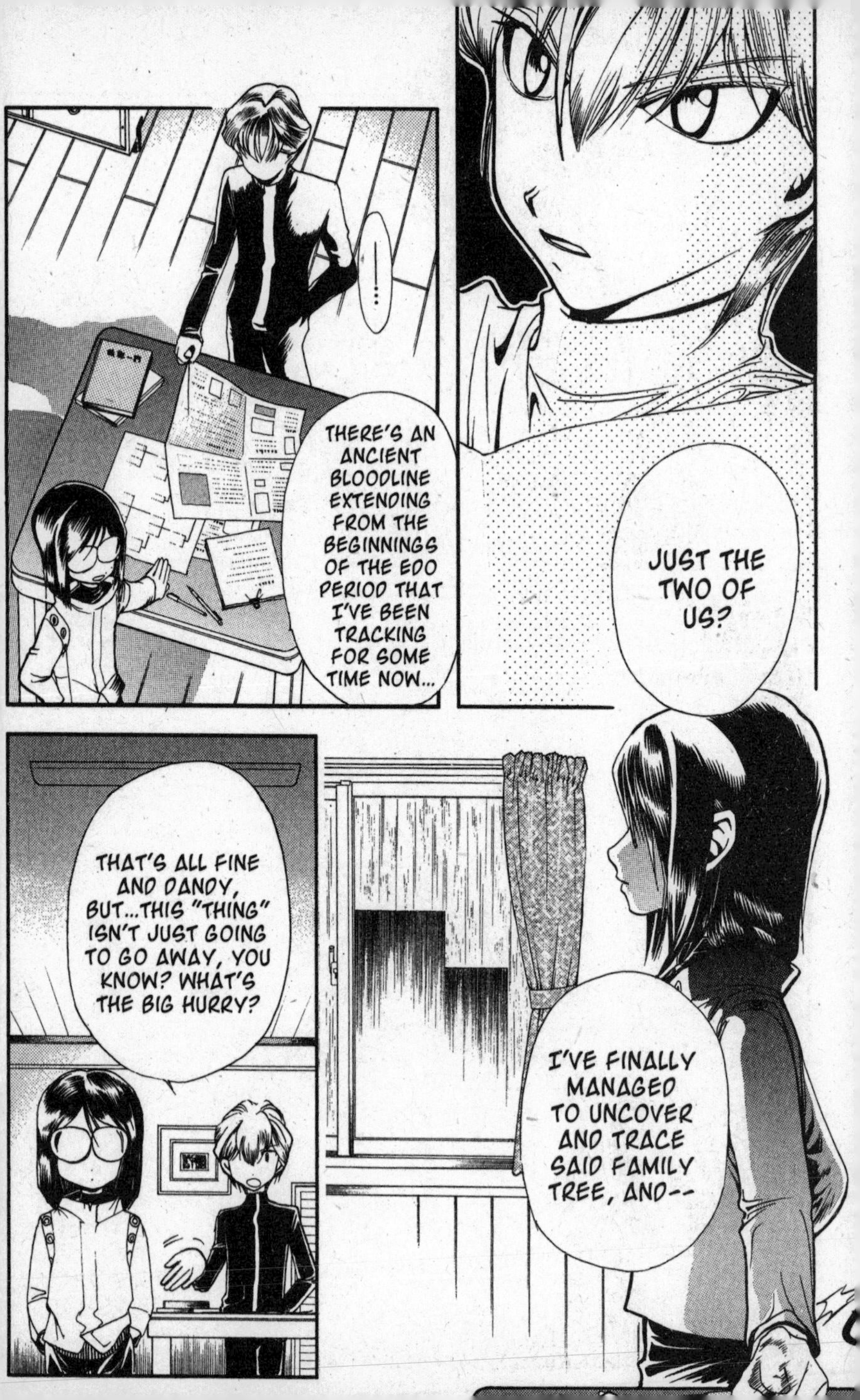
JUST THE TWO OF US?
......
THERE'S AN ANCIENT BLOODLINE EXTENDING FROM THE BEGINNINGS OF THE EDO PERIOD THAT I'VE BEEN TRACKING FOR SOME TIME NOW...
I'VE FINALLY MANAGED TO UNCOVER AND TRACE SAID FAMILY TREE, AND--
THAT'S ALL FINE AND DANDY, BUT...THIS "THING" ISN'T JUST GOING TO GO AWAY, YOU KNOW? WHAT'S THE BIG HURRY?

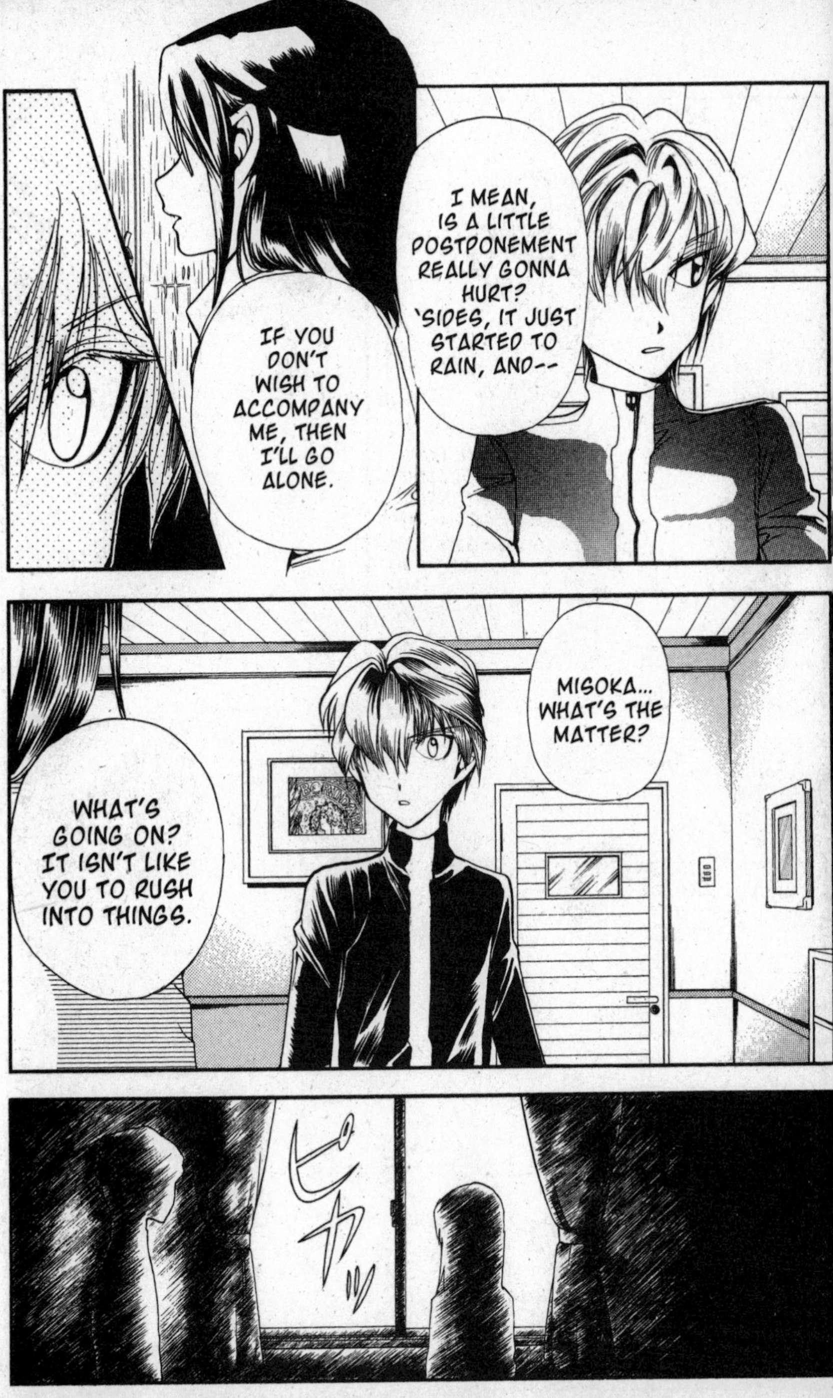
I MEAN, IS A LITTLE POSTPONEMENT REALLY GONNA HURT? 'SIDES, IT JUST STARTED TO RAIN, AND--
IF YOU DON'T WISH TO ACCOMPANY ME, THEN I'LL GO ALONE.
MISOKA... WHAT'S THE MATTER?
WHAT'S GOING ON? IT ISN'T LIKE YOU TO RUSH INTO THINGS.
ピカッ

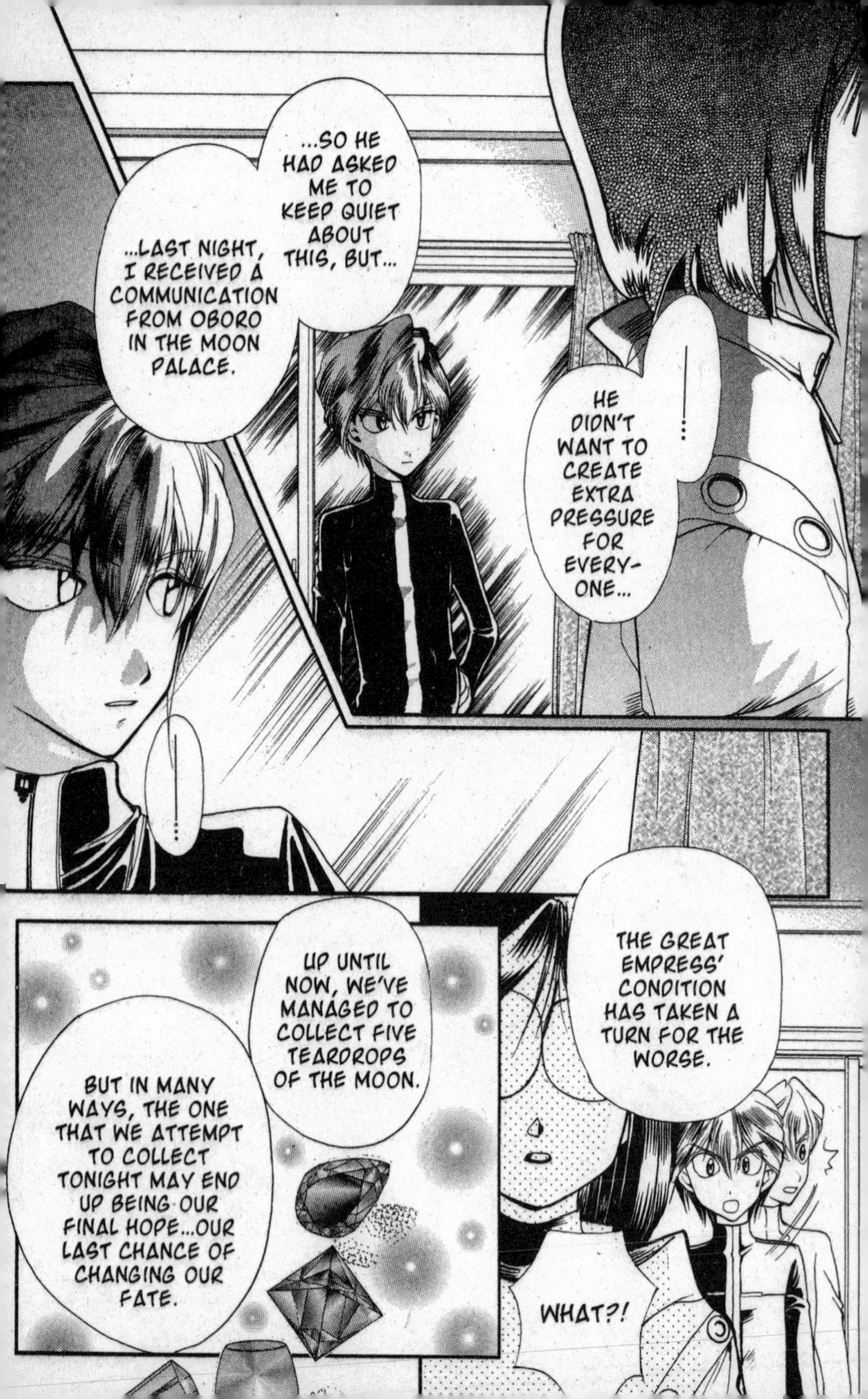
......
HE DIDN'T WANT TO CREATE EXTRA PRESSURE FOR EVERYONE...
...SO HE HAD ASKED ME TO KEEP QUIET ABOUT THIS, BUT...
...LAST NIGHT, I RECEIVED A COMMUNICATION FROM OBORO IN THE MOON PALACE.
......
THE GREAT EMPRESS' CONDITION HAS TAKEN A TURN FOR THE WORSE.
WHAT?!
UP UNTIL NOW, WE'VE MANAGED TO COLLECT FIVE TEARDROPS OF THE MOON.
BUT IN MANY WAYS, THE ONE THAT WE ATTEMPT TO COLLECT TONIGHT MAY END UP BEING OUR FINAL HOPE...OUR LAST CHANCE OF CHANGING OUR FATE.

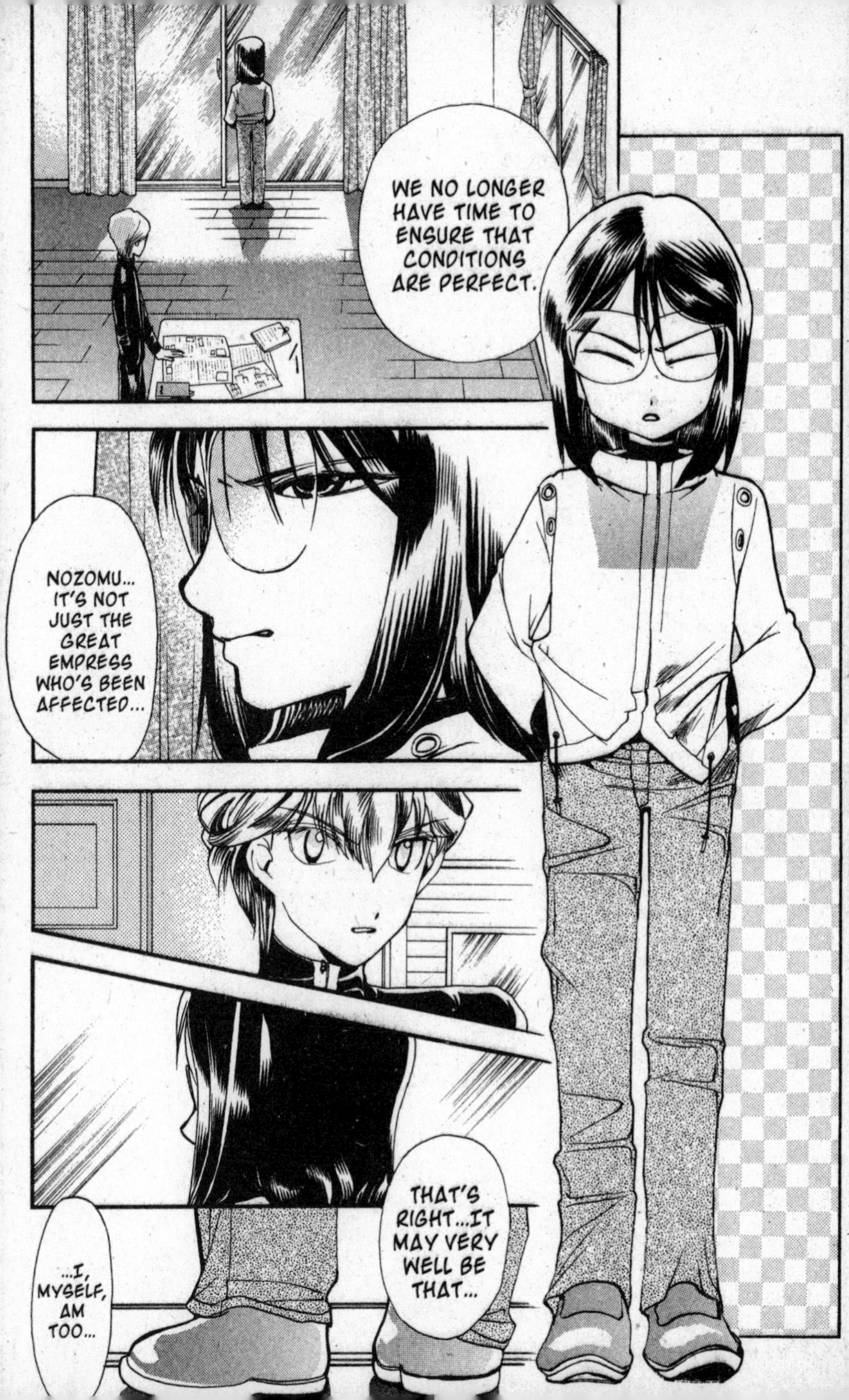
WE NO LONGER HAVE TIME TO ENSURE THAT CONDITIONS ARE PERFECT.
NOZOMU... IT'S NOT JUST THE GREAT EMPRESS WHO'S BEEN AFFECTED...
THAT'S RIGHT...IT MAY VERY WELL BE THAT...
...I, MYSELF, AM TOO...

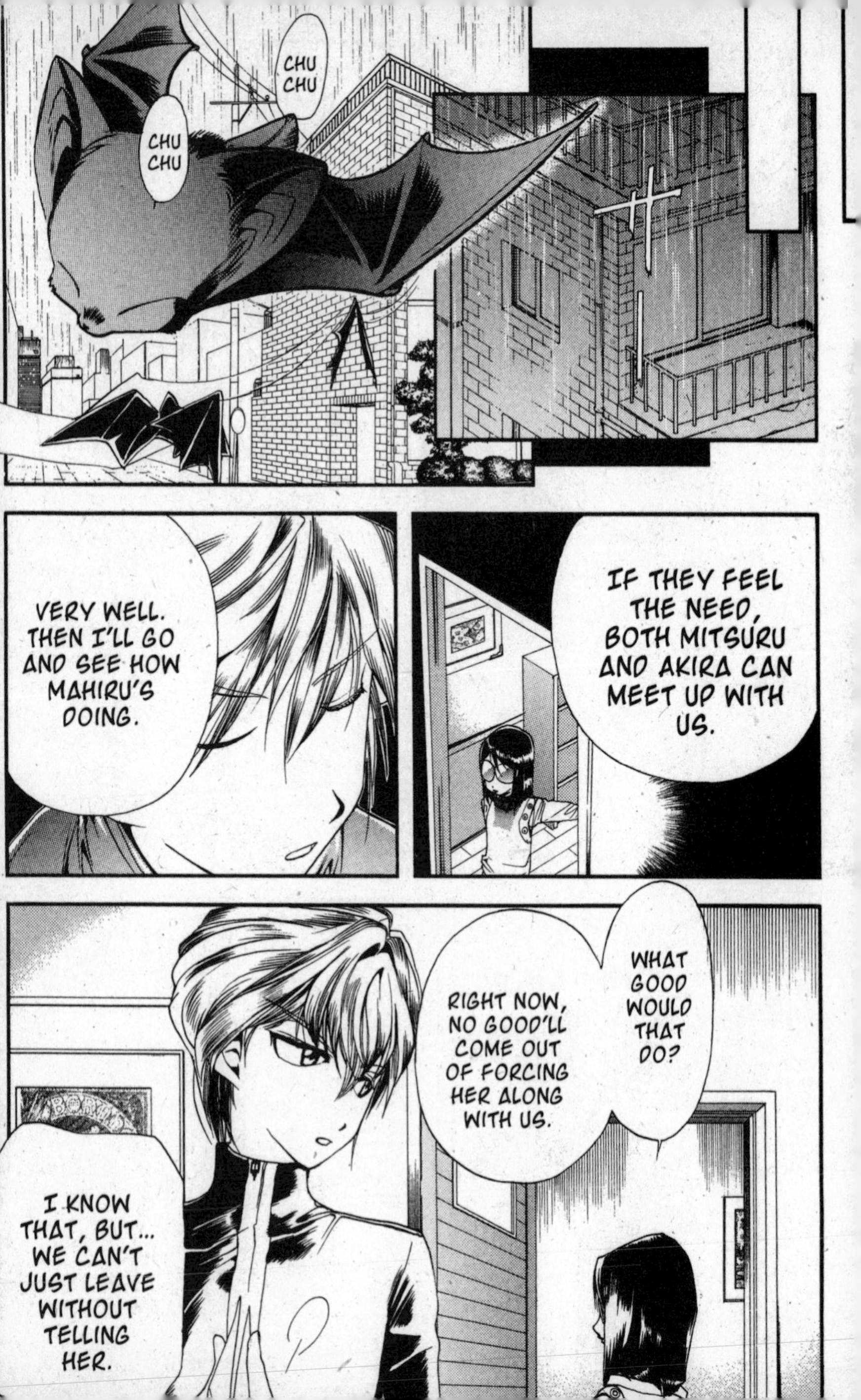
CHU CHU
CHU CHU
IF THEY FEEL THE NEED, BOTH MITSURU AND AKIRA CAN MEET UP WITH US.
VERY WELL. THEN I'LL GO AND SEE HOW MAHIRU'S DOING.
WHAT GOOD WOULD THAT DO?
RIGHT NOW, NO GOOD'LL COME OUT OF FORCING HER ALONG WITH US.
I KNOW THAT, BUT... WE CAN'T JUST LEAVE WITHOUT TELLING HER.

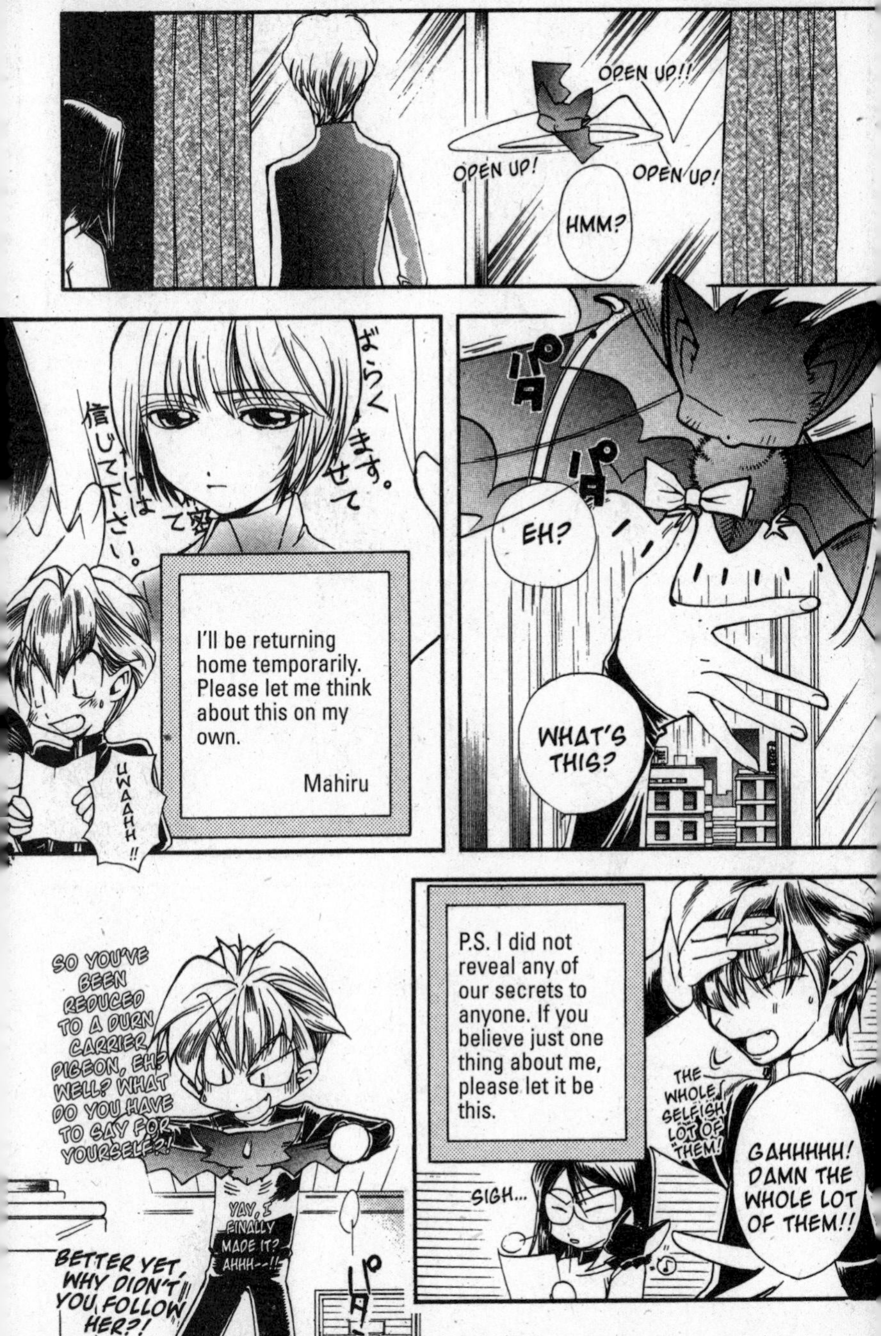
OPEN UP!!
OPEN UP!
OPEN UP!
HMM?
EH?
WHAT'S THIS?
I'll be returning home temporarily. Please let me think about this on my own.
Mahiru
UWAAHH!!
P.S. I did not reveal any of our secrets to anyone. If you believe just one thing about me, please let it be this.
THE WHOLE SELFISH LOT OF THEM!
GAHHHHH! DAMN THE WHOLE LOT OF THEM!!
SIGH...
SO YOU'VE BEEN REDUCED TO A DURN CARRIER PIGEON, EH? WELL? WHAT DO YOU HAVE TO SAY FOR YOURSELF?!
YAY, I FINALLY MADE IT? AHHH--!!
BETTER YET, WHY DIDN'T YOU FOLLOW HER?!

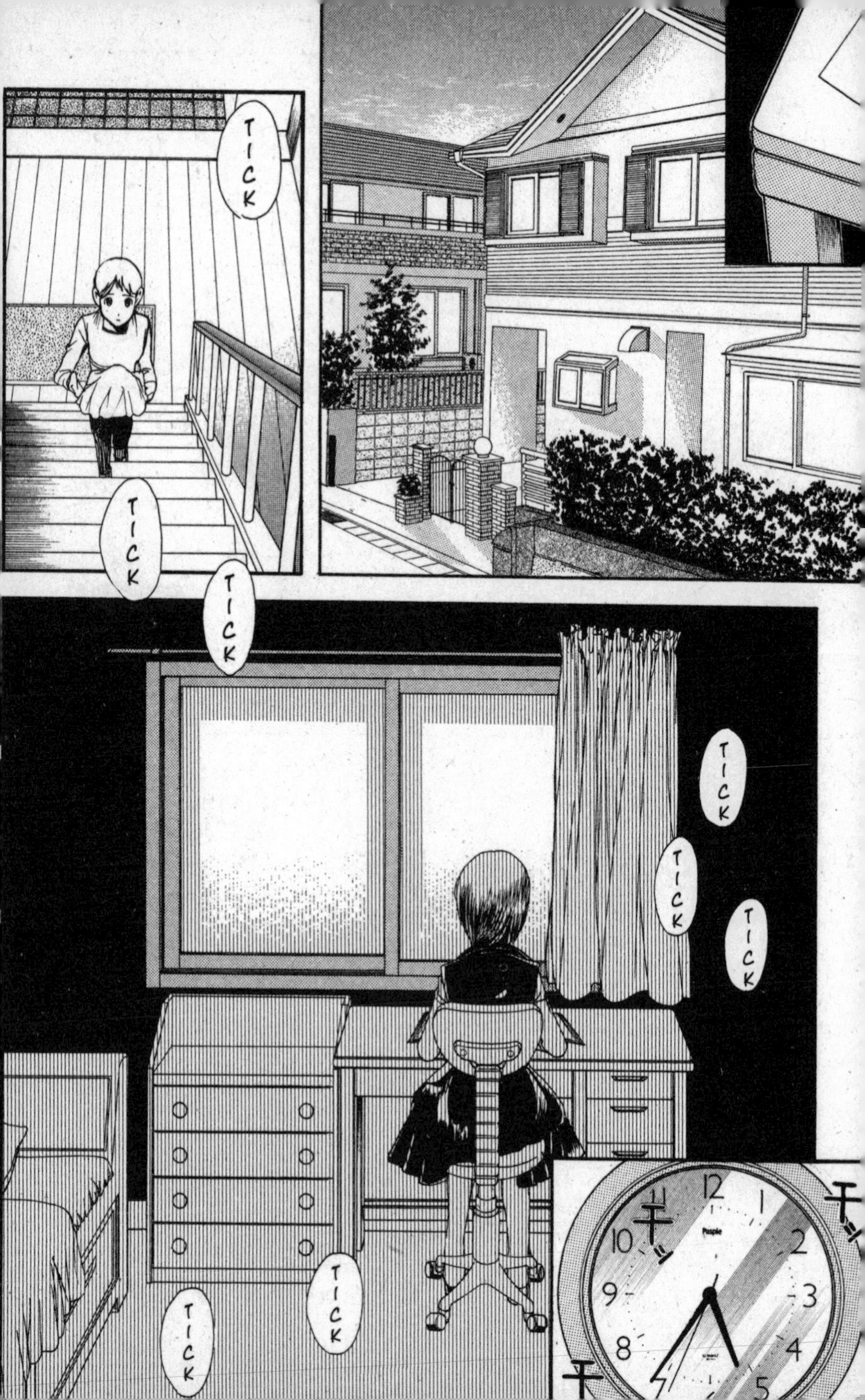
TICK
TICK
TICK
TICK
TICK
TICK
TICK
TICK

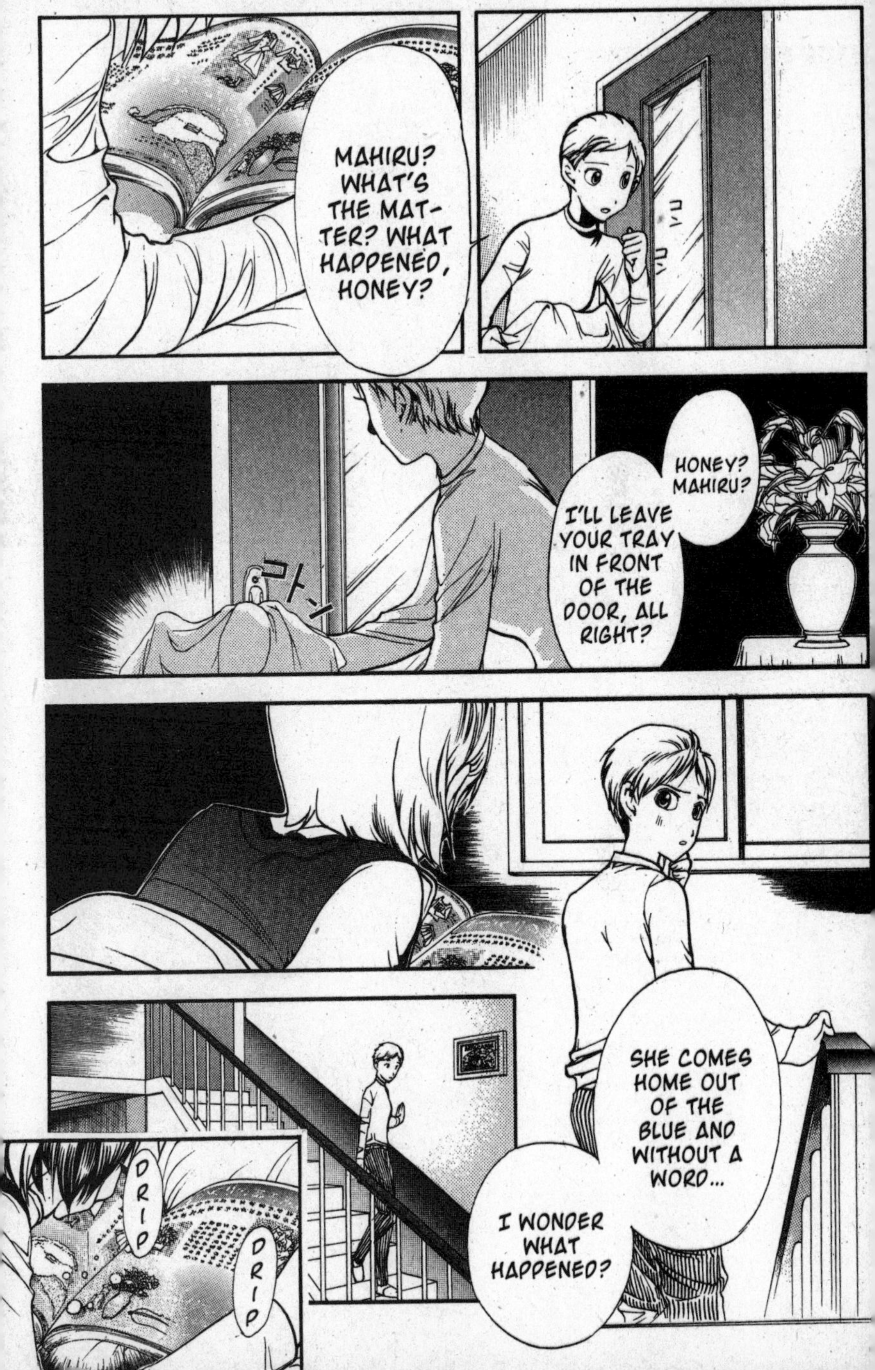
MAHIRU? WHAT'S THE MAT- TER? WHAT HAPPENED, HONEY?
HONEY? MAHIRU?
I'LL LEAVE YOUR TRAY IN FRONT OF THE DOOR, ALL RIGHT?
SHE COMES HOME OUT OF THE BLUE AND WITHOUT A WORD...
I WONDER WHAT HAPPENED?
DRIP
DRIP

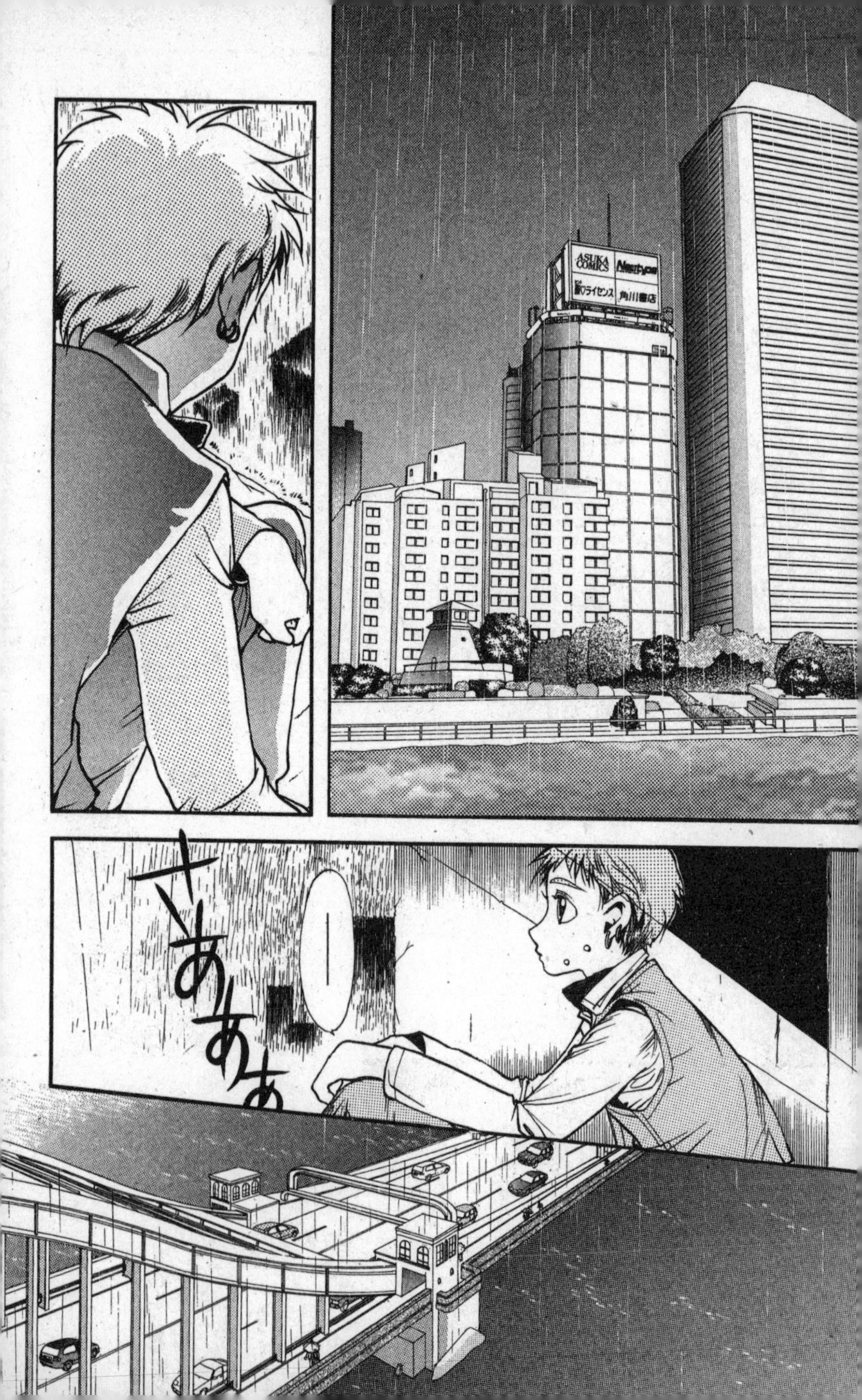
ASUKA COMICS
Newtype
歌♡ライセンス
角川書店
—
さあああ

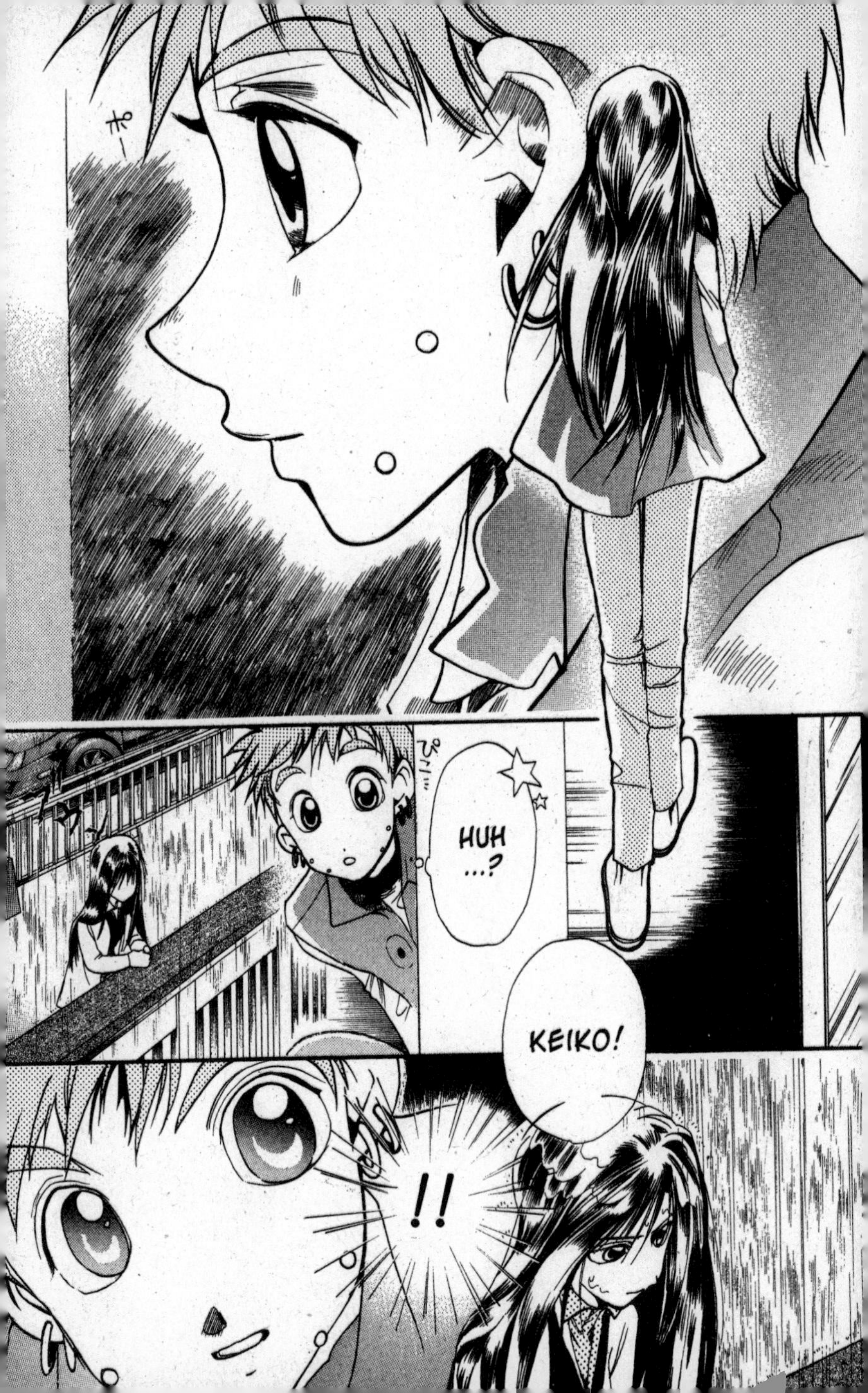
HUH ...?
KEIKO!
!!

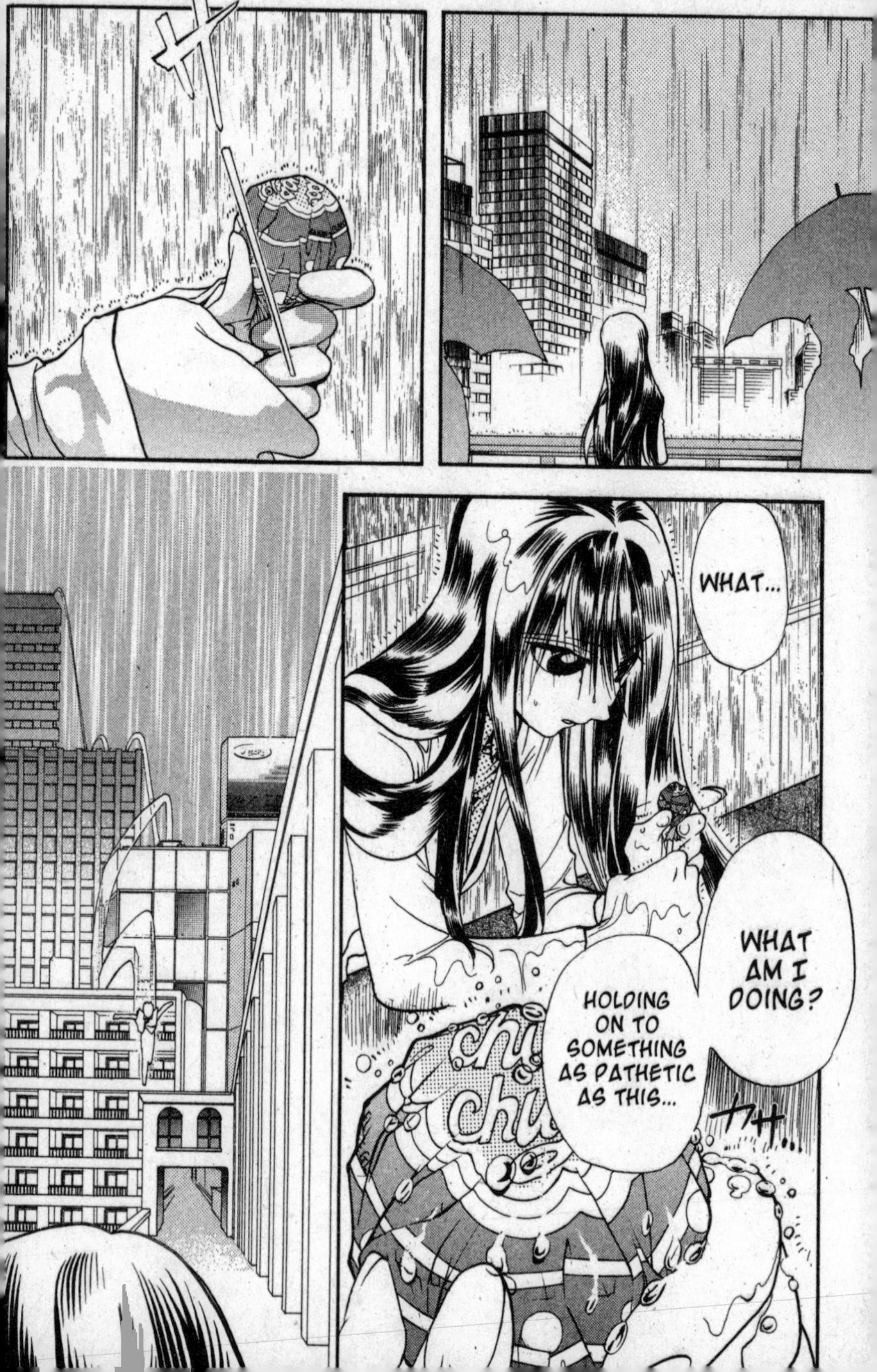
WHAT...
WHAT AM I DOING?
HOLDING ON TO SOMETHING AS PATHETIC AS THIS...

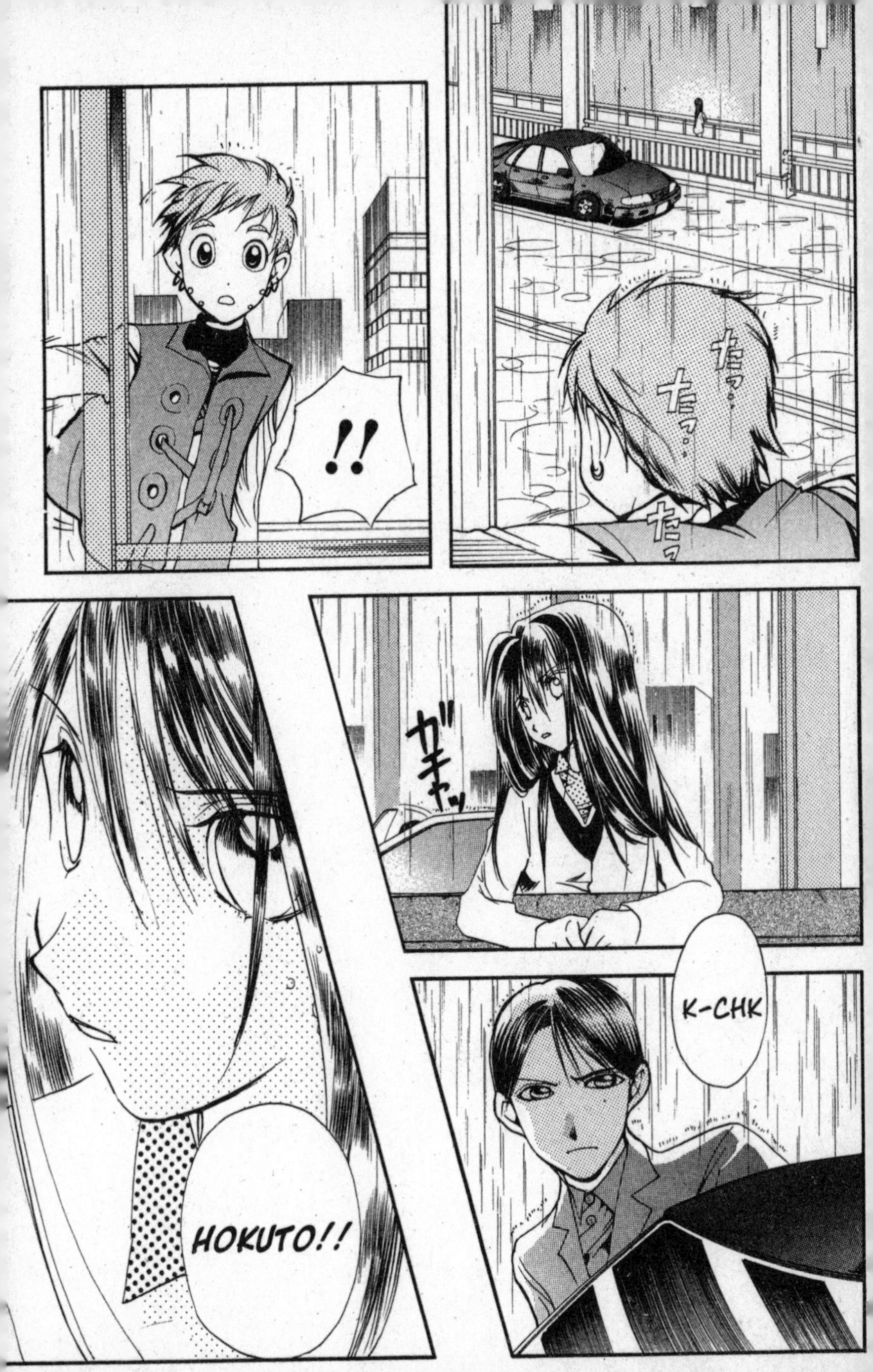
たっ…
たっ…
たっ
!!
ガチャッ
K-CHK
HOKUTO!!

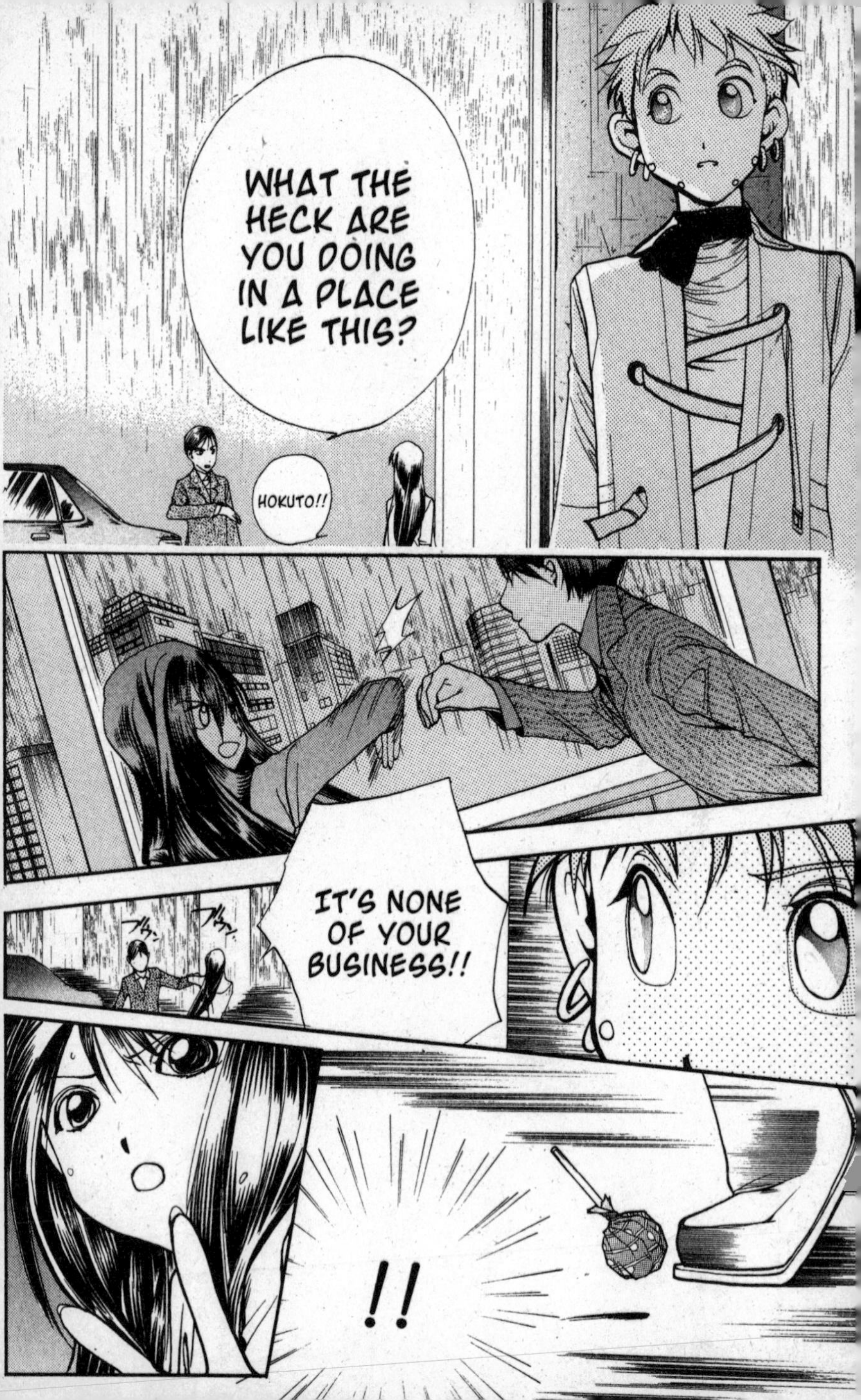
WHAT THE HECK ARE YOU DOING IN A PLACE LIKE THIS?
HOKUTO!!
IT'S NONE OF YOUR BUSINESS!!
!!

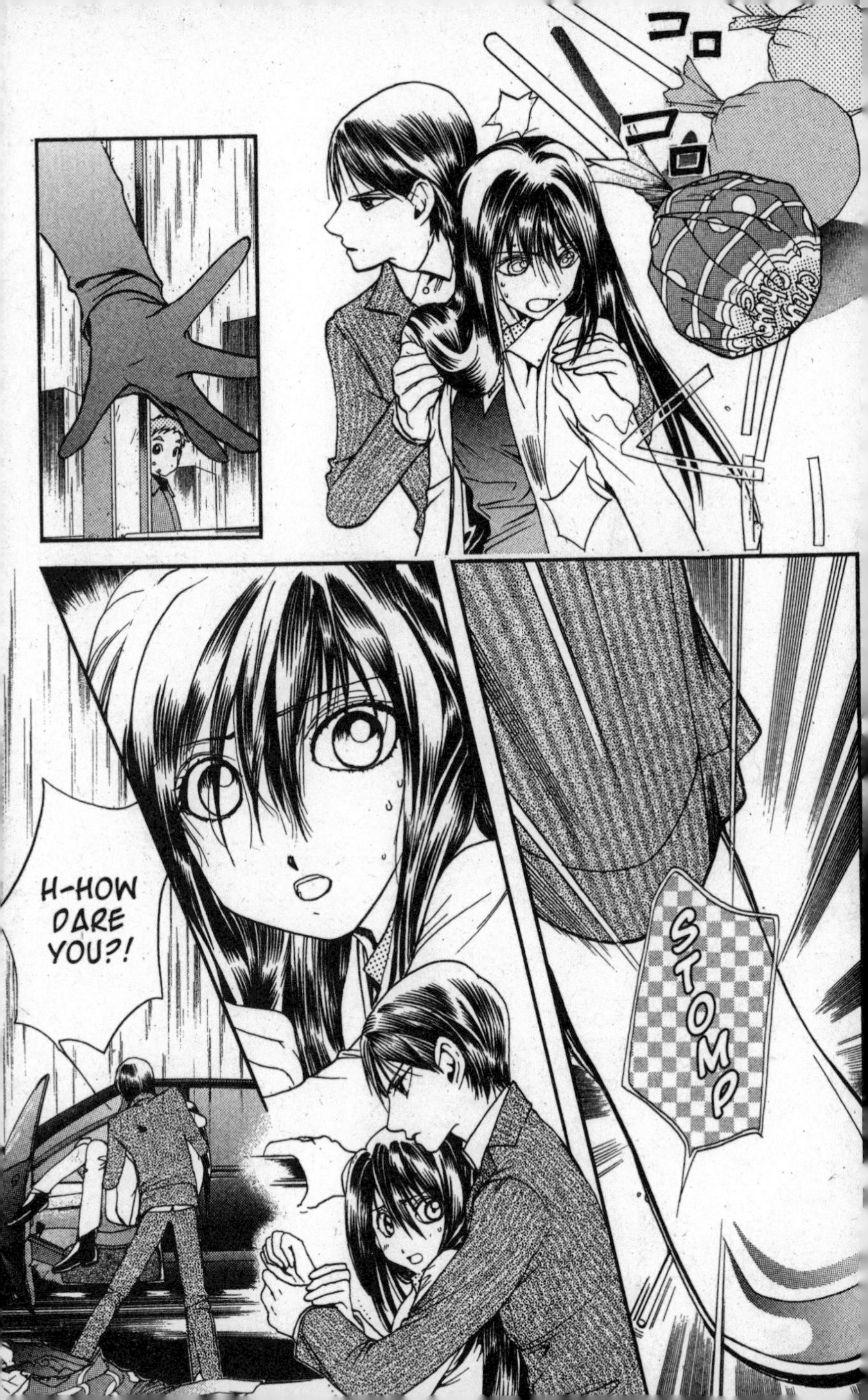
コロ
コロ
STOMP
H-HOW DARE YOU?!

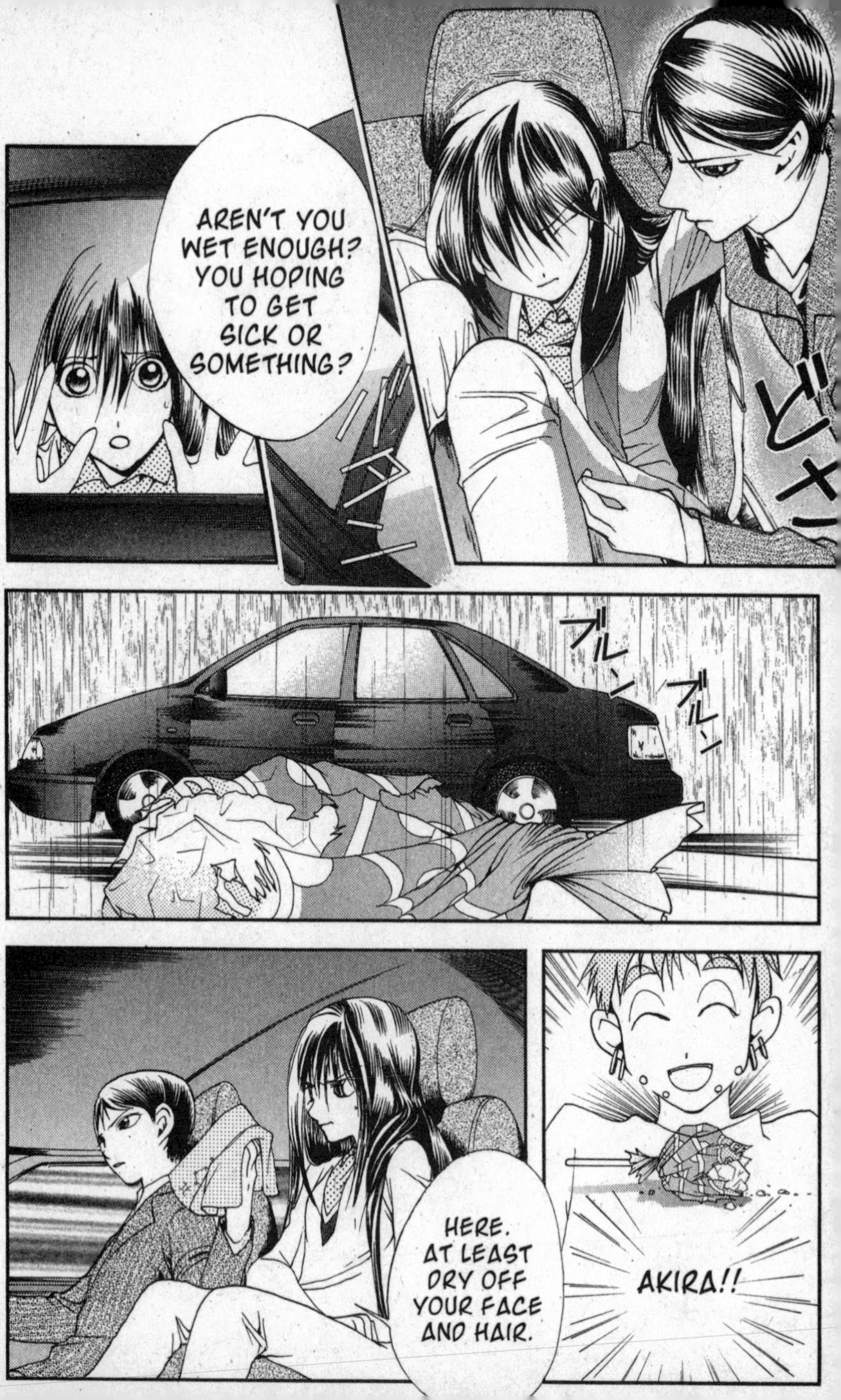
AREN'T YOU WET ENOUGH? YOU HOPING TO GET SICK OR SOMETHING?
ブルン
ブルン
AKIRA!!
HERE. AT LEAST DRY OFF YOUR FACE AND HAIR.

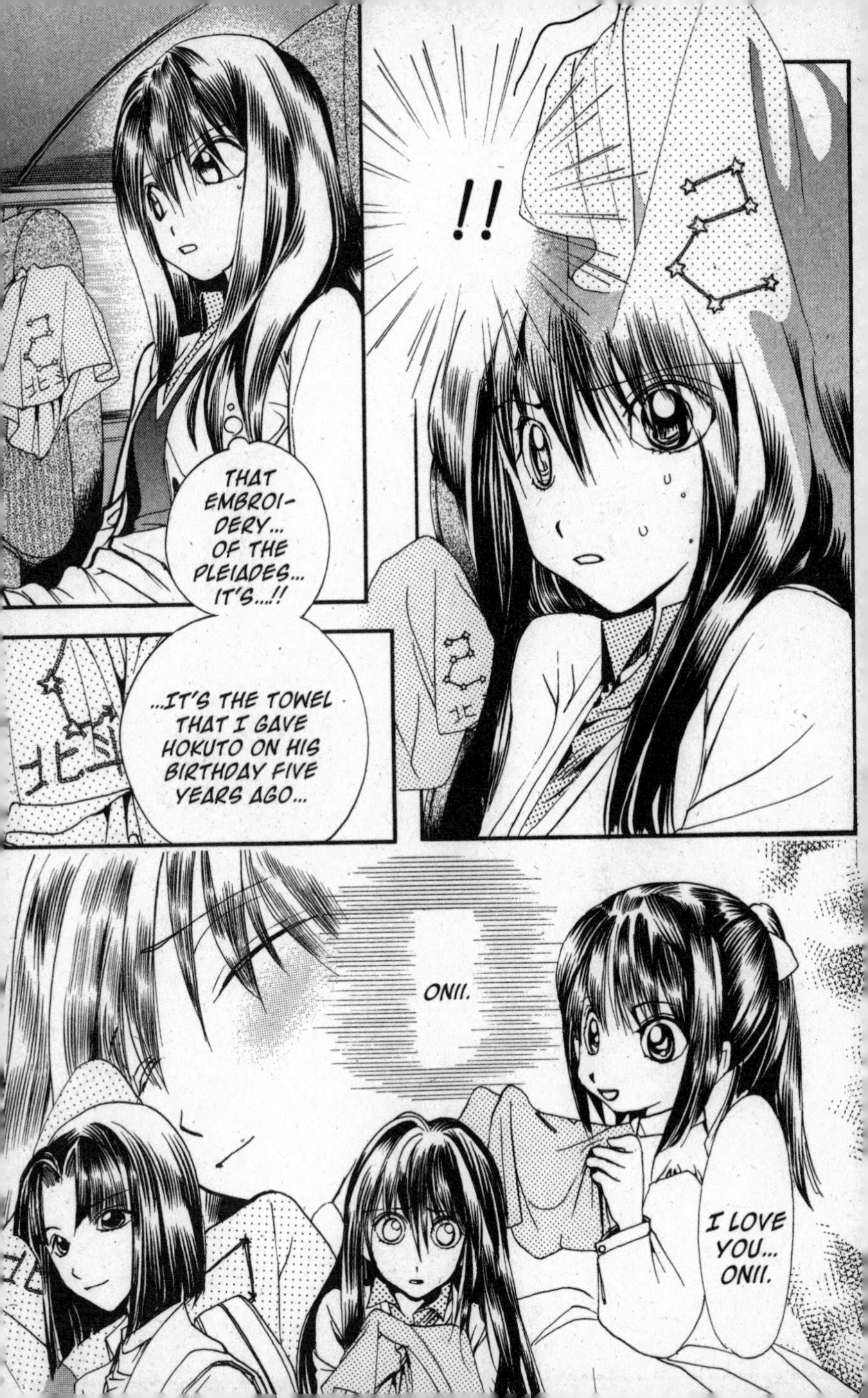
!!
THAT EMBROIDERY... OF THE PLEIADES... IT'S...!!
...IT'S THE TOWEL THAT I GAVE HOKUTO ON HIS BIRTHDAY FIVE YEARS AGO...
ONII.
I LOVE YOU... ONII.

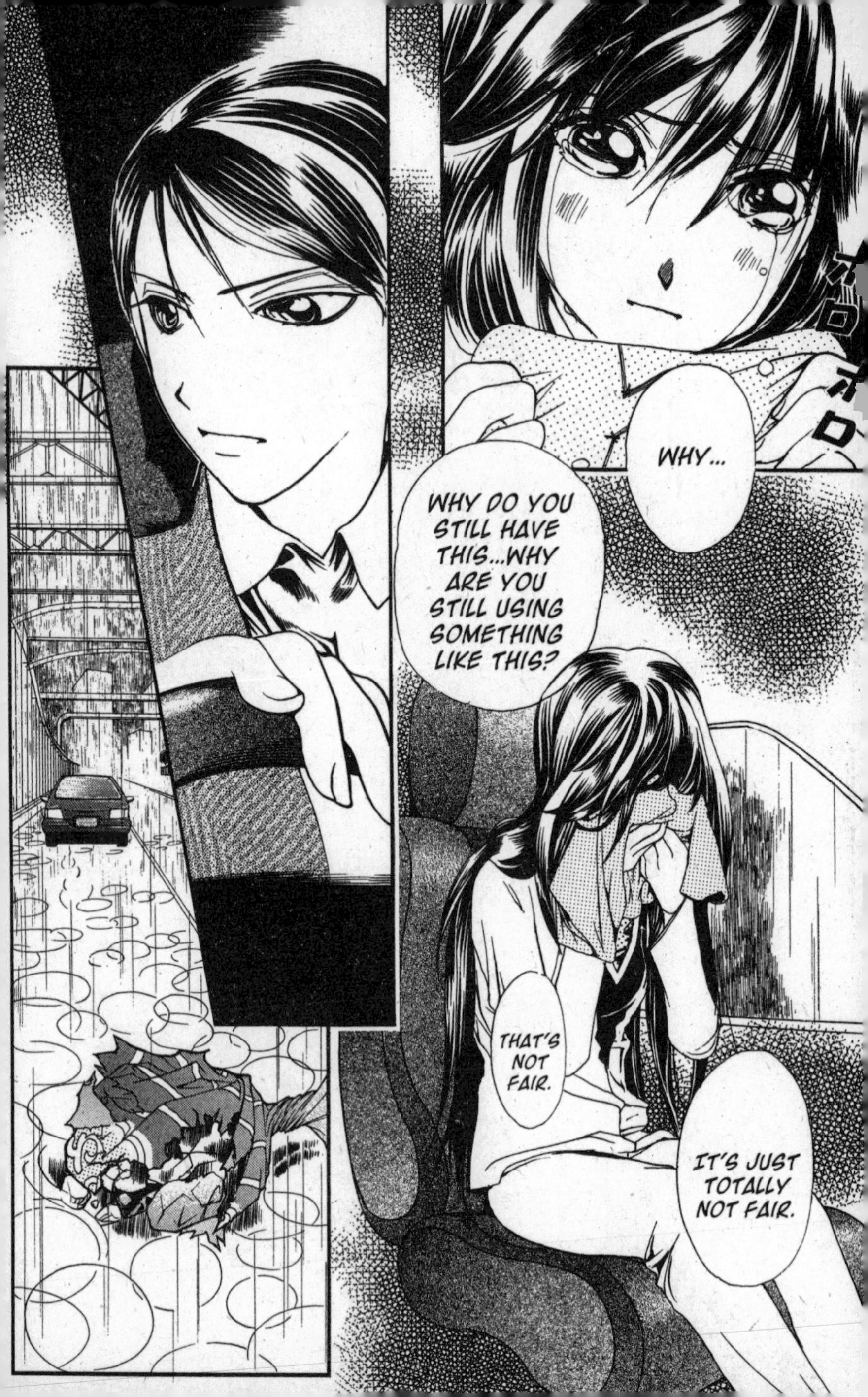
WHY...
WHY DO YOU STILL HAVE THIS...WHY ARE YOU STILL USING SOMETHING LIKE THIS?
THAT'S NOT FAIR.
IT'S JUST TOTALLY NOT FAIR.

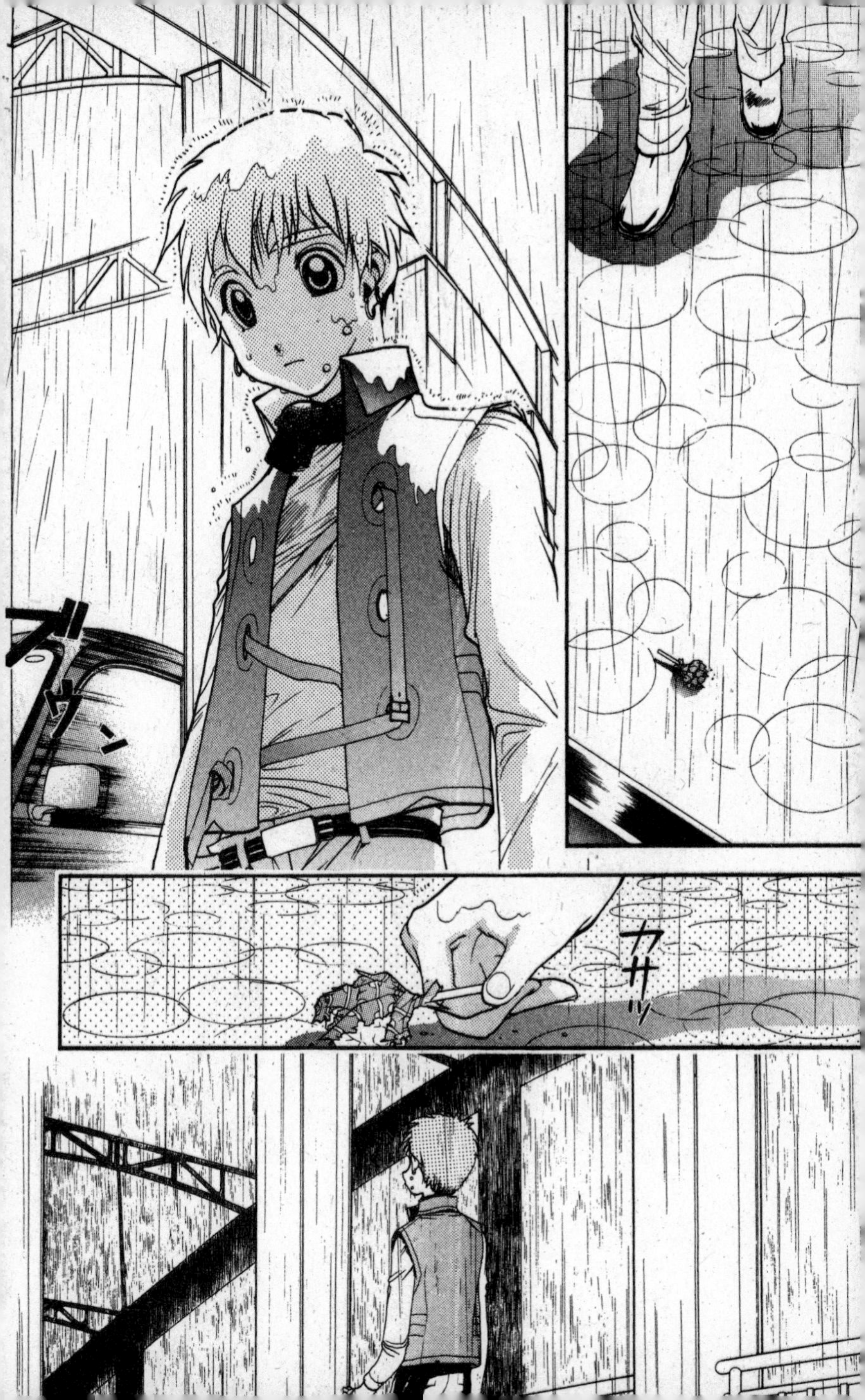
ブゥン
カサッ

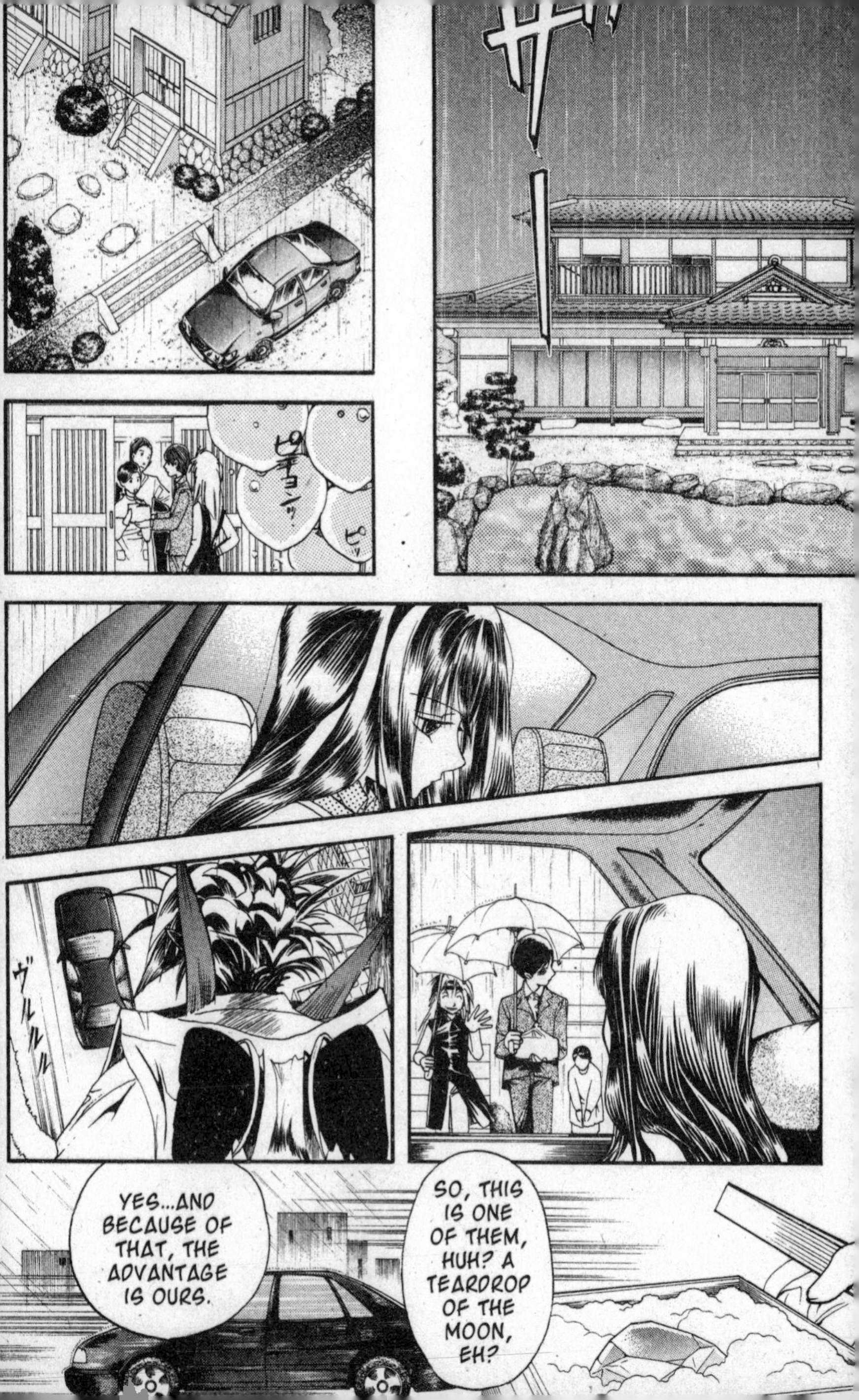
ヴルルル
SO, THIS IS ONE OF THEM, HUH? A TEARDROP OF THE MOON, EH?
YES...AND BECAUSE OF THAT, THE ADVANTAGE IS OURS.

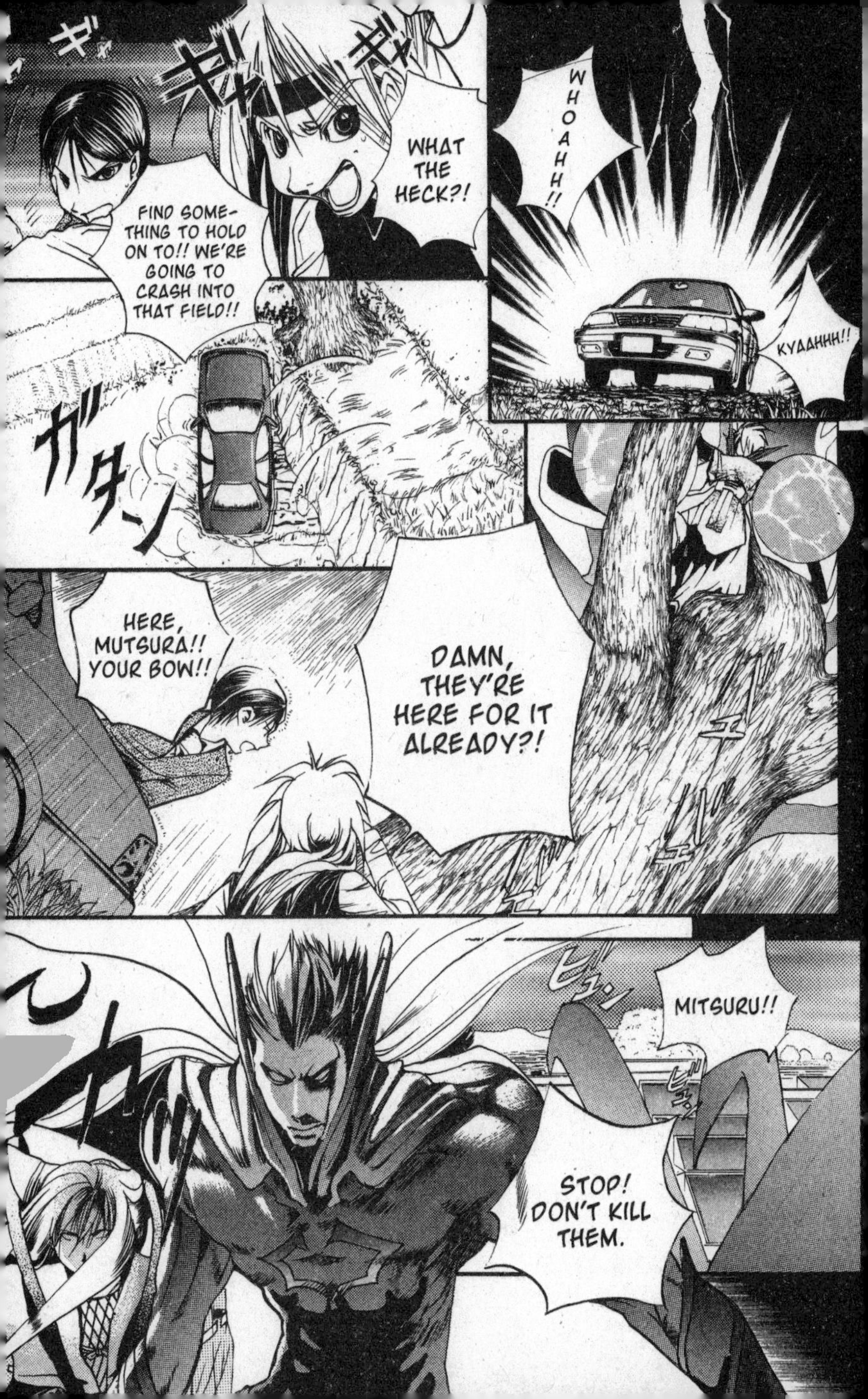
WHOAAHH!!
KYAAHHH!!
WHAT THE HECK?!
FIND SOME-THING TO HOLD ON TO!! WE'RE GOING TO CRASH INTO THAT FIELD!!
DAMN, THEY'RE HERE FOR IT ALREADY?!
HERE, MUTSURA!! YOUR BOW!!
MITSURU!!
STOP! DON'T KILL THEM.

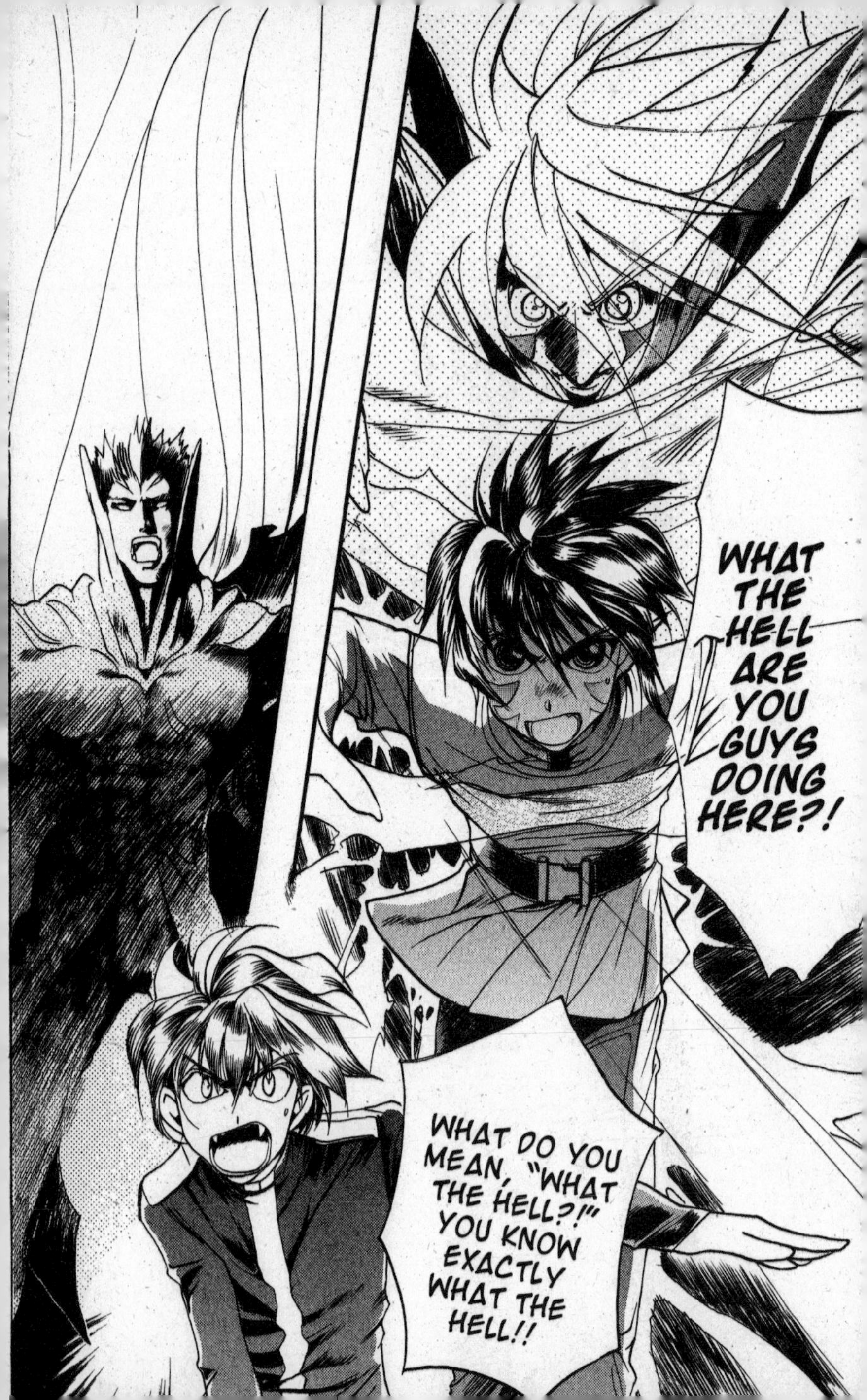
WHAT THE HELL ARE YOU GUYS DOING HERE?!
WHAT DO YOU MEAN, "WHAT THE HELL?!" YOU KNOW EXACTLY WHAT THE HELL!!

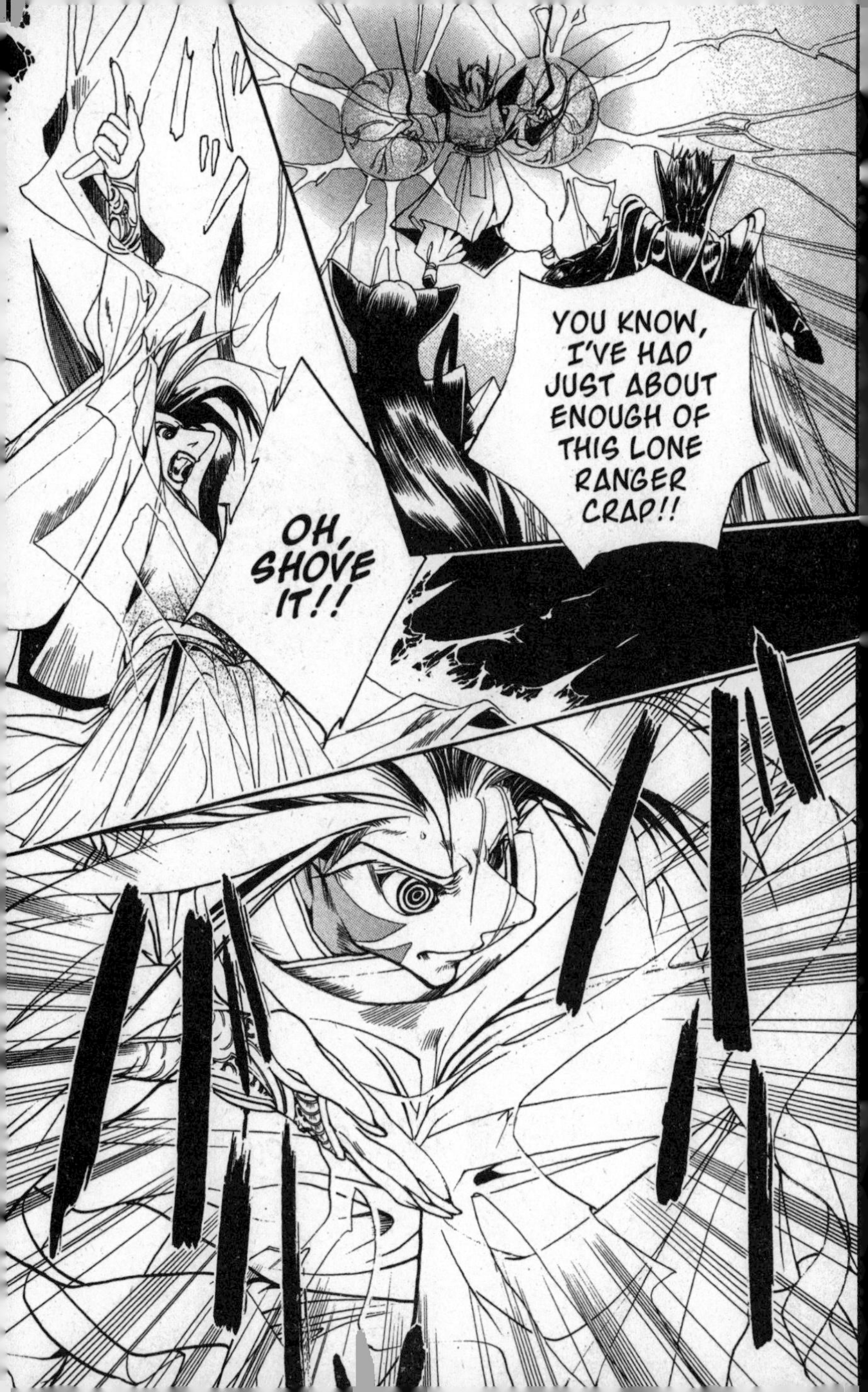
YOU KNOW, I'VE HAD JUST ABOUT ENOUGH OF THIS LONE RANGER CRAP!!
OH, SHOVE IT!!

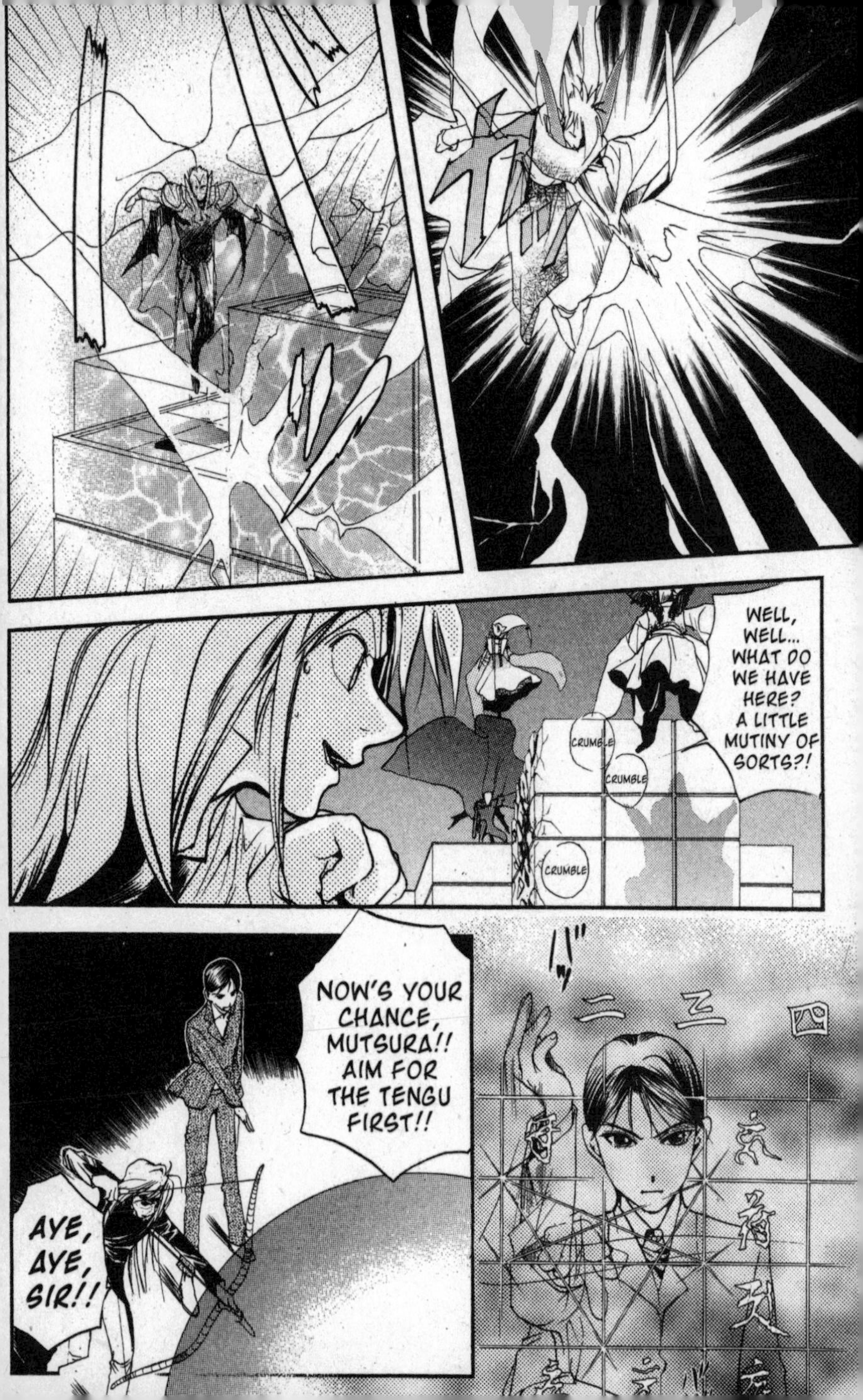
WELL, WELL... WHAT DO WE HAVE HERE? A LITTLE MUTINY OF SORTS?!
CRUMBLE
CRUMBLE
CRUMBLE
NOW'S YOUR CHANCE, MUTSURA!! AIM FOR THE TENGU FIRST!!
AYE, AYE, SIR!!

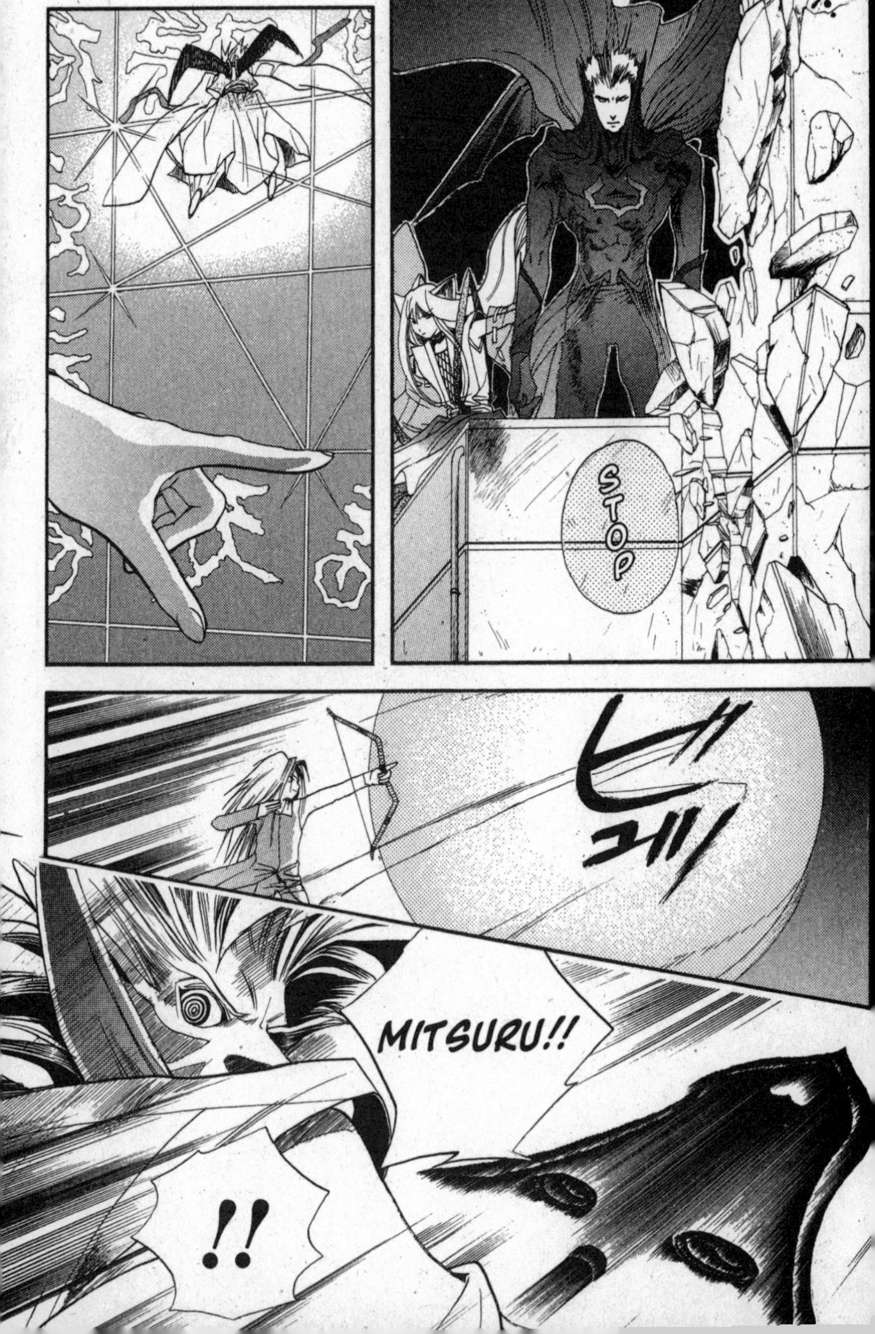
フワリ.
STOP
MITSURU!!
!!

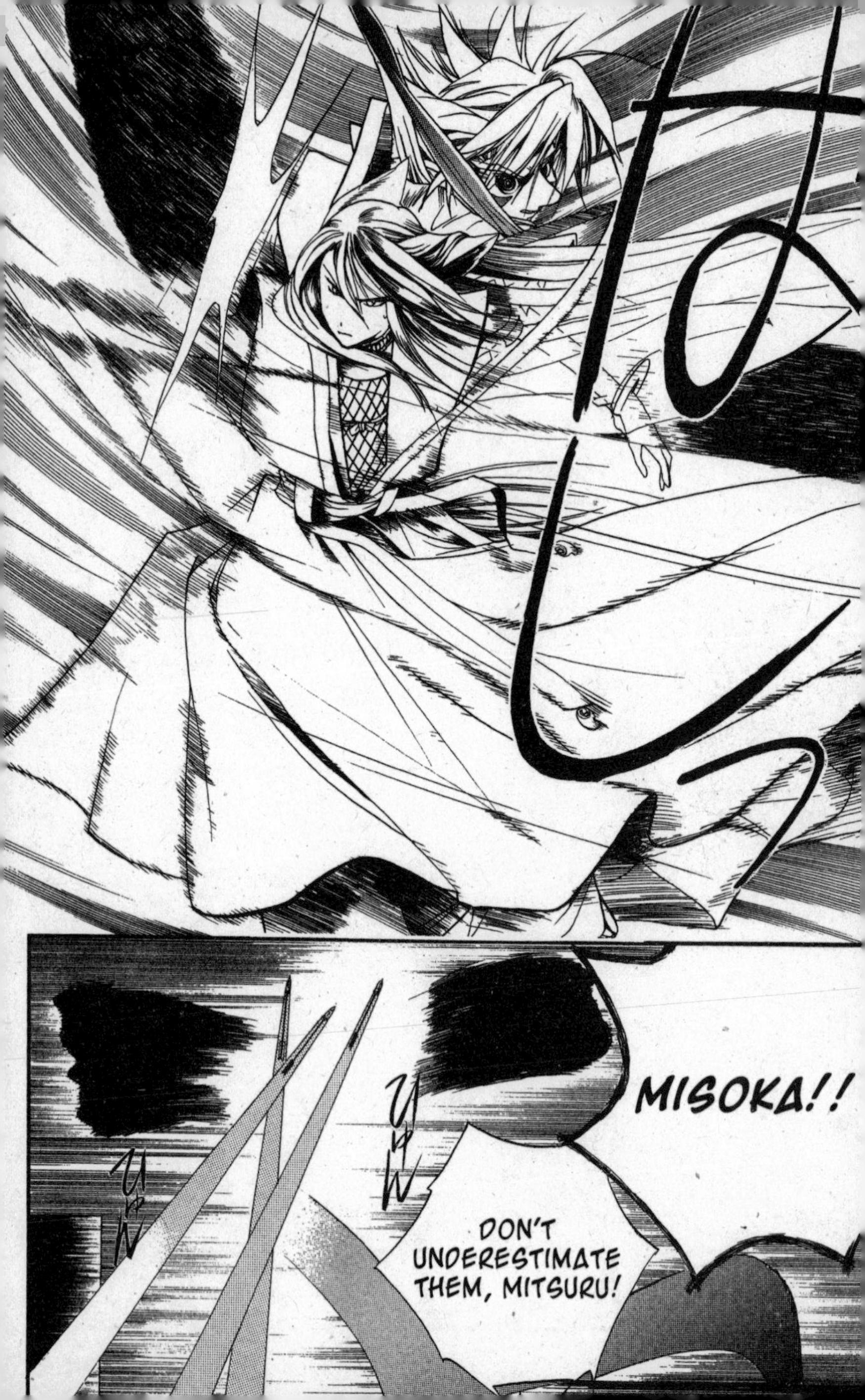
MISOKA!!
DON'T UNDERESTIMATE THEM, MITSURU!

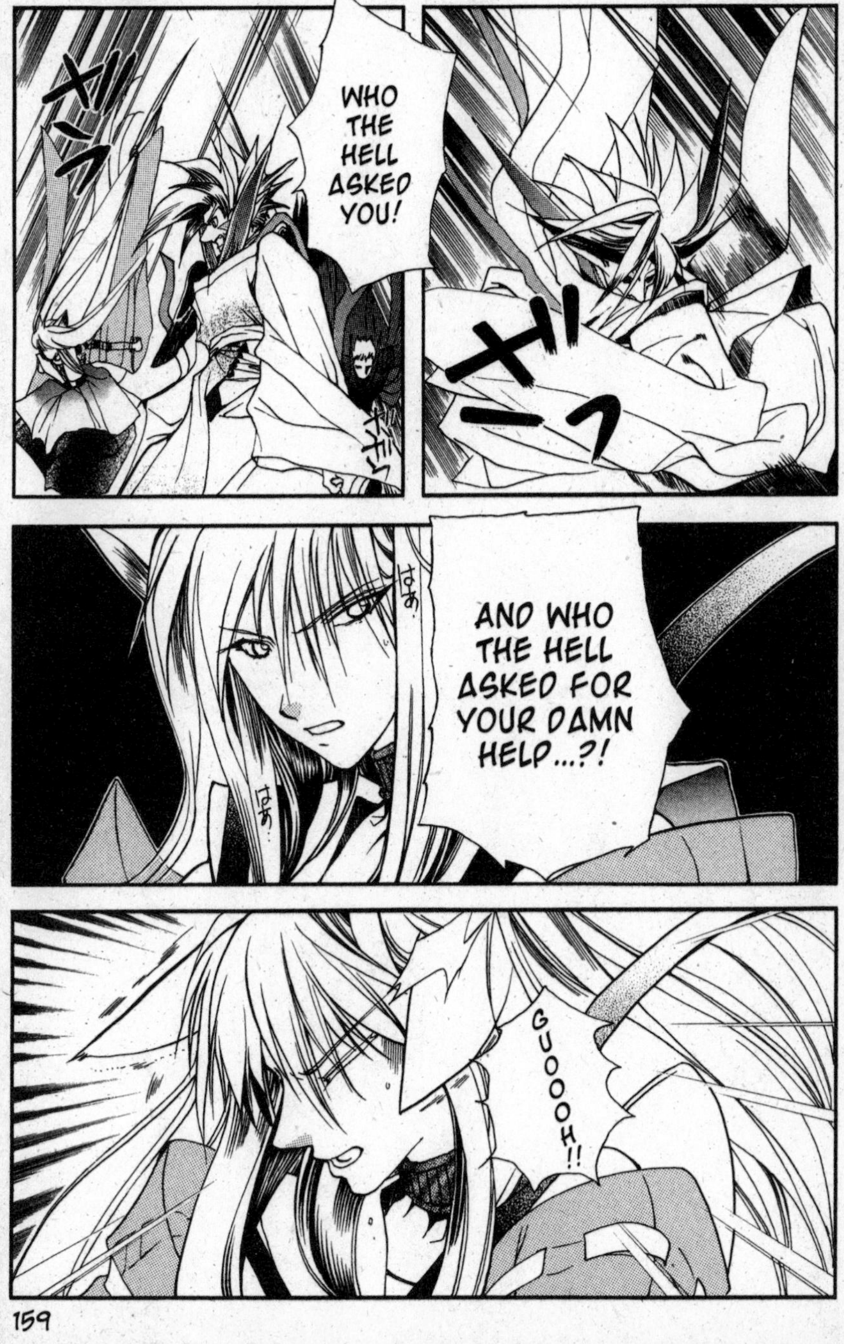

WHO THE HELL ASKED YOU!
AND WHO THE HELL ASKED FOR YOUR DAMN HELP...?!
GUOOOOH!!

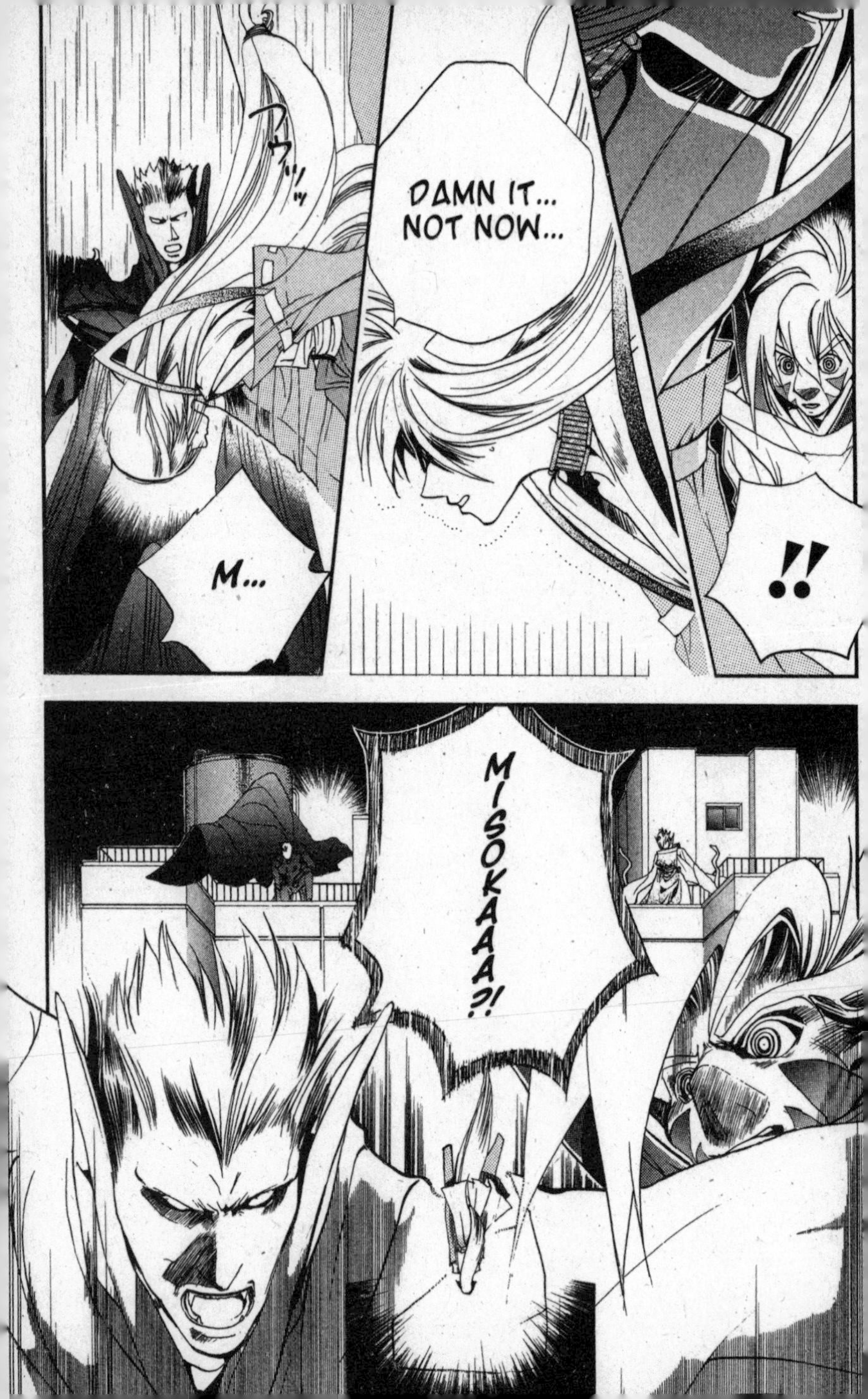
!!
DAMN IT... NOT NOW...
M...
MISOKAAAA?!

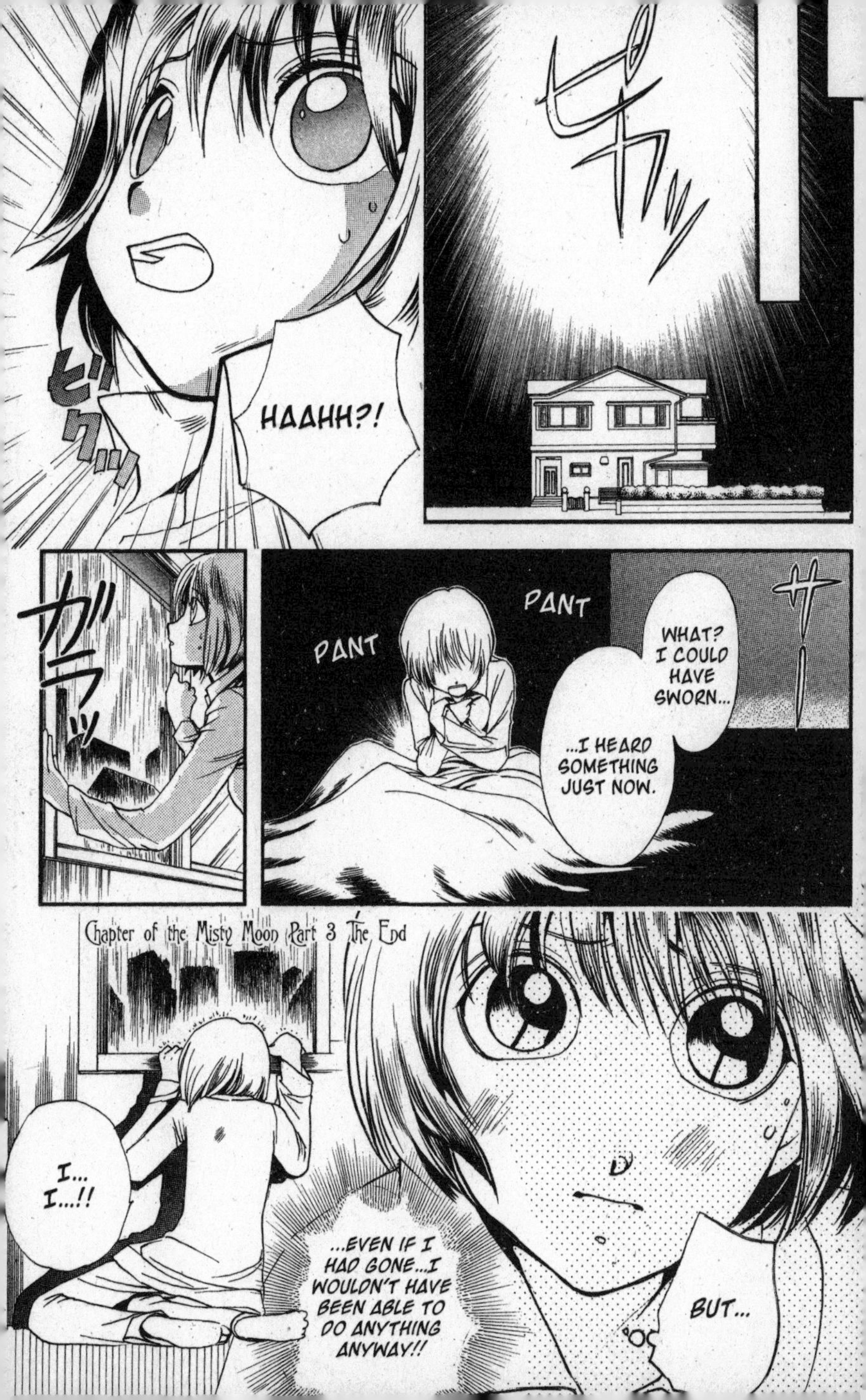
HAAHH?!
ビクッ
PANT
PANT
WHAT? I COULD HAVE SWORN...
...I HEARD SOMETHING JUST NOW.
ガラッ
BUT...
Chapter of the Misty Moon Part 3 The End
...EVEN IF I HAD GONE...I WOULDN'T HAVE BEEN ABLE TO DO ANYTHING ANYWAY!!
I... I...!!

キャラクタープロフィール

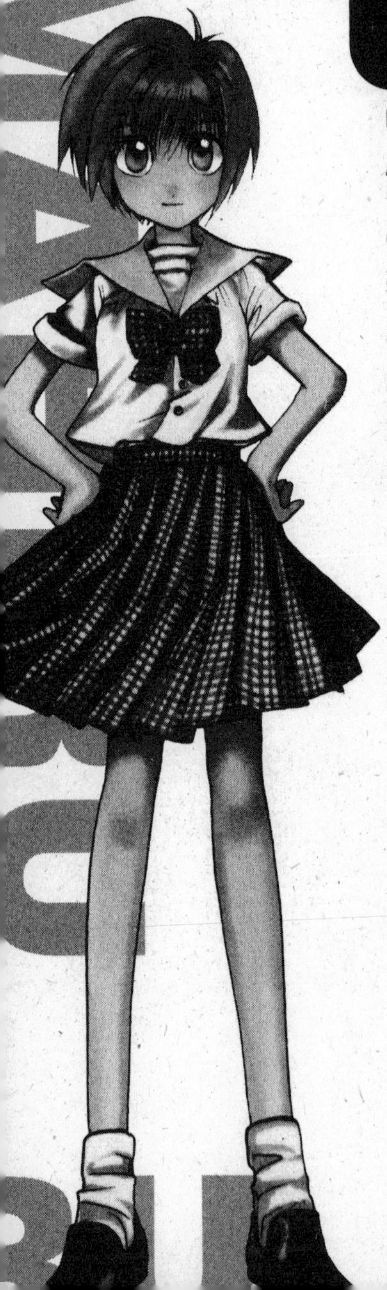

Mahiru Shiraishi

DOB: June 29th.

Age: 17 years old (Junior in High School). Blood Type O.

Club: Member of the Swim Team.

Stats: 160 CM. 48 KG.

Birthplace: Tokyo.

Ability: To bring out the power possessed by the Lunar Race. Senses where the Teardrops of the Moon are located.

Hobbies: Collecting plush aquatic creatures (fish, clams, dolphins, etc.)

Talent: Swimming.

Fave Food: Anything sweet.

Secret: Eats a lot more than she looks like she could.

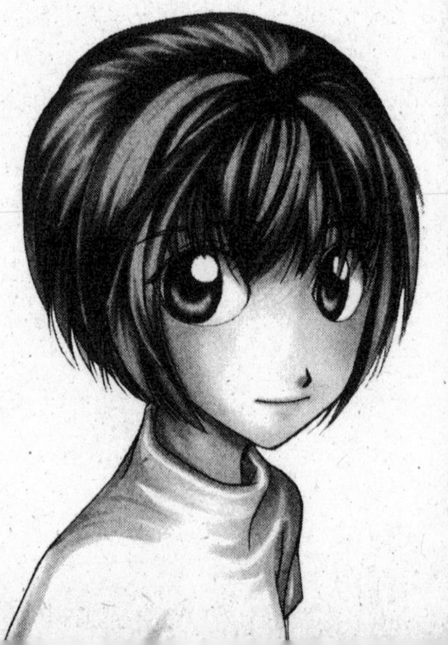

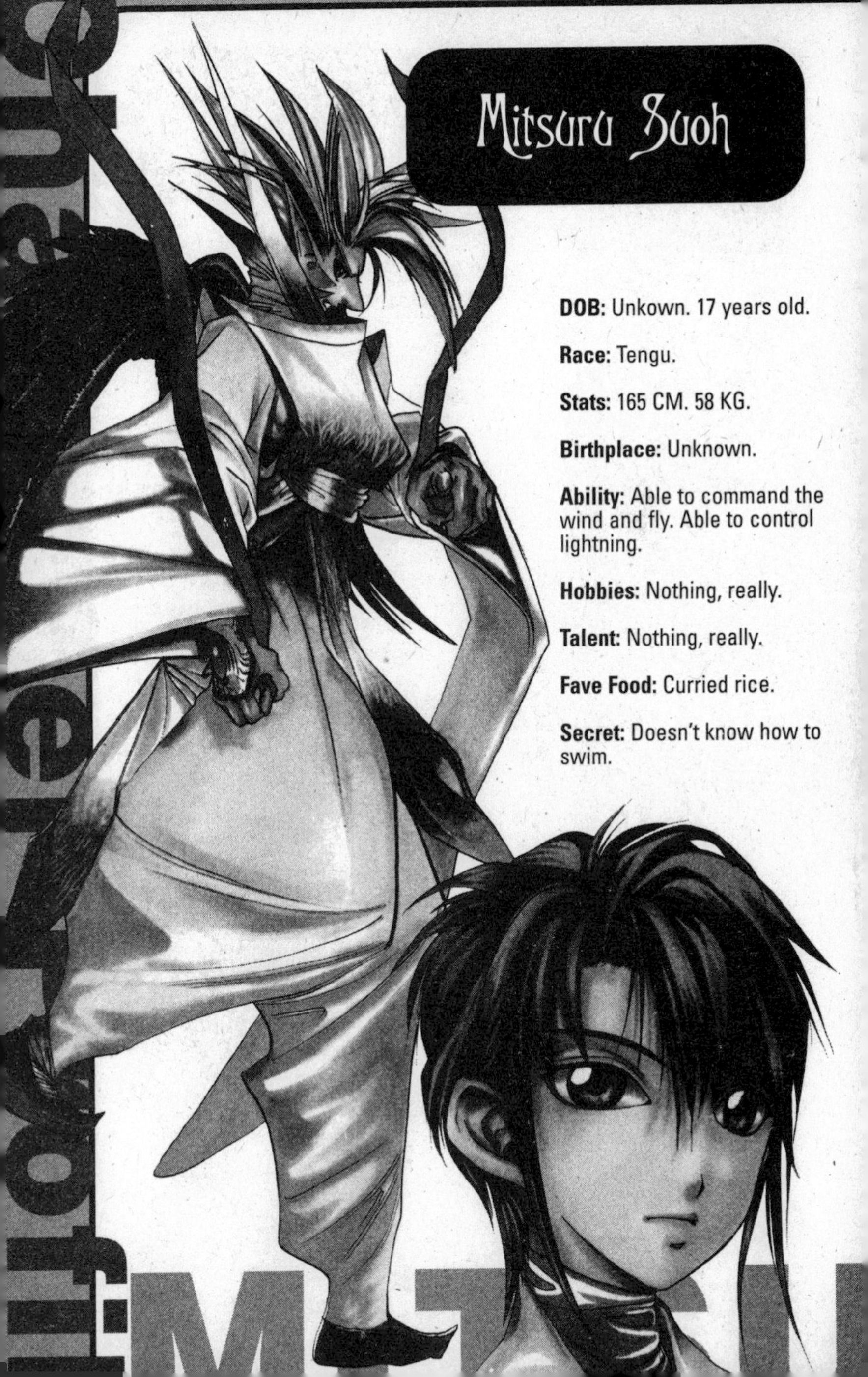

Mitsuru Suoh

DOB: Unkown. 17 years old.

Race: Tengu.

Stats: 165 CM. 58 KG.

Birthplace: Unknown.

Ability: Able to command the wind and fly. Able to control lightning.

Hobbies: Nothing, really.

Talent: Nothing, really.

Fave Food: Curried rice.

Secret: Doesn't know how to swim.

Nozomu Moegi

DOB: September 27th. 19 years old.

Race: Vampire.

Stats: 173 CM. 60 KG.

Birthplace: Osaka.

Ability: Using his bats to gather intelligence.

Hobbies: Tinkering with machinery.

Talent: Tinkering with machinery.

Fave Food: Probably human blood!

Secret: Cannot partake of anything that isn't a liquid. Is currently sustaining self on soup and juice.

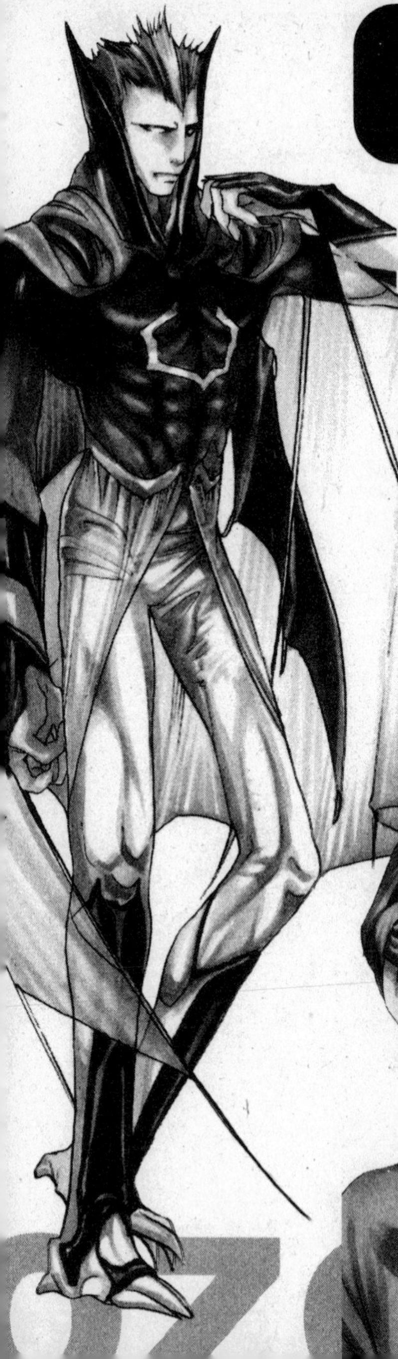

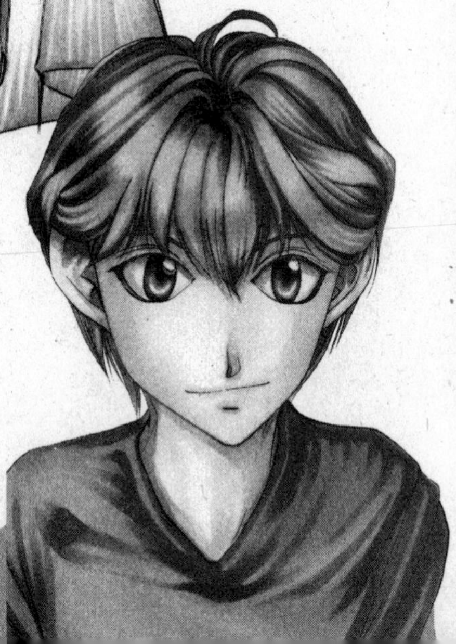

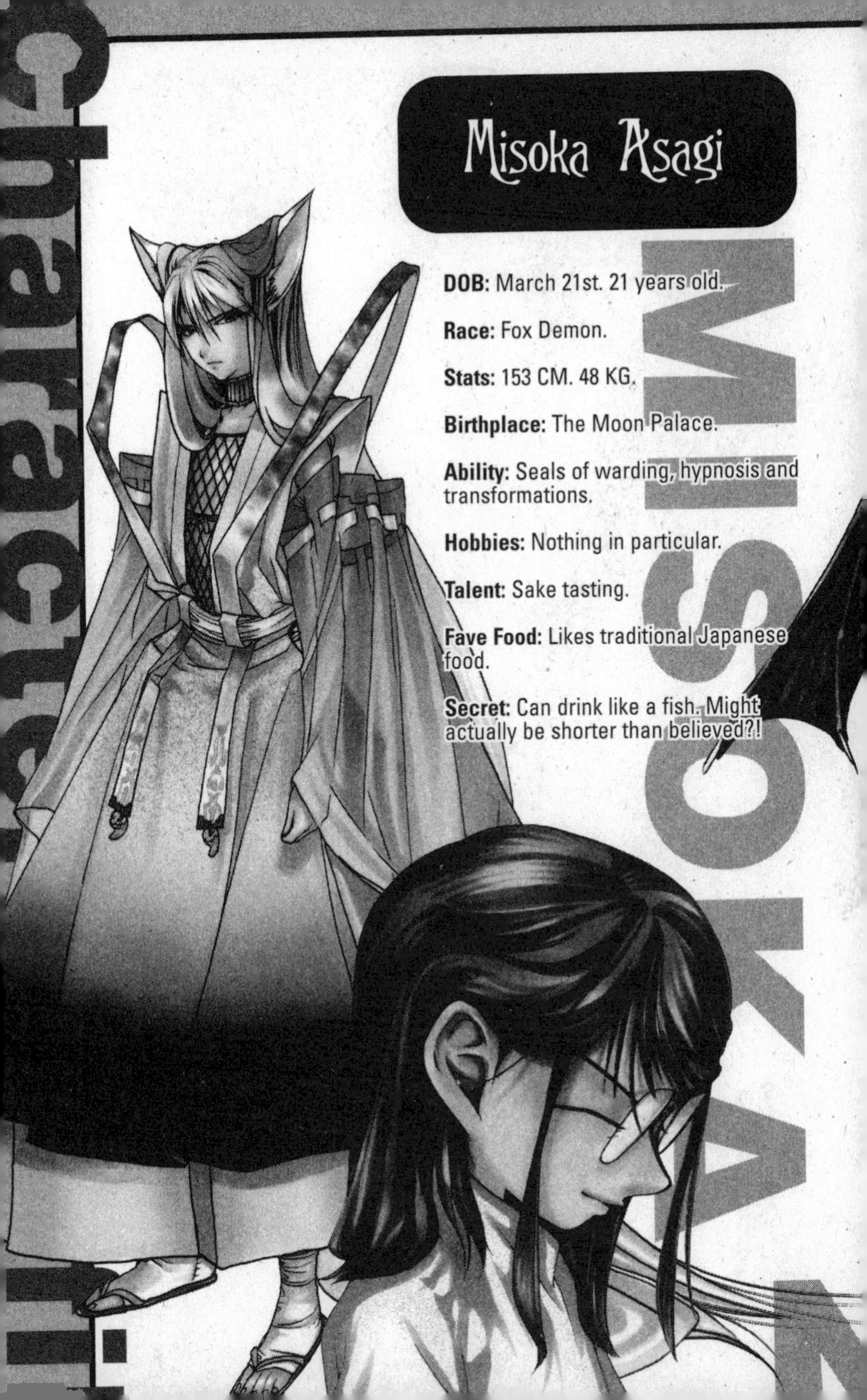

Misoka Asagi

DOB: March 21st. 21 years old.

Race: Fox Demon.

Stats: 153 CM. 48 KG.

Birthplace: The Moon Palace.

Ability: Seals of warding, hypnosis and transformations.

Hobbies: Nothing in particular.

Talent: Sake tasting.

Fave Food: Likes traditional Japanese food.

Secret: Can drink like a fish. Might actually be shorter than believed?!

キャラクタープロフィール

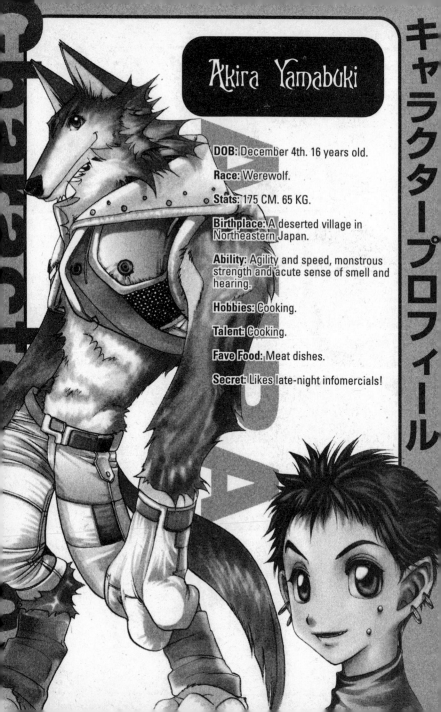

Akira Yamabuki

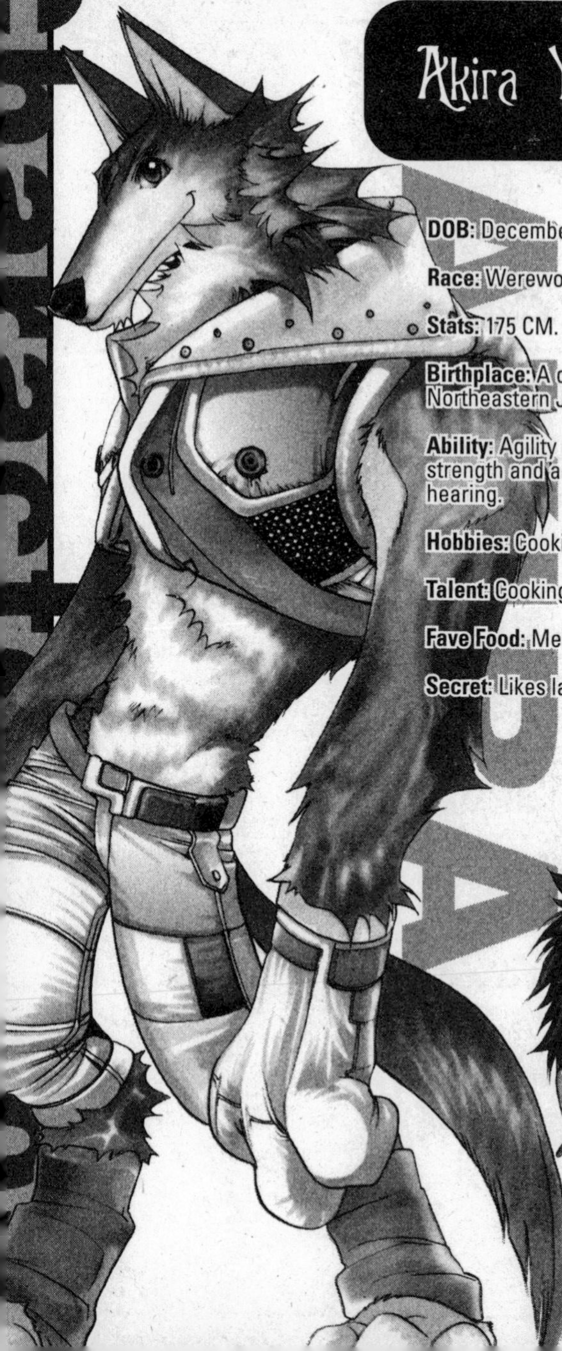

DOB: December 4th. 16 years old.

Race: Werewolf.

Stats: 175 CM. 65 KG.

Birthplace: A deserted village in Northeastern Japan.

Ability: Agility and speed, monstrous strength and acute sense of smell and hearing.

Hobbies: Cooking.

Talent: Cooking.

Fave Food: Meat dishes.

Secret: Likes late-night infomercials!

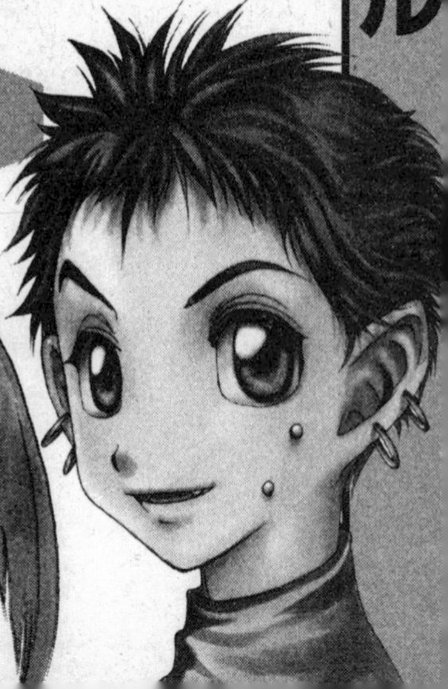

The Rules of Favoritism

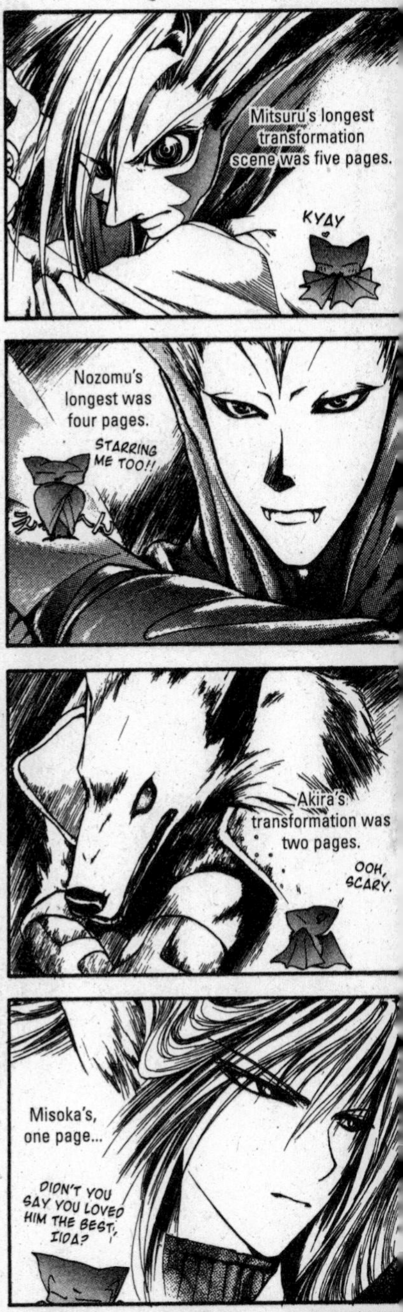
Mitsuru's longest transformation scene was five pages.
KYAY
Nozomu's longest was four pages.
STARRING ME TOO!!
Akira's transformation was two pages.
OOH, SCARY.
Misoka's, one page...
DIDN'T YOU SAY YOU LOVED HIM THE BEST, IIDA?

YESSIR! IIDA ZOO.........EDITED BY IIDA

Silly Hokuto

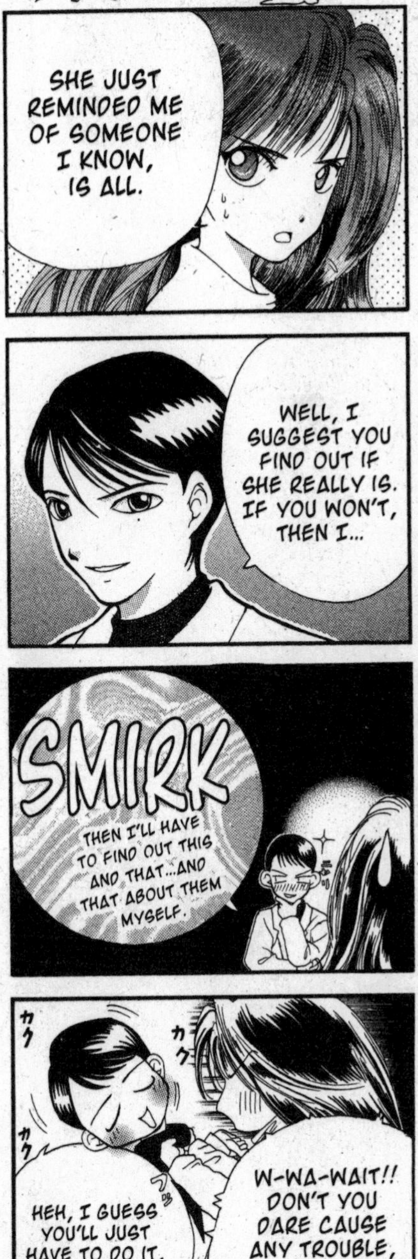
SHE JUST REMINDED ME OF SOMEONE I KNOW, IS ALL.
WELL, I SUGGEST YOU FIND OUT IF SHE REALLY IS. IF YOU WON'T, THEN I...
SMIRK
THEN I'LL HAVE TO FIND OUT THIS AND THAT...AND THAT ABOUT THEM MYSELF.
カク
カク
カク
W-WA-WAIT!! DON'T YOU DARE CAUSE ANY TROUBLE, YOU HEAR?!
HEH, I GUESS YOU'LL JUST HAVE TO DO IT, WON'T YOU?

NO, LET ME!!

Piyo's Day at "Mikan no Tsuki"

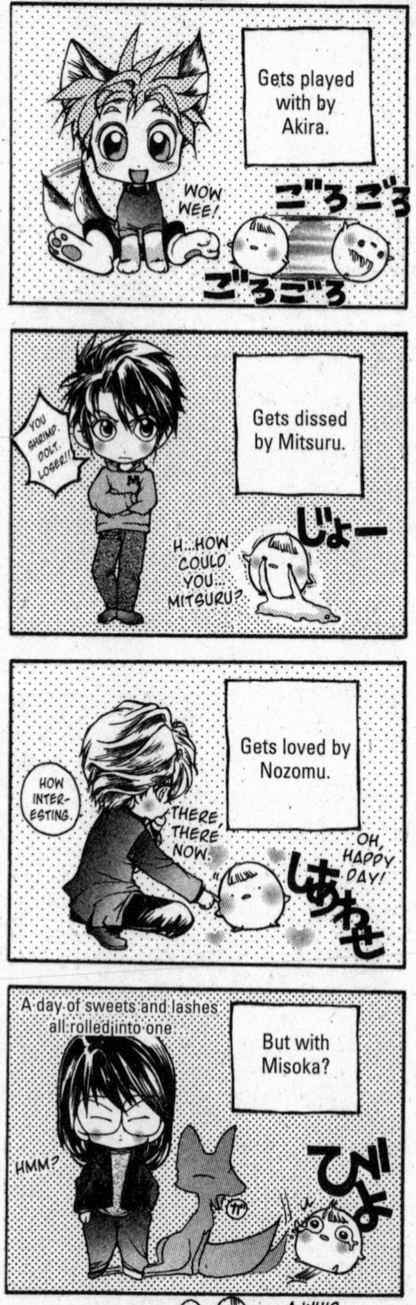

Gets played with by Akira.
WOW WEE!
ごろごろ
ごろごろ
Gets dissed by Mitsuru.
YOU SHRIMP. DOLT. LOSER!!
じょー
H...HOW COULD YOU... MITSURU?
Gets loved by Nozomu.
HOW INTER-ESTING.
THERE, THERE NOW.
OH, HAPPY DAY!
しあわせ
But with Misoka?
A day of sweets and lashes all rolled into one.
HMM?
ぴよ
A WHIP.

Misoka's Secret #1 by Chunta

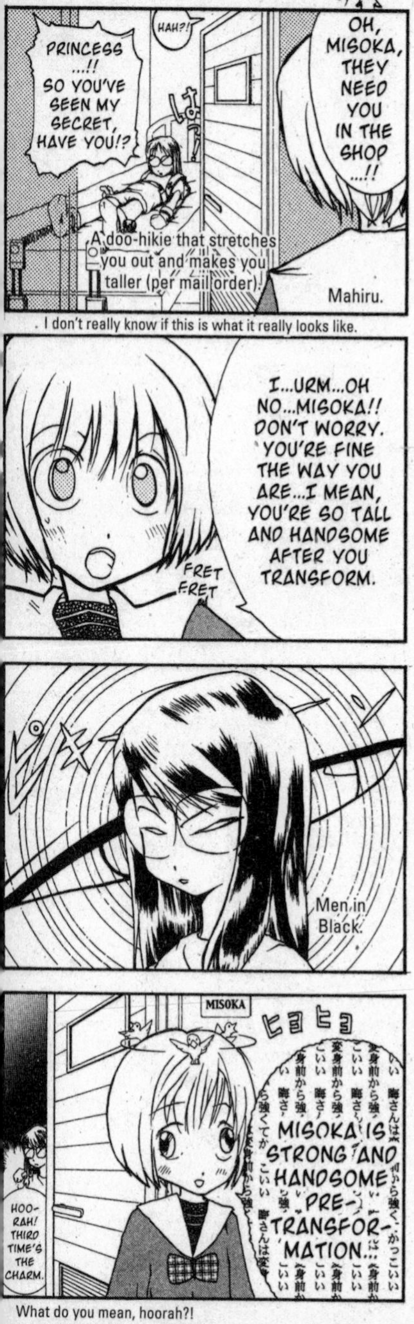

OH, MISOKA, THEY NEED YOU IN THE SHOP...!!
HAH?!
PRINCESS...!! SO YOU'VE SEEN MY SECRET, HAVE YOU!?
Mahiru.
A doo-hikie that stretches you out and makes you taller (per mail order).
I don't really know if this is what it really looks like.
I...URM...OH NO...MISOKA!! DON'T WORRY. YOU'RE FINE THE WAY YOU ARE...I MEAN, YOU'RE SO TALL AND HANDSOME AFTER YOU TRANSFORM.
FRET FRET
Men in Black.
MISOKA
ヒヨヒヨ
MISOKA IS STRONG AND HANDSOME PRE-TRANSFOR-MATION...
HOO-RAH! THIRD TIME'S THE CHARM.
What do you mean, hoorah?!
SERIOUSLY.

Crescent Moon

Preview: Volume 5

THE BLOODY BATTLE BETWEEN THE MOONLIGHT BANDITS AND DAWN'S VENUS WAGES ON, WITH DEADLY RESULTS! VOLATILE LOVE MAY BE LOST IN THE FRAY, WHILE ONE RELATIONSHIP COMES TO AN END AND ANOTHER ONE BEGINS TO BLOSSOM. AND WHEN MAHIRU IS TAKEN TO THE MOON PALACE, WILL SHE BE ABLE TO OVERCOME HER OWN FEAR AND UNCERTAINTY IN ORDER TO SAVE THE EMPRESS?

vol.5

ALSO AVAILABLE FROM TOKYOPOP®

ALSO AVAILABLE FROM 🐾 TOKYOPOP®

08.20.04T

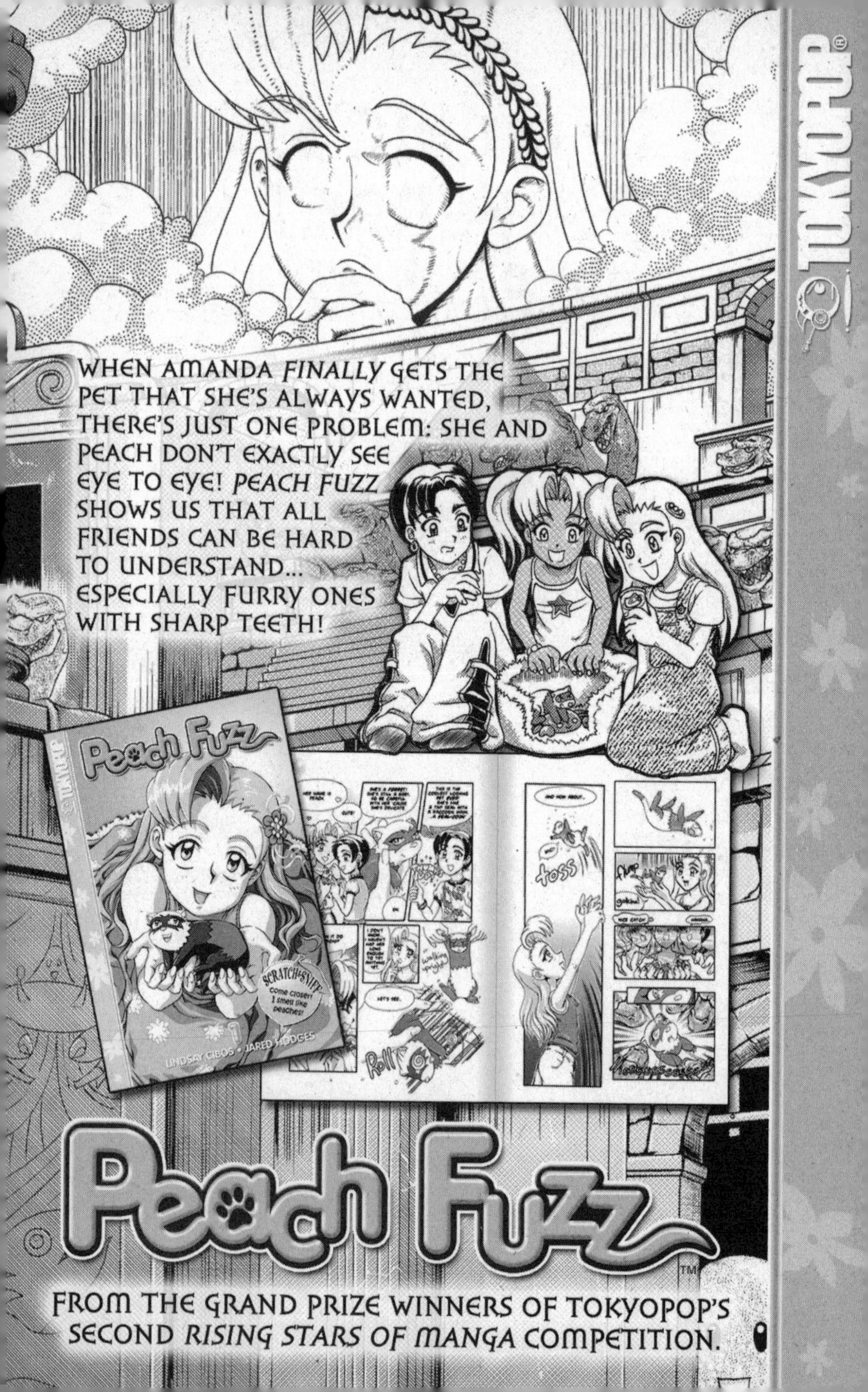
TOKYOPOP®
WHEN AMANDA *FINALLY* GETS THE PET THAT SHE'S ALWAYS WANTED, THERE'S JUST ONE PROBLEM: SHE AND PEACH DON'T EXACTLY SEE EYE TO EYE! *PEACH FUZZ* SHOWS US THAT ALL FRIENDS CAN BE HARD TO UNDERSTAND... ESPECIALLY FURRY ONES WITH SHARP TEETH!
Peach Fuzz
TOKYOPOP
SCRATCH & SNIFF
Come closer! I smell like peaches!
LINDSAY CIBOS • JARED HODGES
toss
Roll
Peach Fuzz™
FROM THE GRAND PRIZE WINNERS OF TOKYOPOP'S SECOND *RISING STARS OF MANGA* COMPETITION.

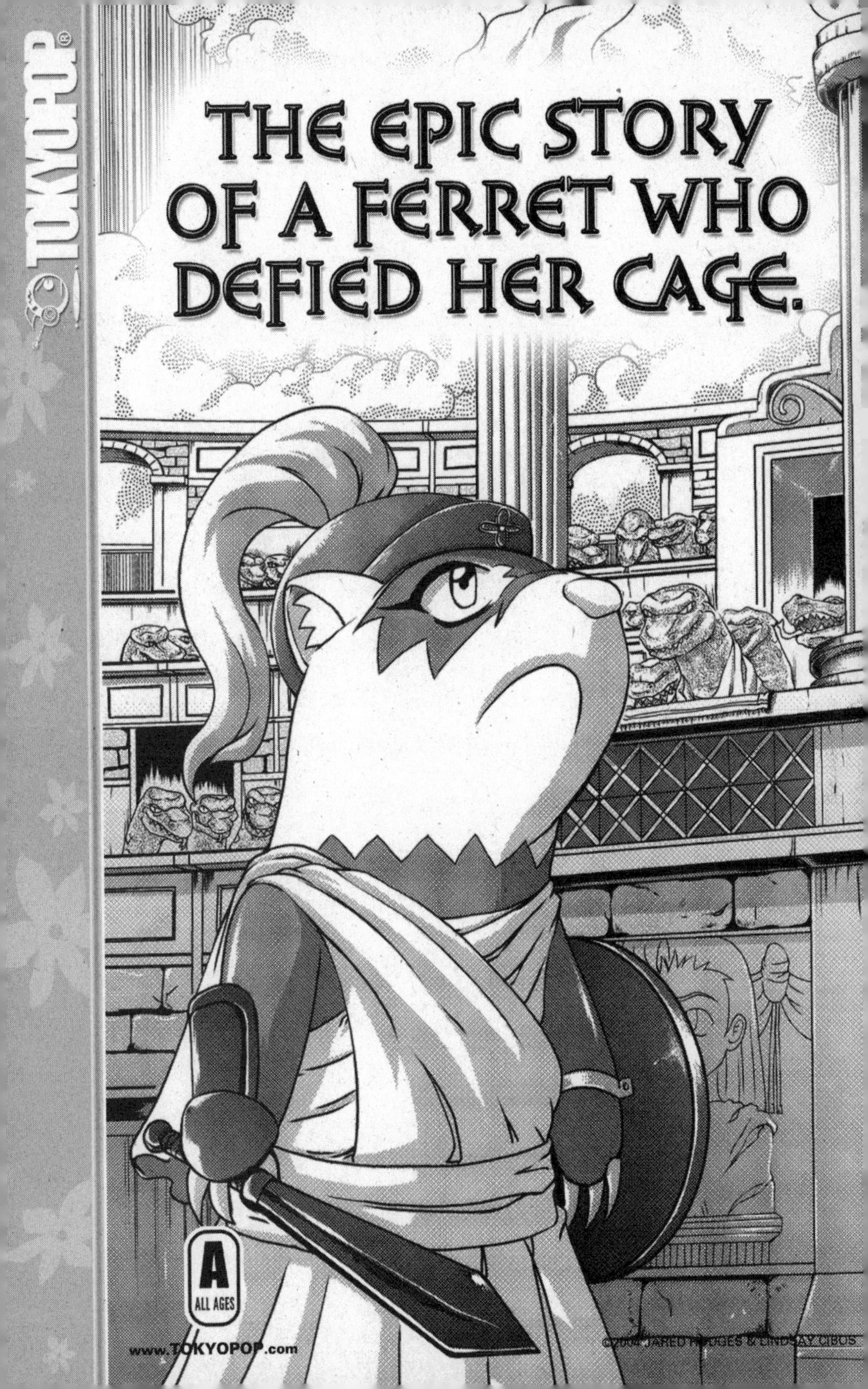
TOKYOPOP
THE EPIC STORY OF A FERRET WHO DEFIED HER CAGE.
A ALL AGES
www.TOKYOPOP.com
©2004 JARED HODGES & LINDSAY CIBOS

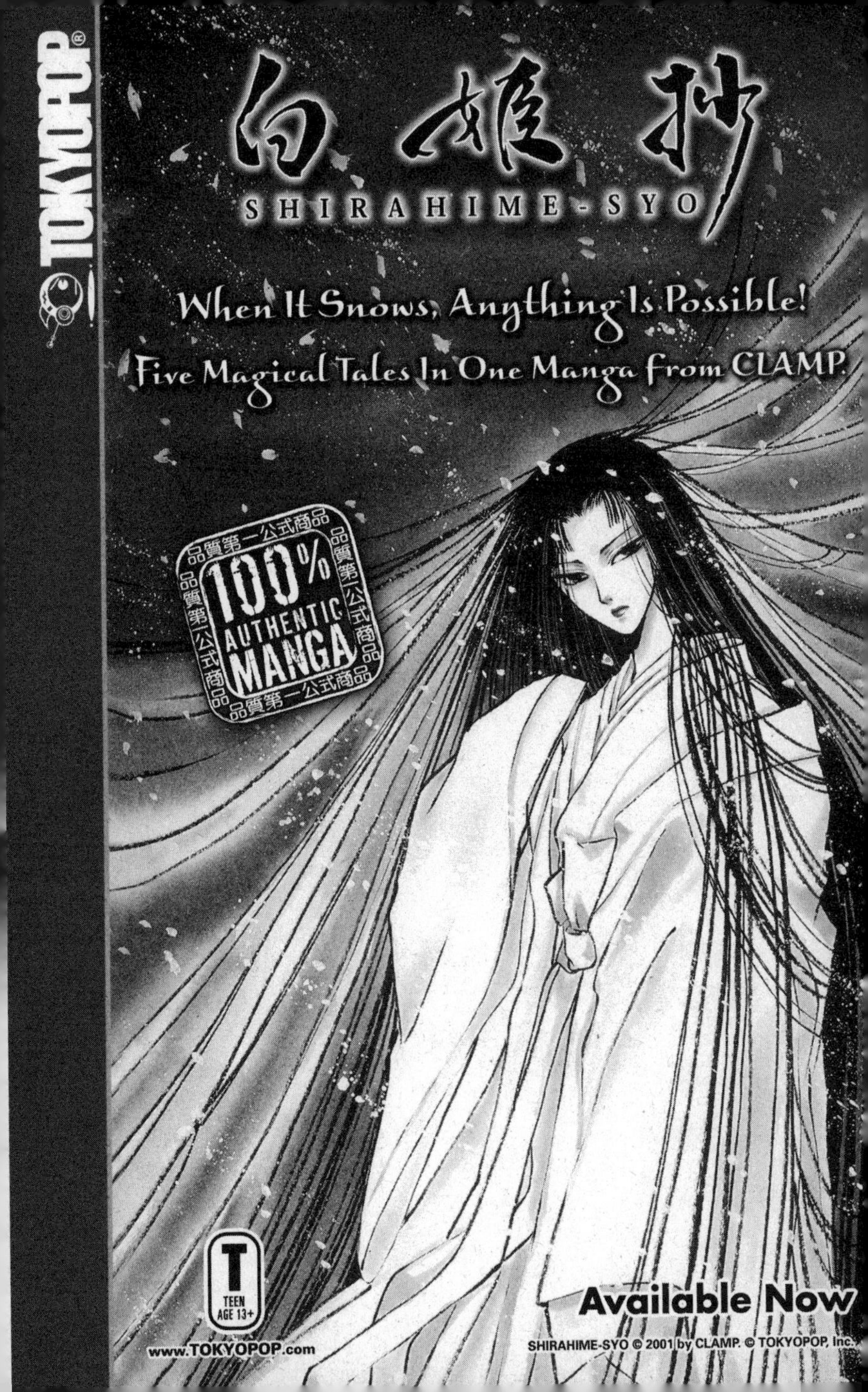
TOKYOPOP®
白姫抄
SHIRAHIME-SYO
When It Snows, Anything Is Possible!
Five Magical Tales In One Manga from CLAMP.
品質第一公式商品
100% AUTHENTIC MANGA
T TEEN AGE 13+
Available Now
www.TOKYOPOP.com
SHIRAHIME-SYO © 2001 by CLAMP. © TOKYOPOP, Inc.

STOP!

This is the back of the book.
You wouldn't want to spoil a great ending!

This book is printed "manga-style," in the authentic Japanese right-to-left format. Since none of the artwork has been flipped or altered, readers get to experience the story just as the creator intended. You've been asking for it, so TOKYOPOP® delivered: authentic, hot-off-the-press, and far more fun!

DIRECTIONS

If this is your first time reading manga-style, here's a quick guide to help you understand how it works.

It's easy... just start in the top right panel and follow the numbers. Have fun, and look for more 100% authentic manga from TOKYOPOP®!